Food Aid After Fifty Years

The United States' 1954 Agricultural Trade Development and Assistance Act effectively began the modern era of food aid. In the past fifty years the lives of hundreds of millions of people worldwide have been improved or saved. Food aid nonetheless remains one of the most misunderstood and controversial instruments of contemporary international policy.

Food Aid After Fifty Years explores the motivations and modalities of food aid and examines issues which impinge on its effectiveness. This book uses analytical and empirical accounts of food aid to resolve key misunderstandings and explode longstanding myths. An alternative, evidence-based strategy is presented for recasting food aid so as to make it more effective in alleviating poverty, hunger, and vulnerability.

Food Aid After Fifty Years provides a clear, comprehensive, and current explanation of a wide range of issues surrounding food aid policy and operations and will prove vital to students of development studies, international agriculture and those working in the field.

Christopher B. Barrett is International Professor of Applied Economics and Management, Co-Director of the African Food Security and Natural Resources Management program at Cornell University, New York, and Editor of the *American Journal of Agricultural Economics*. **Daniel G. Maxwell** is the Deputy Regional Director for CARE International in Eastern and Central Africa.

Food Aid After Fifty Years

Recasting its role

Christopher B. Barrett and Daniel G. Maxwell

LONDON AND NEW YORK

First published 2005
by Routledge
2 Park Square, Milton Park, Abingdon Oxon OX14 4RN

Simultaneously published in the USA and Canada
by Routledge
270 Madison Ave, New York 10016, USA

Routledge is an imprint of the Taylor & Francis Group

Transferred to Digital Printing 2007

Typeset in Baskerville by Keystroke, Jacaranda Lodge, Wolverhampton

British Library Cataloguing in Publication Data
A catalogue record for this book is available from the British Library

Library of Congress Cataloging in Publication Data
A catalog record for this book has been requested

ISBN 0–415–70124–4 (hbk)
ISBN 0–415–70125–2 (pbk)

Publisher's Note
The publisher has gone to great lengths to ensure the quality of this reprint
but points out that some imperfections in the original may be apparent

Contents

Illustrations

Figures

Tables

Boxes

Foreword

Chris Barrett and Dan Maxwell have written the most comprehensive and up-to-date review of food aid available. On the basis of a thorough and analytical review, they provide a series of policy recommendations for recasting the role of food aid. The book is a valuable resource for scholars, practitioners, and policymakers in economic development in general, and development assistance and food aid, in particular.

As pointed out by the authors, food aid is a real resource which can be used to further development and humanitarian goals. Alternatively, it can be misused to serve other purposes. Food aid can be effective in alleviating acute hunger and malnutrition, in building human capital, and in protecting or building assets. Poorly designed food aid can have negative effects on small farmers in recipient countries by putting downward pressures on domestic food prices, affecting trade, production incentives, and labor markets. The book identifies a number of ways in which such negative effects can be avoided, including a sharp targeting on low-income or acutely food-insecure people that would enhance food demand right along with the increasing supplies. Using food aid as an integral part of a food security policy is likely to be more beneficial to recipient countries than simply using food aid as a disposal mechanism for rich countries' surpluses. Dumping surplus food on developing country markets through program food aid and monetization can harm the 75 percent of the world's poor and food-insecure people who reside in the rural areas of those countries. The very simplistic argument frequently heard, that if people are hungry we should simply give them food, has justified inappropriate use of food aid.

The empirical evidence the authors present demonstrates that food aid does not benefit OECD farmers. So decoupling food aid from farm policy and instead making it an integral part of development and food security strategy would not hurt donor country farmers but could greatly help poor people worldwide. One main reason is that food aid availability tends to be inversely correlated to international food prices. Thus, when net food-importing, low-income, developing countries are faced with high international prices and most need free food, less food aid is likely to be available unless food aid is made an integral part of an appropriate food security program. This cannot happen as long as the availability of food aid is heavily influenced by agricultural policies in OECD countries. Meanwhile, the impact of OECD farm subsidies on developing countries can be negative and severe. Food exports by OECD countries at prices below the cost of production make agricultural development and poverty reduction in low-income developing countries extremely difficult.

Slow growth in the demand for staple food commodities is a bottleneck to rapid agricultural development in many low-income developing countries. Successful productivity increases by farmers in such countries may result in surplus production which either drives domestic prices down below production costs or is simply left to rot in the field. If procured in such countries, food aid could serve as an important stimulus to agricultural development and poverty reduction, not only in the aid-recipient countries but also in the countries where the food aid is procured. Such new markets for marketable surpluses in developing countries would be most successful if the food aid procurement is based on long-term contracts and if the procurement is accompanied by the development of the domestic markets and rural infrastructure. Unfortunately, since most of the food aid continues to originate in OECD countries, this potential additional benefit for developing countries with periodic marketable surpluses has not been fully realized. In fact, even in cases where food aid is procured in developing countries, it is usually done on very short-term tenders which do not give farmers enough time to adjust their production. Furthermore, the opportunity to use food aid as a development tool in these countries by adding investments in market development, institutions, and infrastructure has simply not been utilized to any significant degree.

A short foreword cannot do justice either to the subject or the content of this book which is a "must read" for those who have dedicated their professional lives to fighting poverty, responding to humanitarian disasters and hunger, and addressing chronic malnutrition, and to those who would simply like to understand the history of food aid and the prospects for using it more effectively in the future.

Per Pinstrup-Andersen
2001 World Food Prize Laureate
Cornell University
Ithaca, New York

Acknowledgments

We thank Andrea Besley, Kevin Heisey, Joy Learman, Erin Lentz and Jacqueline Murphy for extremely helpful research assistance. Trish (Schmirler) Long and her colleagues at Food Aid Management provided invaluable help in tracking down data and documents. Paul Dorosh, Eleni Gabre-Madhin, Joel Greene, Ted Jastrzebski, Thom Jayne, Asfaw Negassa, Ray Nightingale, David Sexton and George Simon all generously provided data as inputs to some of the empirical analysis. Bob Bell, Arthur Brooks, Jeff Brooks, Jim Firth, Douglas Hedley and Phil Thomas provided very helpful background information.

We were stimulated by discussions, and in some cases past collaborative work, with Awudu Abdulai, Harold Alderman, Bob Bell, Michelle Cachaper, the late Pat Carey, Dan Clay, Susan Farnsworth, Getachew Gebru, Isam Ghanim, Lena Heron, Stein Holden, Marieke Husentruyt, Robin Jackson, Judit Katona-Apte, Werner Kiene, Ellen Levinson, Peter Little, Angela Martin, Nick Maunder, John McPeak, Stephanie Mercier, Sandeep Mohapatra, Rob Paarlberg, David Pelletier, Tom Reardon, Shlomo Reutlinger, Vern Ruttan, David Sahn, Joe Scalise, Nancy Schwartz, Matt Shane, Kevin Smith and Michael Trueblood, from each of whom we have learned much.

We received very helpful comments on chapter drafts from Jim Barrett, John Becker, Cheryl Christensen, Ed Clay, Stuart Clark, Jim Cornelius, Joanne Csete, Steven Devereux, Jim Firth, Jean Pierre Habicht, John Hoddinott, Allan Jury, David Kauck, Marianne Leach, Frans Lammersen, Erin Lentz, Tom Marchione, Matias Margulis, Susan Offutt, David Orden, Frank Orzechowski, Jose Quiroga, Barry Riley, Lawrence Rubey, Curt Schaefer, Shahla Shapouri, Steve Vosti, Patrick Webb, Dennis Weller, Will Whelan and seminar participants at Columbia University, Cornell University, the University of California at Davis and the World Bank. Janet Hou, Cheryl Mrozowski and Alison Wadsworth helped with the manuscript preparation. Chris Barrett's work was partly supported by the Cornell University Agricultural Experiment Station. The findings and claims made in this book in no way represent either our employers or agencies that have helped underwrite any of the research reflected in here. The views expressed here are purely our own.

Finally, and most importantly, we thank our families for their patience and support as we devoted long hours to this project. Our wives, Clara and Joyce, deserve great credit for their patience and generosity. This book would not exist without their support. We dedicate this book to them and to our children, Brendan, Mary Catherine, Joanna, Julia, Elizabeth, Patrick and Emma Clare. May all the world's children have the same opportunities they enjoy. Our prayer is that they and their peers witness substantial progress in combating food insecurity and poverty in their lifetimes.

Abbreviations

ACDI	Agricultural Cooperative Development International
ADRA	Adventist Development and Relief Agency
ASA	American Soybean Association
AUSAID	Australian Agency for International Development
CAP	Common Agricultural Policy
CAP	Consolidated Appeal Process
CARE	Cooperative for Assistance and Relief Everywhere
CBT	community-based targeting
CCC	Commodity Credit Corporation
CDC	Canadian Dairy Commission
CFF	Compensatory Finance Facility
CHE	complex humanitarian emergency
CIDA	Canadian International Development Agency
CIF	cost, insurance, and freight (import value)
CPE	complex political emergency
CRS	Catholic Relief Services
C-SAFE	Consortium for the Southern Africa Food Security Emergency
CSSD	Consultative Sub-Committee on Surplus Disposal
DAC	Development Assistance Committee of the Organization for Economic Co-operation and Development
DAP	Development Assistance Program
DOD	Department of Defense
DPRK	Democratic People's Republic of Korea
EAF	Emergency Assistance Facility
EEC	European Economic Community
EFSR	Ethiopian Emergency Food Security Reserve
EU	European Union
EWS	early warning system
FAC	Food Aid Convention
FACE	Food Aid Co-ordination and Evaluation Centre
FAD	food availability deficit
FAIR	Federal Agriculture Improvement and Reform
FAO	Food and Agriculture Organization of the United Nations

FAP	food assistance programs
FAPC	Food Assistance Policy Council
FAS	Foreign Agricultural Service of the United States Department of Agriculture
FEWSNET	Famine Early Warning System Network
FFE	Food for Education
FFP	Food for Peace
FFW	Food for Work
FHI	Food for the Hungry International
FIAN	Food First Information and Action Network
FIVIMS	Food Insecurity and Vulnerability Information and Mapping Systems
FOB	freight on board (export value)
FSA	Farm Service Agency of the United States Department of Agriculture
GAO	General Accounting Office of the United States
GATT	General Agreement on Tariffs and Trade
GFAC	Global Food Aid Compact
GFE	Global Food for Education
GIEWS	Global Information and Early Warning System
GM	genetically modified
ICESCR	International Covenant on Economic, Social, and Cultural Rights
IDP	internally displaced persons
IFB	invitations for bids
IEFR	International Emergency Food Resource
IFECNP	International Food for Education and Child Nutrition Program
IFEP	International Food for Education Program
INTERFAIS	International Food Aid Information System
IRCRCS	International Red Cross and Red Crescent Societies
ITSH	internal transport, storage, and handling
JICA	Japanese International Cooperation Agency
KR	Kennedy Round
LDC	least developed country
MCH	maternal and child health
MDG	Millennium Development Goals
MSF	Médecins sans Frontières (Doctors Without Borders)
MT	metric tons
MSGR	Malawi Strategic Grain Reserve
MSP	Maritime Security Program
NASS	National Agricultural Statistical Service
NDDB	National Dairy Development Board
NFDM	nonfat dry milk
NGO	nongovernmental organization (see also PVO)
NRC	National Research Council of the United States
OCHA	Office for the Coordination of Humanitarian Affairs

ODA	overseas (or official) development assistance
OECD	Organization for Economic Co-operation and Development
OFDA	Office of Foreign Disaster Assistance
OMB	Office of Management and Budget
PCI	Project Concern International
PL 480	United States Public Law 480
PRISMA	Projects in Agriculture, Rural Industry, Science, and Medicine, Inc.
PRSP	Poverty Reduction Strategy Paper
PVO	private voluntary organizations (see also NGO)
ROW	rest of the world
UMR	usual marketing requirements
UNICEF	United Nations Children's Fund
URAA	Uruguay Round Agreement on Agriculture
USAID	United States Agency for International Development
USDA	United States Department of Agriculture
VAM	Vulnerability Assessment and Mapping
VOCA	Volunteers in Overseas Cooperative Assistance
WFP	World Food Programme
WHO	World Health Organization
WIC	Women, Infants, and Children
WISHH	World Initiative for Soy in Human Health
WTO	World Trade Organization
WVRD	World Vision Relief and Development

Introduction

Food aid[1] comprises one of the most complex and misunderstood instruments of contemporary international policy, though it is widely perceived in simplistic terms of providing life-saving succor to an emaciated child in a desolate refugee camp. In donor countries, it is at once an instrument of domestic agricultural policy, development assistance, and foreign and trade policies, managed through both bilateral and multilateral agencies with heavy involvement from the private nonprofit sector as well as profit-seeking agribusinesses and maritime interests. All these actors make it difficult to appreciate the full range of motivations at play, how the appealing humanitarian image of food aid often gets manipulated for less honorable purposes, and the myriad effects food aid has in various arenas. Widespread misunderstanding feeds ongoing controversy over food aid and undermines food aid's potential as an instrument of humanitarian and development policy, in particular, due to the use of food aid to serve multiple – and often inherently incompatible – donor objectives.

The core objective of this book is to lay out an evidence-based approach to using food aid more productively as one element of a broader strategy to reduce poverty and food insecurity in low-income, food-deficit nations. In order to accomplish that objective, we must first present a clear and reasonably comprehensive analytical and empirical account of food aid as historically and currently practiced so as to explode a few longstanding myths. Food aid has been a deeply flawed instrument over the past half century. But with limited substitute resources available globally from donors to support humanitarian operations and development assistance, it has nonetheless played an important role. Moreover, many of food aid's flaws are remediable through concerted action by key donors and operational agencies.

This book represents the joint reflections of an academic economist and a senior manager and food security advisor with an international nongovernmental organization (NGO) on the role food aid plays, and might prospectively play in the future, in addressing these interrelated problems. We approach this task first by introducing, in Chapter 1, basic concepts, terminology and trends for readers who might not already be familiar with food aid. Chapters 2 through 9 then review the evolving patterns, motivations and modalities of food aid over the past fifty years since the passage of United States **Public Law 480 (PL 480)**, the Agricultural Trade Development and Assistance Act of 1954, which effectively launched food aid as it is known today. We include a number of case study boxes intended to illustrate key points. The core objective of the first nine chapters is to explore the key analytical and operational issues one must consider in understanding contemporary food aid policy and operations.

In the final two chapters, we integrate the preceding nine chapters' findings to outline a strategy for recasting food aid so that it can effectively help alleviate poverty, hunger and vulnerability, and protect and fulfill basic human rights. This requires situating food aid within the broader range of agricultural and development policies of which it is properly a part, and to establish when, where, and why food aid can prove an effective instrument to promote income and productivity growth as well as humanitarian response. Implementing such a strategy will require concerted efforts to restrict the abuse of food aid and to concentrate its use on the most effective procurement and distribution modalities, as well as some redesign of the institutions surrounding food aid.

A glossary is provided at the back of the book, giving definitions of the main terms used in this book.

Throughout the volume, we aim to explode a number of popular myths about food aid – see the thirteen "myth" boxes included in the first nine chapters – in order to bring to light the complex constellation of interests that underpin present food aid policies, and to point the way toward a more sensible approach to food aid. In the final analysis, we argue that the only justification for food aid lies in three key roles. The first is short-term humanitarian assistance aimed at protecting the basic human rights of food-insecure populations, if and only if a problem of food availability underlies the inability of individuals and groups to access sufficient food to meet their nutritional requirements, and particularly where market failures limit the usefulness of other forms of humanitarian assistance. The second justification is the provision of longer-term safety nets to protect the scarce productive assets of vulnerable peoples, albeit under restricted circumstances. The third and most limited defensible use is for asset building among poor, food-insecure populations where other resources are simply not available and food can demonstrably do good without doing harm. Other (non-food) forms of assistance are typically preferable in cases where there is not an underlying food availability shortfall and market failure, or when food insecurity is chronic, even if the aggregate value of the non-food resources is somewhat less than might be available in the form of food.

Literally scores of millions of people have been assisted, and in many cases their lives have been saved, by food aid. These historical achievements of food aid should not be underestimated or devalued. Presently, however, food aid is driven primarily by political economy considerations that make food the primary form in which overseas development assistance is available in many contexts. The political economy of food aid – especially in the United States – sharply limits its effectiveness in humanitarian emergencies by, more often than not, impeding good targeting, slowing responsiveness, distorting recipient and intermediary incentives, and adding considerable costs. Essential complementary resources, particularly cash, are often not made available alongside food. For that reason, food aid's use in development programs is often straightforwardly a substitute for cash resources, a very inefficient one that too often proves to have counter-productive side effects. Contemporary food aid may be the least bad of a number of resource options, but it can and should be substantially improved through reforms such as those we advocate in Chapters 10 and 11.

Proponents have long argued for free or heavily discounted international shipments of food on humanitarian grounds, using the relatively straightforward argument that surpluses produced in food-exporting countries can and should be used to ensure the food security of poor peoples in other countries who cannot afford to buy enough food to meet their immediate needs. There is indisputable intuitive appeal to that argument. And there is good evidence that food aid has often had a positive effect in relieving human suffering, in facilitating human nutrition and child growth, and even in stimulating productivity growth among recipients.

Nonetheless, the empirical evidence also shows that food aid only sometimes helps the poor and hungry. Indeed, on occasion it can worsen their plight. Food aid has long been based on a false assumption that the best way to fight hunger is with food. This may be true if food aid is well targeted to food-insecure recipients when their need is acute, if local food availability is limited, and if commercial food markets do not function well enough to ensure that cash transfers might significantly increase people's access to food. But that is a lot of "ifs." In reality, over the past decade, roughly half of global food aid shipments have been converted into cash by recipients anyway and the emphasis on food occurs largely due not to the humanitarian objectives publicly used to justify food aid, but because of donors' commercial and political objectives. Food aid can prove a terribly inefficient means for transferring resources to poor people, although it need not always be thus.

If there is a single main cause for the inappropriate and ineffective use of food aid for the expressed purpose of reducing hunger, it is surely the complex set of subsidies and interest groups that comprise domestic farm policy, foreign policy, and trade policy in donor countries today. Relatedly, the key problems allegedly plaguing food aid – displaced international trade, depressed producer prices in recipient countries, labor supply disincentives, delivery delays, misuse by intermediaries, diversion to resale or feeding livestock or alcohol brewing, dependency, inattention to beneficiaries' micronutrient needs, etc. – all revolve ultimately around questions of targeting in distribution, procurement, or both. The issue of **targeting** concerns the who, where, when, what, and how questions surrounding transfers: is food aid reaching people who need it (and not flowing to people who do not need it),[2] when they need it, in appropriate form, and through effective modalities? Targeting is inherently difficult for myriad technical reasons we discuss in Chapter 8.

But food aid targeting gets distorted by food aid's political dependence on multiple masters, who often cause food to be overused or misused as a resource in order to serve donors' parochial interests. If the donor community could improve the targeting of food aid, perhaps especially the primary choice of the appropriate circumstances under which to use food as a resource, it could improve the effectiveness of food aid in accomplishing its primary humanitarian and development aims – the maintenance of valuable human capital, the protection of basic human rights and critical productive assets, and the promotion of productivity-enhancing private and public investment – and reduce many of the errors that sometimes make food aid controversial, ineffective, or both.

In this book, we explore where and why food aid is often merely an ineffective symbol – sometimes even a somewhat cynical cover for grossly self-serving, non-humanitarian objectives – when and how it is an effective tool for addressing poverty and food insecurity, and the means by which we can achieve significant improvement in food aid's efficacy as a tool for economic development and the protection of basic human rights. There has been much progress over the past generation in food aid operations on the ground. Because the devil is in the details, the chapters that follow go into some depth in an effort to pin down precisely where policymakers and operational agency managers need to focus in order to improve the efficacy of food aid as a tool for humanitarian relief and development.

Questions about access to adequate food involve both normative and positive elements. We take the approach in this book that access to adequate food is a basic human right, enshrined in both the Universal Declaration of Human Rights and other international treaties. But we also recognize that governments do not always respect, protect or fulfill the right to adequate food, in large part because of competing political interests. We therefore attempt to address both the normative (human rights) elements of access to food, as well as the positive (political and economic) constraints to achieving these goals. The United Nations' Millennium Development Goals (MDGs) provide one key reference point that has been agreed to by at least all the major donor governments. One of the key MDGs is reducing by half the proportion of people living on less than a dollar a day, and reducing by half the proportion of people who suffer from hunger. As public declarations of commitment, the MDGs are, in effect, the political means to address critical human rights issues in development, and we make reference to them in an attempt to address both the moral imperative of and the political constraints on reforming food aid.

This volume focuses disproportionately on the United States as a donor and Sub-Saharan Africa as a recipient region. This partly reflects the fact that the authors are Americans whose professional experience has been primarily in Africa. We therefore feel more confident about our knowledge of and prescriptions for this combination than we do for others. The core points we make nonetheless generalize readily to other donors and regions, not only because we draw on many examples from elsewhere to demonstrate broader patterns, but because the United States remains the world's preeminent food aid donor and Sub-Saharan Africa is the region of greatest development and humanitarian concern, the only continent where hunger is projected to grow rather than recede over the coming generation.[3] A significant rethinking of food aid is especially necessary in both these places.

1   The basics of food aid

As with much of the development business, food aid practitioners employ a bewildering array of opaque terms and peculiar acronyms that can make it a bit difficult for outsiders to comprehend even the broad contours, much less the details, of conceptual, policy and operational debates. This brief chapter, supplemented by the Glossary at the end of the book, aims to introduce the basic concepts, terminology, and patterns that must be understood prior to serious reflection on the role and design of an effective food aid strategy.

The misunderstanding of food aid begins with an ongoing, basic definitional issue.[1] The term "food aid" is commonly, but inaccurately, used to refer to the donation of food to recipient individuals and households. By this standard, Americans would be among the world's most numerous food aid recipients because of the extent of the school feeding in the United States, temporary assistance to needy families, food stamps, and other "food assistance programs."[2] Indeed, even private donations for neighborhood feeding programs – including such common activities as parental programs to provide mid-morning snacks to school children[3] – would qualify as "food aid" under such a broad definition, underscoring how such an expansive definition quickly loses its usefulness. The defining feature of food aid relates neither to the identity of final recipients, who may or may not need additional food beyond that they can produce or procure on their own, nor to the form of transfer. As we will discuss, much food aid gets turned into cash by **nongovernmental organizations** (NGOs) or **private voluntary organizations** (PVOs) and governments and therefore is not distributed as food to hungry people, while "food aid" can likewise take the form of cash donations used to purchase foods in surplus regions of the recipient country for distribution elsewhere. Rather, three core characteristics distinguish food aid from other forms of assistance:

(1)   the *international sourcing*
(2)   of *concessional resources*
(3)   in the form of or for the provision of *food*.

Without some cross-border flow of food or cash for the purchase of food and without there being a significant grant element, the flow is simply not food aid. Food aid is thus as much an issue of procurement as one of distribution, and it is most fundamentally an entry into nations' balance of payments. Food transfers that do not have corresponding balance of payments entries – such as school feeding programs in the United States, European prenatal nutrition programs, and food subsidies in much of the world – are not *internationally sourced*, they do not involve donations from another country. Such programs are not food aid even though they involve assistance related to food. Similarly, commercial international trade in food fails to meet the *concessional* element of the definition because there is no donation involved. Finally, international flows of financial aid that are unrelated to food (e.g., for military equipment or technical assistance) obviously do not qualify as food aid.

Modest flows intended to make a big difference at the margin

Food aid's visibility during crises masks a meagerness that many observers do not fully appreciate. While food aid was once a central part of **overseas development assistance** (ODA) provided by wealthier countries to poorer ones,[4] since 1995 it has averaged less than 2 percent of ODA (Figure 1.1). Not only is food aid a small portion of total foreign aid flows, it pales in comparison to domestic production and commercial trade flows as a source of food. Figure 1.2 underscores how food production and commercial food trade dwarf food aid flows today.[5] (Notice that production is measured against the right-hand axis, which is ten times larger than the left-hand axis against which aid and trade flows are measured!) While commercial food trade flows have grown steadily over time, accelerating especially sharply in the 1960s and 1970s, with slower growth in food trade thereafter, food aid flows have fallen by about two-thirds, averaging only 2 percent of food trade flows, from 1995–2000, and 0.15 percent of food production volumes over that period.[6] Even food aid flows to the poorest countries have halved in per capita terms since 1992.[7]

Globally, the volume of food aid is too limited to supplant production or trade as a source of food other than for very brief periods in very localized situations. Rather, the humanitarian objective of food aid is to make a big difference at the margin by relieving shortfalls in food availability that contribute directly to widespread, often acute **hunger, malnutrition**, and **undernutrition**, shortfalls that local markets cannot fully correct if poor people are just provided cash.[8]

Enough food is produced globally to meet every person's dietary requirements adequately. In 2000, the world enjoyed a daily per capita supply of more than 2,800 kilocalories and 75 grams of protein, more than enough to keep every man, woman, and child well nourished.[9] Such ample global food supplies are a relatively recent phenomenon. In 1961, the equivalent figures were only 2,256 kilocalories and 62 grams of protein daily per capita. The world has enjoyed an increase in daily average nutrient supply per person of 21–24 percent in just forty years, an historically unprecedented achievement. The technological advances in agricultural productivity that brought about such growth have resolved the global food aggregate supply problem, at least for current generations.

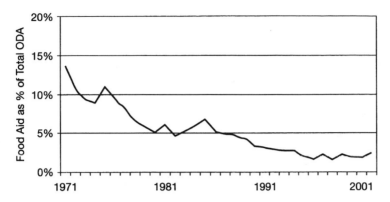

Figure 1.1 The decline of food aid within ODA

Source: OECD/DAC

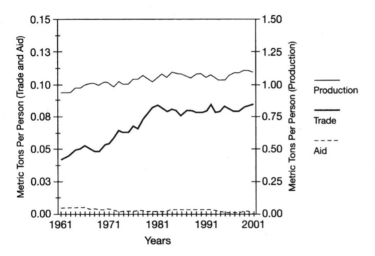

Figure 1.2 Global annual food flows

Source: OECD/DAC

In spite of this global plenitude, the most recent estimates of the Food and Agriculture Organization of the United Nations (FAO) suggest that roughly 852 million people – more than one person in eight worldwide – do not get enough to eat.[10] Many more than that are at risk of having insufficient access to food to maintain good health at intermittent points in time. The aggregate global food availability figures mask tremendous discrepancies among individuals and communities around the world, both within and between countries. Inequitable distribution within countries, within communities and even within households, is distressingly high. For example, the most recent data show that one in ten households in the United States – the country with the greatest per person food supplies in the world – experiences hunger or the risk of hunger.[11] Such intra-national variation is the subject of domestic policy, especially with respect to food assistance programs such as food stamps, food subsidies, school feeding programs, food price stabilization policies and the like.[12] While we recognize and are concerned about discrepancies in equitable food distribution at all these levels, the broader challenge of alleviating hunger and undernutrition globally lie beyond the scope of this book.

International food policy must address sharp discrepancies between countries in **food availability**. An expert consultation convened by the FAO established a **daily caloric intake** minimum of 2,350 per person as a goal.[13] Yet even in terms of average national consumption, a very rough indicator of food security, FAO food balance sheet data[14] suggest that about sixty countries fall below this threshold. Roughly two-thirds of these are in Sub-Saharan Africa. While the roughly 280 million people in the United States enjoyed daily supplies per person of 3,772 calories and 114 grams of protein in 2000 – up 30 and 20 percent, respectively, from 1961 – the equivalent figures for Sub-Saharan Africa's more than 600 million people were only 2,226 calories and 54 grams of protein – up only 6 and 3 percent, respectively, since 1961. Stagnant productivity per capita and limited hard currency earnings with which to import food generate large-scale food availability shortfalls in much of the world. Food deficiencies at national and even continental scales in a world of global surpluses underscore that the contemporary food security challenge is partly a problem of stimulating agricultural productivity in some poorer countries, especially in Africa, and partly a problem of ineffective and inequitable distribution. The question at the heart of this volume is when might food aid be an effective instrument for resolving problems of **food insecurity** associated with inequitable global food distribution and, relatedly, how can its effectiveness then be maximized, and its potential harms mitigated or even prevented?

Although undernourished people live in every nation on earth, residents of some countries are much more likely to be hungry than people elsewhere, as shown in Table 1.1, which lists the ten nations in which at least half the total population was declared undernourished by the FAO in 1998–2000. In four countries, Burundi, Afghanistan, Somalia, and the Democratic Republic of Congo (formerly Zaire), more than two-thirds of the residents are undernourished. As the right-hand column of Table 1.1 makes clear, however, food aid allocation is not especially highly correlated with the undernourished proportion of a country's population.

The causes of hunger – especially mass hunger and its extreme manifestation, famine – are complex, depending not only on food supply per capita, but also on the demand side, on the income people earn with which they can buy food, livelihood alternatives they face, the responsiveness of commercial food distribution channels to changing supply and demand, **safety nets** put in place by governments, non-governmental organizations (NGOs),[15] social or family networks, health factors that affect the efficiency of nutrient absorption and utilization by consumers, and awareness of proper storage, handling and preparation techniques by households. As many readers will realize from the countries listed in Table 1.1, war is strongly associated with widespread hunger, certainly as a cause but also as an effect.[16]

Table 1.1 Countries with greatest undernourished share of population

Country	Percent of total population undernourished, 1998–2000	Per capita food aid receipts, 1998–2000 (kg)
Democratic Republic of Congo	73	0.56
Somalia	71	3.72
Afghanistan	70	7.90
Burundi	69	2.22
Tajikistan	64	16.75
Eritrea	58	40.47
Mozambique	55	7.86
Angola	50	13.66
Haiti	50	16.82
Zambia	50	1.81

Source: FAO (2002)

These myriad factors must not obscure the fact, however, that food supply also matters. And in many countries there simply isn't enough food around to meet everyone's needs. Figure 1.3 plots average calorie and protein availability per person in 2000 for each country in the world. The figure is divided into quadrants according to somewhat arbitrary minima of 55 grams of protein and 2,350 calories per day per person.[17] Those nations in the upper-right quadrant enjoyed sufficient food supplies to provide every resident with an adequate diet. Those countries in the other three quadrants suffer a food supply shortage that effectively condemns many of their citizens to hunger. This latter group encompasses nearly 30 percent of the world's countries. Notice too that few countries suffer a shortfall in protein availability without an accompanying calorie deficit. This reflects the empirical regularity that energy and protein availability are strongly correlated, hence the emphasis within the nutritional sciences on "protein-energy malnutrition." This

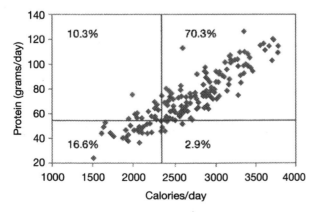

Figure 1.3 Per capita nutrient availability, 2000

Source: FAO Food Balance Sheets

provides part of the rationale for food aid's heavy reliance on basic grains, the lowest-cost sources of calories in the global food economy.[18] If a person's energy needs are met, their protein needs will typically be met as well.

These distributional patterns provide the basic humanitarian motivation for food aid. Nearly one-third of the nations of the world lack the food necessary to feed their populations adequately, in large measure because they lack the income necessary to purchase enough food on the global market to make up for domestic production shortfalls. They require outside assistance to import food to meet residents' dietary **needs**. Richer countries try to fill the gap with domestic food surpluses or with cash used to purchase food aid, either from donor or developing country farmers. A majority of these needy countries are in Sub-Saharan Africa, although most of the world's hungry people reside in Asia, primarily in a few populous, poor countries such as India, Bangladesh, Indonesia, and China.

The players in the food aid game

In part, because global patterns of hunger have changed over time, the geography of food aid has likewise evolved over the past generation. As Figure 1.4 shows,[19] until the mid-to-late 1970s, food aid went primarily to Asia, home to most of the world's hungry people. However, rapid economic growth in Asia over the 1960s and 1970s brought historically unprecedented reductions in hunger and growth in global commercial food trade, as reflected in Figure 1.2. In 1970, the seven largest food aid recipients in the world – India, South Korea, Indonesia, Pakistan, Israel, Turkey, and Vietnam – accounted for nearly 75 percent of global cereals aid flows. In 2001, they cumulatively accounted for only 5 percent.

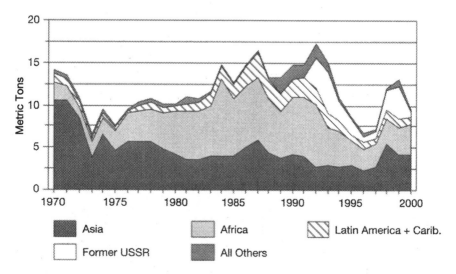

Figure 1.4 Food aid flows by recipient (1970–2000)

Source: INTERFAIS

The nations of Sub-Saharan Africa meanwhile suffered a combination of economic stagnation, rapid population growth and widespread civil strife that contributed to increased hunger on that continent. After a series a serious droughts and food emergencies in the mid-1970s, Africa became the primary destination of food aid globally. That situation persisted until the early 1990s, when a sharp, temporary reduction in food aid flows from the United States and a rapid reallocation of food aid toward the struggling states of the former Soviet Union brought a disproportionately sharp contraction in food aid volumes shipped to Africa.

At the start of the twenty-first century, Asia was once again receiving the largest share of food aid flows globally, the largest share of it destined for North Korea, the world's leading per capita food aid recipient, although Africa remained home to the nation that received the largest annual total food aid shipments over the period 2000–2: Ethiopia. Table 1.2 shows how the list of leading food aid recipients has evolved since 1960.

While the geography of food aid receipt has changed sharply over time, the sources of food aid donation have been remarkably constant. Ever since it began massive commodity shipments to Europe under the Marshall Plan following World War II, then formalized its food aid programs through PL 480 in 1954, the United States has been by far the world's principal source of food aid. PL 480 food aid grew rapidly, accounting for more than half of US food exports and most of the US total overseas aid budget by the early 1960s. Today, although food aid accounts for a much lower share of world food production and trade or overseas development assistance than it did in the 1960s or 1970s, the United States continues to provide most of the world's food aid. In 2000, the United States donated nearly two-thirds of global food aid flows, an increase from a decade earlier, as

Table 1.2 Fifteen leading global food aid recipients (in gross volume terms), selected years

Rank	1960	1970	1980	1990	2000
1	India	India	Egypt	Egypt	North Korea
2	Poland	South Korea	Bangladesh	Bangladesh	Ethiopia
3	Egypt	Indonesia	South Korea	Ethiopia	Bangladesh
4	Pakistan	Pakistan	India	Poland	Kenya
5	Brazil	Israel	Indonesia	Jordan	Russia
6	Israel	Turkey	Somalia	Sudan	Morocco
7	South Korea	Vietnam	Pakistan	Romania	Indonesia
8	Uruguay	Brazil	Portugal	Mozambique	Afghanistan
9	Turkey	Tunisia	Tanzania	Peru	Eritrea
10	Yugoslavia	Morocco	Ethiopia	Tunisia	Angola
11	Taiwan	Egypt	Sri Lanka	Pakistan	Yemen
12	Indonesia	Sri Lanka	Sudan	India	Jordan
13	Italy	Algeria	Kenya	Mexico	Tajikistan
14	Spain	Colombia	Mozambique	Bolivia	Sudan
15	Greece	Lebanon	Senegal	Jamaica	Serbia-Montenegro

Source: FAOStat and USDA data

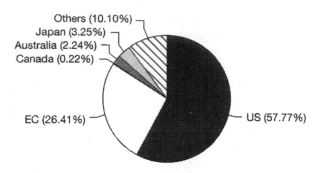

1990 Food Aid Flows By Donor

Others (10.10%)
Japan (3.25%)
Australia (2.24%)
Canada (0.22%)

EC (26.41%)

US (57.77%)

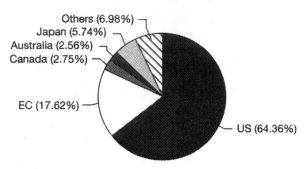

2000 Food Aid Flows By Donor

Others (6.98%)
Japan (5.74%)
Australia (2.56%)
Canada (2.75%)

EC (17.62%)

US (64.36%)

Figure 1.5 Food aid donors, 1990 and 2000
Source: WFP

reflected in Figure 1.5. The European Union (EU) comprises the next largest source of food aid, but has always provided somewhat less that half the volume of the United States. Moreover, EU food aid contributions have fallen in the wake of major reforms in the mid-1990s, which we discuss in Chapter 3. Japan, Canada, and Australia are other significant individual food aid donor countries.

The major food aid donors are, with the exception of Japan, also the world's primary food exporters. This underscores that food aid involves the sometimes awkward marriage of conventional, commercial food trade, geopolitical activity by the world's most powerful democracies, and humanitarian activity motivated by a concern about hunger. As a result, food aid involves myriad distinct objectives.

Upstream, one finds the farmers who grow the food and the agribusinesses who process, package, and sell it; the government and international agencies that raise funds and then use those resources to purchase the food; and the shippers who transport it from the procurement point to destinations worldwide. Food aid is then received by either recipient country governments, multinational organizations such as the **World Food Programme** (**WFP**) or the United Nations Children's Fund (UNICEF), or a range of NGOs, many of them well-known international humanitarian agencies – such as CARE, Catholic Relief Services, or Save the Children – who store it, distribute it directly to recipient populations, and in some cases, sell it on the open market locally and use the cash to support development programs in the field. In short, the food aid distribution channel draws in all the players who are involved in international commercial food trade – growers, processors, export promotion boards, distributors, shippers, warehousing agents, export financiers – as well as government agencies in multiple countries, and international organizations such as WFP and NGOs. The number of different players and interests predictably adds to the complexity of the coalition alignments that drive food aid policy, especially in the United States.

Food aid distribution modalities and channels

This complexity can be found as well in the range of different forms of food aid shipped around the world and the varying modalities through which it is procured. Food aid has classically been broken down into three different types: **program**, **project**, and **emergency**, the latter sometimes called **humanitarian** or relief food aid. Precise definitions of the categories vary somewhat across analysts and agencies, often posing analytical problems for those who work with data from multiple sources. The basic spirit of the differences, however, runs as follows.

Program food aid is provided directly on a government-to-government basis, typically for sale on local markets. This is really nothing more than foreign aid provided in the form of food. Just as with cash assistance, donors often impose conditions on the provision of program food aid. Such policy **conditionality** can take any of a wide variety of forms, from agreeing to negotiate on military and diplomatic matters, to placing the proceeds from the sale of food aid into a **counterpart fund** to be used for particular sorts of development interventions (for example, maternal and child health projects or rural infrastructure investment), to changing macroeconomic, trade or agricultural policies. Chapter 2 discusses some such cases.

Project food aid is provided to a recipient government, its agent, a multilateral development agency (e.g., WFP) or NGOs operating in the recipient country for use in development projects. Initiatives commonly supported by project food aid include the establishment or maintenance of strategic grain reserves, school feeding initiatives, **food for work** programs, or supplemental feeding centers for mothers and young children. Some of this food aid may also be sold or "monetized" and the cash proceeds used to support related programs. We discuss such projects in greater detail in Chapter 7. As will become clearer when we discuss food aid-supported projects in greater detail, it has become increasingly difficult to differentiate project from program food aid flows as the former has become increasingly monetized by NGO recipients much as the latter has been monetized by government recipients. These two categories together are referred to sometimes as *developmental* or *non-emergency* food aid.

Emergency food aid, sometimes called *humanitarian* or *relief* food aid, flows in response to emergencies resulting from natural disasters, such as droughts, floods or hurricanes, economic shocks, or civil strife or war. The general intent is to provide short-term relief to persons who are not able to meet their food requirements due to some kind of acute shock or emergency. Most people associate food aid more generally with emergency food aid because of widely broadcast images of food aid distribution in areas stricken by natural disasters or war, especially for refugees and **internally displaced persons** (IDPs).[20]

Until about 1990, program food aid was by far the dominant form of food aid, as Figure 1.6 plainly shows. Since then, sharp changes – discussed in detail in Chapters 2 and 3 – have prompted a dramatic reduction in program food aid and an associated shift toward emergency food aid. With the exception of 1999, when an extraordinary conjuncture of events brought about massive program food aid shipments to Russia, emergency food aid shipments have exceeded program food aid shipments since 1996, after having been consistently less than half the volume of program food aid until as recently as 1993. Hoddinott *et al.* (2004) find that emergency food aid response has been most pronounced with respect to conflict-related emergencies, while per capita food aid flows to persons affected by natural disasters have actually fallen somewhat since 1990.

The rise of emergency food aid has been accompanied by a shift in food aid distribution channels. Until the world food crisis of 1973–74,[21] the overwhelming majority of food aid was distributed bilaterally, generally on a government-to-government basis. This reflected the dominance of program food aid from the United States to the governments of various pro-American countries around the world. Since the late 1980s, however, one-quarter to one-third of global food aid has been channeled through the WFP. The USA is now the only donor that continues to disburse a majority of its food aid on a bilateral basis. Today, **multilateral aid** channels account for a plurality of food aid flows – 38 percent in 2000, versus 34 percent through **bilateral aid** channels and 28 percent through NGOs – with the WFP accounting for 99 percent of multilateral distributions on average, 1998–2000.

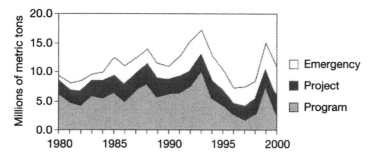

Figure 1.6 Global food aid flows by type

Source: WFP

The WFP, as an agency of the United Nations, receives its support through contributions from member states. The United States is overwhelmingly the primary contributor to the WFP, providing 63.3 percent of the agency's resources in 2001 and 51.7 percent in 2002, nearly ten times as much as the second largest donor, the European Commission, and roughly twice as much as the next ten largest donors combined.[22] US contributions are almost entirely in kind, in the form of donated food,[23] while many other donors (e.g., Canada, the Netherlands, the UK) offer much or all of their donation in cash. Thus, the rise of WFP signals a change in distribution channels, in some cases reflecting a shift in bilateral donors' mode of resourcing food aid, by providing cash rather than commodities.

WFP often uses NGOs for local distribution, however, and NGOs have become a major player in their own right, serving as the international distribution channel for 28 percent of global food aid flows in 2000, a historic high. According to WFP data, in 2000 NGOs sold 26 percent of all the food aid they handled on the open market in recipient countries, a phenomenon known as **monetization** of food aid. This relatively high rate of monetization underscores that food aid is widely used by NGOs as a resource to fund programs that attempt to address the causes of food insecurity, rather than merely treating its symptoms through direct distribution of food to hungry people. In this sense, NGO food aid distribution becomes somewhat like bilateral (i.e., government-to-government) program food aid distribution, 73 percent of which was monetized in 2000, providing recipient governments with resources to deploy wherever they saw fit. Program food aid shipments have typically been governed by a formal agreement by the recipient to channel the counterpart funds generated into particular uses approved by the donor. But given the fungibility of budgetary resources, recipients could effectively use these resources without *de facto* restriction. No one has yet, to the best of our knowledge, produced any empirical evidence that program food aid agreements have significantly affected recipient budget allocations in key productive and social sectors such as agriculture, education, and health.

In large measure, the rapid growth of WFP reflects the partial disengagement of food aid from donor country farm programs due to declining domestic surpluses, as we discuss in more detail in Chapters 2 and 3. And it has grown large indeed. As Charlton (1992, p. 46) notes, "although the WFP has frequently not received much publicity, it has emerged as the second largest source [globally] of development funds after the World Bank."[24] Nearly half of WFP's budget now comes from cash contributions, giving it greater flexibility in delivery modalities than many bilateral donors.

WFP often uses the cash it receives from high-income country donors to supply food aid in low-income countries. Some of these purchases are made in surplus regions of the countries in which the aid is ultimately distributed – a procurement method known as **local purchase** – while other food aid shipments are purchased in third countries (i.e., distinct from the donor or recipient countries) – a procurement modality known as **triangular transactions**. In 2000, more than 25 percent of food aid distributed by multilaterals (principally WFP) was procured through local purchases or triangular transactions. By contrast, NGOs and bilateral providers procured less than 10 percent of the food aid they distributed in 2000 through triangular transactions or local purchases – largely because they receive food directly rather than cash with which to purchase it.

By weight, cereals comprise the vast majority of food aid, at least 90 percent most years, although non-cereal food aid has increased modestly in the wake of an expanded list of non-cereal commodities eligible under the Food Aid Convention that took effect in July 1999. Historically, wheat and wheat flour, the major surplus commodities in the United States, Canada, and Europe until farm program reforms began in the late 1980s, represented two-thirds or more of global food aid flows, as Figure 1.7 shows, with rice and coarse grains (e.g., maize, sorghum) together accounting for most of the rest.

As government-held cereals stocks have fallen, however, and food aid appropriations have increasingly gone toward new purchases of commodities, the commodity composition of food aid has been diversified somewhat. By 2000, the non-cereals share of food aid flows had doubled in fifteen years, to 13 percent, principally in the form of nonfat dry milk powder and vegetable cooking oils. There has also been significant expansion over the past decade or so in shipments of **blended or fortified foods**. These are typically milled cereals to which essential minerals and vitamins – and sometimes milk powder – have been added so that porridge made of the blend provides most of a day's minimum required nutrients.[25] Blended foods have become especially important in emergency distribution and in supplementary feeding programs for children, refugees and internally displaced persons, so their rise mirrors the growth in emergency food aid shipments.

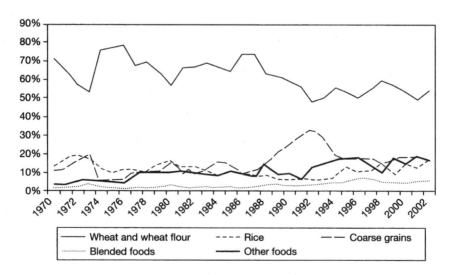

Figure 1.7 Commodity composition of global food aid flows

Source: WFP INTERFAIS

Conclusion

Food aid involves a complex array of players and distribution modalities, many of which have changed significantly over the past fifty years, especially in the past decade or so. The next eight chapters trace out the history of contemporary food aid so as to situate the analysis of key operational and strategic issues surrounding the design and implementation of food aid policy.

One might reasonably conclude that food aid matters less today than it did a generation ago, given absolute and relative declines in donated volumes. But where food aid still matters – perhaps most notably in areas of conflict and complex political emergencies – it continues to matter a lot, and emergency food aid has been growing sharply as a share of overall food aid flows. This only serves to underscore the inappropriateness of a "food aid strategy" distinct from broader agricultural, development, human rights and trade strategies intended to reduce poverty, vulnerability and hunger. The gradual shift from bilateral program food aid of cereals toward humanitarian shipments through multilateral channels, with an increasing proportion in the form of non-cereals, especially blended foods intended for recipients facing extraordinary nutritional risk, reveals desirable movement in the direction of making food aid first and foremost an instrument of relief, with highly targeted and specialized uses in support of safety nets and asset building in poor communities. But there remains much to be done.

2 Donor-oriented food aid
The United States of America

Food aid has long been inextricable from donors' geopolitical, agricultural trade promotion and surplus disposal objectives. Many contemporary observers nonetheless appear surprisingly unaware of food aid's origins and the constellation of interests that support and shape it in practice. In this chapter and the next, we explore the various donor objectives that have motivated food aid, as well as food aid's efficacy in addressing those donor objectives that are distinct from recipient objectives for improved food security.

The USA and Canada each launched their contemporary food aid programs in the immediate post-World War II era, Canada in 1951 and the United States over a period of years, culminating in the July 10, 1954, enactment of Public Law 480 (PL 480) that created what became the world's primary food aid program over the past fifty years.[1] The North Americans dominated both concessional food aid flows and commercial food exports well into the 1980s. As domestic farm programs in both countries generated sizable domestic food inventories that were costly for government to store, North Americans became concerned with developing lasting overseas markets to absorb surplus production. Furthermore, in the wake of the two world wars and the Korean war, Canada and the United States were also concerned about acute humanitarian need overseas and were quite willing to use food as an instrument of foreign policy in the Cold War against the Soviet Union. Over the past thirty or so years, the European Union has joined the North Americans as a donor similarly trying to attend to multiple interests – agricultural, commercial, geopolitical, and humanitarian – through its use of food aid. These multiple motives have long accommodated strong, diverse domestic constituencies supporting food aid.

The domestic political benefits of food aid serving multiple masters has come at a serious cost in terms of its effectiveness. Although trade promotion, surplus disposal, geopolitical and humanitarian assistance motives all support food aid as a general phenomenon, these objectives almost inevitably conflict over the specifics of food aid policy. The complex interest group politics of food aid reflect the nature of the process in contemporary democratic governance systems. Yet, where other donors have significantly simplified the politics and practice of food aid in recent years (see Chapter 3), significant reforms have yet to occur in the United States.

While food aid will never be free of politics, we think it unnecessarily fatalistic to simply accept the political status quo *ex ante* surrounding food aid, especially as it exists in the United States.

The ineffectiveness caused by trying to use food aid to serve multiple, but ultimately inconsistent objectives, should come as no surprise. The Nobel Prize-winning economist Jan Tinbergen long ago cautioned that a single policy instrument can only coincidentally address multiple objectives effectively.[2] The **Tinbergen rule** stipulates that optimal policy requires one policy instrument for each objective. As Vern Ruttan and other expert commentators on food aid have pointed out repeatedly for more than a decade, the failings of the global food aid system derive directly from ill-advised efforts to circumvent the Tinbergen rule, trying to serve multiple objectives that have ultimately proved mutually inconsistent with a single policy instrument: food aid. This has been especially true with respect to US food aid policy.[3]

The core contention of this chapter is that over the past fifty years food aid has been oriented primarily toward a variety of donor concerns, rather than toward the interests, needs, and rights of recipients. There has been some movement since 1990 in both rhetoric and practice in the direction of attending to recipient country needs, inserting food security objectives explicitly into the PL 480 continuing legislation in 1990, improving non-emergency food aid programming a bit in the past decade, and, most recently, the US government's curtailment of Section 416(b) shipments (described below). These changes hint at the potential for more sub-stantive, necessary change, but they should not be mistaken for serious reforms of American food aid.

It should come as no great surprise that food aid, especially US food aid, remains donor-driven, given the empirical regularity that rich countries tend to subsidize heavily small and declining agricultural sectors, known as the **developmental paradox**.[4] Food aid is but a legacy, manifestation, or both, of rich donor countries' efforts to support their own farmers and to advance these nations' own parochial aims. Because world markets transmit price signals from rich countries to poorer ones, heavy farm subsidies in the former tend to have a sharp, adverse effect on developing country agriculture. These linkages between food aid and donors' domestic farm policies, on the one hand, and between rich country farm subsidies and depressed agricultural profitability – and thus retarded agricultural and rural development – in developing countries, on the other, lead many observers to erroneously blame food aid for slow or nonexistent progress in combating poverty and food insecurity in many low-income nations.

Food aid is not inherently problematic as an instrument of development and humanitarian policy. Nonetheless, by attempting to use food aid for too many purposes, especially in pursuit of donor-oriented objectives for which it is inherently ill-suited, donors have compromised food aid's effectiveness in accomplishing most goals well, particularly the humanitarian objectives that underpin most public rhetoric in support of food aid. This ineffectiveness sparks disputes among donors, especially in disagreements over the effects of food aid on commercial trade in foodstuffs.

In Chapters 6–9 we will review how food aid has been changing, gradually but perceptibly, and some of the remaining problems with what appears to be the slow emergence of recipient-oriented food aid. First, however, we need to review the history of contemporary food aid programs in order to make clear why donor-oriented food aid so commonly fails to address the food security needs of vulnerable peoples around the world and even donors' more self-interested objectives. We start with the massive US programs.

US food aid programs[5]

For fifty years, the United States has been the primary provider of food aid globally. The nature of US food aid programs is of disproportionate importance both because of their sheer volume and because US influence manifests itself in food aid funded by other donors. We therefore begin by briefly reviewing how American food aid has evolved in response to domestic and foreign policy concerns unrelated to the alleviation of hunger and food insecurity around the world.

US food aid policy has shifted over time, although it has changed less substantively than have food aid policies of Canadian and European donors. Food aid from the United States continues to be especially heavily tied to American agricultural, foreign policy, and trade interests, often to the detriment of genuine benefits to recipients. Because it dominates worldwide food aid, reform of American food aid is a necessary condition if significant progress is to be made in adapting the global food aid system to serve humanitarian objectives effectively. So it is important to understand where the problems lie in US food aid programs. And the problems appear many. As just one current indicator, President Bush's 2001 management review identified US food aid as one of fourteen government areas most in need of reform.

With six different programs administered by two different Cabinet-level agencies, each operating similar bureaucracies, and involving several other executive agencies as well, the US food aid system is not only the world's largest, but also indisputably the most complicated. An interagency Food Assistance Policy Council (FAPC), chaired by the **United States Department of Agriculture (USDA)** Under-Secretary for Farm and Foreign Agricultural Services, coordinates all US food aid policies and programs. FAPC includes representatives from the Office of Management and Budget (OMB), the **United States Agency for International Development (USAID)**, the US Department of State, the National Security Council, and USDA. At the staff level, program planners in USAID and USDA meet on a regular basis to review and coordinate plans. The Department of Transportation also gets involved through its Maritime Administration, which reimburses USAID and USDA for a portion of the shipping costs incurred under the cargo preference requirements that restrict 75 percent of US food aid shipments to US-flag carriers.

The overwhelming majority of US food aid flows currently and historically fall under the three titles of Public Law 480, and are funded through annual and supplemental appropriations by the Congress. The 1990 Farm Bill sharpened lines of authority over food aid, with USDA taking clear responsibility for surplus disposal and export market development objectives under Title I, with USAID – a semi-autonomous agency within the Department of State – handling Titles II and III, with a stated focus on emergency relief and promoting economic development. Title III had previously been run by USDA, but in converting it from a credit program to one based on outright grants, the program joined grant-based Title II programs under USAID direction. The 1990 Farm Bill was perhaps most important for food aid in its rhetoric, because it changed the stated overall purpose of PL 480 to the reduction of food insecurity worldwide.

Table 2.1 lists the US food aid programs, along with some basic descriptors of the year the program began, the managing agency, and recent expenditure levels. PL 480 Title I programs, administered by the **Foreign Agricultural Service** (**FAS**) of the USDA, offer concessional credit sales of agricultural commodities by the US government to developing countries. The United States is the only donor that continues to ship food aid on anything other than a completely free ("grant" in development assistance jargon) basis. This provokes complaints from other agricultural exporters that at least the Title I PL 480 component of US food aid is a disguised export credit program in contravention of international trade disciplines under the World Trade Organization. We discuss this and related trade issues in more detail in Chapter 4.

Historically, Title I sales have been to governments,[6] although since the **1996 Farm Bill** (the Federal Agriculture Improvement and Reform Act of 1996), sales can now also be made to private entities in recipient countries. For many years, Title I sales came from government-held food surplus stocks. Now, private businesses in the United States respond to invitations for bids (IFBs) from the USDA's Farm Service Agency (FSA), which handles commodity procurement for US food aid programs and coordinates commodity purchases with shipping. Countries (called "participants" in program language) finance Title I market purchases through long-term, low-interest rate loans provided through the **Commodity Credit Corporation** (**CCC**) of the USDA. The terms of sale on credit typically involve quite a substantial **grant element** (i.e., effective discount relative to the open market cost). Recipient governments generally agree to sell ("monetize") shipments received and to use the proceeds for a range of other purposes, typically negotiated in advance with the USA. These programs are explicitly targeted at promoting American agricultural export markets and at advancing US strategic interests. In the fifty years of its history, there has rarely been any serious pretense of Title I serving development objectives.

PL 480 Title II programs, administered by USAID, provide donations of food to meet humanitarian and development needs abroad. To provide for emergency needs, a varying proportion of Title II aid is channeled through recipient governments, NGOs or multilateral organizations such as the World Food Programme. Food aid is also furnished to NGOs to carry out non-emergency programs aimed at stimulating long-term economic development, generally of a type intended to improve household or individual food security and nutritional well-being. Commodities and transport costs for Title II programs are furnished

Table 2.1 US food programs, 1992–2002

Program	PL 480 Title 1	PL 480 Title II	PL 480 Title III	Food for Progress	Section 416(b)	Bill Emerson Humanitarian Trust	International Food for Education and Child Nutrition
Year Begun	1954	1954	1954	1985	1949	1980	2003
Managing agency	USDA	USAID	USAID	USDA	USDA	USDA	USDA
Cumulative 1992–2002 budget (US$ billion)	$4.38	$9.62	$1.34	$1.33	$2.41	N/A	N/A
FY 2001 Total spending (US$ million)	$105	$915	$0	$107	$630	N/A	N/A

Notes: N/A = not available or not applicable

Data sources: USAID, *International Food Assistance Report 2001*; Yager (2002).

by the Commodity Credit Corporation, arranged through USDA's FSA, just as with Title I programs. Over only the past ten or so years has Title II become the primary source of US food aid shipments, a striking reversal from the first thirty or so years under PL 480, when Title I always dwarfed the other programs. Figure 2.1 shows how rapidly Title II has supplanted Title I as the main food aid program over the past two decades. Program food aid (Title I) has declined more than 90 percent since 1980 in inflation-adjusted terms, while emergency and project food aid under Title II have increased significantly since the end of the Cold War in 1989–90, when food security was made a formal objective of American food aid.

PL 480 Title III programs, also administered by USAID, donate commodities to developing country governments that then generally sell the food to generate funds, ostensibly to support long-term economic development programs. Title III funding was effectively phased out in 1999, although it currently remains on the books as an unfunded facility that could be used if Congress appropriated funds for it.

Food for Progress programs, directed by USDA, involve donations of agricultural commodities to developing countries and emerging democracies in exchange for commitments from recipient countries to promote free enterprise and competition in their agricultural economies. Food for Progress focuses on private sector development of agricultural infrastructure such as improved agricultural techniques, marketing systems, farmer education and cooperative development, expanding use of processing capacity, development and introduction of new foods, and agribusiness development. Created by the Food for Progress Act of 1985, this program is funded by annual and supplemental appropriations by the Congress under Title I PL 480 or **Section 416(b)** accounts to serve an array of prospective recipients, including not only developing country governments, but also NGOs, cooperatives and international organizations.

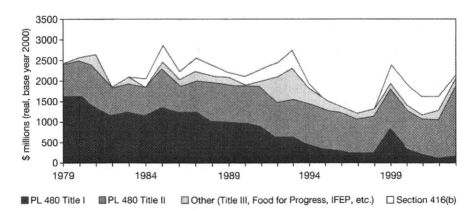

Figure 2.1 US food aid programs, 1979–2003

Sources: US Dept. of Agriculture, General Accounting Office, Bureau of Economic Analysis

Section 416(b) of the Agriculture Act of 1949 authorizes the donation of CCC-owned commodities in surplus of domestic program requirements to carry out programs of assistance in developing and friendly countries.[7] In the past, these commodities were commonly held as government stockpiles built up through farm price support programs. The Section 416(b) program was originally intended to prevent spoilage in government-held stocks by ensuring grains left storage within a reasonable period of time. In more recent years, the CCC has more commonly gone out and purchased commodities for shipment overseas in response to weak prices and political pressures to stimulate demand for agricultural commodities. The commodities are donated to foreign governments, NGOs, cooperatives, and the World Food Programme. The oldest of the food aid programs currently operated by the United States, Section 416(b) shipments are purely responsive to CCC purchases from US farmers and thus best understood as a surplus disposal instrument used to support American farm incomes. Their timing, volume and commodity composition are not related to recipient need unless purely by coincidence. The Bush administration signalled in 2002 that it intends to sharply curtail the use of Section 416(b) shipments and to employ the **Bill Emerson Humanitarian Trust** when faced with increased need for emergency food aid.

The Bill Emerson Humanitarian Trust is a food reserve administered by USDA that is used to respond to emergency food aid needs in developing countries. Up to 4 million metric tons of US wheat, corn, sorghum, and rice can be kept in the reserve and can be used for emergency food aid needs that cannot otherwise be met through PL 480, for example, when the annual PL 480 appropriations have already been committed or when domestic supplies available for procurement through standard channels prove insufficient. Originally established by the Agricultural Trade Act of 1980 as the Food Security Wheat Reserve, it was renamed in 1998 for the late Missouri Congressman, who had been a champion of efforts to expand food donations to the poor. The law permits USDA to release up to 500,000 metric tons annually, plus up to another 500,000 metric tons that could have been released in prior years but were not released, or to release food for use under PL 480 Title II if the domestic supply of that particular commodity is in short supply and would not meet the availability criteria of PL 480. As of spring 2003, there had only been ten releases from the Trust in its history, the most recent to Iraq following the US-led invasion of March 2003 (Table 2.2). The Emerson Trust is thus the most infrequently used of all the US food aid facilities. The main reasons for this are that commodity producers express concern that releases might put downward pressure on market prices, although there is no evidence of this having ever been true, and that by statute Emerson Trust releases must be reimbursed by the procuring agency. Although the repayment requirement is open-ended, the Office of Management and Budget has historically pressed hard for rapid repayment because this is effectively an interest-free loan and because of pressure from storage and warehouse providers who receive payment for services only on stocks held in the Trust. These costs can be covered by supplemental appropriations by the Congress, but that has been a rare occurrence.

Table 2.2 History of release authorizations from the Emerson Humanitarian Trust (through March 2003)

Date	Release
Mar. 20, 2003	200,000 metric tons, with an additional 400,000 tons as needed, for use in PL 480 Title II for unanticipated emergency needs in Iraq. If not all needed in Iraq, commodities could be used in Title II for emergency needs in Africa.
Mar. 19, 2003	200,000 metric tons authorized for use in PL 480, Title II, for unanticipated emergency needs in Africa, particularly Ethiopia and Eritrea.
Aug. 28, 2002	300,000 metric tons authorized for use in PL 480, Title II, for unanticipated emergency needs in southern Africa.
Jun. 7, 2002	275,000 metric tons authorized for use in PL 480, Title II, for unanticipated emergency needs in southern Africa.
Jan. 22, 1996	1.5 million metric tons authorized for use in PL 480, Titles I, II, and III, because of limited domestic supplies.
Jul. 19, 1994	200,000 metric tons authorized for use in PL 480, Title II, for unanticipated needs in Caucasus region.
May 31, 1991	300,000 metric tons authorized for use in PL 480, Title II, for unanticipated needs in the Middle East, Asia, and Africa.
Sept. 14, 1989	2.0 million metric tons authorized for use in PL 480, Titles I and II, because of limited domestic supplies.
Oct. 26, 1988	1.5 million metric tons authorized for use in PL 480, Titles I and II, because of limited domestic supplies.
Dec. 5, 1984	300,000 metric tons authorized for use in PL 480, Title II, for unanticipated needs in Africa.

The 2002 Farm Bill (the Farm Security and Rural Investment Act of 2002) authorized the creation of a new US food aid program, the McGovern–Dole International Food for Education and Child Nutrition Program, named for former Senators George McGovern and Robert Dole, each former champions of food aid in Congress. Senator McGovern also served as the US Ambassador to the Rome-based United Nations agencies (the Food and Agriculture Organization, the International Fund for Agricultural Development, and the World Food Programme). The McGovern–Dole program, administered by USDA's FAS, donates food commodities purchased by the CCC for school feeding and maternal and child nutrition projects in low-income countries. It will be interesting to see how this program evolves, since the pilot program was better funded than the initial appropriations once it was made a permanent part of the USDA food aid portfolio.

Understanding the genesis and evolving uses of and balance among these various programs requires some attention to broader US policy goals. We begin with the relationship between US food aid and farm policy because the domestic agricultural agenda has long been the prime driver behind international food aid policy.

Support from the domestic agricultural lobby and its champions on Capitol Hill, such as Senators Dole, Humphrey, and McGovern, has historically been vital to Congressional approval of food aid appropriations. Changing foreign policy objectives and modalities have likewise had an important effect on food aid and will be discussed in the subsequent section. These historic pillars of American policy have, however, been waning in their interest in food aid, signaling emerging opportunities to recast food aid for the twenty-first century.

American farm policy and food aid

If there is a single main cause for inappropriate use of food aid for the expressed purpose of reducing hunger and its structural causes, it is surely the complex set of subsidies and interest groups that comprise American farm policy. USDA has played the central role in American food aid programming, procurement and management, although various agencies within the Departments of State and Treasury and the Office of Management and Budget, especially USAID, have been involved to varying degrees, as just discussed. As one would expect, USDA's principal concerns have always revolved around domestic surplus disposal and export promotion objectives, not the interests of recipients in humanitarian relief and economic development, who are not the USDA's charge. The USDA's actions have been driven by Congressional pressure and legislative directive, including through appropriations, at least as much as by Department initiative in response to domestic agribusiness pressure. By reducing supply through surplus disposal and stimulating demand through market promotion, it has long been believed that food aid can help support agricultural commodity prices and, thus, farm incomes in the United States – rightfully a principal policy objective of the Congress and USDA.

In the 1940s and 1950s, American farm price support programs generated enormous surpluses of basic grains. Various Congressional initiatives were enacted to try to offload some of these stocks abroad. PL 480 became the largest and most lasting such program. Passed by Congress and signed into law by President Eisenhower in July 1954, PL 480 was the direct byproduct of the collapse of agricultural commodity prices following the Korean War and mounting government stockpiles of grain procured under generous farm price support programs.[8] This was only the largest to date in a long series of surplus disposal measures enacted by a succession of US administrations, and the innovativeness of the Congress and future administrations would lead to further manipulations of the food aid system for surplus disposal as well as, ultimately, the development of alternative, more effective surplus disposal mechanisms and significant changes in American farm policy.

These domestic objectives have long trumped food aid's other goals. As far back as February 1958, a Senate study of PL 480 operations and policy entitled *Food and Fiber as a Force for Freedom* decried the use of the program purely for surplus disposal objectives, with little attention paid to humanitarian or foreign policy aims. The USDA, the farm lobby and its champions in the Congress have consistently used the humanitarian labels and images of food aid as "a convenient public relations device to paper over the reality of surplus disposal."[9] But it would be rather hard to defend concessional shipments of cotton, tobacco and other non-food commodities – which have been included in American food aid programs at various periods – as dietary interventions based on humanitarian or economic development objectives. As the Nobel Laureate T.W. Schultz trenchantly observed in 1960:

> It is easy to rationalize our farm surpluses into international assets. But thoughtful people and informed leaders abroad are not deceived by what we say; they see clearly that we have been making our foreign economic policy fill our internal convenience.[10]

Domestic food stocks peaked in the late 1950s and early 1960s, and food aid flows, predictably, peaked not long thereafter, as shown in Figure 2.2. (Note that year-end wheat stocks are plotted against the right-hand axis, on a different scale than food aid flows, which are plotted against the left axis.) Then, over the course of the Kennedy and early Johnson administrations, food stocks fell steadily as the expansion of farm income supports slowed. A bit of a recovery in the late 1960s came to an abrupt end as a combination of adverse weather – especially in the Soviet Union in 1972 – and fiscal crisis in the USA led to a sharp fall in global cereals stocks by the early 1970s, and helped precipitate the **World Food Crisis of 1973–74**. Year-end carryover stocks of wheat that had stood at more than one billion bushels in the early 1960s dipped to less than 20 million bushels by the end of 1973.[11] Food aid volumes plummeted as a result.

Domestic food stocks grew again over the course of the Ford, Carter and Reagan administrations, with renewed generosity in domestic farm price support programs following the 1981 Farm Bill and the collapse of overseas export markets in the wake of the second oil price crisis of 1979 and the debt crisis that struck most middle-

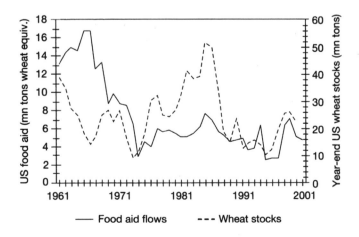

Figure 2.2 US food aid flows, wheat stocks

Source: USDA Economic Research Service

income countries in the 1980s. Although the rise of alternative export promotion instruments and growth in domestic food surplus disposal through school feeding and emergency food assistance programs lessened pressure to use food aid as a vent for surplus during the 1970s and early 1980s,[12] food aid volumes nonetheless increased in response to growth in carryover grain stocks in the United States. Then, once the 1988 drought and resurgent agricultural exports had brought grain stocks back down, food aid shipments fell to historic lows in the early 1990s.

The 1985 and 1990 Farm Bills made incremental changes toward liberalization of American agriculture. The 1996 bill, known as the Federal Agriculture Improvement and Reform (FAIR) Act, however, gutted most government stock accumulation by eliminating supply management provisions and changing the income-support mechanisms enjoyed by wheat, corn, rice, barley, and sorghum growers, among others.[13] As a consequence, food aid had to make a final transition from a government surplus-based to a budget-based regime. This change could have major implications for US food aid policy, in that shipments no longer have to come from extant government-held stocks. To date, however, this potential for reform has gone untapped. Indeed, and perhaps ironically, food aid now tracks domestic food stocks more closely than ever because fluctuations in food aid volumes arise primarily from "emergency" supplemental appropriations by Congress that direct the CCC to purchase commodities for shipment overseas in an effort to prop up a weak commercial market.[14]

The US 1996 Farm Bill also identified food aid as one of four programs to be used in support of commercial agricultural exports. This became perhaps most evident in the 3.7 million metric ton food aid package the Congress approved for Russia in 1998–99, described in Box 2.1. This extraordinary program for Russia exceeded the sum of all US food aid shipments just two years earlier and underscores the continued use of food aid for surplus disposal and export promotion purposes. The agricultural community now looks to food aid episodically to relieve transitory marketing problems rather than as a steady source of demand. Of course, that just tightens the linkage between food aid and aggregate supplies, as manifest most plainly in carryover stocks. The 2002 Farm Bill reauthorized Title I PL 480 flows aimed at trade promotion and, for the first time, authorized agreements with private entities in addition to foreign governments. It is plain that the trade promotion objective of food aid persists, even though it has historically proved an ineffective tool for expanding US commercial food exports.[15]

Box 2.1 Self-serving food aid to Russia

American enthusiasm for US food aid to Russia in the 1990s was driven overwhelmingly by American economic and geopolitical interests. Immediately prior to its dissolution, the Soviet Union suffered a serious economic crisis characterized by rampant inflation and shortages of food and other necessities. In response, President Gorbachev launched a series of economic reforms which proved largely ineffective. The ensuing attempted coup of August 1991 did not succeed in re-establishing central planning. However, it did greatly disrupt national grain purchases by the state procurement organization. The resulting distribution problems were exacerbated by a bad harvest and meager grain reserves which could last only until January 1992.

At the same time, American wheat production jumped 25 percent in 1992 while domestic consumption slumped in the sluggish economy that brought down the first Bush administration. The administration, desperately seeking Midwestern electoral support and concerned to safeguard a fragile Russian state, launched a massive program of food aid shipments. In 1992, it sent more than 1.1 million tons of cereals and another 70,123 tons of non-cereal foods in the first donations ever to the Russian Federation. The next year, food aid shipments to Russia hit nearly 2.5 million tons of cereals, representing almost 30 percent of American shipments worldwide, and non-cereals shipments multiplied eightfold over 1992.

Of course, Russian food shortages were only relative to a very high level of nutrition. FAO data show that in 1992, Russians consumed on average 2,924 calories, 91.7 grams of protein and 80.8 grams of fat per day, well more than internationally accepted nutritional targets and more than 35 percent more energy than was consumed by residents of Sub-Saharan Africa that same year. Some claim that Russia actually had a national surplus of food in 1992.[1]

Despite unconfirmed need, aid to Russia presented an opportunity for the US to change its relationship with its former Cold War enemy. Then-Presidential candidate Bill Clinton stated, "a democratic Russia means lower defense spending, a reduced nuclear threat, a diminished risk of environmental disasters, fewer arms exports . . . and the creation of a new, major market for American goods and services,"[2] thus highlighting the domestic benefits of food aid for the US.

Inflated, self-serving US food aid to Russia reappeared in 1998–99 when Russia's banking system and currency collapsed. Russian farm production plunged approximately 40 million tons from the previous year to only 47 million tons, the lowest since 1946,[3] and Russia threatened to default on its international debt repayment obligations. At the same time, a sharp recession in Asia had dramatically cut US grain exports in a year of record-setting wheat yields, with carryover grain stocks up more than 250 percent since 1995. Agriculture Secretary Glickman argued passionately for massive food aid shipments, claiming that

> In terms of our own economic, strategic and national security interests, the United States has a major stake in supporting Russia's transition and building a closer relationship with it. . . . Until the ruble devaluation, Russia was a major commercial market, the tenth largest export market for US agricultural products in the last few years. Russia was the leading

export market in the world for US poultry meat, and a leading market for pork. All that ended with the Russian financial crisis.[4]

Facing a hotly contested mid-term election in which several farm states were key battle grounds, the US government authorized massive CCC purchases for Section 416(b) food aid shipments to Russia. From less than 6,000 tons each in 1994 and 1996 and 41,000 tons in 1997, US food aid flows to Russia jumped to 1.2 million and 1.9 million tons in 1998 and 1999, respectively, representing 19 and 27 percent, respectively, of US shipments worldwide those years, up from 1 percent in 1997. Figure 2.3 shows the extraordinary volatility in American food aid flows to Russia over the 1990s in response largely to domestic phenomena. We also plot flows to Peru – the only nation in the world to have received food aid flows from the United States every year since the enactment of PL 480 in 1954 – as a comparison against the persistent, modest flows of US food aid to most low- and middle-income countries.

Once again, the availability of food in Russia if there had not been US food aid would have placed it in the top third of the world's rankings of nutrient availability. Food scarcity in Russia was not the true driving force behind extraordinary food aid shipments. That was the collapse of international grain markets in the wake of the east Asian financial crisis and a production spike during a crucial mid-term election year. There should be little surprise that there is no credible evidence of any lasting, positive effect of this massive shipment.[5]

Not all Russians agreed with the US approach to alleviating the food crisis of 1998–99. A former deputy agriculture minister for Russia argued that

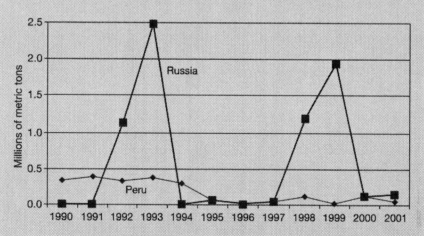

Figure 2.3 US food aid shipments to Russia (as compared against Peru)

Source: WFP INTERFAIS database

the type of aid granted by the US "distorts the market, hurts domestic producers, and will in no way benefit the poorest layers of the population." Russian farmers reportedly exported more than 900,000 tons of grain in 1999 – nearly half the volume of US food aid inflows – pointing to shortcomings in internal markets and distribution rather than harvest shortages, and leaving Mr. Kholod to ask: "Would Americans accept aid if their own farmers couldn't sell anything on their own market?"[6] The motivation behind US food aid shipments to Russia in the 1990s can at best be only partly explained as a response to Russian food shortages. Rather, national security interests, particularly the desire to build a new relationship with a former adversary, and, above all, concerns about American farmers in key election years drove the historically unprecedented shipments.

Notes:
[1] Michael Claudon and Tamar Gutner (eds) (1992) *Putting Food on What Was the Soviet Table* (New York: New York University Press).
[2] As quoted in "Aid for Russian Democracy," *Washington Post,* April 2, 1992.
[3] USDA's Russian Food Aid Program hearing before the Committee on Agriculture, House of Representatives, 106th Congress, First Session, October 6, 1999. p. 18 (http://commdocs.house.gov/committees/ag/hag10636.000/hag 10636_0f.htm).
[4] USDA's Russian Food Aid Program hearing before the Committee on Agriculture, House of Representatives, 106th Congress, First Session, October 6, 1999, p. 19. (http://commdocs.house.gov/committees/ag/hag10636.000/hag 10636_0f.htm).
[5] Moreover, the US General Accounting Office (2000) published a highly critical evaluation of the 1998–99 Russian food aid program, noting that less than one-quarter of the targeted regions within Russia received an amount equivalent to or near their planned allotment, that severe lack of internal controls created widespread opportunities for fraud and abuse, not least of which because US food aid was monetized at a sharp discount to Russian wholesale prices: approximately 50 percent less in the case of rice shipments and 40 percent in the cases of corn and wheat.
[6] Mark Whitehouse, "Many Ask Whom US Food Aid in Russia is Helping," *New York Times,* March 16, 1999.

Food aid has long served as a vent for surplus, as a means of trying to reduce the downward pressure on food prices that would result from the donated commodities entering the domestic or world market, although there is no evidence that food aid has had any discernible effect on domestic farm prices in at least twenty-five years. Food aid has also, secondarily, limited government expenditure on stocks maintenance during periods when government-held surpluses have been considerable, and on government price support programs. One should not be lulled into believing, however, that the discontinuation of government farm price support programs that once generated massive government-held stocks used to source food aid somehow signals a break in the connection between domestic farm surplus disposal objectives and food aid volumes. So long as USDA bears responsibility for procurement and Washington can use food aid to respond to market pressures faced by US farmers, surplus disposal and food aid will remain closely coupled.

Of course, there is an automatic linkage between food stocks and food aid flows that operates through grain prices. As stocks fall, prices rise, and as prices rise, food aid volumes purchased from a fixed dollar budget necessarily fall. This can be seen clearly in Figure 2.4, which plots global wheat food aid flows against international wheat market prices. The negative correlation between wheat prices and food aid flows is obvious. So to a certain degree, co-movement between stocks and food aid flows is merely an artifact of monetary budgeting.

The tight linkage between US domestic food stocks and food aid flows goes well beyond this accounting relationship, however. Food prices respond only modestly to changes in year-end carryover stocks. Yet for long periods, total US food aid flows have tracked year-end wheat stocks in the United States almost perfectly.[16]

Historically, the commodity composition of democratic donor countries' food aid reflects those items currently in surplus in the donor economy and the political power of particular commodity interest groups. As a consequence, while food aid represents a small share of total agricultural exports from donors, there are a few commodities – notably US soybean oil and EU skimmed milk powder in the 1990s – for which food aid accounts for half or more of all shipments overseas. Producers of those particular commodities are especially dependent on food aid.

In the United States, the emergence of strong, commodity-specific subcommittees in the House Agriculture Committee has shifted influence from broad-based farm groups to crop-specific lobbies that provide key information and staff for the subcommittees.[17] As a consequence, several commodity groups push hard for increased use of food aid channels for sale of their particular food products, using the apparent humanitarian benefits as excellent public relations cover for plainly

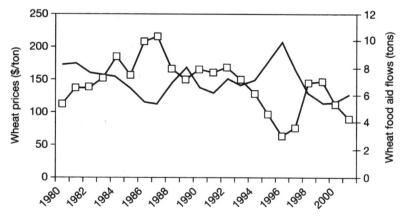

Figure 2.4 Wheat prices and food aid flows

Note: Prices are for US number 1 hard red winter wheat, fob Gulf of Mexico.
Sources: IMF, WFP

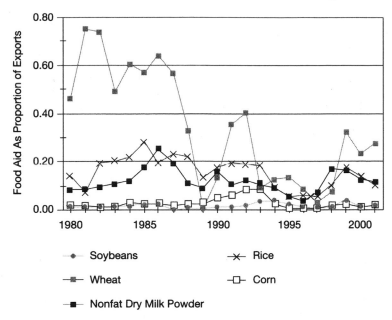

Figure 2.5 Food aid and exports

Source: FAOSTAT

self-serving aims. American wheat, rice, and nonfat dry milk powder producers and exporters, in particular, derive a large share of their income from food aid shipments. As Figure 2.5 shows, US food aid flows have historically been very large relative to commercial export volumes of these three commodities, averaging 33.7 percent of exports of nonfat dry milk powder, 15.5 percent of rice exports, and 12.1 percent of US wheat exports, 1980–2001. Not coincidentally, they have been especially active proponents of food aid.

Four recent examples underscore the efforts and influence of especially powerful commodity groups. In February 2001, in a clear attempt to piggyback on momentum building behind international development assistance related to health, the American Soybean Association (ASA) launched the World Initiative for Soy in Human Health, with the pleasant-sounding acronym WISHH, to promote the use of soy products in food aid around the world. The aim of the initiative is to create short- and long-term market opportunities for US farmers through increased acceptance of soy-based foods by encouraging NGOs to incorporate more soy-fortified and soy-protein products into their international feeding programs, by developing new soy products for WFP emergency feeding programs, and by expanding concessional sales and donations of soybeans, soybean oil and soybean meal through USDA, ASA president Tony Anderson explained.[18] Predictably, soybean product food aid from the Unites States increased in the wake of the launch of WISHH, although, as discussed in Chapter 1, protein deficiency is rare in the absence of dietary energy shortfalls, and energy (calories) is typically much cheaper to provide. WISHH has been a relatively bald attempt to manipulate food aid for the benefit of a small group of growers and processors.

Faced by a *de facto* moratorium by the European Union on imports of genetically modified foods that had allegedly cost US corn growers nearly $1 billion in sales, the US Grains Council and the National Corn Growers Association delivered a joint letter to President Bush in late January 2003, asking him not only to begin dispute settlement action in the World Trade Organization, but also to agitate against resistance to acceptance of genetically modified corn in food aid shipments.[19] This ignited a strong response by the US government. Within months, President Bush began assailing the Europeans on this issue, using African hunger and food aid as a lever with which to try to pry open European markets for American growers. In a speech at the US Coast Guard Academy May 22, 2003, President Bush said:

> Our partners in Europe have blocked all new bio-crops because of unfounded, unscientific fears. This has caused [*sic*] many African nations from investing in biotechnology for fear that their products will be shut out of European markets. European governments should join, not hinder, the great cause of ending hunger in Africa.[20]

Speaker of the House Hastert (R-Illinois) reiterated these points forcefully in testimony before the House Science Committee.[21]

Our third example borders on the silly. In August 2003, at the behest of California raisin producers suffering a market glut, USAID capitulated to Congressional pressure led by Rep. Devin Nunes, a member of the House Agriculture Committee and representative of California's San Joaquin Valley raisin heartland, to include raisins on the menu of food items to be included in humanitarian rations sent to Iraq and other countries. No humanitarian group had called for the inclusion of raisins in humanitarian rations. The pressure had originated entirely with a small group of growers with good access to an influential legislator.

Our fourth and final example, like that of genetically modified corn, underscores the linkages between food aid and international trade disputes. In three successive meetings, from September–November 2002, of the Consultative Committee on Surplus Disposal, the international regulatory body established to oversee global food aid flows, Australia and the European Community registered concerns about sharp growth in US nonfat dry milk (NFDM) food aid donations.[22] NFDM had been reintroduced into Title II programs after a lapse of more than a decade, largely in response to the accumulation of USDA surplus stocks of more than half a million metric tons. American NFDM donations more than doubled from US fiscal year 2001 to 2002, to more than 57,000 metric tons, with signficant further expansion in fiscal year 2003 before slowed milk production and rapid price increases cut NFDM donations back sharply midway through fiscal year 2004.[23] In fall 2002, USDA NFDM stocks were available to Title II programs for only $155/metric ton plus freight, only about 10 percent of prevailing world prices. This therefore looked a lot like **dumping**[24] for export promotion purposes to other food aid donors who are likewise commercial NFDM exporters. The Australian delegation also objected to food aid distribution running through US-based, non-profit divisions of commerical entities whose other divisions commercially export the same products and sell the same products into the US Section 416(b) and PL 480 Title I programs. The US delegation defended increased shipments as responding to humanitarian need, especially in feeding school children under the US's new **Food for Education** program. This last example underscores the difficulty of disentangling development assistance from donor support for its domestic producers' surplus disposal and export promotion objectives.

Cumulatively, these examples and this history clearly indicate that United States food aid programs have not been and are not now primarily about assisting food-insecure populations worldwide. Rather, these programs have largely been driven by the opportunity to use assistance to vulnerable groups abroad to advance domestic producer objectives. As we document extensively in subsequent chapters, this comes at a high cost of foregone effectiveness in addressing food insecurity problems around the world.

Myth 1 American food aid is primarily about feeding the hungry

The US government's food aid programs have always aimed to advance self-serving goals of surplus disposal, export promotion and geopolitical leverage to benefit privileged domestic interest groups. While the rhetoric of American food aid has always emphasized its altruistic appearance, the design and use of US food aid programs have always been driven primarily by donor-oriented concerns, not by recipient needs or rights.

In spite of such examples, food aid has ultimately proved ineffective as an instrument for broader farm policy in that it has failed to generate any measurable increase in prices fetched by American growers relative to the counterfactual in which there had been no food aid shipments. Rather, food aid has merely responded to changes in US farm policy. When price supports and production subsidies generated massive government food stockpiles as market prices steadily fell, food aid was used as a vent for surplus in the 1950s and 1960s. As food prices rose and surpluses dwindled in the 1970s, US food aid stagnated and, as we discuss in the next section, an opening emerged for foreign policy to play a dominant role in shaping food aid allocation patterns and distribution modalities. As domestic **farmgate prices** fell over the 1980s, the farm lobby turned to direct export enhancement programs as more effective, lower cost and less bureaucratic instruments than food aid for advancing foreign market promotion objectives.[25]

Since 1986, the government has moved aggressively from farm price supports to income support programs. The Farm Bill of 2002 perhaps best exemplifies this transition, as it increased subsidies by up to $180 billion over a period of ten years, bringing them back to record levels after a period of decline during the Clinton administration, but without increases in food price supports. Although the decoupling of support programs from production means farm programs no longer have marginal output effects – i.e., they no longer directly encourage increased production volumes – because they enable farms to cover fixed costs and stay in operation during downturns, the new farm support programs following the 1996 and 2002 Farm Bills may overstimulate American farm output even more than before. When food surpluses have emerged and farmgate prices have collapsed since the start of serious decoupling of payments from production and prices, as in the 1998 farm crisis, the government has quickly used extraordinary increases in food aid flows to try to mop up excess domestic supply. Unless the US government becomes more disciplined in its supplemental appropriations for CCC purchases of grain for Section 416(b) food aid shipments, one should expect the 2002 Farm Bill to lead to still greater and more volatile food aid flows in response to natural commodity market cycles.

Of course, the main effect of American farm policy on food aid recipients comes not through food aid but through the effects on global food prices. OECD agricultural subsidies exceed $300 billion annually and are set to surpass $1 billion/day by the end of 2004. American, European, and Japanese farmers receive more in subsidies in a five-day work week than the world spends on food aid in the course of a year. European dairy subsidies alone amount to almost $2.25 per cow per day, more than the daily income of half of the world's population. Such massive subsidies enable American (and Canadian, Australian, Japanese and, most of all, European) farmers to sell profitably on global markets for significantly less than their true cost of production. This quasi-dumping, including but far broader than just food aid, depresses world market prices for goods in which many developing country farmers hold comparative advantage, knocking down their incomes by far more than the value of any food aid transfers they might receive. As the *New York Times* put it, "The world's farming system is rigged in favor of the rich."[26] Food aid represents but a drop in the ocean as compared against the adverse effects American agricultural and trade policies have on low-income countries. Food aid is primarily a manifestation of the policies that injure food insecure populations abroad, not the salve for those injuries that some advocates make it out to be – and certainly not part of a coherent strategy for preventing them.

Even in the United States, food aid is tiny in comparison to other components of domestic farm policy. For example, in fiscal year 2001, food aid appropriations of only $1.8 billion paled in comparison to more than $16 billion in farm loans (directed and guaranteed) to 130,000 American farmers and nearly $20 billion in net government transfers, representing more than 35 percent of total net farm income in the country.[27] Because food aid represents such a small share of the US food market – only $1–2 billion annually in a domestic market exceeding $900 billion plus an additional $60 billion or so in commercial agricultural exports – it has proved too small to move markets in a way that generates any identifiable effect on farmgate prices in all but very exceptional circumstances. Senior officials with USDA and with its Canadian counterpart, Agriculture Canada, both acknowledge this privately. They recognize that North American food producers are too well integrated into the global market, in which food aid is but a drop in the ocean, for domestic food aid procurement to benefit anyone other than perhaps a privileged few with preferential access to procurement processes (on which more in Chapter 5). Rather, the benefits to American farmers come purely through image and the "warm glow" of knowing that their crops are being shipped to poor countries and peoples, even if the food aid largely displaces commercial imports of the same commodities. Given the inefficiencies and volatility of US food aid, as we document in Chapter 8, this is a very expensive "feel good" operation.

Myth 2 Food aid is an effective form of support for American farmers

Food aid has always been a *product* of support for American farmers, rather than a *source* of support for them. There are sub-sectors – most notably nonfat dry milk, rice, wheat, and soybean meal – where domestic farm lobbies have routinely been able to masquerade domestic subsidies as international charity. But there exists *no* solid empirical evidence that food aid has had any significant positive effect on domestic farmgate prices. Moreover, direct export enhancement programs have been more effective than food aid in increasing domestic producers' access to overseas commercial markets.

Food aid and American development assistance policy[28]

One lens through which one can usefully view food aid is that of American development assistance policy more generally. Food aid dominated all other components of US foreign assistance in the mid-1960s, peaking at 17.2 million tons shipped in 1965, before beginning a precipitous decline to only 2.5 million tons shipped during the global food crisis of 1974. Food aid fell to less than 10 percent of total US overseas development assistance in the 1990s and stood at only 8.2 percent in 2002.[29]

Ruttan (1993, 1995) identifies a succession of "six visions" he sees as having shaped US development assistance policy over the past half century or so. The first vision was the push of economic and political liberalism in the immediate post-World War II era in response to the widespread perception that autarky[30] and political repression were primary causes of both the Great Depression and World War II. The first inklings of contemporary food aid emerged during this period with significant free food shipments to Europe and East Asia under the Marshall Plan and a series of small Congressional and executive initiatives.

The second vision was outlined in President Harry S. Truman's inaugural address of January 20, 1949, in which he proposed "a bold new program for making the benefits of scientific advances and industrial progress available for the improvement and growth of underdeveloped areas." Food aid as we know it today was really born of this vision. The primary foreign policy objective underpinning food aid during this era was security. This view was especially ably and ardently articulated by Senator Hubert Humphrey, who argued in July 1953, "[w]ise statesmanship and real leadership can convert these [food] surpluses into a great asset for checking communist aggression. Communism has no greater ally than hunger; democracy and freedom no greater ally than an abundance of food."[31] Government food stocks had come to be viewed as yet one more weapon that could be deployed for strategic gain in the rapidly intensifying Cold War against the Soviet Union and its allies. Recall from Chapter 1 that the leading recipients of US food aid during the 1950s and early 1960s were countries such as India, Egypt, Pakistan, Poland, South Korea, Taiwan, Turkey, and Yugoslavia, all nations seen as central to the struggle between the capitalist West and the communist East. As a direct consequence, Europe received more than half of all US food aid in the 1950s. This would shift sharply in the coming decade or so, as US food aid shifted dramatically towards Asia.

The third vision pushed beyond the narrower security orientation that preceded it, toward a more general emphasis on development assistance, as summarized by John F. Kennedy in his repeated assertion during the 1960 presidential campaign that "a more prosperous world would also be a more secure world."[32] Pushed by Senate advocates such as Hubert Humphrey and George McGovern, the United States Agency for International Development (USAID) was created in 1961 as a semi-autonomous unit within the Department of State with the mission to implement America's foreign aid programs. The Kennedy and Johnson administrations pushed hard for a recasting of food aid programs as tools for development and humanitarian assistance. The Food for Peace Act of 1966 explicitly encouraged the recasting of food aid as a development assistance tool rather than as purely an instrument for domestic surplus disposal. For the first time, **Food for Peace** was authorized to use commodities that were not in surplus and was barred from distributing commodities that recipients could obtain on their own. At the same time, the Kennedy administration strongly backed the emergence of new multilateral approaches to food aid, ultimately enshrined in the creation of the World Food Programme in 1963.[33]

While it is true that the 1960s brought the first serious attempts to imbue American food aid with genuinely humanitarian and development objectives, it is important not to overstate the extent of the shift in policy. As Ruttan observes:

> In retrospect it is clear that the Kennedy administration's positive attitude toward food aid was due more to the flexibility it gave the administration in pursuing foreign policy objectives than to its value as an instrument of humanitarian assistance and economic development. The use of food aid as

an instrument for political and strategic leverage would be refined and intensified during the Johnson and Nixon administrations.[34]

Over the course of the 1962–74 period, food aid allocation swung sharply to (and later, back away from) countries such as Algeria, Cambodia, Egypt, South Vietnam and, above all, India – the largest US food aid recipient 1958–71 – in response to emerging geopolitical concerns. Where Europe had been the main US food aid recipient continent in the 1950s, by 1973, on the eve of the World Food Crisis centered on Africa – which would prompt yet another geographic redirection of American food aid flows – Asia had become the primary destination, as Cambodia, India, Indonesia, Pakistan, South Korea, and South Vietnam together received roughly three-quarters of all US food aid shipments.

Minnesota Senator Hubert Humphrey perhaps articulated the strategic objectives behind food aid most baldly during 1957 Congressional hearings when he said, "[I]f you are really looking for a way for people to lean on you and to be dependent upon you, in terms of their cooperation with you, it seems to me that food dependence would be terrific."[35] One former USAID official shared his own experience in the early 1970s in Jamaica, to which the Department of State insisted increased food aid shipments be sent so as to maintain support for the then pro-US government, which faced a serious socialist opposition. Although Jamaica's granaries were already full, the US State Department wouldn't relent. USAID officials involved referred to the problem as exceeding Jamaica's "stuffability quotient."[36]

This pattern of food aid for strategic foreign policy objectives, albeit dressed up as humanitarian relief and economic development assistance, persists to this day. Two of the best current cases, North Korea and Afghanistan, are described in Boxes 2.2 and 2.3. In North Korea, food has been used as an extraordinary instrument to induce diplomatic negotiation over the communist government's nuclear program and general demilitarization of the peninsula. The economist Marcus Noland insightfully labeled this phenomenon "food for talks"[37] (i.e., food for negotiations), playing on the obvious, distant similarity to "food for peace" and "food for work." In Afghanistan, food aid was transparently used to soften the public relations effects of intense media coverage of the US military assault on the Taliban regime, with food aid deliveries peaking as the fighting grew most intense and controversy swirled around the installation of Hamid Karzai as Afghanistan's new ruler.

Box 2.2 Food for talks in North Korea

Food aid to North Korea provides an excellent example of donations driven by mixed motives, wherein donor geopolitical interests often seem to the unaware as purely humanitarian. There is no doubt that many North Koreans are severely undernourished nor that their nation cannot meet its nutritional needs on its own. However, need alone has never been a sufficient condition for aid. Donor countries, led by the United States, have used food aid to keep the Democratic People's Republic of Korea (DPRK) engaged in diplomatic talks, an approach Marcus Noland of Washington's Institute for International Economics aptly labeled "food for talks" and others have termed "food for nukes."

Since the end of the Korean War in 1953, North Korea has espoused a policy of economic self-reliance, or *juche*. The pursuit of food self-sufficiency is ill-advised for most countries, but *juche* has been especially harmful in a land with only 150–180 frost-free days per year and much land that is ill-suited to agricultural production.[1] With scant access to foreign exchange after the collapse of the Soviet Union, North Korea has been unable to purchase agricultural inputs from abroad in sufficient volumes to maintain its farm productivity. Combined with recent episodes of drought and flooding, North Korea's chronic food shortages reached a crisis point in the mid-1990s, and, by at least some estimates, over two million North Koreans died from starvation and related diseases between 1994 and 1998.[2]

North Korea has received international food aid since 1994, primarily from China, the USA, Japan, and South Korea (even though the two Koreas are still technically at war), with WFP as the primary food distributor. All donor countries have faced conflict with North Korea and have at times renegotiated or delayed their shipments due to diplomatic disagreements. Even the NGO Médecins Sans Frontières (MSF) announced in September 1998 it would withdraw its services due to counterproductive activities on the part of the communist government, reporting that DPRK agents curtailed MSF's activities and had distributed food mainly to those loyal to the government.[3] Sadly, the selective distribution of food represents another level of manipulation of aid for political gain, this time by the DPRK regime.

Food aid shipments to North Korea sometimes resemble a diplomatic arm wrestling match more than an attempt to help the hungry. For example, the USA and South Korea insisted that the bags of grain they donate bear their emblems or flags, so as to receive due credit for their donations. This, however, embarrassed Kim Jong Il's government, which believed the markings would imply the failure of the *juche* policy and that the more prosperous South Korea had food and wealth to spare. The donors eventually won this battle and were able to deliver grain emblazoned with their emblems.

Each of the donors uses food aid to extract concessions from the DPRK regime. Japan uses aid as a bargaining chip with North Korea as it tries to resolve kidnappings, hijackings, and missile tests. China and South Korea use their own rice surpluses to try induce cooperation with the North over refugees.[4]

The USA meanwhile has grave concerns over North Korea's nuclear and long-range missile capabilities and its suspected support of terrorist organizations and has manipulated food aid shipments to the country explicitly so as to bring the North Koreans to the negotiating table. The Clinton administration had no qualms about interrupting American (and, derivatively, South Korean) shipments at the height of the North Korean famine. Revealingly, this act elicited no international uproar. Then, only a year after declaring North Korea part of an "axis of evil" in early 2002 and as rice stocks began being replenished in the DPRK, the Bush administration announced the resumption of US food aid shipments to North Korea. The clear motivation behind food aid resumption was its utility as a bargaining chip in ongoing diplomatic confrontations over the US unwillingness to sign a non-aggression treaty and North Korea's production of nuclear weapons.

Of course, those bearing the risk in these repeated games of chicken against the United States are the food-insecure peoples of North Korea. Kim Jong Il's regime is unpredictable. But from the donor's perspective, the US benefits no matter how negotiations over food aid end.[5] If the regime agrees to their conditions for aid, then the United States succeeds in engaging the regime in talks, scores a diplomatic victory, gains access to the North Korean population, and can argue that it has achieved important humanitarian impacts. If the regime rejects the offer of food under the prescribed conditions, then the health of the country's economy and its citizens falters, thus creating an environment in which the population could revolt.

The USA and other donor countries continue to offer food shipments despite doubts that the food will reach the most needy groups and with scant solid evidence of any sustainable impact.[6] Commitment to aid and actual shipments do not appear to respond to changing food availability. Rather, aid has responded primarily to diplomatic exigencies, pulled by one or another donor in protest over an act by the North Korean government or begun or resumed by a donor in an effort to engage the North Koreans in dialogue and thereby be able to stop undesired behaviors.

Notes:
1 FAO Global Information and Early Warning System, Special Report: FAO/WFP Crop and Food Supply Assessment Mission to the Democratic People's Republic of Korea. July 29, 2002, p. 4.
2 Cohen (2002).
3 Aaltola (1999).
4 BBC News. "Seoul Reviews Rice Deal with North," July 3, 2002.
5 Aaltola (1999).
6 According to a World Food Programme press release dated 21 February 2003, a child nutrition survey carried out in October 2002 found that the proportion of underweight, acutely malnourished and chronically malnourished (i.e., "stunted") children had dropped significantly relative to a 1998 survey, although the statistics from the two surveys are not directly comparable. The North Korean government

publicly attributes the gains to substantial humanitarian assistance and the WFP claims in its 2002 annual report that this demonstrates "that WFP's food assistance made a significant contribution to improving the nutritional status of vulnerable groups" (Allan Jury, personal communication). These claims notwithstanding, the 1998 point of comparison reflects the tail end of a famine during which food aid shipments were likewise massive and credible monitoring of food aid distribution is notoriously absent in North Korea (GAO 1999). Whether or not positive nutritional impact can ultimately be established rigorously, our core point stands: food aid flows to North Korea have been driven by geopolitical considerations far more than by humanitarian ones.

Ruttan's fourth "vision" of American development assistance became popular especially within the Carter administration and among key members of the Congress, such as Senator Hubert Humphrey, the long-time champion of food aid. This fourth vision emphasized basic human rights as a central objective of foreign policy. Especially in the wake of shocking famines in Bangladesh, Ethiopia and the Sahel in the mid-1970s, development experts began emphasizing the importance of factors other than mere food availability in addressing poverty and malnutrition. This helped provide an intellectual and rhetorical justification for sharply reduced food aid shipments necessitated by precipitous drops in government-owned stocks. Cuts in food aid flows during this period came out of program flows because a cap had been put on Title I distributions to middle-income countries, effectively limiting the usefulness of program food aid for diplomatic and market development purposes. This was, of course, fine with the NGOs that championed the basic human rights agenda, since they played little to no role in program food aid and viewed it, correctly, as less well targeted towards basic human needs than were project and emergency assistance flows. The real importance of this era of American food aid was the rise of the rights-based perspective, which we discuss in considerably more detail in Chapter 6.

The fifth vision, emerging during the Reagan administration of the early 1980s, once again drew a close linkage between economic and security assistance. At the same time, a gradual ideological transition away from a belief that governments have to run food production and distribution picked up steam. Policymakers and analysts increasingly came to recognize that public or private nonprofit distribution is rarely much more efficient than commercial, private distribution and that trade has historically proved far more effective in stabilizing and increasing food availability per capita in developing countries than food aid has.[38] As a consequence, food aid appropriately fell as a share of aid flows and even of flows directed toward agricultural and nutritional objectives in developing countries. This ideological shift was reflected in the emergence of a new form of political conditionality for food aid policy, the Food for Progress Program. Originally authorized by the Food Security Act of 1985, Food for Progress allowed PL 480 Title I or Section 416(b) food aid shipments to be used to assist agricultural policy reforms in recipient countries attempting market-oriented economic reforms and a move to multiparty democracy.

This ideological adjustment was complemented by enactment of new budgeting rules under the Gramm-Rudman-Hollings Act in 1985. Where USAID had previously received a separate food aid appropriation from its financial appropriation by the Congress, Gramm-Rudman-Hollings capped the Agency's total budget, imposing a direct trade-off between food aid and other forms of assistance that had never previously been faced. Where USAID had discretion over how to spend its budget, it increasingly opted against food aid. Combined with sharp decline in US food stocks, US food aid flows began dropping precipitously again in the late 1980s and into the early 1990s.

The sixth vision, brought a sharply increased emphasis on NGOs as key development actors in the 1990s. Building on increasingly widespread belief that developing country governments were often an impediment to improved food security, international donors began relying more heavily on NGOs to distribute food aid.

This was not entirely new. NGOs had long been involved in food aid distribution. They had been the primary food aid distribution channel used by the American Relief Administration in Russia and western Europe in the aftermath of World War I, and played a central role in food aid under the Marshall Plan as well. Section 416 of the Agricultural Act of 1949 institutionalized NGOs' role by directing the Secretary of Agriculture to donate CCC stocks to registered NGOs for distribution overseas. But NGOs were largely pushed aside by the Johnson, Nixon and Ford administrations, before regaining influence during the Carter and Reagan administrations.

What was truly new in the 1990s' resurgence of NGO food aid activity was the NGOs' success in making the case that the best use of food aid might be to "monetize" (i.e., sell) food resources so as to obtain funds with which (i) to support in-country costs of managing direct food distribution (e.g., transport, storage and handling costs); and (ii) to pursue other interventions not involving direct food distribution to food insecure groups. This was an important shift, as it acknowledged that food had come to be viewed as a liquid resource, and not as a necessary input for conducting humanitarian operations in low-income countries. The NGO lobby effectively argued for the lifting of monetization limits in the 1990s. The 1998 Farm Bill increased the *target* share of Title II commodities to be sold under non-emergency programs from 10 to 15 percent and the conversion of the *target* share to a *minimum* share. Then the 2002 Farm Bill[39] authorized the monetization of commodities for US dollars, not just local currencies, encouraged USAID approval of multiyear and multicountry agreements, and more than doubled the maximum level of funding for overseas administrative support.[40]

These developments were all pushed heavily by NGOs who stood to benefit from longer-term, more stable and more fungible flows of food aid as well as from more generous reimbursement of administrative expenses. These innovations underscore the increased influence of the NGO lobby over the terms set for American food aid programs by Congress. Title II and Section 416(b) food aid shipments that had previously gone almost entirely to direct distribution have come to look increasingly like Title I, an in-kind transfer cashed out by recipients. The main difference has been that the Title II and Section 416(b) recipients were NGOs, not recipient country governments, as was the case under Title I. The practical effect of the programs is increasingly the same.[41]

The most recent visions of food aid within development assistance revolve around the use of food to support education and to combat terrorism. In 2001, the US government launched a Global Food for Education (GFE) Pilot Initiative using commodities procured domestically under Section 416(b) to support school feeding and pre-school nutrition programs in developing countries. Over the objections of USAID but with strong support from WFP, the 2002 Farm Bill replaced the GFE with the McGovern–Dole International Food for Education and Child Nutrition Program (IFECNP), launched in 2003 and administered by USDA's Foreign Agricultural Service and operated very similarly to its predecessor pilot program. The big difference between IFECNP and GFE is that the former's appropriations include significant amounts of cash, while the latter effectively operated from only food commodities.

Recent food-for-education initiatives extend internationally the popular and successful domestic school feeding programs likewise run by USDA. The question arises, however, whether food aid sourced abroad – in this case, in the United States – is the best way to finance domestic food assistance programs such as school feeding. The momentum currently behind food-for-education programs underscores the need to distinguish between **food assistance programs** intended to ensure the food security of vulnerable populations regardless of where the resources originate, and **food aid**, the international shipment of free or heavily discounted food, sometimes but not always in support of food assistance programs in recipient countries. Chapter 7 will emphasize this issue as we explore effective mechanisms for supporting important food assistance programs – such as school feeding and pre-school nutrition interventions – via food aid.

After the terrorist attacks of September 11, 2001, on New York and Washington, the second Bush administration began tying much of its development assistance to the overarching counter-terrorism thrust of its foreign policy. This was strongly evident in Afghanistan in 2001–2, as described in Box 2.3. More recently, the International Federation of Red Cross and Red Crescent Societies noted in the launch of their annual World Disaster Report in July 2003 that within days of President Bush's declaration of the end of the Iraq War, US$1.7 billion had been raised for relief efforts in Iraq, a nation of 26 million people. At the same time, a consolidated appeal by the United Nations to avert famine among 40 million people in twenty-two African countries had raised less than half the amount provided to Iraq, remaining more than $1 billion underfunded after more than a year's efforts at marshalling the resources necessary to tackle one of the most intense humanitarian crises the world had faced in a generation. The American WFP Executive Director, James Morris, described these different donor responses as "a double standard," noting that donors "routinely accept a level of suffering and hopelessness in Africa we would never accept in any other part of the world."[42] Plainly, the resources were available, but only to support geopolitically important efforts related to "the war against terror." That agenda is increasingly driving aid allocations, including those for food aid.

Box 2.3 War and food aid to Afghanistan

The case of Afghanistan in 2001–2 highlights the tendency of food aid donors to favor high-profile efforts in geopolitically strategic situations rather than to attend to acute or chronic emergencies, even in the same place, but at a less politically advantageous time.

By 2001, Afghanistan had suffered 22 years of internal conflict and five years of Taliban rule. It had experienced drought and famine for the previous three years and its people, most of whom had used up any savings or provisions they had, were without means for coping with the growing food crisis. Seven million refugees had fled to neighboring countries and many of those who remained suffered undernutrition. According to UNICEF and WHO, in 2001 the infant and under-five mortality rates were 165 and 257 per 1,000 live births, respectively, and the maternal mortality rate was 1,700 per 100,000 live births.[1] Nutrition and health standards and food availability were woeful in Afghanistan.

Afghanistan had long been one of the largest recipients of US humanitarian food aid, with $174 million spent in FY2000. However, tensions were rising and aid was becoming more difficult to deliver. In the summer of 2001, eight faith-based humanitarian aid workers were arrested, leading many agencies to withdraw their expatriate staff from the country. Food aid declined as the situation worsened and Afghanistan rapidly became one of the most unlivable places on earth.

Then came the September 11, 2001, terrorist attacks on the United States. Believing that the Taliban had helped and was harboring Osama bin Laden and Al Qaeda, the United States began bombing Afghanistan in early October, 2001. On October 4, President George W. Bush announced $320 million in additional humanitarian aid, followed shortly by a call to American children to donate coins and dollar bills to help Afghan children. As Afghanistan rapidly became even more unlivable, food aid flows quite suddenly turned around sharply, as Figure 2.6 shows.

The sentiment that "our opponents are terrorists and the Taliban regime that protects them; we are not at war with the Afghan people"[2] was expressed by representatives throughout the US government. To ease domestic and international public concern over the plight of the Afghan people, the Bush administration complemented military action with humanitarian relief for the Afghan people, both those left inside the country and the growing number of refugees in neighboring countries. This sentiment was summarized in a Congressional hearing on America's assistance to the Afghan people: "The critics of the United States both in this country and abroad better take notice of the extraordinary compassion and commitment of the American people to relieve suffering in Afghanistan, as elsewhere, while simultaneously fighting a war against international terrorism."[3]

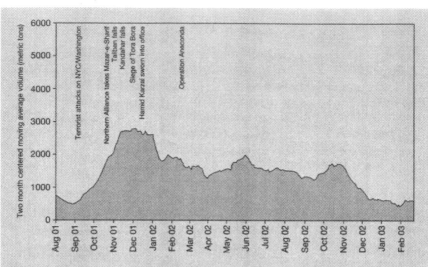

Figure 2.6 Daily food aid flows into Afghanistan, August 2001–February 2003

Source: World Food Programme database

There were many challenges to implementing a food aid program in the middle of a war. Virtually all relief workers had been evacuated. Rampant lawlessness and abysmal road conditions made the logistics of delivery difficult, especially in rural areas as harsh winter weather began to set in. All of the earlier reasons for reducing food aid flows had become magnified several fold. Yet donors' resolve, especially in the United States, had been fixed by the war. Donor political interests thus spurred food aid flows in a situation in which tangible human misery in the form of acute food insecurity had been an insufficient justification for intervention.

In the early stages of the relief effort, the United States used extraordinarily expensive airdrops for food distribution. However, this tactic proved to be ineffective, even dangerous. There were reports that pallets of food aid landed on homes, damaging or destroying them, or in mine fields, perilously attracting hungry villagers. There was further criticism that the yellow food ration packets too closely resembled unexploded ordnance (yellow bomblettes left by cluster bombs) and that the contents of these packages were nutritionally inappropriate.

In October 2001 a group of international NGOs called upon the United States to halt bombing of Afghanistan long enough for aid agencies to get necessary food into the country before the harsh winter would make distribution even more difficult. Christian Aid asserted that although they did not support the Taliban, they had been able to effectively distribute aid in Afghanistan prior to September 11. "Following that date, the fear of US military action meant that international aid workers had to leave the country and the aid shipments stopped."[4] The American position was that they should "first finish the war against Osama bin Laden,"[5] and bombing continued.

Disappointment continued after the Northern Alliance's taking of Mazar-i-Sharif in early November. American officials insisted that the Northern Alliance would be responsible for patrolling the roadways and, contrary to the aid community's expectations, no troops were sent to secure the area for relief workers and their convoys.[6] Food aid delivery fell in mid-November although the allied victory over the Taliban at Mazar-i-Sharif had finally opened up overland access into Afghanistan from Uzbekistan, where staging access had been prepared for trucking in humanitarian aid relief shipments. This called into question American officials' commitment to the well-being of the Afghan people, which it had so recently cited as justification for war on their country.

WFP was using international funding including donations from the USA to buy up grain in neighboring countries to distribute in Afghanistan. The national wheat lobby protested loudly, but ultimately unsuccessfully, in Washington to completely stop WFP's purchase of grain in central Asia that could be delivered rapidly. The fact that such a proposition was aggressively pushed by a powerful lobby and discussed at senior levels underscores that food aid to Afghanistan in 2001–2 was less about attending to the immediate needs of a desperately food insecure population than with the Bush administration's need for political cover for the significant civilian casualties it caused by its invasion of Afghanistan.[7] As the *Christian Science Monitor* reported:

> The US acknowledges that the food drops, which began with such fanfare, were never a serious answer to Afghanistan's pending famine: They constitute only a quarter of 1 percent of estimated needs. But they were meant to give high profile to America's humanitarian take on the war.[8]

Food aid shipments into Afghanistan reached their peak as the war intensified with the siege of Tora Bora and as diplomatic attention intensified with the installation of Hamid Karzai as the new Afghan leader in December 2001, although capacity to deliver food to needy communities and individuals was at perhaps its nadir. From that peak of public visibility, however, food aid deliveries into Afghanistan steadily declined over the course of 2002, as shown in the accompanying Figure 2.6, returning to pre-September 11 levels in just one year, even though humanitarian agencies have yet to be able to re-establish operations in large parts of the country due to continued violence, destroyed infrastructure, and the continued presence of and attacks on foreign soldiers. US transitory assistance plainly had far more to do with the

politics and public relations of war than with food security in a land of intense
and widespread suffering.

Notes:
1   Ferdous (2002).
2   Chairman Rep. Henry J. Hyde, International Relations Committee Hearing,
    November 1, 2001. p. 2. (www.house.gov/international_relations, viewed
    September 23, 2002).
3   Rep. Tom Lantos, International Relations Committee Hearing, November 1,
    2001. p. 4. (www.house.gov/international_relations, viewed September 23, 2002).
4   *Guardian.* "Afghanistan on Edge of Humanitarian Catastrophe", Sunday, October
    21, 2001. (www. Guardian.co.uk, viewed March 30, 2002).
5   Cohen (2001).
6   Becker (2001).
7   Moreover, US food aid into Afghanistan in 2002–3 fell under PL 480 domestic
    procurement and cargo preference restrictions, which ultimately added $35
    million to assistance costs and delayed deliveries by 120 days, on average, relative
    to if the United States had provided cash or regionally procured commodities to
    international operating agencies in Afghanistan (GAO 2003b).
8   LaFranchi (2001).

Ultimately, US development assistance policy has always been constrained
by its broader foreign policy, particularly national security, objectives. Today, most
foreign assistance resources are tied up in advancing geopolitical objectives for
peace in the Middle East, in maintaining domestic political stability in Russia, in
trying to defuse hostility on the Korean peninsula, and in efforts at nation-building
and **refugee** assistance accompanying or in the immediate wake of US military
action in the Balkans, Afghanistan and, most recently, Iraq. After attending to these
demands, there are limited resources available for relief assistance or authentic
economic development in other areas of acute need, although the United States
has stepped up to the challenge in especially severe cases, as in Ethiopia and
southern Africa in 2002–3. Thirty years ago, as the Vietnam War drew to a close,
US food aid was heavily concentrated on South-east Asia, with nearly half of all
flows going to Cambodia and South Vietnam in 1973. Although the countries
involved have changed over time, food aid allocations have remained subject more
to geopolitical calculus than to nutritional accounting.[43]

Yet there is scant evidence that US food aid allocations have had any significant
effect in advancing US geopolitical objectives. Indeed, a respected American
political scientist has concluded that food aid consistently has had more foreign
policy drawbacks than successes.[44] Meanwhile, the massive, forgotten emergencies
of strategically unimportant places, such as the Great Lakes region of Africa
(Burundi, Democratic Republic of Congo, and Rwanda) continue.

The foreign and farm policy constraints on food aid create a major gap between
rhetoric and resources. The United States simply cannot accomplish much with the
meager resources it presently puts on the table. The volumes involved are too small

to provide an effective demand stimulus to US farmers just as they are too meager to make a discernible difference in global diplomacy. The most significant and lasting gains, unfortunately, result from the "warm glow" and public relations effects of food aid flows. At one level, the remarkable thing is that anything is accomplished at all. As Ruttan writes "the gap between America's pretensions and its willingness to support them had led to inevitable disillusionment."[45]

In the final analysis, food aid has been deployed mainly in the service of donor-oriented objectives related to surplus disposal, export market promotion, and strategic geopolitical ambitions. It has proved relatively ineffective in each of these tasks. Domestic food assistance programs (such as school breakfast and lunch programs, Women, Infants, and Children (WIC) or food stamps) and export enhancement programs have proved to be far more effective and low-cost means of surplus disposal and farm price support. Meanwhile, the farm income support programs that begat enormous commodity stockpiles have gradually become recognized as wasteful welfare disproportionately benefiting relatively wealthy landowners. Food aid has never succeeded on any broad scale in promoting commercial exports. The US General Accounting Office's evaluation of Title I PL 480 pointedly remarked, for example, that there was no good evidence of food aid having any important effect on the development of long-term agricultural markets overseas.[46] Nor has it been an effective lever to induce policy reform in recipient countries.

The complex constellation of political advocates who have fostered this state of affairs is to a certain degree inevitable in the messy interest group politics of contemporary America. The politics is not necessarily worse than that which characterizes US foreign aid or agricultural policy more generally. The major difference, however, is that food aid could be put to effective use in many low-income food deficit nations around the world if its funding, procurement, and distribution modalities were reformed. And such reforms need not cost the major domestic constituencies anything since food aid presently generates effectively no widespread benefits either to American agriculture or to US foreign policy. Indeed, if efficacy and flexibility could be improved while reducing the overall cost of food aid programs to the US government – a feasible target, given the gross inefficiencies of the present system that we document in Chapter 8 – then new constituencies could potentially be enlisted to support the reform of US food aid policies, as we outline in Chapter 11.

In part, because food aid has rightly come to be understood as a weak instrument for advancing these goals, the domestic political constituencies supporting food aid for farm income support, export market development, and diplomatic strategic purposes have grown far less supportive of US food aid over the past twenty or so years. There remain some vocal supporters of food aid domestically, especially the commodity-specific interest groups, millers, processors, baggers, freight forwarders, shippers, and NGOs that reap most of the domestic gains from food aid (see Chapter 5). But the manifest ineffectiveness of donor-oriented food aid has perhaps created an opportunity, at long last, for substantial, genuine reform (see Chapter 11).

Myth 3 American food aid is no longer driven by short-term self-interest

The United States has always employed food aid in the service of short-term self-interested goals related to surplus disposal, export market promotion, and geopolitical strategy. Although food aid has proved relatively ineffective in advancing any of these goals, short-term self-interest continues to prevail, as manifest most recently in Afghanistan, Iraq, and North Korea. Longer-term self-interest in using food aid effectively for humanitarian assistance and economic development in countries afflicted with widespread chronic poverty and food insecurity remains merely a residual claimant on whatever limited resources might be left over.

3 Multilateral and other bilateral donors

Nearly all food aid programs have been inextricable from donor agricultural, trade and geopolitical objectives at one time or another, as was just argued to have been true of US food aid programs as a whole over the past fifty years and is typically true of overseas development assistance more generally. But the balance between enlightened self-interest that is truly oriented toward responding to recipients' basic human right to food and that which exploits images of food-insecure peoples to serve other policy objectives has varied over time for most donors and among donors at any given point in time. In recent years, all donors have made some movement in the direction of food aid systems based on (i) the recognition of recipients' basic human rights (or at least the "food needs" of vulnerable populations); and (ii) the need to situate food aid within a broader strategy for reducing poverty and vulnerability to hunger. The degree to which reforms have been substantive rather than merely rhetorical has nonetheless varied a great deal and reforms remain at best partial among all donors.

The greatest progress has occurred outside of the United States. Although the United States has consistently been the world's largest food aid donor for at least the past fifty years, others have long been involved as well, heavily in some particular settings or over specific issues. The World Food Programme (WFP) and bilateral donors other than the United States are leading the way in edging food aid toward a more recipient-oriented system. In order to envision a more sensible, recipient-oriented global food aid regime and to recognize that other donors have succeeded in breaking from a politics-as-usual of food aid that is rooted in myths such as those discussed in Chapter 2, it is important to understand the genesis of these other donors' food aid programs and why they have been able to change over time more than the US program has. This chapter sheds some light on this issue by briefly reviewing several of the other key donors' food aid programs.

Canada[1]

Canada was historically the most generous per capita donor of food aid. The Canadian food aid program began in 1951, three years prior to the signing of PL 480 in the United States, when Canada joined the Colombo Plan to assist Asian members of the British Commonwealth and negotiated with Ceylon and India to accept part of the aid in the form of Canadian wheat. The South Asian countries had substantial food deficits, Canada enjoyed large wheat surpluses and food donations allowed the Lester Pearson government to secure both agricultural and foreign policy support for Canadian participation in the Colombo Plan. Over the ensuing two decades, the two North American behemoths of the international wheat market sought in parallel to relieve excess supply pressures on global prices and, perhaps in the process, pursue some export market development, foreign policy or humanitarian and development goals at the same time. The surplus disposal goal dominated discussions and policy on North American food aid throughout the early years.

Unlike the United States, all Canadian food aid has been provided as a grant through the Canadian International Development Agency (CIDA) from the nation's domestic surpluses, rather than as concessional sales, *à la* PL 480 Title I shipments. As a consequence, Canadian food aid never came to play a major role in agricultural exports, almost always comprising less than 4 percent of Canadian grain exports, a lower share than the United States experienced prior to the late 1980s. Canada's relatively greater emphasis on foreign policy over trade promotion objectives was reflected as well in its extraordinary concentration on just a few recipient countries. Bangladesh, India, Pakistan, and Sri Lanka – the core of the Colombo Plan – together accounted for fully three-quarters of Canada's food aid shipments over the first thirty years of its program.[2]

Canada consistently was placed second globally in food aid donations in absolute terms, behind the United States, until the rise of European food aid in the late 1960s. Canada and the European Economic Community (EEC) – now the European Union (EU) – then traded second and third place in the global food aid standings from year to year until European food aid pulled ahead for good in the mid-1980s. In recent years, Japan's food aid donations have likewise surpassed Canada's in absolute terms.

Canada's population of a bit more than 30 million people, however, is far smaller than that of the United States (about 290 million), the European Union states (about 375 million) or Japan (roughly 125 million). In per capita terms, therefore, Canada was the world's most generous per capita food aid donor through the end of the 1980s. Then, with the policy changes we discuss momentarily, Canadian food aid declined somewhat in favor of cash assistance and the Canadians began to fall behind their southern neighbors in per capita food aid donations. Nonetheless, the Canadians continue to provide nearly three times as much food per Canadian as the Europeans and the Japanese combined, albeit less than half of what the United States now provides. Food aid has thus been an important and potent symbol of Canadian generosity to the world.

Part of the recent relative decline in Canadian food aid can be attributed a "period of turbulence and uncertainty"[3] in the 1970s, followed in the late 1990s by strategic rethinking of food aid's place in Canada's broader overseas development assistance operations. World wheat prices spiked with the food crisis of 1972–74, prompting a sharp rollback of concessional shipments in favor of commercial exports. Then unprecedentedly visible famine in Africa and Bangladesh prompted considerable soul searching as to the appropriateness of food aid in Canadian development assistance programs.

A series of substantial reviews of Canadian food aid practices ensued, beginning in 1975, the most recent of which was conducted in 1997. The central strategic theme emerging from those reviews and ensuing policy debates was that henceforth Canadian food aid would be used first and foremost to address humanitarian concerns, aimed at closing any extant "food gap," rather than at the balance of payments gap, and at addressing primarily the nutritional needs of poorer segments of the recipient population. Canadian food aid was thereafter intended to serve only as a short-term palliative meant to complement and reinforce recipient country agricultural development strategies. As Charlton (1992, p. 176) writes, "[It] can no longer be said, as was the case in the 1970s, that the Canadian food aid program is nothing more than a diverse collection of unconnected programs pursuing disparate objectives." This sensible aid allocation philosophy and bureaucratic design stands in stark contrast to the prevailing approach in the USA and several other donors, wherein multiple agencies and objectives overlap without any serious systematic coordination of policy and programming.

In the interests of ensuring coherence in its food aid programming, in 1978 CIDA created the Food Aid Co-ordination and Evaluation Centre (FACE), the first bilateral bureaucratic unit charged with overseeing all strategic and operational aspects of a donor food aid program. FACE was subsequently renamed the Program Against Hunger, Malnutrition and Disease, signaling the absorption of food aid within broader development programming. In the 1990s, CIDA aggressively pursued food aid monetization through NGOs to support health and nutrition activities seen as having a greater impact on malnutrition. In the late 1990s, the CIDA Minister was able to get the terms and conditions of the food aid program changed somewhat, enabling him to move money between food aid and other activities, rather than having to use monetization as a slow and inefficient way to trade between food and non-food interventions.[4] He then directed a shift of funds from food aid to health and nutrition activities. Food aid has recovered somewhat in the past couple of years, as Canada failed to meet its minimum commitments under the Food Aid Convention (more on this in Chapter 4) and in the face of effective lobbying by WFP.

Through the 1970s, Canadian food aid was comprised primarily of bilateral, government-to-government donations. Since 1979, however, most Canadian food aid has flowed through multilateral channels, overwhelmingly WFP, with a little bit flowing through NGOs, primarily the Canadian Foodgrains Bank. These donations continue to be almost entirely in kind, contributions of bulk Canadian food (primarily grains, especially wheat) rather than of cash.[5] Unlike many other donors who channel most contributions through WFP, the Canadians make very little use of triangular transactions or local purchases.[6] Canadian agricultural and foreign policy interests have been very reluctant to lose the visibility and perceived good will that comes from distributing food aid clearly marked as originating in Canada. This underscores how, in spite of a sharp movement in both rhetoric and programming in the direction of food aid's humanitarian and development objectives, it remains somewhat constrained by domestic agricultural and foreign policy goals.

Canadian agricultural policy has long involved a complex of state trading enterprises, most notably for food aid the Canadian Wheat Board, a farmer-controlled organization created in 1935 and given a monopoly over the export marketing of Canadian grain since 1943, and the Canadian Dairy Commission (CDC), created in 1966. All CIDA wheat procurement must be purchased from the Wheat Board at its designated "card price," typically above international market prices. CIDA (2003) reports that CIDA paid approximately C$200 million more for food than the shipments would have cost at international market prices for wheat, 1980–94, a period when it was authorized to pay prevailing international prices. CIDA likewise paid more than the average export prices during the period when it was authorized to pay prevailing export prices.[7] Similarly, CIDA has been compelled to purchase nonfat dried milk powder at CDC support prices, rather than market prices. Canadian food aid procurement has thus been more expensive than open market commodity purchases because of agricultural policy restrictions on procurement modalities.

These procurement premia are part of Canadian policy to support domestic grains prices, although there is no evidence that Canada's relatively modest food aid procurements actually have any effect in moving prices in the Canadian or global wheat market. Indeed, Agriculture Canada officials privately tell us that unpublished results from modeling alternative uses of farm support appropriations have consistently showed that food aid is ineffective in supporting the nation's farmers, especially compared to alternative subsidy or transfer policies of similar cost. And when food aid took disproportionate cuts when Canada reduced its aid program in the 1990s, there was negligible opposition from the agriculture lobby, given food aid's relative unimportance to their incomes or export markets. Food aid is less a direct farm price support tool than an instrument of foreign policy constrained in its cost-effectiveness by government regulation related to a different sphere of policy. While Canada has untied most of its aid programs,[8] Canadian food aid remains closely coupled to domestic procurement, albeit less closely tied to domestic production patterns and farm policies than was previously the case.

While Canada's federal cabinet has increasingly taken the view that it is desirable to decouple Canadian food aid from management of Canadian grain, dairy and other food surpluses, this has proved somewhat difficult to accomplish quickly. Nonetheless, unlike the US government, which has been regularly besieged by domestic farm producer groups to make extraordinary procurements of grains for Section 416(b) shipments, the Canadian government has been able to avoid addressing such requests through a clear policy that it must avoid the hypocrisy of objecting in international fora to surplus disposal and then itself indulging in such acts. Although domestic farm and foreign policy interests continue to constrain Canadian food aid, substantial progress has been made in the past decade or so in focusing Canadian food aid on fundamental humanitarian and development objectives.

Europe

European food aid takes two broad forms. Individual states have long appropriated resources for contribution to food-deficit countries, partly for foreign policy reasons, partly in support of domestic farm programs, including surplus disposal and export market development, and partly to advance humanitarian and development goals in recipient countries. But European food aid has grown more distinctive in its steadily increasing reliance on cooperative, multi-donor procurement and distribution through the institutions of the common market and, most recently, the European Union (EU).[9] Not all European states are members of the EU (e.g., Norway and Switzerland remain outside the Union, while Sweden only joined in 1994). But especially among those nations within the EU, European food aid has been the vanguard of multilateralism in the global system.

The creation of the European Economic Community (EEC) by the Treaty of Rome in 1957 began a new, unprecedented era of intra-European cooperation on matters of domestic and foreign policy. The Common Agricultural Policy (CAP), agreed in 1962, advanced a distinctively European concern with food self-sufficiency, introducing a suite of policies to ensure Europe could meet its own food needs internally. The CAP has been among the most significant, expensive and controversial manifestations of European cooperation over the past forty years. The CAP, most ardently advocated and defended by the French, has long provided uncommonly generous financial support to European farmers. At roughly $90 billion annually, EU payments to farmers are significantly greater than those in the United States. Through an elaborate maze of farm price supports, substantial tariff and non-tariff barriers to food imports, European farmers have been able to overcome a clear comparative disadvantage on the world market to become and remain the major global player, after the United States, in global agriculture.

CAP reform has long been an ongoing topic of heated discussion within the EU. Most recently, the EU agreed in July 2003 to begin breaking the link between the subsidies farmers receive and their production levels. Bloated EU agricultural subsidies continue – eating up roughly half of the Union's budget – but many analysts believe the decoupling of farm payments from output volumes will reduce overproduction. Overproduction of food in Europe (as in the United States, Canada and other countries that heavily subsidize their agricultural sectors) puts downward pressure on international market prices, hurting farmers in other countries, perhaps especially the low-income food-deficit countries to which surpluses are commonly shipped as food aid. These issues have been front-and-center at the current Doha Round of World Trade Organization negotiations over further multilateral trade liberalization.

As the Kennedy Round of negotiations of the General Agreement on Tariffs and Trade (GATT) wound down, the United States insisted on greater burden sharing on international food aid as a price for agreeing to a new international wheat agreement that the Europeans desperately wanted. The EEC had never previously provided food aid to developing countries and there had been scant bilateral programs among the individual member countries, chiefly France and

West Germany. The Food Aid Convention (FAC) – which Chapter 4 discusses further – created as part of the 1967 International Grains Agreement, required all signatory countries to pledge a minimum contribution of wheat, another cereal grain, or cash for food aid overseas. The American objective behind this was to further reduce international market supplies without requiring any marginal contribution from the United States, which had an obligation of only 1.9 million metric tons, far less than it had ever shipped. The EEC took on a minimum commitment of better than one million metric tons, 23 percent of the FAC floor. The United States had effectively used the FAC to engineer the use of non-American resources to reduce food supply on global markets.

This was, of course, perfectly consistent with the CAP's mechanisms for driving up farm prices so as to support European food self-sufficiency and agricultural productivity growth. Indeed, in many ways, European Union food aid under the CAP looked a lot like food aid from the United States in the 1950s and 1960s, when high farmgate prices were the agricultural policy objective and surplus disposal was the chief concern. European food aid was donated out of surplus agricultural stocks generated by the CAP, especially wheat and animal products. With the creation of the CAP, which had increased agricultural productivity as its main goal, wheat production within the member countries increased by 50 percent in less than a decade, in spite of reduced acreage in production, with sharp increases likewise in dairy and sugar beet production. Big surpluses induced by profligate agricultural policy created both pressure and opportunity to use food as a resource for overseas development.

The EU runs a food aid program for the Union as a whole that now accounts for more than half of all European food aid contributions. But each of the Union's member states also operates a separate, bilateral food aid program. This complexity has led to considerable operational problems and regular reorganization.[10] Because agricultural policy and political pressures in each nation are slightly different than in the others, the complex web of bilateral food aid programs complemented by a larger, multilateral food aid program have had two major effects. First, this situation has predisposed the Europeans toward multilateral food aid. This has had a major effect on WFP, the world's primary multilateral food aid agency. Europe has been the main champion of WFP since its creation, even though the United States has always been the main donor. Second, the internal contradictions among member states' national-level farm and trade policy objectives have forced articulation of some shared vision for European food aid, necessarily elevating this common rationale relative to its place in motivating food aid from purely bilateral donors such as the United States or Canada.

That overarching rationale has become development assistance. The Europeans have always taken the development and humanitarian objectives of food aid more seriously than the Americans, perhaps in part because of cultural and economic ties due to historical colonial relations and in part due to their own experience in the immediate post-World War II period. Perhaps it is because European food aid came of age during the world food crisis of 1973–74 and the mid-1970s, when food aid advocates argued successfully that food was a resource of uniquely high priority because of the physiological necessity of good nutrition and the basic right to food recognized under the 1948 Universal Declaration of Human Rights. Concerns about potential market disincentive effects were largely dismissed as of lower-order importance during this period.

The EU has never offered concessional export credits for food aid, as the USA does through PL 480 Title I exports, but has opted instead for pure donations to recipient country governments and NGOs, like the Canadians. The character of European food aid has therefore always been more like that of Canada than like US food aid. The European Commission long argued that food could be a uniquely beneficial resource to help recipient countries' agricultural and rural development and their nutritional programs. It has been loathe to acknowledge any self-interest in food aid through surplus disposal or export market development, quite in contrast to the US government's trumpeting of the domestic benefits of its foreign food aid programs. Indeed, in one well-documented case, the Danes drastically reshaped their bilateral food aid program, in the face of considerable opposition from the domestic farm lobby, so as to improve its cost-effectiveness in delivering nutrients to developing country recipients (see Box 3.1). Similarly, the Netherlands, Sweden, Switzerland, and the UK have all effectively broken the links between domestic agricultural lobbies and food aid disbursements from their nations. If European nations with farm support programs even more far-reaching and generous than US programs have proved able to break these chains that had previously shackled European food aid, it should be similarly feasible to reform food aid in the main donor country, the United States.

Box 3.1 The enlightened transformation of Danish bilateral food aid[1]

Denmark has made one of the most remarkable shifts in bilateral food aid strategy of any donor nation. Like most donors, Denmark had long contributed from the domestic output according to self-interest. In Denmark's case, this implied significant donations of canned pork, beef and chicken, processed cheese and split peas, all high-value commodities perceived as internationally competitive. Danish food aid policies had long been strongly supported by the Ministry of Agriculture and the Agricultural Council of Denmark as an important tool for price support and export market development. However, these foods are also very expensive per gram of calorie or protein. In 1988, the Danish parliament froze the rate of increase of Denmark's contributions to WFP at the suggestion of the Ministry of Foreign Affairs, which maintained that WFP had reached a satiation point at which it could not use additional resources effectively. This elicited a storm of protest from the Ministry of Agriculture and the Danish farm lobby, which wanted continued increases in food aid.

The ensuing debate induced the Ministry of Foreign Affairs to commission a study of the effectiveness and appropriateness of Danish food aid by the eminent agricultural economist Per Pinstrup-Andersen. Professor Pinstrup-Andersen's study concluded that a large increase in Danish contributions to WFP should be considered based on likely increases in WFP's near-term needs, its manifest effectiveness, and the common vision between WFP and Danish development policy. He also argued, however, for a radical change in the basket of foods donated, with a shift toward basic grain commodities that could sharply increase the total volume of calories and protein available to recipients within the Danish food aid budget. Moreover, he pushed for Denmark's food aid contribution to be untied financial aid rather than contributions in kind of Danish food products. When asked for its opinion on the study, WFP offered its support of the recommended changes.

The Ministry of Foreign Affairs swiftly recommended a change in the food aid commodity basket, although it maintained two-thirds of the Danish contribution in kind and declined to recommend an increased contribution to WFP, and the Prime Minister adopted these changes in the spring of 1992, over stiff opposition from the well-organized meat and dairy industries. The Prime Minister also moved administrative responsibility over Danish food aid from the Ministry of Agriculture to the Ministry of Foreign Affairs. In October 1992, canned meat and processed cheese were replaced by wheat flour, peas and vegetable oil in the Danish contribution basket.

As a direct result of these relatively simple changes, by 1997 (after a gradual phase out of cheese and meat donations) Danish contributions to the World Food Programme were able to provide six times more calories and three times more protein than the 1990 Danish food aid basket, and at lower cost. Total sales from Danish agriculture were unchanged, although there was some redistribution of earnings and employment from the processing, dairy, and meat subsectors to the grains, peas, and vegetable oil subsectors, with perhaps a very modest loss in aggregate agricultural sector employment (on the order of perhaps 100 jobs total) because the higher-value commodities are more labor-intensive. This was a clear case of major gains at limited-to-no cost based on timely, skilled policy analysis and enlightened and courageous policymaking.

Note:
[1] Abstracted from Colding and Pinstrup-Andersen (1999).

The developmental focus of European food aid has prompted more innovation with alternative procurement and distribution modalities, especially local purchases and triangular transactions. A major break point in European food aid policy came when the European Union enacted Regulation 1292/96 in 1996 that initiated an important transition from food aid in kind to cash transfers in support of food distribution programs. This came on the heels of the Single Market Act of 1995 that required EU-wide tendering of all but exceptional contracts, which significantly reduced member states' capacity to use food aid appropriations to stimulate demand for food from domestic producers.

These actions marked a significant departure from past supply-driven policies toward more demand-driven operations. Then the Joint Evaluation of European Program Food Aid (Clay *et al.* 1996) delivered a scathing evaluation of the efficacy and efficiency of European program food aid based largely on surplus disposal. To the EU's credit, it responded to the criticism by substantially overhauling the budgeting and programming of European food aid. The Europeans have subsequently been reallocating resources away from food aid in kind toward financial transfers through its Forex facility, whereby hard currency is provided to private sector operators for the import of agreed food commodities from a set of European and other countries deemed eligible by the EU. This is rightly seen as far less costly and more supportive of development of private food distribution systems in low-income countries.

As a consequence, Europe – through the EU, its members and non-member states – has been the leader in pushing triangular transactions and local purchases in an effort to (1) reduce delivery lags; (2) ensure that food aid distributed is suited to local tastes and dietary habits; (3) achieve greater cost-efficiency in food aid procurement and delivery; and (4) channel the demand stimulus from food aid procurement so as to benefit developing country farmers. While European food aid has not entirely lived up to this promise, perhaps especially regarding reduced delivery lags, this nonetheless represents a sharp break from traditional food aid reliant entirely on sourcing food in the donor's domestic market. Sweden, the Netherlands, and Germany have gone almost entirely to these procurement modalities in their bilateral food aid, while Switzerland, the United Kingdom, Norway, and Belgium all now give roughly three-quarters of their food aid in this form. EU collective donations remain largely in kind contributions but are now more than one-third local purchases or triangular transactions. The contrast is striking with the United States, which uses these procurement methods for less than 1 percent of its food aid and Canadian flows that remain more than 90 percent in kind commodity contributions. Of course, not all of the Europeans are progressive in this respect. The French, for example, still make scant use of triangular transactions or local purchases in their limited bilateral food aid program.

In spite of the Europeans' far greater emphasis than the Americans on employing food aid for economic development in recipient countries, the effectiveness of European food aid "as a development resource . . . is not at all clearly demonstrated by the results of its [programs] over the past twenty five years."[11] The 1996 Joint Evaluation of EU food aid offered an even harsher judgment, calling for "radical changes" in recipient country selection, choice of form of assistance, management of counterpart funds, and coordination among donors and with recipient country governments (Clay *et al.* 1996). While the evaluation concluded that the impacts of European program food aid were "on balance, marginally positive," it also decried extraordinarily high transactions costs that sharply limit effectiveness and efficiency.

Partly in response, food aid flows from Europe have fallen in both absolute and relative terms over the past decade, reinforcing American dominance of the global food aid regime.

The relatively more progressive European approach to food aid in the early twenty-first century does not reflect a more enlightened approach to domestic agricultural policy or less harm done to the global food trading system and developing country farmers. Many of the problems that US food aid causes for developing country agriculture are not dissimilar to those caused by massive EU farm subsidies under the CAP. It just happens that the EU, as a net food importer, does its damage to the global food economy primarily through import barriers that have little effect on food aid policy, while food aid more prominently reflects agricultural policy distortions in the United States because it remains a major net food exporter. When the discussion focuses purely on food aid, the Europeans appear far more sympathetic to developing country agriculture and global humanitarian and development objectives more generally. But if viewed from the perspective of developing country agriculture, the Europeans fare no better than the Americans.

Other bilateral donors

The United States, Canada, and Europe combined account for about 85 percent of global food aid flows, somewhat down from proportions in excess of 90 percent through the late 1970s. Most of the remaining bilateral food aid flows through WFP are targeted for particular recipients and procured from specially designated sources.

Japan was a major food aid recipient in the decade following World War II. It then gradually became a food aid donor and was one of the original signatories of the 1967 Food Aid Convention agreed during the conclusion to the Kennedy Round (KR) of the General Agreement on Tariffs and Trade, the predecessor to the World Trade Organization (WTO). Japanese food aid is thus often termed "KR aid," because of its origins with the Kennedy Round. The Japan International Cooperation Agency (JICA) administers all of its food aid programs.

For a number of years now, Japan has been a larger food aid donor, in absolute terms, than Canada. Its overall overseas development assistance budget has expanded far more rapidly than the OECD average and food aid has advanced with the broader expansion in Japan's aid budget, pushed further by new obligations under international trade agreements. Up through the mid-1980s, the overwhelming majority of Japanese food aid was bilateral assistance. Over the past fifteen years, however, it has reoriented much of its food aid toward multilateral distribution. Today, most of Japan's food aid donations are in cash to WFP.[12] Nonetheless, most Japanese food aid is made available through arrangements coordinated between WFP or recipient country governments and private Japanese traders from its Grain Importers Association.

The reason for this arrangement stems from the uniqueness of Japan's food aid program. It is the only major food aid donor that is a significant net food importer. The United States, Canada, Australia, and China are all net food exporters, and

Europe, a net food importer in aggregate, includes important net exporter member states. Japanese food aid donations are closely related to its trade policy, as it uses food aid procurement to meet food import obligations under international trade agreements. In order to keep prices high for its domestic farmers, Japan imposes very high import tariffs on grains, especially rice, that price imported cereals beyond the reach of most Japanese, who commonly pay four to five times the global market price for rice. Because the WTO agreements require signatory countries to allow at least 5 percent of all food consumed to be imported tariff-free from the world market, Japan uses the minimum required level of tariff-free food imports as a window for procuring food aid.

Australia was the world's third largest food aid donor for several years, behind the USA and Canada, until the EU became a major player with the agreement of the Food Aid Convention in 1967 and Japan began to contribute significantly. Unlike Japan, Australia has always shipped its own surplus food to recipient countries, making very little use of triangular transactions or local purchases, although that has been changing in the last few years. But since Australia has never provided income or price support programs to its domestic food producers on the scale of the European or North American countries, its government has never faced significant surplus disposal pressures and its food aid program, administered by the Australian Agency for International Development (AusAID), has long been relatively more focused on recipient country need and humanitarian objectives.

There are a few other food aid donors who ship food bilaterally to particular recipients. Probably the most important and largest such relationships are between China and South Korea, as donors, and North Korea. With the mercurial treatment of food aid to North Korea by the United States in recent years, China has in many years been the primary provider of food aid there, while South Korea episodically donates rice when its own harvests generate a domestic surplus. These examples are noteworthy largely because they are among the very few examples of non-American donor use of food aid for strategic geopolitical purposes.

Multilateral food aid[13]

Multilateral food aid flows have grown rapidly over the past quarter-century, tracking the rapid expansion of emergency food aid, as shown in Figure 3.1. The World Food Crisis of 1973–74 and the World Food Conference were significant events marking the rise of multilateral efforts to prevent famine. The World Food Programme (WFP) became a central part of that agenda.

WFP was established by parallel resolutions of the UN Food and Agriculture Organization (FAO) and the UN General Assembly in 1961, over the active opposition of the FAO leadership, which perceived WFP's creation as a vote of no confidence. WFP subsequently began operations in 1963 on a three-year experimental basis, becoming a permanent part of the UN system in 1965. In 1976, the International Emergency Food Reserve (IEFR) was established as a contingency reserve with annual replenishment under the joint supervision by WFP and its sister UN agency in Rome, the FAO.

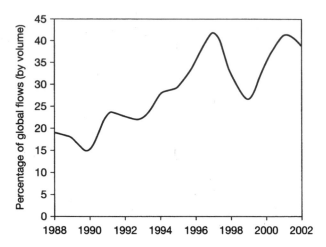

Figure 3.1 Food aid flows through WFP

Source: WFP INTERFAIS

WFP's central role in emergency food aid distribution is a relatively recent phenomenon. WFP was established to use food aid to advance economic and social development objectives through project food aid flows.[14] It proved relatively successful in responding to humanitarian crises in Africa and South Asia in the early to mid-1970s, however, and from that point on WFP became the focal point for coordinated international efforts at delivering food aid in emergencies. Then, a 1993 joint evaluation sponsored by Canada, the Netherlands, and Norway proved highly critical of WFP's performance in development efforts, citing a general lack of evidence of positive impacts. When European food aid donations (especially of milk powder) dropped sharply in the latter 1990s in response to changes in internal agricultural policy, a key resource for WFP's development projects dried up. The net effect was a sharp fall in nominal WFP operational expenditures on development projects from just under US$500 million in 1989–90 to only US$185 million in 2000, while WFP emergency operations multiplied fivefold over the same period.[15]

Today, WFP is the world's dominant multilateral food aid organization, responsible for more than 95 percent of multilateral food aid allocated and 30–40 percent of all food aid worldwide.[16] WFP's mission statement calls for it to use food aid to support economic and social development, meet refugee and other emergency food needs and associated logistics support, and promote world food security. Supplier interests in expanding export markets and reducing surplus stocks – central features of most bilateral food aid programs – are noticeably absent from WFP's mission. Its multilateral nature has helped WFP to depoliticize food aid to a significant degree, although because it depends almost entirely on bilateral donors for contributions (in kind or in cash), WFP can only distance itself so much from bilateral donors' potentially parochial concerns. Most importantly, WFP's Executive Board has majority representation from developing countries, who might reasonably be expected to insist on responsiveness to measurable need in recipient countries. Partly as a consequence of developing country representation and partly under pressure from donor countries concerned with responding to – but not always preventing – humanitarian emergencies, WFP now concentrates far more heavily on emergency humanitarian assistance. It therefore makes far greater use of emergency appeals and more responsive acquisition and distribution modalities, such as local purchases and triangular transactions, than do major bilateral donors such as the United States, the European Union, Canada, or Japan in their direct food aid distributions.

These factors have jointly led to a widespread belief within the donor community that multilateral assistance is more effective in reaching intended recipients in a timely and cost-effective manner, partly because it is allocated more according to recipients' needs than donors' needs and because it has made more extensive use of creative modalities for food aid procurement and distribution, including triangular transactions and local purchases.[17] The multilateral organizations' dependence on bilateral donations somewhat limits their ability to avoid donor country politics with respect to food sources, but WFP appears far less politically constrained with respect to the distribution of food aid.

Politics nonetheless play a role, and perhaps increasingly so. For example, USAID faces considerable political pressure from US-based NGOs that wish to handle American food aid flows, especially as monetization has become the norm for non-emergency Title II PL 480 shipments. Some NGO officials see WFP as a competitor for non-emergency shipments, especially those who do little direct distribution of food, focusing instead on development interventions that depend heavily on food aid monetization. Other NGOs commonly serve as implementing agencies for WFP in emergencies, distributing food and working together in emergency management. Those NGOs perceive themselves more as partners with WFP than as competitors. This varied relationship with the NGO community is a major reason why US donations to WFP tend to fall disproportionately in the emergency assistance category, where US-based international NGOs more commonly see themselves as WFP's implementing partners, than in non-emergency, food aid for development.

As just one microcosm of this issue, USAID has historically resisted school feeding programs of the sort that WFP has placed at the center of many of its non-emergency food aid projects for the past decade or so.[18] In the United States, the USDA bears responsibility for domestic school feeding programs, which have been highly successful in improving child nutrition and school attendance indicators.[19] USAID, on the other hand, has no tradition of school feeding and has tended to view such efforts as desirable but of lower priority than prenatal and preschool feeding programs targeted that affect child growth in the first 24–36 months of life, when long-term impacts are greatest. In 2002, after considerable, sustained pressure from former presidential candidates George McGovern, serving since March 1998 as US Ambassador to the United Nations agencies in Rome, including WFP, and Robert Dole, a former Kansas Senator and champion of food aid to help Midwestern farmers, the US Congress finally launched a food for education program over the objections of USAID, donating surplus commodities from CCC inventories. The program was based in USDA and, in spite of a scathing evaluation of the pilot program by the US General Accounting Office (2002) and strong pressure from USAID, the Office of Management and Budget and other executive agencies to move it to USAID under the 2002 Farm Bill, the global food for education initiative remains within USDA.[20]

In spite of the growth in multilateral flows as a share of total food aid, there is nonetheless growing concern about the "bilateralization" of humanitarian response to emergencies.[21] The concept of bilateralization refers to the growing use of earmarked contributions to multilateral agencies (i.e., flows restricted by a donor for use only in a particular destination) in an effort to increase bilateral donor visibility and to exert greater political control over the use of donated resources. As is apparent in Figure 3.2, there has been rapid growth in earmarking of WFP food aid flows in recent years, to more than 80 percent of all WFP-mediated food aid flows in the initial years of the twenty-first century. This partly reflects the rise of consolidated appeals, wherein WFP raises funds specifically targeted for a particular emergency. Yet it also raises a question as to the degree to which the apparent multilateralization of food aid is real, rather than just a façade for bilateral donations increasingly dispensed through WFP. Clay (2003b, p. 697) raises particular concerns about what he sees as "the gradual erosion of the multilateral character of WFP."

WFP raises a significant share of its resources through extraordinary, consolidated appeals to donor governments for supplemental food aid appropriations in response to emerging crises, as in southern Africa in 2002–3, Afghanistan in late 2001 and the Horn of Africa in 1999–2000, and again in 2002–3.[22] In 2002,

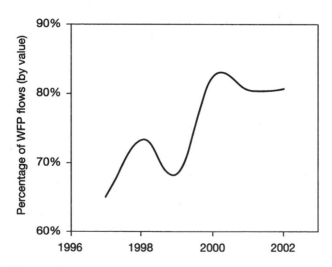

Figure 3.2 Earmarking of WFP flows

Source: WFP INTERFAIS

83 percent of WFP's operational expenditures were on relief activities (emergency and protracted relief and recovery operations), with emergency operations alone accounting for 57 percent. By tying food aid volumes to emerging needs rather than just to *ex ante* monetary appropriations, appeals tied to specific humanitarian emergencies can help break the procyclical straitjacket of monetary food aid budgeting, and thereby perhaps generate better timed and targeted food aid allocations to recipient economies than year-in-and-year-out project programming, which has been shown to be highly persistent across years in the case of PL 480.[23] Chapters 7 and 8 discuss these principles and phenomena in greater detail, including the variable success of these appeals.

WFP's clearer focus on assessed need (as opposed to other, donor-specific objectives) is widely perceived to give it a significant comparative advantage in increasing and stabilizing food availability in poor, food-deficit countries. For example, the empirical evidence indeed suggests that WFP food aid flows have historically proved considerably more responsive to recipient country need than US food aid flows have. Where US food aid flows have been uncorrelated historically with either levels of recipient country per capita food availability or temporary shocks to recipients' per capita food availability, WFP flows have been strongly and negatively related to both of those measures, helping to plug gaps where they emerge – i.e., to stabilize food availability – and to address chronic shortfalls.[24] This responsiveness is reflected as well in the high degree of concentration of WFP emergency aid flows among countries in any given year, with 73–83 percent going to its six largest recipients in any given year between 1995 and 2002.[25] The main shortcoming of WFP flows in response to fluctuations in recipient country food availability has been the modest magnitude of the offset they provide against short-term food availability shortfalls. While the statistical evidence suggests that multilateral food aid can make a real difference for good at the margin, it can never be a foundation for a national level food security strategy.[26] Also, its impact could plainly be improved if generalizable lessons could be learned from the significant number of countries where multilateral food aid has proved highly responsive to need and if those lessons could then be applied elsewhere, where food aid seems to fail to stabilize food availability effectively. Furthermore, there is some reason to fear that the efficacy of WFP food aid in stabilizing recipient country food availability could be compromised as the agency comes to depend increasingly on US donations, given the supply-driven nature of US food aid contributions, and links to geopolitical objectives.

In theory, multilateral food aid also helps resolve donor coordination problems associated with food aid's effects on international trade, migration, and political stability. There is some limited empirical evidence supporting this as well.[27] Insofar as well-targeted, timely food aid helps to avert emergency-induced population movement and political instability and to the extent that it stimulates recipients' immediate or future demand for commercial food imports, food aid's benefits accrue to a wide array of international actors. A bilateral approach creates the potential for a classic "free rider" problem, wherein each donor has an incentive to wait and let other donors bear the cost of emergency response because the benefits to the donor governments' other domestic or foreign policy objectives depend relatively little, in most acute emergencies, on who provides the support. As a consequence, it can prove difficult to raise the necessary resources in a timely fashion. Multilateral management of international food assistance can help induce donors to (at least partially) coordinate, even match each others' contributions, thereby helping to obviate the natural tendency to free ride on each other's humanitarian assistance.[28]

Conclusion

Contemporary food aid remains more a manifestation of donors' broader agricultural, foreign, and trade policies than an independent policy unto itself in support of food security objectives in recipient countries. The Nobel Prize-winning economist T.W. Schultz's 1960 caution about rationalizing food aid rings true still today: "[T]houghtful people and informed leaders abroad are not deceived by what we say; they see clearly that we have been making our foreign economic policy fill our internal convenience."[29] The donor orientation of food aid has been reflected at various times in programs in the United States, Canada, Europe, and Japan, as well as other donor countries. The design and size of food aid programs have shifted in response to changing domestic agricultural programs, foreign policy objectives, and shifts in the balance of power among different constituencies lobbying for food aid to better serve their particular interests. But the basic pattern of donor-oriented food aid has persisted.

The United States – and, less importantly, Japan – excepted, however, there has been noteworthy progress in breaking food aid from many of the shackles imposed by donors' domestic agricultural policies. Reforms have been slow and incomplete, to be sure. But in many donor countries, progress has been tangible, especially in the elimination of concessional sales programs, in the increased use of multilateral channels, local purchases, and triangular transactions, in more flexible movement between cash and food resources as dictated by the particular needs of programs, and in explicit decoupling of farm programs from food aid resourcing. The potential of food aid thus appears in both the substantial progress made in several bilateral food aid programs and in the demonstrably greater efficacy of multilateral food aid, relative to bilateral food aid, in responding to chronic and temporary shortfalls in food availability in low-income countries.

Given its checkered history over the past half-century, especially in the United States, it would be easy, but wrong, to dismiss food aid as an inherently poor instrument for addressing food insecurity worldwide. The key is that as long as food aid procurement and distribution remain largely a bilateral affair, focused on procurement in and shipment from donors' domestic markets, it will be exceedingly difficult to break free of the inherent donor orientation of the resource. Even Canadian and European food aid policies, while becoming less explicitly donor-oriented in their modalities, remain nested within exceptionally protectionist farm policies that are reforming at glacial speed thanks to resistance from countries such as France, Germany, and Ireland. If the inappropriate use of food aid is to be reduced, there will need to be a concerted push toward an authentic multilateralization of food aid.

The problem is that by attempting to use food aid for too many purposes, donors have compromised its effectiveness in accomplishing the core goals well, particularly the humanitarian objectives that underpin most public rhetoric in support of food aid. Food aid has had little effect on domestic food prices in major donor countries, on the efficacy of foreign policy (as in Vietnam, North Korea, or Afghanistan), on agricultural trade promotion, on maintaining the competitiveness of the US maritime industry, etc. Indeed, food aid has been a source of regular tension among the major donor countries because of its potentially disruptive effects on international food markets and trade patterns, as we discuss in the next chapter.

Because so many different interests have a stake in the system, food aid becomes a terribly expensive and slow means of transferring resources to low-income, food-deficit countries, as we discuss in greater detail in Chapter 8. As modern food aid reaches its half-century mark, the task now is to free food aid from the donor-oriented shackles that presently keep it from realizing its humanitarian and economic development potential – and to meet the other erstwhile policy objectives with different policy instruments more appropriate to and effective in advancing donor-oriented objectives.

4 International regulatory mechanisms and trade disputes

As the preceding two chapters have made clear, donors' varying interests surrounding food aid lead to a complex landscape of food used in different ways at different times by different agencies for different purposes. Not surprisingly, this sometimes sparks conflicts among donors. This chapter reviews some of those conflicts and the institutions that try to pre-empt or mitigate rows related to food aid.

There exist international regulatory mechanisms over food aid intended to ensure the availability of adequate supplies of food to fulfill humanitarian or development objectives in low-income, food-deficit countries and to prevent the abuse of the global food aid system by donors seeking to advance their own objectives, especially in the area of export market development. But these strictures have grown increasingly ineffective over time. Partly as a result, the role of food aid as a form of disguised agricultural export subsidy has become a hot issue again in international trade negotiations associated with the current Doha Round under the World Trade Organization. At the same time, trade disputes between, chiefly, the United States and Europe over genetically modified foods have spilled over into the food aid domain as well, as recipient countries have become battlegrounds in which the exporting and donor behemoths battle for supremacy. These issues of international trade and regulation provide an important arena for a potential recasting of food aid in the near future.

International regulatory mechanisms

Precisely because of the range of prospective conflicts between donors, a body of international regulatory mechanisms has emerged around food aid. The mechanisms are associated with several different institutions, each with a limited mandate, no one of which has overall responsibility for or authority to coordinate (bilateral and multilateral) donor and operational agency actions related to food aid.

The most visible of these is the **Food Aid Convention (FAC)**, the legal agreement that establishes food aid guidelines for donors. The Food Aid Convention (1999) is a legal agreement among twenty-two donor nations (and the European Commission) that guides international cooperation on food aid matters. It was originally agreed in 1967 as part of the International Grains Agreement within the

Kennedy Round of the GATT trade negotiations and most recently revised in 1999.[1] As a result, the FAC is housed at the International Grains Council, a body organized to promote international commercial trade in cereals. Recipient countries do not participate in the FAC.

The multiple objectives of the FAC are to make "appropriate levels of food aid available on a predictable basis," "to ensure that the food aid provided is aimed particularly at the alleviation of poverty and hunger of the most vulnerable groups, and is consistent with agricultural development in those countries," to maximize "the impact, the effectiveness and quality of the food aid provided as a tool in support of food security," and to provide "a framework for cooperation, coordination and information-sharing among members" so as to improve efficiency and coherence between food aid and other policy instruments. The FAC expired on June 30, 2002, and has yet to be renewed, having instead been extended annually since its expiration.

The Convention commits donors to minimum annual food aid disbursements. Minimum aggregate international commitments increased during the early agreements, but have fallen steadily over the past three FAC renegotiations, to only 4.895 million metric tons in the 1999 Convention (down from 5.5 million tons in the 1995 Convention).[2] The United States, following longstanding tradition, once again comprised more than half of the commitments agreed in the most recent Convention. The Convention also limits shipments of some higher value commodities, putting the emphasis squarely on basic grains, pulses, root crops, and edible oils.[3] The FAC explicitly encourages increased distribution of food aid through multilateral channels, particularly the WFP. But the FAC has never been formally evaluated, so it is difficult to clearly establish the degree to which the Convention has succeeded, if at all, in achieving its aims.[4]

The FAO **Consultative Sub-Committee on Surplus Disposal (CSSD)**, established in 1954 with the passage of PL 480 in the United States and based in Washington, monitors food aid donors' disposal of agricultural surpluses. CSSD comprises 41 member states, including both donors (e.g., Australia, Canada, Japan, and the United States) and recipients (e.g., Bangladesh, India, Malawi, Myanmar), with 16 additional states and 7 international organizations (e.g., International Federation of Agricultural Producers, International Monetary Fund) holding "observer" status. The basic objective behind the CSSD is to safeguard exporter interests by ensuring that food aid does not encroach on the **usual marketing requirements (UMR)** of food aid recipient countries. The UMR is a commitment by food aid recipients to maintain a "normal" level of commercial food imports in order that food aid not displace trade.

In practical terms, the UMR is operationalized as the average of the preceding five years' commercial imports for the particular recipient country and commodity in question. Under the FAC, the UMR is used to gauge whether food aid will displace normal commercial imports or adversely affect domestic production. The maximum level of food aid permitted under the FAC – with exceptions for acute emergencies due to natural or manmade disasters – is the difference between the country's consumption needs[5] and the UMR plus domestic supplies (production and stocks). If the food aid is given to a government, the recipient country agrees to maintain the specified level of commercial imports. The UMR is also taken into account prior to considering grants to NGOs.[6]

The rules guiding CSSD have been agreed by all the major food aid donors and are captured in the Sub-Committee handbook, *Principles of Surplus Disposal and Consultative Obligations of Member Nations*. The rules include a reporting requirement for all food aid donors. Reported shipments are recorded in the Register of Transactions, as it is officially called, and are then reviewed when the CSSD meets each quarter to discuss these reports and broader matters of food aid policy, especially as it relates to commercial international trade in foodstuffs.

In recent years, however, the reporting requirement has effectively been ignored. In 1991–93, 80 percent of global food aid flows were reported. By 1997, less than 50 percent of food aid was reported through the CSSD, and by 2000–1, less than 5 percent of food aid had been reported to CSSD each year.[7] The decline in notification arises at least in part because the proportion of reported food aid that requires the establishment of a UMR has also declined rapidly in recent years. This reflects: (1) the relatively small size of most transactions; and (2) the vastly increased proportion of food aid channeled through NGOs or multilateral agencies or provided in response to emergency situations. The UMR requirement is waived entirely in order to relieve any potential burden on recipient countries that are in difficult economic situations. The extent of use of UMR waivers is a subject of some contention between donor and recipient countries, although the basic principle is universally agreed.

The real concern about the sharp decline in notification over the past decade arises mainly because some members of the CSSD are understandably concerned that non-notification effectively prevents the Subcommittee from fulfilling its mandate of ensuring food aid does not impact adversely on commercial transactions in international agricultural markets. Given the long history of bilateral donors' use of food aid for surplus disposal and trade promotion objectives, and given stricter disciplines surrounding export subsidies in agriculture since the Uruguay Round Agreement on Agriculture in 1994, decreased reporting has helped fuel renewed concerns that food aid is being exploited to evade WTO restrictions on trade in food, especially by the United States, and to a lesser degree, by France.

In recent years, the EU and the Cairns Group, a coalition of agricultural exporting countries that serves as a bit of a counterweight to the EU and the United States,[8] have pushed for strengthening the rules and disciplines on food aid so as to ensure that food surplus disposal through food aid donations does not circumvent export subsidy commitments embodied in the World Trade Organization's **Uruguay Round Agreement on Agriculture (URAA)**, does not displace normal commercial imports, and does not depress prices and thereby create a disincentive for domestic producers in recipient countries.

For reasons we discuss in more detail in the next section, however, the objective of non-displacement of commercial imports is infeasible. Expert observers such as Per Pinstrup-Andersen and Shlomo Reutlinger have long pointed out that food aid inevitably replaces some portion of the food that recipients would otherwise purchase. The simple reason follows directly from one of the most basic empirical regularities of agricultural economics, Engel's Law, which says that food consumption increases more slowly than income. Since aid flows are an income transfer in the form of food, the additional food consumed will be less than the additional food received. Some of the food aid, therefore, necessarily displaces purchases.[9] This was not readily noticed for many years when food aid flowed mainly to Asian economies that enjoyed steady economic growth, so that food imports naturally increased because of economic growth, masking the adverse effects of food aid on commercial food imports by recipient countries. In countries that are not growing, however, the concept of the UMR violates basic laws of economics. The degree to which food aid displaces food purchases in a recipient economy depends fundamentally on how well targeted program the program is – does the food go almost exclusively to very poor people, for whom displacement is low? – and whether the food aid is monetized, in which case it competes directly with commercially marketed food. It is therefore curious that UMRs *do not* apply to emergency food aid shipments that are typically better targeted and less likely to be monetized – and thus where commercial market displacements are typically least – but UMRs *do* apply to program and project food aid shipments where monetization is the norm and thus UMR compliance is a fallacy that can only be masked by the simultaneous effects of economic growth.[10]

Myth 4 Food aid is wholly additional

The UMR concept depends fundamentally on a belief that food aid is wholly additional, meaning that each extra kilogram of food aid received increases food consumption by a whole kilogram (i.e., there is no displacement of purchases). This is false because food aid represents an in-kind income transfer. Even very poor people do not spend all of an extra dollar of income on food, even if it comes to them in the form of food. As a result, each extra kilogram of food aid sent to a country tends to increase food consumption by much less than a kilogram. As a result, food aid inevitably displaces some commercial food purchases or recipient country food production, regardless of whether or not food aid recipients agree to maintain a usual marketing requirement.

Food aid and commercial food trade[11]

The displacement of commercial food purchases by food aid gives rise to trade disputes. Indeed, food aid has been a contentious issue in trade policy since the earliest US food aid programs at the outset of the twentieth century elicited protests from foreign allies who were competitors with American producers in overseas agricultural export markets.[12] Disputes have intensified again in recent years in the wake of changing US farm policy. In the 1950s and 1960s, farm policy basically involved price support programs and import tariffs that kept food prices high, not just for American producers, but also for competing exporters from Canada, Australia, New Zealand and, as the Common Agricultural Policy came online, the European Community.

But as US farm support programs have transitioned over the past decade from what were effective high-price policies to ones that provide general income support to enable American farmers to weather market downturns and to invest in technology improvements, increased American food supplies and reduced import protection have lowered real (inflation-adjusted) global food prices, intensifying global market competition. When American farm policy – including food aid – basically worked to their advantage, the other major agricultural exporters would complain a bit in the hallways but food aid was not a source of serious dispute. However, now that American farm policy hurts competing exporters, they shout about American food aid from the rooftops, identifying it as a form of export dumping and protesting that it therefore violates the rules of the World Trade Organization (WTO).[13] The US government has begun taking such concerns reasonably seriously in the past two years, reducing PL 480 Title I concessional sales volumes and proposing no new Section 416(b) shipments from surpluses procured by the CCC. Whether these proposals ultimately hold or not remains to be seen.

It is important to note, however, that concerns about food aid in the context of international trade are not concerns for the efficacy of food aid in addressing food insecurity or hunger around the world. These are purely donor governments' self-interested concerns about the potential international market displacement and price effects of food aid. Those market effects can impact as well on domestic food producers in recipient countries, an issue we tackle in Chapter 8. But the real hue and cry about food aid in a trade context is focused on donor concerns for their domestic constituents.

Despite many policy changes over the past ten years, especially in Europe and Canada, and in spite of a dearth of hard empirical evidence that food aid offers an effective tool for this objective, export market development remains an important political justification for food aid, especially in the United States. PL 480 Title I shipments by the US Department of Agriculture – rather than the US Agency for International Development – still comprise a significant share of global food aid flows, and there has been significant resurgence in use of Section 416(b) and Food for Progress flows from the United States in the past decade.[14] USDA's websites trumpet food aid as an agricultural export instrument. Recall that Title I is subsidized credit for food aid bought at market terms in the United States, or at least on something approaching market terms. So from the producers' perspective, Title I food aid recipients are just another customer, increasing sales volumes, revenues and profits, but in effect, subsidized by the US government. Hence the concerns voiced by other exporting countries about food aid as a means for circumventing trade agreements.

Agricultural export subsidies have been and continue to be reduced under the disciplines of the URAA, signed at Marrakesh, Morocco, in April 1994. But food aid programs are not subject to the same restrictions. Under Article 10 of the URAA, WTO member countries that are international food aid donors are nonetheless prohibited from tying food aid directly or indirectly to commercial exports of agricultural products to recipient countries. This restriction was intended to prevent the circumvention of the export subsidy commitments made under the URAA. The URAA also stipulates that food aid is to be given in full grant form to the maximum extent possible, or on terms no less concessional than those provided for in Article IV of the 1986 Food Aid Convention. Furthermore, all food aid transactions (including bilateral food aid) are to be carried out in accordance with the Food and Agriculture Organization of the United Nations' (FAO) "Principles of Surplus Disposal and Consultative Obligations," including the system of Usual Marketing Requirements discussed previously. Recall that reporting of food aid shipments to the CSSD has largely collapsed in recent years, both causing and reflecting tensions over the effect of food aid on commercial agricultural trade.

These tensions have spiked in the past two years as American food aid has come under severe attack by various other agricultural exporting nations as the Doha Round of WTO negotiations has proceeded. Indeed, food aid was one of several key agricultural issues that led to the impasse that caused talks to collapse at the Cancun ministerial meeting in September 2003. At the mini-ministerial meeting in Montreal in July 2003, the United States for the first time said it would negotiate on food aid terms, including placing food aid credits (e.g., Title I PL 480 shipments) within the purview of WTO disciplines on export subsidies, which are aimed at preventing commercial displacement through food aid, as proposed by the Europeans and supported by India, the Cairns Group, and the Mercosur countries of South America.

The FAC, CSSD, and WTO disciplines on food aid likely have far less impact on the trade-distorting effect of food aid than does the efficacy of food aid targeting, however. Ultimately, the primary trade displacement effects arise when food aid leaks out to those whose need for food is limited and who therefore substitute transfers received in kind for food they would otherwise have purchased. If the agricultural trade community wants to work at limiting the distortions created by food aid in the global marketplace – just like recipient country governments that want to limit the adverse market price effects of food aid in domestic markets – then they need to pay far more attention to the practices that guide food aid targeting in its various forms: who provides and receives it and how, when it flows, and what commodities are involved. For example, program food aid such as PL 480 Title I shipments, and monetized project food aid shipments are not targeted at all within a recipient country and thus inevitably have significant trade displacement effects.

Differences in climate, technology, and the availability of land and water create sharp differences in agricultural productivity around the globe. On balance, the world today enjoys significant and growing food surpluses. These surpluses are concentrated in a relatively small number of countries, especially in North America, Europe, Australia, and the southern cone countries of South America. Most commercial food trade takes place between these countries and the large economies that do not enjoy significant, regular domestic food surpluses, such as China, Japan, and Russia. Food trade has grown quite rapidly over the past generation as increasing incomes and falling costs of commerce have stimulated faster expansion in trade than in output. Nonetheless, a large share of the world's population continues to suffer food insecurity or hunger and many low-income countries have insufficient food available to provide nutritionally adequate diets for all their citizens even if food were evenly distributed throughout the population. Food aid could, in theory, help to address the commercial food distribution problem that leaves 800 million or more people hungry in a world enjoying considerable food surpluses.

As already mentioned, the central questions about food aid's effects on global food markets revolve around targeting, a topic we will cover in much greater detail in Chapter 8. Were food aid to flow exclusively to those who would otherwise go hungry, and only in amounts and forms so that those vulnerable recipients did not correspondingly reduce their own production or commercial purchase of food, then food aid would result in nearly completely additional consumption. That is, there would be no significant reduction in the amount of food purchased or produced in the economy of the recipient country.

The question of **additionality** is a purely short-run concern, however, and not even the only factor influencing the short-run effects of food aid on international food trade. The remainder of this section explains the various factors that determine food aid's inherently ambiguous short- and long-run effects on commercial food trade, both exports by food aid donors and spillover effects on exporters other than the donor country. Beyond the first question of additionality, however, there has been scant empirical research. As a consequence, it remains difficult to make any strong, scientifically defensible statements about the actual extent to which food aid affects trade.

First, we consider the effects of food aid on recipient behavior. One can usefully identify four distinct effects of food aid on recipient country food markets. First, food aid adds to the income of the recipient and thereby affects consumption and purchasing patterns. Economists call these "static income effects." Second, because some of that extra income is invested, either directly in new projects or equipment, or indirectly, such as by protecting human nutrition and health, food aid can also have longer-term, dynamic income effects. Third, as incomes increase, people tend to demand greater variety in their diet, which will affect how aid impacts on trade. Finally, in so far as food aid has any effect on recipient country food market prices, then it will affect domestic food producers' supply patterns in the medium-to-long run, if not always immediately. We address each of these concepts in turn.[15]

The most obvious consequence of food aid receipt is the static income effect associated with the transfer of resources in the form of food, for which the income elasticity of demand is less than one. As one would expect on the basis of Engel's Law, the empirical evidence suggests overwhelmingly that food aid partly substitutes for contemporaneous commercial food imports, thereby providing a net foreign exchange transfer, generally of the order of 40–70 percent of the value of the food aid delivered.[16] Put differently, only 30–60 percent of food aid seems to add to recipients' food consumption, with the remainder functioning almost as if it were instead a cash transfer, displacing commercial purchases through markets, whether from domestic production or international trade.

One conclusion that comes through in the case study evidence is that the additionality of food aid depends to a considerable degree on the design and implementation of the program – targeting, timing, etc. – variables that are difficult to quantify and capture in formal, quantitative analyses.[17] Key features include the extent to which food aid is monetized in local markets and the use to which recipient country governments and NGOs put counterpart funds generated by monetization, in particular, whether these funds are spent on subsidizing demand or supply. Poorly targeted and heavily monetized food aid shipments have greater market displacement effects, for reasons we detail in Chapter 7. When counterpart funds are used to stimulate food production, commercial imports decrease, and when they are used to subsidize demand (through income transfer to the poor), commercial imports increase.[18]

Because **income elasticities of demand** fall sharply as one approaches and moves beyond the poverty line,[19] additionality is highest when food aid reaches almost exclusively the intended (typically poor) recipients. Leakage to richer, unintended recipients necessarily increases the contemporaneous market displacement effects of food aid. Food aid's additionality therefore depends fundamentally on how well targeted it is. And it is very difficult to target effectively, as we discuss in detail in Chapter 8. Even reasonably well-executed transfer programs incur significant **errors of inclusion** (of unintended recipients) **and errors of exclusion** (of intended recipients). Significant errors of inclusion result in relatively large market displacement of food purchases.

The macro-level evidence generally corroborates the micro-level evidence. Quite a few studies have found at best weak relationships between various indicators of nonconcessional food availability (i.e., domestic production plus commercial imports) in recipient countries and the food aid volumes received.[20] One reason is that food aid – especially program food aid – is multi-targeted, first to a recipient country with a particular bundle of commodities, and then to a subpopulation within the recipient country through a specific food assistance modality. More importantly, however, food aid allocations have traditionally been made largely on the basis of political criteria, and there has been only modest movement in recent years toward targeting food aid to low-income, food-deficit countries. Moreover, once in the recipient economy, food aid disproportionately facilitates explicit or implicit consumer food subsidies, few of which are well targeted.[21]

The magnitude of contemporaneous displacement is not the only issue. Displaced commercial sales could be taken from donor country exporters, third country exporters or domestic producers. In so far as displacement of donor country exports is not of great concern – this effectively constitutes a relabelling of the flow[22] – the concern within donor countries and the WTO tends to revolve around induced reductions in third country commercial exports. The contemporaneous displacement effect results entirely because the extra increment of income received by the recipient comes in the form of food. The one empirical study to date that explores how food aid affects recipient country imports from the donor country versus from other countries found that food aid has nearly identical negative effects on recipient country commercial imports from the United States and from the rest of the world.[23] For each kilogram per capita of food aid received, both the donor and other foreign exporters lose an estimated 0.3 kilograms of commercial sales. So the very limited available empirical evidence suggests that other exporters pay a price for donor country food aid programs. Hence their displeasure.

There may also be important dynamic income multiplier effects, stimulating recipients' productivity and income with a lag, thereby increasing future commercial demand for food. The whole idea of trade promotion rests on a belief in the positive dynamic income and trade effects of food aid. The export market development claims associated with food aid are heard commonly in national capitals of donor countries. It is certainly true, as claimed by advocates in the United States, for example, that major food-importing nations such as Japan, Morocco, the Philippines, South Korea, and Taiwan were once food aid recipients. But the causal relation between food aid and later commercial food imports has never been credibly established. Increased market demand for food in these countries is almost surely the consequence of income growth, which may have been (very mildly) abetted by food aid, but there is no evidence that food aid has stimulated incomes growth any better than financial aid, good economic policy, cheap energy, or a host of other factors that underpin economic growth. Two different farm lobby representatives in Washington, for example, used exactly the same "fact" in interviews with us, that "43 of the top 50 importers" of US farm products once received PL 480 food aid. These are facile claims since roughly 90 percent of the world's economies have at one time or another received PL 480 food aid. So one would randomly predict about 45 of the top 50 importers to have once been US food aid recipients. More fundamentally, the longest-standing recipients of US food aid (Peru, Haiti, India, Indonesia, Jordan, and the Philippines) are relatively small markets for US agricultural exporters.

The common claim by agricultural producer groups advocating for food aid is thus that while in the short run food aid may significantly substitute for commercial food imports, it nonetheless stimulates long-run demand for commercial food imports, especially from the donor. Put differently, the combination of short-term displacement of commercial food purchases and stimulus of long-term (demand for and thus) purchases of food suggests the existence of what economists term a "J-curve effect." At the time of food aid delivery, commercial imports fall, but as time goes by, dynamic income effects kick in and commercial food imports recover and then grow beyond the baseline level, creating a plot of commercial imports versus time that is shaped like the letter J. The only empirical study that directly explores this question finds support for the hypothesized J-curve relation between food aid and commercial food trade.[24] Food aid seems to initially depress recipients' commercial imports and then, with a lag of a few years, to stimulate commercial food imports in excess of pre-food aid volumes, as shown in the left-hand panel of Figure 4.1.

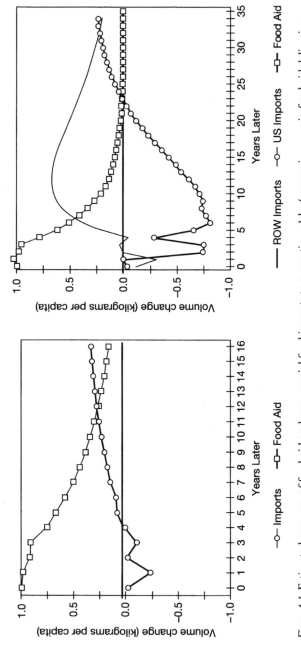

Figure 4.1 Estimated response of food aid and commercial food imports to a one-time, 1 kg/person increase in food aid deliveries

Source: Adapted from Barrett *et al.* (1999)

Of perhaps even greater interest, however, when one distinguishes between recipient country imports from the donor (in this case, the United States) and from other exporters, program food aid primarily stimulates medium-to-long term commercial imports from other producers, not from the donor. So while food aid builds future commercial food export markets, it is largely for others' exports, not the donors'.[25] As a consequence, food aid simply doesn't pay as a long-term export promotion strategy. Estimated internal rates of commercial export return on US program food aid (PL 480 Titles I and III) shipments have been negative at all meaningful time horizons.

If food aid also helps to shape consumer preferences for the imported foodstuff instead of indigenous foods, this could further reinforce the dynamic trade gains resulting from food aid, although induced change in consumer preferences directly pits local producers against foreign suppliers, drawing understandable criticism from the development community. Free samples are a familiar marketing tactic used by firms in all sectors of the economy to try to broaden their customer base by convincing new consumers of the quality and value of the product. In many farm groups' and Agriculture ministries' eyes, food aid is little more than another free sample marketing campaign. Indeed, Minnesota Senator Edward Thye made this tactic explicit in his remarks at a 1957 Congressional hearing:

> If they ever develop the taste for powdered milk or for butter . . . or if they develop a strong habit for wheat, where they are rice consuming, then we will always have a market there . . . We put these foods at their disposal for a period of six months or a year, after which they are always going to be looking for that type of product.[26]

Champions of food aid-as-trade promotion hope to shape recipient country consumer preferences for the donated commodity so as to turn them into future commercial customers. The United States has explicitly tried to encourage shifts in consumer preferences from rice to wheat and from soft wheat to hard wheat in which North America holds a comparative advantage. Yet there seems to be little direct empirical evidence as to whether food aid really induces shifts in consumer tastes and thereby inducing substitution of imported foods for indigenous ones over time.[27]

At least three studies have claimed that consumer taste for variety may stimulate lagged recipient country demand for food exports from countries other than the donor or transmission of price effects from one commodity market (e.g., donated yellow maize) to another (e.g., domestically grown white maize).[28] Yet none of these studies offers direct evidence in support of the hypothesized taste-for-variety mechanism. There are certainly plenty of anecdotes relating how food aid recipients receiving a sack of wheat or corn–soy-blend will happily trade much of it for meat and alcohol. But there is scant rigorous empirical evidence on the cross-commodity effects of food aid and any associated international differences.[29]

There do not appear to be any studies to date on the potentially differential trade effects of different food aid procurement modalities, such as local purchases versus triangular transactions versus direct shipments from the donor country. One major obstacle to such research is data availability. Only about 10 percent of global food aid shipments were procured via local purchases or triangular transactions in the past decade. Figures are not available on the share of the remainder that was purchased by donors rather than donated from their existing stocks (or from purchases to which they were otherwise committed, for example, due to domestic farm support programs). Without developing such data series, it will be difficult to establish either the extent to which food aid actually expands market demand for food or the markets in which this happens.

The issue is nonetheless of considerable current importance. For example, in the United States, the Office of Management and Budget is presently pushing to transition food aid away from dependence on surplus stocks under Section 416(b) and toward cash appropriations under Title II PL 480. One can well imagine that such changes, if implemented at significant scale, could have a measurable effect on US and presumably international food markets.

Just as aggregation across time can prove misleading, so can aggregation across commodities. The demand for dietary variety has been well documented.[30] When food aid is concentrated in just a few commodities, this not only increases local supply of the donated commodity, it also stimulates additional demand in markets for different foods, especially complementary foods such as meats, fresh fruits and vegetables, and other higher-value products. The aggregate effects on food trade may therefore differ from the effect on individual commodity markets. Increased supply of the donated commodity may cause that product's price to fall and may displace commercial purchases of that commodity, while increased demand for complementary goods boosts prices and purchases of those foods.

The market effects of food aid also depend fundamentally on the nature of food aid procurement. Until the early 1970s, food aid was almost always procured from extant government food stocks created by domestic farm support programs. With the decline in farm surpluses in the European Union, Canada, and the United States over the 1990s, a significantly increased share of food aid now arises from cash appropriations. Open market procurement of food necessarily moves the aggregate demand curve for food on the source market(s), thereby potentially driving up local prices and benefiting commercial suppliers on the source market. This is the core logic behind local purchases and triangular transactions, the idea that food aid can benefit not only poor consumers in the location where it is to be distributed, it can also benefit poor producers elsewhere in the recipient country (in the case of local purchases) or in another, nearby low-income country (in the case of triangular transactions). The same logic also motivates many donor country commodity groups to lobby for food aid, which they perceive as generating domestic price support effects separate from any export promotion benefits that might result. Of course, these effects depend fundamentally on food aid procurement being of sufficient volume to affect the market. Given that global food aid flows represent less than 2 percent of global food production, it is naïve to believe that a single food aid procurement activity might discernibly influence prices in markets well integrated in the global economy.

When food aid originates in donors' domestic surplus stocks, food aid does not stimulate demand, rather, it changes the nature and perhaps the volume of supply. Food aid supplied out of surplus stocks permits the donor to undertake price discrimination, charging one price (the world market price) to commercial buyers with a higher willingness to pay and another, lower price (often zero) to aid recipients with a lower willingness to pay.[31] Price discrimination always benefits producers since it permits them to capture a greater share of the economic surplus generated by exchange. Suppliers' capacity to price discriminate successfully depends fundamentally on market segmentation so that food aid recipients do not turn around and sell the aid on the world market to other buyers. Hence the UMR restriction on recipients under the FAC. And hence historical agribusiness opposition to food aid monetization by NGOs. PL 480 Title I agreements prohibit the resale or transshipment of donated commodities and may prohibit or limit the export of similar commodities in order to ensure that Title I commodities are not used to increase the commercial exports of the importing country. In fact, leakage almost inevitably occurs in the form of reduced commercial imports, which should reduce world market prices relative to what they would be if donors could enforce UMRs and thereby accomplish perfect price discrimination between commercial customers and food aid recipients.

As soon as one recognizes that food aid provided by net exporting countries enables *de facto* price discrimination, it becomes plain that the effects of food aid on world market prices depend on one's counterfactual: should one assume that the surplus stocks would otherwise be held off the market or that they would otherwise be indistinguishably commingled with the commercial aggregate supply? If one conjectures that stocks would otherwise be completely held off the market, then the leakage inherent to food aid distribution implies that food aid depresses market prices, thereby hurting commercial suppliers. On the other hand, if one believes stocks would be marketed commercially if they were not given away as food aid, then food aid increases world market prices by removing supplies from commercial distribution channels. This then amounts to an involuntary transfer from those who buy food on the global market to those who receive food aid.

Food aid shipments have ripple effects on markets that depend fundamentally on the degree to which markets are integrated across space, time and commodities. The question is, if cash procurement of food stimulates commercial demand in the source market or, if the limited additionality of food aid increases aggregate supply in recipient economies, are the resulting price effects transmitted to other source or destination markets internationally and, if so, to what extent and with what speed? How does food aid in the form of one commodity affect market equilibria in markets for other commodities, including for processed products derived from the same commodity (e.g., how does maize distribution affect the market for maize flour)?

Most recent studies suggest that world agricultural markets are reasonably well integrated and that price shocks in one major market transmit relatively completely and quickly to spatially distant markets.[32] Increasingly open markets in the wake of the URAA and prospective further liberalization through the WTO and regional agreements should reinforce this pattern. Nonetheless, low-income country markets tend not to be as well integrated with global markets – particularly local markets in rural areas – so price transmission of shocks due to deliveries or procurement in low-income countries may be less than price transmission due to procurement in donor country economies. Understanding such patterns is essential to mapping out the spillover effects of food aid on commercial producers around the world.[33]

In summary, if food aid could be perfectly additional, it would cause no trade distortions. Income transfers in the form of food do not – and never will – add to food consumption one-for-one, not even among very poor populations. On average, less than half of every extra dollar's worth of food aid adds to recipients' food consumption. The rest displaces food they would have otherwise grown themselves or purchased on commercial markets. The empirical evidence suggests that the bulk of this displacement falls on the shoulders of exporters, both those from the donor country and from third countries. Hence disputes among donors.

Although food aid seems to provide some longer-term stimulus to food import demand in recipient economies, most of this appears to benefit countries other than the donor. So not only does food aid displace short-term exports for donors, it seems to fail to generate long-term commercial markets for donor country agricultural exporters as well. The only available rigorous estimates show that food aid has a negative internal rate of return as an investment in donor country commercial exports. Thus, the use of food aid for trade promotion purposes seems a failure and a costly one at that, since it sparks trade disputes.

Myth 5 Food aid builds long-term commercial export markets for donors

Farm lobbies have long argued for food aid as a means to open up foreign markets for future commercial sales. While this sounds reasonable and there are some isolated cases in which food aid indeed seems to have effectively cultivated a new taste for foreign commodities among recipients, the long-term, aggregate evidence shows that food aid does not work as a market development tool. Because food aid displaces commercial exports in the short run and because food aid persists, the internal rate of return on US food aid has been negative at horizons out to twenty years.

Current discussions within the WTO focus on efforts to improve the disciplines applicable to food aid transactions, emphasizing the need to ensure that food aid allocation is based on humanitarian considerations and recipient need, so as to minimize distortions to international trading patterns. But one must keep in mind that ultimately whatever trade-distorting effects food aid might have result ultimately from targeting errors.

Genetically modified foods[34]

The use of genetically modified (GM) foods has been a contentious issue since the first products came onto the public food supply in the early 1990s. The United States and a few other countries – including several large, developing countries such as Brazil, China, and India – have been cautious supporters of GM foods development and marketing, perceiving GM technologies as ways to reduce environmental damage and production costs associated with chemical applications. Most of Europe, by contrast, has resisted GM foods because of uncertainty surrounding the foods' effects on human health and possible genetic contamination of the natural environment. The transatlantic dispute over these issues has intensified over the years, fueled by sometimes quite acrimonious exchanges between agribusiness and environmental activist groups.

There are important, difficult questions facing developing country governments about GM crops. Initially, GM technology had little applicability to developing country agriculture. As GM crops arguably become more appropriate for developing country agricultural systems, these nations have had to explore competing concerns about agricultural productivity growth, food safety, environmental protection, and trade.

Different governments have come to markedly different conclusions as to the relative merits of GM foods for their production and marketing systems, much as the OECD nations have thus far arrived at different conclusions. The issue has been forced to an unprecedented degree in Sub-Saharan Africa, however, by a fierce 2002 dispute concerning food aid that pitted Europeans and their anti-GM foods supporters against Americans and their pro-GM foods allies. Once again, food aid was fundamentally caught up in donor, rather than recipient, interests, not least of which because the resulting, extraordinary politicization of the issue makes it extremely difficult to have the sort of rational domestic policy debate about the pros and cons of GM technologies that low-income agrarian countries urgently need to undertake.

As early as February 2002, international agencies began alerting the world to an impending humanitarian disaster in southern Africa as repeated, severe drought, HIV/AIDS and continued political turmoil in Angola and Zimbabwe were conspiring to make as many as 14 million people vulnerable to food insecurity. The staple food of the region is maize and the United States offered to supply significant quantities of maize ("corn" to Americans) food aid. But because 34 percent of the area planted in corn in the USA in 2002 used genetically modified (GM) seed[35] and because many commercial outlets for corn will not accept this grain, American corn food aid is disproportionately comprised of GM corn. Moreover, GM corn is not stored and shipped separately from non-GM varieties in exporting channels, so it is practically impossible to prevent commingling of the two. Of course, WFP has been using some GM foods in ration packages for several years, so this was not to be the first time that food aid recipients were to receive donated GM grain or grain products.[36] This time, however, the issue exploded.

The governments of Angola, Lesotho, Malawi, Mozambique, Swaziland, Zambia, and Zimbabwe strongly resisted accepting any food aid shipments containing GM corn. Angola and Swaziland ultimately agreed to accept GM grain, while Lesotho, Malawi, Mozambique, and Zimbabwe ultimately agreed to accept GM food aid only so long as it was milled prior to delivery into the country.[37] The purpose behind the prior milling requirement was to prevent the possibility of farmers planting the seed and thereby introducing GM varieties into local agroecosystems or feeding the corn to their livestock and thereby potentially compromising access to meat export markets in Europe. In Zimbabwe, at least, the detritus from the milled grain, which is valuable livestock feed under normal circumstances, had to be destroyed at the government's insistence. Although feed availability had plummeted and many small farmers were losing their herds, the government was concerned that cattle fed GM maize milling by-products might compromise the nation's access to European export markets.[38]

Zambia, however, refused to accept GM food aid under any conditions, including milled flour produced from corn potentially containing GM varieties, on the basis of human health concerns and especially worries about potential contamination of domestic crops and livestock feed.[39] The bitter irony is that Zambia's food security situation deteriorated significantly after the ban went into effect. South Africa had volunteered to mill the grain en route to Zambia, but in late October 2002, President Levy Mwanawasa turned down this offer in announcing the total ban. The World Health Organization had certified the grain for human consumption, but the Zambian President labeled it "poison." A Zambian Department of Agriculture spokesman explained the government's decision as a "precautionary measure to protect the local crop varieties and [that] there is a risk of losing its export market if it grows GM crops."[40] To a certain degree, this concern about export markets seems unfounded since the likelihood of Zambia ever exporting raw or processed maize to Europe is negligible. More likely, Zambia would export meat from livestock fed GM maize and the EU does not (presently) ban imports of livestock fed GM grains.[41] While the export market risk may have been exaggerated, the risk of losing crucial European financial assistance for agricultural development likewise exists for countries permitting GM foods into their production and distribution systems. Moreover, the introduction of GM foods, especially unprocessed seed, would force national governments to develop and implement potentially complex and expensive biosafety frameworks that had not previously been a priority.

The logistics problems in this situation were legion. Maize shipped from outside the region in large ocean-going vessels arrives in one of a few large ports from whence it is, under normal circumstances, shipped overland to distribution nodes where it is subsequently either monetized or broken out for truck transport in smaller volumes to final distribution points. Given the distances and poor infrastructure involved, especially in reaching landlocked countries such as Malawi, Zambia, and Zimbabwe, this is a slow and expensive process under the best of conditions. Fears of agroecosystem contamination motivated the Mozambican government to refuse to allow its ports to be used for transshipment of whole grain GM corn to Malawi and Zimbabwe. This further exacerbated local transport bottlenecks and forced some shipments to the Tanzanian port of Dar es Salaam, a considerably greater and more expensive distance from key distribution points in Malawi and Zimbabwe.

Adding a milling requirement complicates matters considerably because the only processing facilities able to handle such volumes are in South Africa, requiring redirection of grain to Durban, a more expensive port than its Mozambican competitors, and inland shipment to milling points elsewhere in South Africa and then on to recipient countries. This significantly delayed deliveries and added a lot to costs, including those due to spoilage since the shelf life of milled grain is less than that of whole kernel grain. There was significant dispute among donors, distributors and recipients over who should bear the milling costs. Ultimately, South Africa offered to mill GM food aid donations for its neighbors, in some cases through services donated by private millers, who in exchange keep the by-product for animal feed, and in other cases at cost, paid by the South African government. Taking the transport and milling problems into account, Margaret Zeigler of the Congressional Hunger Center in Washington referred to this as "a logistical nightmare for the humanitarian agencies trying to respond to the impending crisis."[42]

The Zambian GM food aid ban added to costs in other ways as well. The WFP had to remove about 15,000 tons of US food donations that had already been delivered, but not distributed, from Zambia for distribution in other countries in the region that would accept the food donations. Some GM food aid deliveries were seized by intended recipients when they were told that they would not receive the grain supplies.[43] Additional security expenses were therefore also required to facilitate removal of the delivered GM grain.

So why the controversy and the logistical problems and expense? Much of this boils down to competing donor interests. The United States (and, to a lesser extent, Canada) insists on contributing food procured on its domestic markets. It has been unwilling to procure food from regional suppliers from whom GM content would not be a problem.[44] Anti-GM food activists have also accused the USA of manipulating hunger to open up foreign markets for a crop of more uncertain quality and safety that is being refused by many commercial buyers within the United States and abroad. Once introduced through food aid, market access for GM foods becomes a *fait accompli*, a point understood well by American marketing agents.

These activist organizations plainly played an active role in encouraging African resistance to GM food aid, prompting the USAID Administrator, Andrew Natsios, to remark in frustration that "they can play these games with Europeans, who have full stomachs, but it is revolting and despicable to see them do so when the lives of Africans are at stake." US Secretary of Agriculture Ann Veneman similarly protested that:

> It is disgraceful that instead of helping hungry people, these individuals and organizations are embarking on an irresponsible campaign to spread misinformation and create an atmosphere of fear, which has led countries in dire need of food to turn away safe, wholesome food.[45]

Many within the humanitarian community, while not supporting American GM food marketing, have reasonably questioned whether the middle of an acute crisis is the right time to mount a debate about this topic – in effect accusing the anti-GM lobby of scoring political points on the backs of starving people.

The Europeans, while they donated cash for local purchases and triangular transactions to try to meet local food aid needs in a culturally appropriate manner while minimizing logistical delays and expenses, have actively fueled resistance to acceptance of GM food aid due to their own food and environmental safety preferences. The European Union has made it clear for several years that it will not import foods from countries growing GM crops and it has hinted darkly that agricultural development assistance may depend on conformity to a vision of agriculture consistent with Europe's. So the presence of GM crops, whether accidentally or intentionally introduced, could jeopardize access to European export markets and financial assistance.

Perhaps the most troubling part of the GM food aid saga in southern Africa has been the intense, externally driven politicization of the debate that needs to take place in all developing countries over the appropriate role of GM technologies in national agricultural development and food security strategies. Prior to 2002, there was no indigenous view on GM foods and the science of GM crops remains inconclusive, leaving a considerable information vacuum. The debate was begun and flamed by outsiders with strong competing interests, forcing the governments of southern Africa into rapid political and commercial calculus over the risks of antagonizing the Europeans or the Americans.

By contrast, when the Indian government announced in 2003 that it would no longer accept GM food aid, no great international controversy erupted. India has been a leader among developing countries in the genetic engineering of crops, so this stance did not reflect a categorical opposition to GM technologies. Rather, the Indian government expressed concerns about the safety of US corn and soy products processed into the corn-soya blend mix that was then being distributed in non-emergency Title II programs in India. When it did not get assurances from the US government that it found satisfactory, the Indian government agency charged with oversight of GM products refused import permission for Title II cereals or soy food aid. Many observers believe that the GM issue merely offered a convenient cover for the government's desire to end food aid inflows now that it holds considerable domestic stocks and has become a significant food exporter itself, after many years' rapid growth in domestic agricultural productivity. But although India was still a major food aid recipient at the time this decision was reached, its refusal to accept GM food aid went largely unnoticed in the international agriculture and development communities because, unlike the southern Africa crisis of 2002, it was not a firefight between donors.

Conclusion

Food aid, as it is known today, originated from surplus grain production in the major exporting nations of North America and was partly motivated by American and Canadian ambitions to stimulate future export market expansion by giving away current surpluses. It should therefore come as little surprise that trade disputes have often swirled around food aid, although they have perhaps never been more acrimonious than in the early twenty-first century. Increased disciplines under the World Trade Organization have heightened incentives to use food aid to circumvent global trading rules while the Europeans' unilateral reduction of program food aid flows makes them especially impatient with continued American classification of concessional exports as food aid. Transatlantic disputes over genetically modified foods merely fan these flames.

The trade-related problems associated with food aid do not originate, however, in the nature of food-based humanitarian or development assistance, but (i) in operational failures, especially with respect to the targeting of food aid; and (ii) in global regulatory mechanisms that do not meaningfully incorporate recipient countries and that are openly ignored by donor nations. Substantial reforms of global food aid, above all of the US programs and of the international agreements, appear necessary if the world is to reduce trade-related tensions and to improve the efficacy of food aid in addressing food insecurity among poor populations in developing countries. Progress on these two fronts will, however, depend on some explicit decoupling of food aid from donor governments' export promotion and domestic price support objectives, for which food aid has proved itself remarkably ineffective.

5 So who benefits?

The "iron triangle"

Food aid remains heavily donor-oriented, with only modest progress over the past two decades in edging toward a recipient-oriented system, as Chapters 6–9 will document. Yet as documented in the preceding three chapters, food aid has been largely ineffective either in providing income support to farmers through prices support or in export market development or in manipulating foreign governments to support donor foreign policy objectives. So why does food aid-as-usual have such staunch allies in donor countries?

The simple answer is that while there are negligible general benefits to donor country agriculture or foreign policy, primarily because the volume of food aid is far too small to develop or move markets or foreign governments effectively, a few specific, small, but highly influential subgroups benefit handsomely from food aid as presently practiced. In the United States, three in particular stand out and are sometimes referred to by insiders as the "iron triangle" of food aid: domestic food processors, maritime interests, and the NGO community.

The NGO community has arguably become the most powerful, vocal and effective constituency supporting food aid in the past decade or so, not least of which due to the leadership of the Coalition for Food Aid, a Washington-based lobby group that represents fourteen US-based NGOs with international development and humanitarian assistance missions.[1] This is not surprising, given how heavily many prominent NGOs have come to depend on food aid as a resource for their operations. The NGO coalition nonetheless depends on the support of domestic agribusiness and maritime interest groups to secure legislative backing for significant food aid programs. The price for that support has always been procurement modalities that ensure tangible benefits to domestic millers, processors, and shippers. This is a major reason why American food aid has not fully migrated from USDA to USAID, unlike in other donor countries where food aid has been placed wholly under the control of international development agencies rather than ministries of agriculture.

For agricultural and maritime interests, profits are the bottom line. And as we show in this chapter, they fare well under existing food aid policies. Food aid procurement regulations create effective market power that generates considerable economic gains for these constituencies. Producers and processors earn a premium on sales of commodities into the food aid distribution system, while shippers receive significant mark-ups on food aid cargo. The consequence of these premia is the abysmally poor financial efficiency of food aid as a means of providing overseas development and humanitarian assistance. We will return to the issue of resource transfer efficiency in Chapter 8.

For the international NGOs that carry out the bulk of the distribution or monetization of food aid, the bottom line is a mix of humanitarian and poverty reduction concerns, on the one hand, with inevitable institutional preoccupation with program budgets and the longer-term program horizons that food aid programming enables, even though food aid is an unwieldy and often less-than-appropriate resource for achieving the ends that NGO programs seek to achieve. While NGO interventions that rely on food aid have had a favorable impact on food insecurity and malnutrition,[2] food aid nevertheless puts NGOs in an awkward position. A 2000 study by Tufts University noted that virtually all US-based NGOs involved in food aid programming viewed food aid as the "least-bad" resource for any programming beyond emergency response in acute humanitarian disasters, but accepted it routinely because they believed food aid to be the only resource that donors would make available.[3]

But the frank fact of the matter is that the same volume of food could, in many if not most cases, be purchased and shipped at far lower aggregate cost, with greater developmental benefits in recipient countries, and with greater goodwill benefits to donors than under present arrangements. And where food aid is monetized, the same level of cash resources for programming could be secured far more efficiently and with far smaller donor government appropriations if resources were made available in the form of cash rather than food. US food aid has been captured by a small constellation of donor interests. This results in food aid programs that not only underperform their potential as a tool for addressing humanitarian crises and advancing economic progress in low-income countries, but are also ineffective in promoting broad-based donor agricultural or foreign policy interests.

Domestic producers and processors

Until the 1980s, most food aid came out of government-held surplus stocks that resulted from the government's role as a buyer of last resort in farm price support programs. When market prices dipped, the government stepped in to buy up surplus commodities and held them in storage. Stored grains had already been paid for and holding commodities in storage is costly. So food aid donations were effectively the cheap by-product of domestic farm price support programs. The causality here is important because too often one hears people claim incorrectly that food aid caused price supports for farmers when, in fact, it was price supports that caused food aid. Any benefits to domestic agricultural producers and processors from shipping food surpluses abroad was purely indirect, due to any changes in market prices food aid shipments might have induced. We have found no solid empirical evidence anywhere of any such effects. Donor country ministries and departments of agriculture that would have a strong interest in documenting such gains have notably never done so.

Times have changed. As government surplus stocks have dwindled in donor countries and food aid has come to rely increasingly on specific procurement from market sources, the benefits to domestic producers and processors have changed. The theoretical possibility of indirect effects due to higher market prices induced by increased demand remains, although these price effects seem negligible given how tiny food aid procurement is within the broader US economy – less than 0.2 percent of total sales – and have never been convincingly documented.[4]

The more important benefits appear to be direct, accruing to specific vendors with whom food aid donors contract to procure commodities for shipment overseas. This is a major reason why large-scale food processors have consistently pressed for increased levels of procurement of bagged, processed, or fortified commodities in US food aid programs, and why agricultural producer groups have often opposed these demands, favoring bulk commodity purchases that might more directly benefit farmers.

Each group wants to channel the direct benefits of US government food aid procurement toward its own small community. The smaller, better-funded processor lobby has been relatively more successful. For example, the 1985 Farm Bill established that at least 75 percent of the nonemergency minimum tonnage be fortified, bagged or processed, ensuring demand from the federal government for the services of a modest number of vendors registered with the US government in that industry. Few farmers sell bagged, fortified, or processed commodities. Those value-added activities are the domain of agribusiness firms.

Recall the process by which the US government procures food aid today. The US Department of Agriculture's **Farm Service Agency (FSA)** serves as the buying agent for all American food aid programs. FSA extends invitations for bids (IFBs) to prospective sellers of food commodities. Only pre-qualified, US-based agribusinesses are eligible to win such contracts. Elementary economics suggests that regulatory limits on market entry will drive up prices and increase the profits of those firms fortunate or influential enough to be in the market.

The companies securing contracts for "competitive" provision of food aid commodities are limited in number, often just one or two for minor commodities (e.g., buckwheat, raisins, or textured soy protein). USDA research has shown that prices paid in commodity procurement auctions fall as the number of bidders increases.[5] While there are a dozen or more qualified bidders in some commodities, the competition for food aid IFBs is typically quite limited and often dominated by large, privately held corporations such as Cargill, Louis Dreyfus, ConAgra, and ADM/Farmland. According to *The Wall Street Journal*, two agribusiness giants alone, Cargill and Archer-Daniels Midland, combined to ship 1.9 million metric tons of food aid in fiscal year 2003, more than one-third of all US food aid shipments for the year.[6] These agribusiness giants, not American family farmers, are the big agriculture sector beneficiaries of US government food aid procurement programs. But the agribusiness lobbyists effectively dress up programs that directly benefit primarily a small number of downstream processors as support for American family farmers because few legislators or non-specialists understand that farmers are typically far removed from USDA/FSA's food aid procurement system.

There are a few minor exceptions to this rule that the profits from US food aid procurement flow to a relatively small number of very large agribusiness firms. Food aid procurement represents a significant share of the total market for a few niche commodities like lentils and dried yellow peas, for which domestic American demand is limited and for which there are many qualified bidders for FSA procurement operations. But these commodities are an extremely small, albeit variable share of US food aid shipments.

In addition to this basic market entry limitation issue, the General Accounting Office pointed out twenty years ago a variety of problems in procurement operations that inflate food aid procurement costs, most of which remain ongoing issues today.[7] Delayed approvals sometimes bunch procurements into a single, brief period, often toward the end of a federal fiscal year when a "use it or lose it" approach takes over and fiscal discipline often slips. Another common problem is uncoordinated, overlapping purchases by different administrative agencies that cause a sudden surge in demand on a particular day or week, thereby sparking temporarily higher prices. Congressional restrictions on shipping in US flag carriers, on bagging of commodities, etc. also force FSA to award contracts to individual bids that are above the market minimum because the lowest price bids do not always have matching bids for shipping or bagging services from a qualified US firm. The consequence of all of these phenomena is that the government commonly pays more than the open market price for the commodities it purchases to send abroad as food aid.

From conversations with staff in the relevant US government offices, it seems that many of these practices have changed little, if any, in the ensuing twenty years. The GAO recommended that the USDA disapprove Title I bid prices that exceed the comparable export market price, remarking that if it did not, "the price review system for Title I purchases will lack credibility."[8] The Foreign Agricultural Service disagreed; the consequence is continued overpayment for food aid commodities procured in the United States.

USDA's Economic Research Service studied FSA commodity purchases for domestic school feeding programs and selected food aid program purchases of wheat flour and vegetable oil in the early to mid-1990s.[9] They found that the median number of bids in these auctions was two. Their estimates suggested that FSA paid less than prevailing market prices for these commodities. But their method of price comparison relied on comparisons with a single private foodservice wholesaler, not open market prices, and their comparisons are for two commodities that represent a very small share of US food aid shipments.

By looking at detailed USDA records of food aid procurements by the Farm Service Agency of bulk grains that are the main US food aid commodities, and comparing the prices paid against open market prices, we have been able to estimate the direct benefits for those producers and processors who sell into the US food aid programs. Taking the commodities and the place where they are purchased as given, for the moment, we ask how food aid procurement prices compare with prevailing market prices for the same commodity at the same time in the same place. Note that we are not yet asking whether the same food could be purchased cheaper elsewhere, nor whether there might be cheaper sources of nutrients available than the commodities procured, nor higher-return uses to scarce overseas development assistance funding in a particular setting. By taking the average procurement price for specific food aid shipments in 1999 and 2000 and comparing those against open market prices reported by the USDA's Farm Services Agency for the same commodity and week and location of purchase (e.g., hard red winter wheat purchased in New Orleans the second week of June 2000), we can get a reasonably good estimate of what premium, if any, qualified vendors enjoy from sales of commodities to US food aid programs. In the empirical analysis that follows, we establish that federal government food aid procurement regulations and procedures result in higher prices paid for food aid than prevail in contemporaneous domestic commodity markets in the United States.

We constructed a sample of 623,000 tons of corn and wheat shipments to Bangladesh, Ethiopia, and Kenya for which we have clearly comparable data.[10] While one needs to be careful about reading too much precision into the estimates from one small, nonrandom sample, these data show that food aid procurement prices on individual contracts ranged from 6.4 percent less than contemporaneous open market prices to 110.1 percent above. The average procurement premium accruing to wheat vendors was small, only 3.2 percent above prevailing open market prices.[11] Corn food aid purchases, however, cost more than 70 percent in excess of the equivalent market prices faced by private sector buyers. Combining the two grains and weighting by shipment volumes, the average procurement premium paid on bulk grains food aid shipments was 11.0 percent, as shown in Table 5.1. Plainly, a few commodity suppliers make quite a handsome windfall from selling to American food aid programs, but these direct gains are highly concentrated on the relatively few who sell into the food aid system.

This issue of procurement premia has grown in importance as governments have shifted from donation of government-held surplus stocks generated by domestic farm price support programs to open market procurement of food for shipment overseas. Those stocks did not exist for the purpose of food aid donations; rather, food aid existed in large measure for the purpose of disposing of surplus stocks. As a consequence, donations from government-held surplus commodity stocks historically were worth less than the market value of the food due to the savings in management and storage costs (including physical losses). Now that food aid is primarily purchased directly from the market through government procurement – by USDA FSA in the United States – whatever past fiscal savings (of surplus

Table 5.1 Weighted average food aid procurement premia

Produce	(%)
Corn	70.5
Wheat	3.2
Weighted average	**11.0**

storage and management costs) were once achievable by using food as a medium for making international aid transfers no longer apply unless the US government is able to buy food at below-market prices. It does not. Our estimates suggest instead that US government food aid costs about 11 percent more than prevailing market prices. And that figure does not include any of the fiscal costs of maintaining a significant bureaucracy to operate and oversee the food aid procurement process. As a consequence, food is no longer a relatively cheap form in which to provide aid. Indeed, food aid as presently practiced by the United States is not necessarily even a cheap way to provide food!

Beyond the procurement premia they reap from food aid sales, several major agribusinesses also make good money just for holding Emerson Trust grains in their silos and warehouses. Indeed, the history of the Emerson Trust, although the smallest and least frequently used of US food aid programs, sheds useful light on who benefits from US food aid programs and how. The Emerson Trust was created when President Carter imposed an embargo on the Soviet Union in 1980 to protest the Soviet invasion of Afghanistan. The embargo voided several large commercial shipments of American wheat to the Soviet Union. In a hotly contested presidential election year, the grain merchants successfully lobbied the US government to step in and assume all the abrogated contracts. Lacking spare public storage capacity, the government not only bought the grain shipments from the commercial traders, it then paid them handsomely to hold the stocks in their silos. Over the ensuing months, the government gradually liquidated much of these stocks, in many cases, selling the grains back to the original exporter at a sharp discount. The big grain merchants quickly learned that there was good money to be made from government procurement and storage of grains. Ultimately, this group of grain companies championed the creation of a new Strategic Wheat Reserve that was later renamed the Emerson Humanitarian Trust, in honor of the late Missouri Congressman.

Because releases from the Emerson Trust reduce the amount big mills earn for storage, because they are paid only for volumes on behalf of the government, the agribusinesses that benefit from the Emerson Trust have historically been very successful in minimizing releases from this facility. In recent years, non-grain agro-processors have elbowed their way into the action over the objections of the straight grain merchants who charge the government for storage under the Emerson Trust. The 1998 Farm Bill allowed, for the first time, domestic sales of rice, corn, sorghum, and wheat from the Emerson Trust to raise funds to procure processed and fortified products (e.g., vegetable oil, nonfat dried milk powder). Of course, when the Trust holds cash used to procure processed commodities, it transfers the profits from grain silo owners to processors. This has sparked backroom battles between the big agribusiness concerns. Sub-coalitions of agribusinesses jockey for the greatest spoils from this system, lobbying for relatively minor rule changes that effectively redistribute the profits within a relatively small group of corporations that make handsome profits out of what is intended to be a humanitarian mechanism.

Maritime interests

In the United States, maritime interests have always played a major role in food aid policy. In accordance with the cargo preference provisions of Section 901d of the 1936 Merchant Marine Act, as amended several times subsequently, and the Cargo Preference Act, enacted alongside PL 480 in 1954, a minimum share of US food aid must be shipped on American ships. From 1954 until 1985, cargo preferences restrictions required that at least half of the gross tonnage of US food aid commodities be shipped on privately owned, registered US-flag commercial vessels. The 1985 Farm Bill increased that proportion to 75 percent, despite opposition by farm groups, USDA, and USAID, and although the increase did not apply to other government-directed shipments, only to food aid.[12] Moreover, the maritime industry helped to push (and has benefited handsomely from) the 1985 Farm Bill provision mandating that at least 75 percent of the nonemergency minimum tonnage be fortified, bagged or processed. Shippers gain from this because they must surrender subsidies they receive from the Department of Defense (DoD) Maritime Security Program (MSP) on any days that they carry more than 7,500 tons of bulk food aid under cargo preference provisions.[13] Shipping lines can "double dip," however, when they carry bagged food aid commodities, collecting both the substantial premia that accrue from the cargo preference restriction and the MSP subsidy of more than $6,500/day per vessel.[14] These Congressionally imposed restrictions on food aid procurement and distribution have made the maritime industry, including the constellation of related labor organizations, some of the greatest beneficiaries of food aid policy and, therefore, some of its most energetic supporters.

The basic economics of the previous section on commodity procurement carries over directly to the procurement of shipping services. But now the effect is twofold. First, there is a market restriction due to cargo preference laws that require US-flag carriers to carry at least three-quarters of food aid flows. This necessarily generates a windfall premium for US shipping lines. Second, the government procurement process for freight forwarding follows a similar system to the invitation for bids system for commodity procurement, generating additional rents for those firms eligible to bid on contracts on offer, creating further windfall gains for those eligible to participate. For a variety of reasons we discuss momentarily, only a few shipping lines and freight forwarders participate in the system, creating market concentration that cannot help but inflate program costs.

The procurement process works as follows. The food aid recipient or their appointed agents – "freight forwarders" – arrange for the ocean transportation of commodities purchased under Title I or donated under other food aid programs. The relevant US government office determines the quantity of the commodity to be shipped on US-flag commercial vessels. Open public freight invitations for bids (IFBs) are required for both US and non-US flag vessels when CCC is financing any portion of the ocean freight. Unless otherwise authorized by the USDA, IFBs are also required for non-US flag vessels even though CCC is not financing any portion of the ocean freight. Only pre-qualified vendors may bid. According to the

US General Accounting Office, only eighteen shipping companies were qualified to bid on food aid contracts in the 1990s.[15] The USDA/FSA website listed only thirteen registered US-flag carriers as approved shippers in June 2002. Limited competition necessarily drives up costs.

The freight forwarders, who act essentially as general contractors on behalf of operational agencies (e.g. WFP, CARE, World Vision), are an even smaller group. The main reason is that some forwarders also have ship brokers licenses, creating a conflict of interest problem that used to plague Title I PL 480 shipments[16] until the US government declared ineligible any forwarders with brokerage operations or ships of their own. Add to this restriction the complex web of rules that govern food aid handling, involving at least two different administrative agencies, and the number of forwarders able and willing to deal in food aid becomes very small.

In fiscal year 2001, the most recent for which data were available, only twelve freight forwarders won contracts for 276 shipments of Section 416(b) and Food for Progress food aid. These successful bids were heavily concentrated (Figure 5.1). A whopping 84 percent of shipment volumes were handled by just four freight forwarders, a market concentration ratio that would ignite keen interest from anti-trust investigators were these private transactions rather than government procurement operations. Wilson Logistics, a privately held group based in Sweden that is WFP's preferred freight forwarder, alone won 43 percent of the shipment contracts that year (and 64 percent of the Section 416(b) shipments).[17] Because of the limited market competition in freight forwarding and shipping, international transport costs for food aid go through the roof.

Congress has long recognized that cargo preference restrictions force over-payment for freight forwarding and therefore built in complex compensatory mechanisms into food aid contracts. Under a Title I PL 480 agreement – as distinct from other food aid programs such as Title II – CCC responsibility for ocean freight

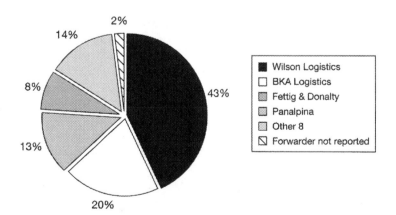

Figure 5.1 Freight forwarders' market shares FY2001 Section 416(b) and Food for Progress shipments

Source: USDA/FSA

is generally limited to payment of the ocean freight differential, if any, between the cost of US flag and non-US flag shipments. In certain exceptional cases, CCC may also finance on credit terms the balance of freight costs on US flag vessels, as well as foreign flag freight charges to selected countries approved by the US Department of Agriculture's Foreign Agricultural Service. For food aid donations, the US government pays shipping costs. The US General Accounting Office found that cargo preference requirements effectively reduced export market creation benefits to American agriculture by requiring buyers to use high-priced US-flagged carriers.[18]

The GAO also reported "an average of about $200 million per year in government funds has been used to pay the added cost of shipping US food aid to foreign countries on US-flag ships rather than on lower-cost foreign-flag ships," up from GAO estimates of $150 million annually just a few years earlier.[19] In 2000–2, nearly 40 percent of total costs of US food aid programs were paid to US shipping companies. The cargo preference law and government procurement regulations create significant market power in ocean freight of concessional food grains exports and donations, leading to substantial overpayment relative to free market costs. The handsome gains they enjoy from the present system give US maritime interests a keen interest in food aid, making them an oft-overlooked but extremely powerful constituency behind US food aid.

Cargo preference restrictions also contribute to the higher prices paid for commodities that we documented in the preceding section. This occurs because availability of appropriate US-flag ships restricts which commodity sale bids can be accepted. GAO documents a variety of cases in which lowest-price offers could not be accepted because no US-flag ships were available to pick up the commodity when and where it was located.[20] As a consequence, higher price bids had to be accepted.

Using 1991–93 data, GAO found that average US-flag carrier shipping rates were 75.9 percent higher than foreign-flag shipping rates for the same routes and commodities on bulk carriers, the most commonly used ship type, 49.3 percent higher for tankers, and 75.7 percent higher on liners.[21] The weighted average premium paid for shipping on US flag carriers came to 68.8 percent in 1991–93.[22] The principal reason for the high costs are US regulations with which ship owners must comply in order to operate a US-flag ship, such as employment solely of American citizens on crews.[23]

When we replicate the GAO's earlier analysis using 1999–2000 USDA data for Section 416(b) and Food for Progress shipments of the same commodity, between the same ports, in the same quarter of the year, we find that the shipping cost mark-ups due to cargo preference restrictions have, if anything, increased. Using 71 different pairs of US-flag and foreign-flag carriers that satisfy the preceding criteria,[24] we find that the mean premium paid for shipping on US ships was 77.7 percent, an 11.3 percent increase over the course of half a dozen years (Figure 5.2). The two periods' series are not strictly comparable across years – although they are directly comparable between US- and foreign-flag carriers – and are expressed in nominal terms (i.e., they are not adjusted for inflation), so we caution against

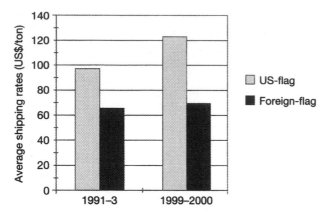

Figure 5.2 Cargo preference premia to shippers

comparison of food aid freight cost changes over time. Regardless, the core points remain: shipping from the US is very costly, an average of more than $120 per metric ton on US-flag carriers, and nearly 80 percent more expensive than shipping the same commodities between the same ports on foreign-flag carriers.

In spite of the enormous profit margins food aid shipments carry, cargo preference laws have proved ineffective in maintaining the viability of the US maritime industry. The reason is simple and perfectly mirrors the reason why food aid has been similarly ineffective in supporting the competitiveness of American farmers. Food aid volumes are a tiny share of global shipments and most ocean freight is not subject to cargo preference restrictions. Thus, while food aid shipments are lucrative for US-flag carriers that get the business, the volumes involved are far too small to keep a shipping line afloat. Food aid merely pads the bottom line for participating shippers, most of whom (e.g., American President Lines, Maersk Sealand, Nedloyd) rely primarily on commercially competitive container vessels not used for food aid shipments. However, a few shippers that operate mainly dry bulk ships (e.g., Waterman Steamship Corporation) depend heavily on food aid business and might not be financially viable without the massive subsidies they draw from food shipments the American electorate thinks are donations not to shipping lines but to poor people abroad.

As a direct consequence of the uncompetitiveness of US-flag carriers in open commercial tender markets – an inefficiency reinforced by cargo preferences that shield them somewhat from competition – the share of commercial international cargo carried by US flagged ships has declined steadily over the past thirty years, accounting for less than 3 percent of US commercial export and import tonnage today. And according to the American Maritime Congress, cargo preference accounts for only 5–15 percent of US-flagged ships' total containerized cargoes.[25] The US merchant fleet has shrunk from 536 vessels in 1991 to less than 260 now, with less than one-third the capacity (in deadweight tonnage) of Greece's, less than half that of Japan, and significantly less than those of Norway or China.[26] Moreover,

74 percent of the US-owned fleet is registered not in the USA (i.e., is not US-flagged), but instead under foreign flags of convenience from nations such as Liberia and Panama.

The GAO concludes that:

> The application of cargo preference to food aid programs does not significantly contribute to meeting the intended objectives of helping to maintain US-flag ships as a naval and military auxiliary in time of war or national emergency or for the purposes of domestic or foreign commerce.[27]

Indeed, in intra-departmental negotiations, the Department of Defense has supported Department of Agriculture and Department of State pleas to scrap cargo preference restrictions since they do not contribute significantly to national security. To date, however, the Department of Transportation and Congressional champions of shipping interests have prevailed thus far.

Cargo preference requirements are terribly expensive and thereby sharply limit what can be achieved with a limited food aid budget. But these windfalls to a small number of shipping lines – many of which might otherwise reflag to another country to save costs or would shut down[28] – do not make a significant dent in the decline of American shipping. The cost to food aid efficiency comes with no discernible long-term benefit to anyone save for a handful of largely privately-owned shipping lines and freight forwarders.

Myth 6 Cargo preference laws ensure the viability of the US maritime industry

Cargo preference laws that require at least three-quarters of American food aid be shipped on carriers registered in the United States generate enormous windfall profits for a small number of shipping lines and freight forwarders. Shipments on US-flag carriers cost nearly 80 percent more, on average, than identical shipments on foreign-flag carriers. This expensive subsidy fails, nonetheless, to ensure the viability of the US maritime industry because food aid volumes are small relative to global commerce. So the US fleet has continued to shrink and to lose market share to other nations' maritime industries. The US Department of Defense has supported the termination of cargo preference restrictions, undercutting the argument that this is essential for national security reasons. Cargo preferences do not ensure a viable American maritime industry in support of national security or broader commercial objectives.

Nongovernmental organizations

The steady and substantial transition from program food aid to project and emergency shipments has spurred NGOs' rise to prominence in the design and implementation of food aid programming. In so far as project and emergency food aid are more clearly motivated by humanitarian concerns to which food aid can respond effectively, this may be a positive development. But just because many NGOs do valuable work among food-insecure populations does not mean that they do not have a strong vested interest in food aid's status quo. While all NGOs would prefer cash to food, most have made the (in our view, mistaken) assumption that food is the only form in which donors will make resources available, and thus they take it irrespective of how inefficient or relatively ineffective it might be.

We should be clear that our focus in this section falls squarely on US-based NGOs. European NGOs have moved much further away from food aid, except for direct distribution during acute humanitarian emergencies, not least of which because most bilateral European donors and WFP do not permit monetization to anything like the degree allowed – even encouraged – by the United States. Furthermore, even within US-based NGOs, there exists a diversity of views on the use of food aid as a resource in development and emergency programming. In spite of this diversity, a few core patterns have become apparent in recent years.

Most American NGOs' strong financial interest in food aid stems from three distinct considerations: (1) its magnitude as a resource; (2) its fungibility through monetization; and (3) its effect on crucial financial indicators that are commonly perceived to affect private contributions to NGOs. We tackle these each in turn using detailed data we assembled on the gross revenues, food aid receipts and food aid monetization volumes over the period 1990–2002 for eight NGOs that regularly received food aid donations from the United States for distribution or monetization in developing countries.[29] These eight – Adventist Development and Relief Agency (ADRA), Africare, CARE, Catholic Relief Services (CRS), Food for the Hungry International (FHI), Project Concern International, Technoserve, and World Vision – account for the overwhelming majority of US food aid distributed to NGOs. They also account for a considerable share of the other bilateral donors' and WFP food aid distributed through NGOs. Between them, they had almost $1.5 billion in gross revenues in 2001. Of these eight, CARE, World Vision, and CRS, in that order, are by far the largest, together accounting for 86.5 percent of annual average aggregate revenues (from all sources, food aid included) of the eight organizations over the 1990–2002 period.[30]

Each organization pays careful attention to its primary funding sources. For development and relief NGOs, food aid is a primary source of resources for programming, as the two panels of Figure 5.3 show. US food aid contributions alone accounted for 30.0 percent of the weighted average[31] share of 2001 gross revenues among these eight NGOs, ranging from World Vision, at only 9.6 percent, to Technoserve, at 49.6 percent. Other than World Vision, each of these NGOs depended on US food aid for between one-quarter and one-half of its budget in

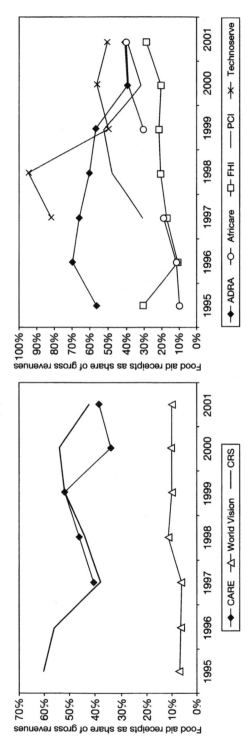

Figure 5.3 Food aid receipts as share of gross revenues for key NGOs

2001. Such financial dependence makes it difficult for the mainstream NGO community to push for any significant reforms to existing food aid programs. In private, one hears plenty of concerns and criticisms of food aid from senior NGO officials. But most have been reluctant to voice these concerns publicly, in large measure because their organization cannot afford to rock the food aid boat without securing the cooperation of the other major NGOs that handle food aid.[32] Nevertheless, given some of the concerns we discuss in Chapters 7–9, some organizations that take a rights-based approach seriously have begun to reconsider the role of food aid. And some agencies oriented toward small business development, like Technoserve, have thrown up their hands in frustration at the US government's renewed insistence on direct distribution rather than monetization.

NGOs' dependence on food aid derives not only from the importance of food aid to their aggregate revenues. It is perhaps even more a function of the fungibility of monetized food aid. NGOs that monetize a large share of the food aid they receive are able to undertake a range of other projects by cashing out the shipments they receive. Many of these highly visible projects relate to education, health, natural resources management, small business development and other important topics that attempt to reduce poverty or improve livelihoods and thereby improve nutrition and food security – and many of them appear successful.[33]

The point is, these NGO projects do not inherently need food resources. But under present foreign assistance appropriations, many such projects would simply not be funded without monetization receipts. Moreover, these projects help leverage other donor funds as well as private voluntary contributions precisely because of their visibility and appeal as interventions that go beyond food distribution. Because few believe that the US food aid budget would be converted one-for-one into cash transfers abroad, the view of many NGOs is that food aid is "the least bad" available resource because, as unwieldy and wasteful as it may be, it does generate cash for use elsewhere. This is true enough in the short term; but this perspective has also abetted, even exacerbated, the business-as-usual approach within US food aid.

The US Congress first authorized the monetization of food aid in 1990, setting a 10 percent minimum monetization rate, mainly to cover cash **internal transport, storage, and handling** expenses related to food distribution in recipient countries. As NGOs discovered the fungibility of food aid, however, monetization rates skyrocketed (Figure 5.4). Congress changed monetization rules, increasing the monetization rate to 15 percent on PL 480 Title II non-emergency shipments in 1998. But as Figure 5.4 shows, while the Congressional minimum target proved reasonably accurate for eventual approved monetization a decade ago, it is now meaningless. Actual, approved monetization of non-emergency Title II food aid shipments hit 70 percent in 2001, up sevenfold in ten years in percentage terms, before dipping back to 64 percent in 2002. We suspect that most Americans, and probably most Congressional representatives, would be shocked to discover that food aid shipped through NGOs is generally not distributed to hungry people these days.

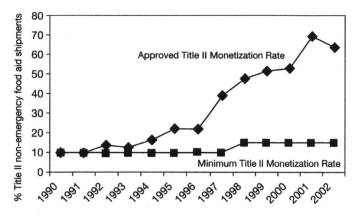

Figure 5.4 Non-emergency Title II monetization rates

Just as Title I food aid is effectively a form of in-kind budgetary assistance to recipient country governments that then liquidate the food on local markets in recipient countries to raise cash for whatever programs they wish to pursue, so too is non-emergency Title II food aid increasingly a form of budgetary assistance to NGOs that do likewise. The data we assembled, reflected in the two panels of Figure 5.5, indicate that the two largest NGO food aid recipients, CARE and World Vision, each monetized more than half of the non-emergency food aid they handled in 2001. Some of the smaller NGOs, such as Technoserve, FHI, and Africare, monetize virtually all the food aid they receive, in part because they handle little emergency food aid.[34] For these agencies, food is in effect merely bulky cash since direct distribution through feeding programs is rare. Indeed, as USAID's Food for Peace office, prodded by the Office of Management and Budget and American food exporters, has pushed for greater direct distribution of food aid in the past year or two – manifest in the reduction in monetization rates between 2001 and 2002 – some NGOs have begun to protest at being compelled to distribute more of the food aid they receive. The most striking case is Technoserve which announced in spring 2003 that it would enter into no new Title II PL 480 food aid agreements as of federal fiscal year 2003–4 (beginning October 1, 2003).

The skyrocketing of NGO monetization rates of course raises a question as to whether, when, where and why food aid is really an effective or efficient resource for development programming, as distinct from its use for operations in situations where food access and food availability both threaten food security. We address this broader issue in Chapters 8–10. NGOs ought to become much more outspoken in their criticism of food aid as an inefficient means of addressing the needs of the poor. Unfortunately, the extent to which the major US-based NGOs are dependent on food aid as a proportion of their gross revenues compromises their position to advocate strongly for reforms in food aid. This situation is changing in some organizations, however, with organizations developing and implementing their own internal food aid policies, and with international codes of conduct (discussed

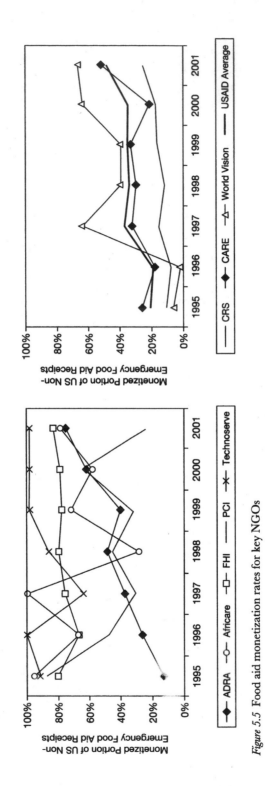

Figure 5.5 Food aid monetization rates for key NGOs

in detail in Chapter 6) being recognized to limit the potentially harmful effects of food aid.

Nevertheless, monetized food aid represents more than 12 percent of the group's weighted average gross revenues, ranging from 6.4 percent for World Vision to 51.5 percent for Technoserve (Table 5.2). NGOs have had favorable impacts using food aid resources, but this is arguably more in spite of than because of the use of food as a resource. As a group, NGOs have a strong financial incentive to perpetuate existing food aid programs. So they should not be seen as objective or disinterested experts with only the interests of food-insecure peoples in mind as they lobby on food aid policy.

Food aid has one further, subtle, but extremely important effect on NGOs' behavior, through its perceived effects on private fundraising. Because the administrative overhead for dealing with USAID on Title II food aid programs – or any major donor on food aid – is almost entirely fixed costs, large food aid programs generate a very low ratio of administrative expenses to overall revenues for NGOs that handle food aid. Note that we are not claiming that there are economies of scale in handling food aid, only that the administrative cost component is not appreciably greater for extremely large food aid operations than for quite small ones.

This matters because the ratio of administrative costs to total expenses is one indicator of NGO effectiveness and efficiency that is tracked by NGO watchdog organizations – and therefore an indicator that NGO managers monitor closely.[35] Such indicators are pushed in current NGO management handbooks, and various outlets publicize NGOs' administrative cost ratios, including Guidestar, which gives financial information for every non-profit organization in the United States, and the Charity Navigator.[36] Regular media ratings of non-profit organizations, by publications such as the *Chronicle of Philanthropy*, *Money*, and *Worth* magazines, routinely incorporate this ratio into their assessments of organizational efficiency and efficacy. Given the attention paid to administrative cost ratios within the sector, it is not surprising that development NGOs and humanitarian agencies harbor deep concerns about reducing food aid volumes and thereby perhaps indirectly inflating their administrative cost ratios. Especially since the stock market bubble

Table 5.2 Monetized US food aid as percentage of NGOs' gross revenues

NGO	2000–1 Average
Adventist Development and Relief Agency (ADRA)	27.0
Africare	26.9
CARE	13.4
Catholic Relief Services (CRS)	10.0
Food for the Hungry International (FHI)	19.7
Project Concern International (PCI)	14.8
Technoserve	51.5
World Vision Relief and Development (WVRD)	6.4
Group Weighted Average	**12.1**

popped early in the new millennium and the terrorist attacks of September 11, 2001, NGOs have found it tougher to attract private contributions for work abroad, making them ever more reticent to diminish their attractiveness *vis-à-vis* domestic charitable organizations. Quite aside from the positive public relations effect feeding programs based on food aid have on an organization's marketability to private contributors, large food aid programs also make NGOs' financial stewardship look better than it otherwise would. The fear among many NGOs is that disengagement from food aid when and where it is inappropriate or ineffective may cause not only a drop in monetizable food aid receipts but also a drop in private giving due to an induced worsening of the organizations' administrative cost ratios.

The good news for NGOs, however, is that the data simply do not support the assumption that administrative cost ratios matter to private donors. Academic research in this area suggests that non-profit organizations that position themselves as cost-efficient fare no better in fundraising from private individual, foundation and corporate contributions than less efficient ones.[37] These studies seem to support the hypothesis that marketing around mission is more effective for private fundraising than marketing around efficiency. Informal, expert opinion from marketing firms that handle fundraising for major NGOs corroborates this view. Marketing professionals think of administrative cost ratios as helpful bits of information they can exploit when the figures look good, but the ratios are neither necessary nor sufficient for effective fundraising. One industry expert told us:

> In focus groups and surveys, donors always say efficiency matters a lot to them. I take that with a grain of salt, because efficiency is not an emotional driver, and giving decisions are made emotionally. . . . Those charities that don't brag about their efficiency hold their own just fine.

As with so much else in food aid, an apparent myth seems to exert heavy influence over current practice.

Myth 7 Nongovernmental organizations are a progressive force in food aid

Most NGOs recognize from considerable field experience the problems that arise from the misuse of food aid. With their commitment to development and/or humanitarian assistance, they could therefore be a progressive force for improvement in food aid policy. However, their revenue streams depend heavily on the amount of food aid that they receive and deliver. Budgetary dependence on food aid tempers their willingness to publicly challenge a system that many privately acknowledge underperforms its potential. Indeed, in public settings the NGO community vigorously defends the status quo as "least bad," fearing that a move away from food aid would result in a drop in total resources available for development programming because they might not find allies in the political battle to make more cash available from donors (especially the United States). As a result, NGOs are reluctant to rock the boat and to bring much of their on-the-ground experience to bear in serious policy discussions on food aid.

Conclusion

A global food aid system that began in the 1950s as North American programs to dispose of government-held grain surpluses in a way that many hoped might advance foreign policy objectives, help develop future agricultural export markets, or both, has metamorphosed over half a century into a complex global system underpinned by cash appropriations for *de novo* food procurement in donor countries and intercontinental shipment of those commodities. The practice of food aid over these past fifty years has thus proved that the primary objective has *not* been providing assistance to food-insecure populations around the world. Rather, food aid has been heavily oriented toward domestic concerns in donor countries.

Nonetheless, and in spite of the rhetoric one commonly hears in Washington, Ottawa and other national capitals, the purported benefits of food aid to farmers in donor countries have never materialized in the form of either higher farmgate prices or increased future commercial agricultural exports. Nor has food aid proved an effective instrument for diplomacy where it has been deployed aggressively, as in Afghanistan, Iraq, Democratic People's Republic of Korea, or Russia most recently. Indeed, the effects of food aid as practiced to date have often been negative in international affairs, as it has sparked disputes between donor countries over the trade-distorting effects of aid shipments and over genetically modified foods.

Meanwhile, a bewildering array of legislative and administrative restrictions on food aid procurement and distribution, especially within the United States, has allowed a small group of influential special interests to effectively capture food aid for their own purposes. In the United States, the big agro-processors and millers, freight forwarders, shipping lines, and the major international NGOs have emerged as the prime beneficiaries and the most influential constituencies driving the design and impeding the reform of global food aid. However, the gains these interests reap from the present global food aid system inflate overall program costs and impede the efficacy of food aid in contributing to either the relief of human suffering or the sustainable development of low-income, food-deficit economies around the world.

As the next four chapters argue, in spite of the severe constraints imposed by the present architecture of global food aid, there have been noteworthy advances in improving the effectiveness with which operational agencies employ food aid to address recipients' real needs in fighting undernutrition and poverty. We are edging toward a recipient-oriented food aid regime. But there is limited capacity for further improvements without substantial structural change to reform donor food aid procurement and distribution policies and to place food aid more firmly and appropriately within a broader strategic framework for global poverty reduction.

6 Edging towards a recipient-oriented food aid system

Food aid, as we presently know it, was born largely of donor concerns for trade promotion, surplus disposal, and geopolitical advantage. At the macro-level, food aid has remained distressingly tethered to donor concerns, as discussed extensively in Chapters 2–5. There are exceptions, such as the reformed Danish food aid policy detailed in Box 3.1, but at the global level, food aid remains heavily tied to donor objectives.

Significant changes have nonetheless taken place since the World Food Crisis of 1973–74 at what might be termed the meso-level, at the operational level of food aid distribution agencies. These changes are driven in large measure by a changed understanding of the etiology of famine and food insecurity, as well as growing emphasis on non-economic, rights-based considerations. In sum, for the past thirty or so years, food aid has been edging slowly toward a more recipient-oriented system. It remains primarily donor-driven at the macro-level, although the rhetoric of food aid has changed even there. For example, the mission statements of the largest food aid donor (USAID/Office of Food for Peace) and the largest food aid agency (World Food Program) now read exclusively in terms of serving the objective of improving the food security of poor and vulnerable people. But donor-level considerations still sharply constrain what can be accomplished with food aid, even though many intriguing advances have been made with food aid. These advances in how food aid is mobilized, how it has been justified, and the way in which food aid can be used to address both humanitarian and development objectives reflect key advances in the general understanding of food security. In order to take full advantage of these advances, systemic changes along the lines of those we propose in Chapters 10 and 11 will be necessary.

First, however, we need to appreciate how food aid can provide an effective instrument for the reduction of food insecurity and hunger around the world. This chapter describes how and why food aid has been edging towards a recipient-oriented approach, beginning with a very brief review of the changing understanding of food security. It thus provides a natural segue between the discussion in Chapters 2–5 of donor-oriented food aid policy – food aid's history – and Chapters 10–11, in which we discuss what a more effective food aid regime might look like during the next half-century.

Changing views of food insecurity: from Malthus to Sen[1]

The problem of food insecurity was long thought to be primarily a matter of insufficient food to feed a population. Although the history of food policy is replete with obvious examples to the contrary – such as the Indian famine codes, for example – food insecurity was long simply regarded as a supply problem, and acute events like famines were caused by a serious and sudden drop in food availability. Such "food availability deficit" (FAD) theories of famine have their roots in the late eighteenth- and early nineteenth-century writings of the Rev. Thomas Malthus. In this Malthusian view, an ever-growing population with more or less fixed land resources is bound to suffer widespread starvation unless advances in production technology allow the production of food to grow more rapidly than human population. From the FAD perspective, acute hunger arose directly from an acute shortage of food, most commonly caused by climatic shocks such as drought, floods or other natural disasters. Food aid was thus easily rationalized in its early days as filling a food supply gap, an obvious humanitarian remedy to an obvious under-production problem.

This Malthusian view was reinforced in the immediate post-World War II period in the strategic orientation of the Food and Agriculture Organization of the United Nations (FAO) around increasing food production as the lynchpin of a strategy to reduce hunger. At the same time, the World Bank championed a theory of economic development founded on the importance of closing balance of payments and budgetary gaps faced by newly independent states of Africa, Asia, and Latin America. Up through at least the World Food Crisis of 1973–74, these prevailing perspectives on the primacy of food production, balance of payments and budgetary support to developing country governments, led to an overwhelming emphasis on supply-side constraints to reduce hunger and food insecurity. Because program food aid is a clear means by which food availability deficits and developing country fiscal and balance of payments gaps can be plugged – and not coincidentally because such shipments satisfied donors' interests – the FAD view of famine and food insecurity underpinned the design of food aid in its formative years.

The Nobel Laureate Amartya Sen revolutionized the analysis of food insecurity with the entitlements theory he proposed in his influential 1981 book, *Poverty and Famines*. Ever since, the implementation of food aid programs has been trying to catch up to theoretical insights on the causality of food insecurity. Sen explained how and why famines (and other forms of severe food insecurity) can occur even when there is a sufficient food supply, emphasizing that an adequate food supply is a necessary but not sufficient condition to prevent hunger and food insecurity. Sen's core insight is that "starvation is a matter of some people not *having* enough food to eat, and not a matter of there *being* not enough food to eat."[2]

Sen advanced a theory of "entitlements," a set of different alternative commodity bundles one can legally acquire, thereby emphasizing demand-side factors where the prevailing Malthusian understanding of food insecurity had focused exclusively on the supply side. Economists' initial interpretations of Sen emphasized individual ownership of productive assets and access to markets through which food could be purchased at reasonable prices. As the entitlements view has matured, it has increasingly become understood more broadly to encompass legal or moral claims to food, which Sen discussed explicitly. Sen emphasized three distinct sources of entitlements:

1   *Production-based entitlements*, describing the food consumption choices available to one by virtue of one's right to the product of one's owned assets, such as labor and land. Production-based entitlements depend fundamentally on the efficiency of production technologies and on biophysical phenomena beyond a food producer's control, such as rainfall, temperature, soil conditions, and insects.

2   *Trade-based entitlements*, which describe the consumption options open to one via exchange of things one owns for other goods or services, as when workers earn wages in the labor market with which they can buy food in commodity markets, thereby effectively trading labor power for food. Trade-based entitlements depend fundamentally on relative prices.

3   *Transfer entitlements*, which refer to the choices created by one's right to that given willingly by others, including gifts and bequests from individuals, as well as transfers by the state such as social security or pensions.

Sen illustrates his entitlement theory with several cases of recent famines. He documents the Bengal (India) famine of 1943, in which food availability does not seem to have played an important role but a rapid, sharp rise in rice prices did, creating trade entitlement failures for those dependent on the purchase of rice. A sharp rise in aggregate urban demand pushed prices higher without the rural poor enjoying the increased purchasing power necessary to maintain a standard of living. This is a classic case of a "boom famine." By contrast, the 1973–74 Ethiopian famine was a "slump famine" in which droughts substantially cut food production in Wollo province. Food availability fell, but it wasn't so much aggregate availability as the local effects of wiping out agriculturalists' total income (including own crop and livestock production) that resulted in famine, as those individuals could not even purchase the food that was available in markets. The entitlements approach thus encompasses food output shortfalls without tying our understanding of hunger to agricultural output measures. A rise in prices or a fall in wages or employment that reduces real incomes of the poor or a reduction in publicly provided services can also cause a reduction in entitlements and lower nutrient intake. Indeed, Sen emphasized that food can and does actually move out of a famine area in slump famines as private traders move the commodity to where demand yields greater revenues and profits.

The major policy insight from Sen's work is that, while overall food availability is still a necessary condition for food security, it is not a sufficient condition. Inadequate overall supply of food necessarily implies that someone, somewhere will go hungry. But there can be acutely food-insecure people even when there is plenty of food to go around because individuals can suffer "entitlements failures" when their production, trade, and transfer entitlements cumulatively do not enable them to command a nutritionally adequate diet. Thus acute food insecurity alone is not sufficient justification for a food aid intervention. Moving food into famine areas will not in itself do much to cure starvation, since what needs to be created is food entitlement, not just food availability.[3] Food security has therefore been viewed, at least since Sen, as being comprised of the overall availability of food as well as **food access** at the level of individuals, households or groups. Further refinements in the late 1980s and 1990s added the issue of utilization of food as well,[4] creating the availability–access–utilization triad most popularly used today in policy discussions of food aid. Perhaps the most commonly used definition of food security remains that proposed by the World Bank: access by all people at all times to sufficient food for an active, healthy life.[5]

Sen's work forms the basis of the sustainable livelihoods approach to food security, which has been widely adopted by much of the anti-hunger/famine industry since the early to mid-1990s. A livelihood

> comprises the capabilities, assets (including both natural and social) and activities required for a means of living: a livelihood is sustainable which can cope with and recover from stresses and shocks, maintain or enhance its capabilities and assets, both now and in the future, while not undermining the natural resource base.[6]

While still focusing heavily on the outcome of food security, a livelihoods approach therefore puts much more emphasis on understanding people's means of achieving this outcome: their asset base at the household level, the strategies on which they rely, the constraints they face, and the coping strategies they are forced to rely on to achieve outcomes in terms of food security and accessing other basic requirements, but the emphasis is on both the means (livelihoods) and the ends (food security, health status, shelter, etc.). A sustainable livelihoods approach also requires looking holistically at the multiple and sometimes competing objectives of poor households, at the trade-offs that poor people must inevitably make between consumption and savings or investment, or even among different consumption choices (spending income on food or health care or education, for example, when income is inadequate to cover all three). Livelihoods are generally analyzed in the context of the key factors in the broader institutional and biophysical environment that make livelihoods – and therefore people – vulnerable.[7] This emphasis on risk and vulnerability, and on the coping mechanisms on which vulnerable households and groups rely, is a recurrent theme in the contemporary literature on food and livelihood security.[8] Food aid fits less easily into such a construct than it did into a straightforward food availability deficit conceptualization of famine and food insecurity.

As operational agencies gained greater programmatic experience with livelihoods approaches, they inevitably began to highlight key factors that were outside the plausible control of poor households and beyond the normal reach of program interventions, such as the national and international policy environment. This recognition further emphasizes the weakness of an approach to programming that relies heavily on food as the input (as distinct from food security as the intended outcome). These new approaches to analyzing food insecurity have necessitated innovative approaches to working with food aid.

The crucial implication for the management of food aid as a policy instrument for the prevention of acute food insecurity is that famines are not simply events, but rather the outcome of underlying processes. While it is the acute event that captures media attention – and therefore widespread recognition in wealthy nations – acute food insecurity simply does not materialize spontaneously. Famines are crises that involve severe malnutrition, starvation, and excess mortality, but also economic destitution and social breakdown, and with important health causes and outcomes as well.[9] Famines may be triggered by environmental, climatic, or economic shocks (as those that Sen analyzed were) or they may have their proximate causes in combinations of conflict or political shocks and other factors (as is becoming distressingly common in what are now known in the industry as **complex political emergencies** or **complex humanitarian emergencies**). But the recognition of all these as processes rather than simply events has led to important new ways of managing food aid as a resource for combating hunger. Given that famine processes follow well-recognized patterns, there is, as one observer notes, no excuse for famines to continue to happen.[10] The limiting factor is less an understanding of the etiology of acute food insecurity and famine than the political will to implement policies consistent with current understanding. In particular, this calls into question continued reliance primarily on food aid as the input of choice, a carryover from the Malthusian days when acute and widespread food insecurity were understood as caused by food availability deficits.

A rights-based perspective to livelihoods approaches

More recently, a rights-based approach – specifically the right to adequate food – has played an increasingly important role in analysis and policy regarding food security and food aid. This builds analytically on the empirical approach implied by Sen and subsequent livelihoods approaches to food security. The key difference is that rights-based approaches incorporate a distinctively normative element, they are not merely descriptive and analytical, as the entitlements and livelihoods approaches tend to be.

The right to food is not new. It is enshrined in both the Universal Declaration of Human Rights (Article 25), drafted in 1948, as well as the International Covenant on Economic, Social and Cultural Rights, or ICESCR (Article 11), drafted in 1966. The latter covers a broad range of rights, of which food is only one. The **World Food Summit** held in Rome in 1996, reaffirmed the right to food and the right to freedom from hunger and malnutrition. Since then, human rights have become an increasingly important rallying call in the global fight against hunger.[11]

By the late 1990s, while retaining an emphasis on understanding livelihoods, the World Food Programme and many of the non-governmental organizations active in food aid had begun to adopt a rights-based approach. The focus of a rights-based approach is not only at the household level, but also explicitly at the policy level, the external forces that shape the way people's livelihoods are constrained, and the norms and obligations of extra-household actors in achieving household food security. Rights-based approaches also focus as much attention on process concerns as on outcomes such as food security. The implications for food aid of a rights-based approach are manifold, and not necessarily straightforward in terms of practice. Food aid is, at best, a problematic tool for the protection of the right to food, not least because of the interlocking nature of rights (and the right to more than just food alone), but in ways that are "sustainable and that do not interfere with the enjoyment of other human rights"[12] such as the right to self-determination, the right to a sustainable livelihood, cultural and consumer preference, etc.

Numerous authors note that the interest in human rights – and particularly the right to food – increasingly dominates humanitarian and development debates. Never has there been a time when the capacity to end global hunger has been greater, yet significant gaps remain between rights and reality. While the global community is adequately providing access to food for 1.5 billion more people than it was able to feed twenty years ago, and as obesity problems associated with excess food consumption become widespread health concerns not only in the high-income countries but in middle- and lower-income countries as well, more than 800 million people remain chronically undernourished and hungry. This undernutrition problem is overwhelmingly concentrated in South Asia and Sub-Saharan Africa, though pockets of hunger and malnutrition remain in all countries, western industrialized societies as well.[13]

In 1999, the United Nations Committee on Economic, Social and Cultural Rights clarified the right to food when it attached a "general comment" on this right to the ICESCR. General Comment No. 12 defines this right as "having physical and economic access to food of adequate quality and quantity, and having the means to obtain it, including access to food via means of production or procurement." Access should be sustainable and protect human dignity. The right to food is generally understood to constitute a claim of the individual *vis-à-vis* the state in which s/he resides, and generates individual entitlements and related obligations potentially enforceable in courts of law. This underlines the difference between needs and rights – rights imply an obligation on behalf of other parties that needs do not.

Beyond this, the right to food also encompasses elements of international humanitarian law, which, for example, prohibit the use of food as a weapon; the starvation of civilians as a method of combat in both international and non-international armed conflict; attacking or destroying civilian food stocks or water sources in time of war; or forced displacement of civilian populations in time of war. The international law of war also states that belligerent parties in armed conflicts must permit humanitarian access to impartial relief operations – including those providing food – when supplies essential for the civilian population are inadequate.

Rights-based approaches vary, and include much more than just the right to food. The principle of the "right to life with dignity" is used by many to encompass the whole range of rights enshrined in the UN Charter and the Universal

Declaration of Human Rights. Life with dignity implies something beyond just the provision of life-saving assistance, and is a powerful organizing principle for both the humanitarian and development communities. Several other common themes can be discerned from the numerous approaches elaborated below.

The first is the relational nature of rights. The Universal Declaration of Human Rights makes it clear that all humans are born with rights, and that with rights come duties. This is the sense in which a rights-based approach differs fundamentally from a needs-based approach: where someone has a right, other parties necessarily have a corresponding duty or responsibility regarding those rights. Whereas needs may or may not be met, rights and responsibilities go together. The distinction between a failure to meet others' needs and a failure to meet one's own responsibilities associated with others' rights may be subtle, but it is powerful. These responsibilities are generally understood to include the following:

- *Respect* human rights (by not directly violating human rights).
- *Protect* human rights (by preventing others from violating).
- *Fulfill* human rights (either directly or by facilitating the efforts of other actors).

Agencies attempting to implement a rights-based approach often take upon themselves a fourth obligation – to promote greater awareness of rights and responsibilities

Second, human rights are by their very nature interrelated and interlocking. The right to food, for example, is fairly meaningless without corresponding rights to health, education, and a productive livelihood. Most advocates for the right to food advocate more broadly for the right to nutrition, incorporating health and basic care, which in turn relate to the rights of women. Picking and choosing among rights undermines the seamless nature of the human rights system.

A third characteristic is the right of people to participate in decision-making processes that affect their lives. This applies equally to localized development projects and humanitarian response as to national politics. An emphasis on equality of access and participation underlies other principles of inclusion and non-discrimination, and the empowerment of the most marginalized and oppressed.

A fourth major theme of the rights-based approach is the obligation to address the underlying causes of poverty and human rights violations. Purely addressing symptoms may fulfill rights in the short term, but if root causes are not addressed, any impact on achieving rights or reducing poverty likely proves unsustainable. In practice, this has led to increased involvement in advocacy at the policy level of organizations that previously restricted themselves to on-the-ground programming. Advocacy may often be thought of as simply promoting certain ideas at the policy level. From a rights-based approach perspective, however, advocacy means more: it means holding other actors (often, but not necessarily, state actors) accountable to their obligations to respect, protect, and fulfill human rights.

A fifth (though not necessarily universal) element of a rights-based approach is the analysis and mitigation of unintended and negative impacts or side effects of programming – that is, holding actors accountable for the consequences of their actions, whether intended or unintended.[14] This emphasis traces its contemporary roots to the evaluation of the negative impacts of the 1994–96 relief efforts in the aftermath of the Rwanda genocide, in which humanitarian aid was clearly implicated in permitting the militias that had committed atrocities to regroup and take control over the refugee camps in Eastern Zaire (now the Democratic Republic of Congo). For most of the time since then, "do no harm" has been a humanitarian mantra – albeit an operational impossibility from a purist's perspective.[15] But other tools have been developed that help practitioners try to weigh both the positive, intended impact of humanitarian or developmental interventions and potential unintended or negative impacts, and to seek ways of mitigating or preventing these impacts. From a rights-based perspective, the emphasis is on holding actors accountable, humanitarian and developmental actors included.

While at one level, the right to food would seem fairly uncontroversial, in fact substantial controversy prevails in the international dialogue over the right to food. At the recent World Food Summit + 5 Conference, held in Rome in June 2002, the United States opposed a resolution supporting the right to food. Instead, the USA advocated greater trade liberalization, an increased role for the private sector, and the promotion of biotechnology to address global food security concerns, an approach that some observers believe produces greater inequalities and therefore further reduces the capacity of some groups of vulnerable people to fulfill their right to food. The US government's primary concern, as is the case with most of its objection to social, economic and cultural rights, revolved around the question of international obligations and domestic legal entitlements.[16]

Implications of rights-based approaches: standards and codes of conduct

Careful consideration of the underlying causes of food insecurity and of sustainable improvements in food security in accordance with operational agencies' efforts to fulfill the right to food raises core questions about the use of food aid. Food aid, almost by definition, addresses acute *symptoms* of poverty and food insecurity, it rarely tackles underlying *causes*. Indeed, food aid may, in some cases, contribute to them – particularly food aid as constrained by the political economy considerations raised in Chapters 2–5. Chapters 10 and 11 explore how these problems might be reduced significantly.

Even restricting the use of food aid only to humanitarian emergencies, in which insufficient food availability commonly – although by no means always – is a proximate causal factor of food insecurity, it quickly became clear in the latter half of the 1990s that so much interpretation of the terminology of rights is required that minimum standards that cut across all operational agencies were necessary. In all cases described below, it has been the non-governmental organizations, not the donor or recipient country governments, which have taken the lead in developing these normative standards.

The Sphere Project

The Sphere Project *Humanitarian Charter and Minimum Standards in Disaster Response* is an effort to improve humanitarian response, and the accountability of humanitarian agencies to the disaster-affected populations they serve. The Minimum Standards "are an attempt to describe the level of disaster assistance to which all people have a right, regardless of political, ethnic or geographical specificity."[17] The book was drafted over a two-year process involving staff from hundreds of organizations, and significant parts of it (including the chapter on food security, food aid, and nutrition) were re-written in 2002/2003. In addition to the humanitarian charter, there are chapters on minimum standards in six key sectors. In the case of food security, food aid, and nutrition, Sphere lays out guidance in terms of assessment and analysis, participation and transparency, protection of assets, production, income and employment, access to markets, nutritional adequacy (including nutritional programs, child feeding, food quality, food safety, food acceptability, food storage, supply chain management and distribution, and of course, caloric, protein, and micronutrient adequacy). Sphere is famous for stating unambiguously that human beings have the right to a minimum of 2,100 Kcal/person/day, and that, at least in emergencies, humanitarian agencies and donors are obligated to ensure access to that amount.

Notwithstanding the fact that there are enormous operational problems of implementing them, the Sphere guidelines have served as a very important rallying point for standardization of inter-agency norms. The guidelines highlight the rights-based approach to programming and provide a means of leveraging donor funding for humanitarian assistance, attempting to hold donors as well as humanitarian agencies accountable to a set of minimum standards.

The Red Cross/NGO Code of Conduct in Disaster Response

Though not restricted to food aid delivery, the Code of Conduct in Disaster Response, developed by the International Federation of Red Cross and Red Crescent Societies in collaboration with a consortium of international NGOs, enshrines important humanitarian principles in the work of responding to emergencies and disasters, building on the long tradition of Red Cross principles.[18] The code of conduct emphasizes first and foremost the humanitarian imperative: the absolute responsibility to provide assistance to emergency-affected people. Other important principles include impartiality, non-partisanship, and the independence of humanitarian action from political or strategic priorities of governments, respect for local customs and the strengthening of local capacities, participation and accountability, and respecting human dignity.

The Food Aid Code of Conduct

The Food Aid Code of Conduct is a much simpler document, drafted in 1995 by a group of European non-governmental organizations and EuronAid – the agency responsible for food aid allocation to NGOs within the European Union. The Code defines food security,[19] and outlines the responsibilities of signatory agencies to the people they serve. The focus on food security is very broad, including (like Sphere, albeit several years earlier) agriculture, income and job creation, health, education, water and environmental issues. Also like the Sphere Guidelines, the Food Aid Code treats access to food as a fundamental human right, in both short-term (emergency) and longer-term (poverty reduction) contexts. Signatories also commit themselves to certain standards of analysis, coordination, implementation, and distribution. More importantly, signatories commit themselves to promoting local or regional purchases wherever surpluses exist side-by-side with food deficits, because local purchase of food "contributes to the development of local markets, reduces costs, improves timing and provides the type of food people are accustomed to."[20] We will return to this issue in Chapter 8 when we discuss local purchases and triangular transactions as food aid procurement modalities. The Food Aid Code of Conduct also provides for the participatory management of resources, good resource management, standards of monitoring and evaluation.[21]

The International Code of Conduct on the Human Right to Adequate Food

Though the drafting was overseen by a non-governmental organization (FIAN, or the Food First Information and Action Network), the International Code of Conduct reflects an attempt to implement the right to food through the Office of the UN High Commission for Human Rights. The right to adequate food, according to the International Code of Conduct, means "first of all, the right to feed oneself or to social safety nets for those who are unable to do so,"[22] the latter making an implicit if not explicit reference to food assistance and food aid. In addition to points stressed in the Sphere Guidelines and the NGOs' Code, the International Code of Conduct also makes reference to non-discrimination, and the abolition of food as a weapon of war or an instrument for political or economic coercion. Most of the obligations mentioned are those of the state, and include, among others, an obligation to provide the resources for food safety nets to countries that cannot afford it themselves, to purchase food for such safety nets from the "nearest available sources," and to organize food aid in ways that "facilitate the return to food self-reliance of the beneficiaries."[23] Though the International Code of Conduct explicitly mentions the role of civil society, it makes it plain that the primary obligations to respect, protect and fulfill the right to food are those of nation-states. The role of non-governmental actors is two-fold: first, they must undertake humanitarian action in certain contexts (conflicts and emergencies), and, second, they must practice advocacy for the right to food.[24]

However, even the elucidation of minimum standards and codes of conduct is not without controversy. One of the major ironies of Sphere is that, while academics, practitioners and lawyers agree on the standards for something like, for example, the 2,100 Kcal of dietary intake per day as the minimum standard to be achieved in humanitarian response, there are many examples in non-emergency cases where populations do not have access to anywhere near that amount of food. Indeed, recall Figure 1.3 from Chapter 1, which plotted national average calorie availability. In 2000, at least 25 different nations did not reach an average of 2,100 Kcal per person per day for the whole country! While food aid may be an appropriate intervention in an emergency where people are cut off from their means of livelihood and the short-term provision of food is required, it is not an appropriate intervention when the nature of livelihoods themselves – or the political, economic, technological, or environmental constraints of the system in which they are carried out – are part of the problem. It is simply infeasible for food aid to make up substantial, persistent deficits that affect entire nations. Thus, agencies are faced with the irony of what amounts to higher standards for the fulfillment of the right to food in "emergencies" than in "development."

While these various normative statements have offered both an important interpretation of the right to food, and a goal to which humanitarian agencies – and the donors who fund them – should and strive to be held accountable, the existence of normative frameworks in and of themselves do not guarantee people access to adequate food. An important, recent criticism of contemporary humanitarian action notes that the twentieth century had some of the best normative statements in history about people's rights and entitlements, about the protocols and conventions to ensure the protection of these rights or the underlying principles, but the bloody reality on the ground in recent history has been totally at odds with the normative statements.[25] As a result, many observers discredit the process of developing and signing up to these normative statements in part because they tend to become an end in themselves – and even when they are only viewed as a means to an end, in and of themselves, they offer little guarantee of achieving those ends. The purely instrumental role of codes of conduct needs to be kept firmly in mind. Their real value comes in so far as they actually – not hypothetically – stimulate better practice in humanitarian and development operations. But simply having the norms to which agencies, governments and donors should be held accountable is a useful tool. Changes in policy have been uneven, and implementation frequently falls short of policy imperatives, but governments and donors have slowly come around to embracing many of the normative standards suggested by the right to food.

Such criticisms notwithstanding, however, a rights-based approach to food security goes well beyond earlier approaches in a number of important ways. First, it expands the range of analysis, looking at the question of food in a much broader context, and demanding that political causes and failures of governance be taken into consideration in addition to environmental or economic causes of food insecurity. Second, it expands the range of interventions, most notably demanding advocacy at the policy level in addition to interventions that make provision of food the sole aim. Third, while participation has long been a "good word" in development and humanitarian work, the emergent approach demands the right of people to participate in decisions and choices about meeting their food security requirements. Fourth, the focus on normative standards has given clear benchmarks for monitoring and evaluation (see the more detailed discussion below).

Finally, the normative element adds "teeth" to the empirical analysis of food and livelihood insecurity by shifting the benchmark to the minimum standards associated with basic human rights rather than focusing on incremental improvements.[26] Without a human rights approach, modest increases from, say, 1,500 to 1,650 Kcal/day may be celebrated as "successes." A rights-based perspective would label this an improvement but not a success until the minimum standard for living with dignity, defined by the Sphere Guidelines at 2,100 Kcal/day, is reached.[27]

Poverty traps and relief traps[28]

The most recent advances in understanding of food insecurity relate to evolving conceptualizations of poverty and vulnerability more generally. Amartya Sen's seminal work stimulated increased scholarly research and policy emphasis on poverty reduction and, most recently, on poverty dynamics, on how standards of living evolve over time. Perhaps the most fundamental lesson of recent economic research on poverty dynamics is the need to distinguish transitory from chronic poverty, between those who become poor temporarily but naturally recover after a short while, and those who remain in poverty for extended periods, often an entire lifetime, and pass their poverty on to their children.[29] A **poverty trap** exists when the natural course of economic growth does not lead an individual, household or sometimes a whole village or region beyond poverty.[30] Time is a natural ally for those who find themselves in **transitory poverty**, but not for those caught in a poverty trap.

Some people suffer **chronic poverty** because of these factors. Poor maternal health and nutrition, early childhood malnutrition, poor health care, limited or no access to education, and scant household productive assets, limit what they have to work with in trying to claw their way out of the poverty and food insecurity into which they were born. Others start out better off, but fall into chronic poverty because of an adverse shock or series of shocks. Natural disasters and civil strife are tragic not just because of the temporary displacement and deprivation they bring but because they can wipe out in a moment what households have labored years to accumulate through disciplined savings and investment. Brief disturbances can have persistent effects. These two effects are often mutually reinforcing as those who start off in poverty are far more likely to suffer serious adverse shocks that knock them back down as they struggle to climb out of poverty. For example, one report notes that "between 1990 and 1998, poor countries accounted for 94 percent of the world's 568 major natural disasters and 97 percent of disaster-related deaths."[31]

Shocks can have persistent effects only in the presence of *poverty traps*. Poverty traps ultimately depend on the existence of threshold effects. Threshold effects exist when people with very similar initial positions nonetheless follow different welfare or asset accumulation trajectories over time. Above the threshold, poverty is only transitory as the natural dynamic of accumulation leads to increasing productivity and standards of living. Below the threshold, however, people find themselves trapped in a low-productivity state of chronic poverty and vulnerability due to a lack of productive assets (e.g., land, livestock, education, capital) and the meager returns they earn on the few assets they do own (e.g., due to poor market access or the rudimentary agricultural technologies they use). Absent access to capital, their only path out of long-term poverty would require unrealistic levels of personal sacrifice and savings in order to make productivity-enhancing investments in new assets and livelihoods. Indeed, in many cases, they cannot even afford to maintain current productivity by investing in the maintenance of the assets they own, instead mining these for current subsistence at the cost of future productivity and continued, chronic poverty and vulnerability.

The thresholds that distinguish transitory from chronic poverty give rise to a crucial policy distinction between **cargo nets** and **safety nets**. Safety nets aim to prevent the non-poor and transitorily poor from falling into chronic poverty. Because people can become temporarily poor up to some threshold level and still recover on their own, often quickly, the role of safety nets is to keep them from crossing that threshold, from becoming chronically poor and food insecure. Emergency feeding programs, crop or unemployment insurance, employment guarantee schemes, and disaster assistance are common examples of formal safety net interventions by governments and operational agencies. While some of these policy instruments can be used as well for cargo net or humanitarian interventions, they are best understood as safety nets when used primarily to insure against asset loss so as to preserve beneficiaries' capacity to recover from shocks and to grow their way out of poverty. Social solidarity networks and systems of informal mutual insurance often provide safety nets internal to communities. The partial displacement of the latter by the former should serve as a caution on the design of safety nets, however, so as to minimize the crowding out of informal safety nets, although most rigorous estimates suggest those effects are reasonably modest.[32] Safety nets catch people, keeping them from falling too far, then people step off the net and climb back up on their own.

Conclusion

Crucial thresholds exist in the domain of nutrition and health, both intrinsically, due to every individual's basic human right to food and health care, and instrumentally, because future productivity depends so fundamentally on human capital, especially among the poor who own little other than their own labor power. The irreversibility of some nutrition-related health problems – for example, blindness related to vitamin A deficiency, brain damage related to iodine deficiency, physical stunting from sustained protein energy malnutrition – makes the insurance of food security especially important. Thus, safety nets with respect to nutrition and health are fundamental to blocking vulnerable people's descent into chronic poverty and food insecurity in the wake of shocks, whether specific to the family (e.g., a farm or road accident) or general to a region (e.g., civil strife or drought).

Cargo nets, by contrast, help climbers surmount obstacles or can be used to lift objects, overcoming the structural forces that otherwise keep them down. Cargo nets are thus meant to lift people who fall below critical thresholds or to help them climb out of chronic poverty and food insecurity. Familiar examples of cargo net policies include land reform, targeted school feeding programs, education and skills training initiatives, targeted subsidized microfinance or agricultural input subsidization projects, etc. As with safety nets, the same instrument (e.g., school feeding) can serve safety net or humanitarian assistance aims when the emphasis of the intervention changes. Cargo net interventions aim at building chronically poor participants' asset stocks and/or improving the productivity of the assets they already possess.

Safety nets block pathways into chronic poverty and food insecurity for the non-poor and transitorily poor. Well-designed and implemented cargo nets can set people onto pathways out of chronic poverty. In order to be effective, cargo net interventions must target the chronically poor and safety nets must target the transitorily poor, meaning they must be set above thresholds at which natural path dynamics break in different directions. This implies a central role for effective targeting, in order that the appropriate policies are applied to the right sub-populations.

The concept of poverty traps and the resulting distinction between safety nets and cargo nets is fundamental to development and humanitarian policy. The longer individuals remain in poverty, the more vulnerable they become to natural disasters and civil strife, and the more likely that overseas aid must be channeled in the form of relief efforts intended to protect basic human rights in acute humanitarian emergencies. As aid becomes concentrated in relief efforts, however, this diverts scarce resources from addressing the structural causes of chronic poverty. Without highly effective safety nets, a vicious cycle thereby ensues, with individuals falling into poverty traps. Moreover, as the population ensnared in poverty traps grows, international assistance becomes ensnared in **relief traps** as emergency operations consume an increasing share of scarce foreign assistance budgets, effectively precluding long-term development assistance through critical investments in non-emergency education, health, agriculture, and infrastructure initiatives. Reduced investment in such areas, however, increases the likelihood of future emergencies, trapping donors in a vicious circle in which they can increasingly finance only relief operations accompanied only occasionally by under-funded structural investments. That's a relief trap. As we document in Chapter 11, global development assistance flows appear to have fallen into this trap.

In this evolving view of poverty dynamics as conditioned by poverty traps associated with multiple dynamic equilibria, the important questions surrounding food aid therefore relate to when, where and how assistance in the form of food can be used to create safety nets to keep people from becoming chronically poor, and when, where and how food aid can contribute to cargo nets. This view complements the rights-based approach, which focuses on the more fundamental question of when, where and how food aid can be used in humanitarian response to meet the basic human right to food. In Chapter 10 we explore how these three levels of assistance – humanitarian response, safety nets, and cargo nets – can be nested into a coherent approach to the use of food aid in support of a coherent, broader strategy to reduce poverty and food insecurity.

7 The uses of food aid to address food insecurity

Over the years, food aid has been deployed in an extraordinary array of uses, everything from general distribution to emergency-affected populations and direct feeding of severely malnourished children in famines to maternal and child health projects with a nutrition focus; as an incentive to education and school attendance; food for work in environmental protection, agricultural production, and infrastructure development; market development; as a tool for the mitigation and care of HIV/AIDS; general balance of payments assistance, and a variety of other indirect, programmatic uses. Historically, food aid has been subdivided into "program," "project," and "emergency" uses (see Chapter 1). From recipients' perspective, program food aid has been almost entirely for balance of payments and local currency budgetary support. In many instances, the line between the project and emergency categories is blurred, although some of the most potentially innovative uses may exist in the blurry area. The current language of operational agencies and donors reclassifies what used to be the categories of project and emergency food aid into three broad applications: (1) acute humanitarian emergencies; (2) safety nets, vulnerability reduction, and asset protection; and (3) "development." These uses of food aid, as presently employed, are briefly reviewed below. Chapter 10 will go into greater detail on the untapped potential of food aid uses at the blurry intersection of project and emergency applications.

There is a second dimension along which one must divide food aid: that which is distributed directly to beneficiaries and that which is monetized by recipients or operational agencies so as to convert the food resource to some other form. Direct distribution prevails in acute humanitarian emergencies, while monetization tends to dominate much of Title II PL 480 food aid for "development" purposes. This two-dimensional characterization of food aid – distinguishing between direct distribution and monetization in one dimension, and between uses (emergency, project, and program in prevailing current food aid accounting) in the other – raises important strategic and operational questions as to when to monetize and when to distribute food aid directly, issues to which we return in detail in Chapter 10. Initially, however, we need to clarify the crucial distinctions between these alternative uses of food aid.

Acute humanitarian emergencies

When most non-specialists think of food aid, they envision direct feeding of or food transfers to destitute, hungry people. The emphasis in relief operations during acute humanitarian emergencies falls on the direct protection of human lives and the food security and nutritional status of groups directly affected by natural disasters, man-made shocks, or some combination of the two. This popular vision of food aid is not without foundation. Food aid for acute humanitarian emergencies accounts for the vast majority of food aid provided through multilateral channels, although it represents a minority (albeit steadily growing) share of bilateral food aid flows.[1]

Food aid used in humanitarian emergencies is largely for the purpose of protecting human nutritional status and human life, although in many kinds of emergencies, protecting livelihood assets is critical as well. The most common applications of food aid for protecting human life and nutritional status in acute humanitarian emergencies are: (1) general nutrition support, primarily through direct distribution of a basic food ration to vulnerable groups (based on some assessment of need); (2) correcting malnutrition via supplementary or therapeutic feeding for especially acutely affected sub-groups; and (3) food for work (FFW) if the emergency intervention is mounted rapidly enough to begin before people have been badly affected by the crisis, since FFW is obviously not an appropriate intervention for already malnourished or acutely food insecure groups or individuals who will lack the energy necessary to undertake sustained physical labor for an extended period.

All these interventions involve some kind of targeting of distributed resources in order to increase their efficacy in providing the desired assistance. People typically think of targeting at household level (for example, by income), as occurs in many non-emergency assistance programs around the world. In widespread acute emergencies – particularly if caused by drought, floods, conflict, or other factors that tend to affect whole populations – however, geographic targeting of affected areas is more common than household targeting for direct distribution of food. Individual-level targeting is always important for therapeutic feeding, and usually for supplementary feeding, as well. Individual-level targeting in emergency settings is typically done on the basis of anthropometric or other health indicators (e.g., disease status).

The demand for targeting at various levels in order to achieve rapid, effective response to humanitarian emergencies implies a clear need for rapidly available information in order to effectively manage these kinds of interventions. Food aid in acute humanitarian emergencies therefore functions best in conjunction with reasonable accurate and timely early warning systems, and solid contingency planning, assessment, and targeting abilities. We discuss these issues in greater detail in Chapter 8.

It is very difficult to get good figures on the impact of emergency food aid operations, given the context in which they take place. Nonetheless, it is no understatement to assert that emergency food aid has protected the life and health of hundreds of millions of emergency-affected people over the past fifty years, and the focus on emergency assistance is growing within the food aid community. WFP reported having devoted 90 percent of its resources to emergencies in 2003 and notes that number of deaths resulting from causes other than direct violence in emergencies dropped 40 percent during the decade between 1993 and 2003.[2]

While operational difficulties beset food aid provision – and most other activities – in acute humanitarian emergencies, the justification for providing food aid in such situations is fairly straightforward and widely accepted.[3] And operational agencies have made important strides in improving program quality in emergencies, both with respect to the timely delivery of food and as regards provision of required non-food complementary inputs. Nevertheless, the use of food in certain situations – complex political emergencies,[4] in particular – is fraught with unanswered policy and ethical questions: To what extent does providing food make recipients targets for attack, or at least for "taxation" of those receipts by parties to a conflict? Is it possible to target humanitarian assistance solely to victims of conflict, without also shoring up oppressive governments or providing assistance to those instigating the conflict, as occurred in the Goma refugee camps in Zaire during the Rwandese refugee crisis during 1994 to 1996? When are the risks to aid workers and the costs of delivery too high to justify emergency food aid distribution operations? While food aid clearly has a role to play in emergencies underpinned by a food availability deficit, these and other questions must be addressed for food aid to play a useful role in complex emergencies. We take up these prescriptive issues in Chapter 10. For now, we wish merely to describe the present state of play with respect to food aid and how the international community has come to the point where we now find ourselves.

Safety nets for vulnerability reduction and asset protection

People are not always born into poverty and food insecurity, nor is it always permanent, as we discussed in Chapter 6. Sometimes people fall into chronic poverty as a result of adverse shocks associated with disease, crime, drought, floods, hurricanes, or other natural or human emergencies that cost them productive assets, whether directly (e.g., homes washed away, permanent injuries or disabilities incurred, or livestock killed) or indirectly, through distress sales of productive assets. Safety nets, including those based on food aid, play a crucial role in helping people to defend current consumption without having to sacrifice future opportunities by selling off productive assets to cope with adverse shocks, and to undertake productive investment in livelihoods improvements with the security that they are not imperiling their families today in their effort to improve their future situation. Well-functioning safety nets ensure that short-term shocks do not have permanent consequences by defending critical asset thresholds that define the poverty traps discussed in Chapter 6.

In safety net operations, the timely provision of assistance becomes just as important as its availability. If, for example, people have to leave their farms in search of food in a drought emergency, by that point they probably have already used up, lost or sold off most of their productive assets and their health and nutritional status may already be severely degraded. In order for safety nets to be effective in reducing vulnerability to downside shocks and in protecting crucial productive assets, they must respond swiftly to emerging needs.

Households or communities threatened with repeated shocks face greater risks of destitution, because they have less time and fewer resources with which to recover. Recurrent shocks that lead to asset divestiture increase the vulnerability of a population to falling into chronic poverty. The closer people live to the threshold between chronic and transitory poverty, the greater importance attached to both a guarantee of a safety net and the timeliness of its operationalization in the event of (even a minor) shock, so as to prevent loss of assets in a timely and equitable manner.[5] Protection of both physical assets and human capital in the face of shocks is always preferable to attempting to rebuild it in the aftermath of a shock – an insight that underlies much of the so-called "developmental relief" approach that exists at the blurry divide between emergency relief and development (see Box 7.1 on the C-SAFE project in southern Africa).

Box 7.1 C-SAFE: a developmental relief food aid program[1]

In 2002, southern Africa suffered its most severe region-wide food security crisis in a decade. An estimated 15.3 million people in six countries (Lesotho, Malawi, Mozambique, Swaziland, Zambia, and Zimbabwe) needed food aid by March 2003. The three hardest hit countries were Zimbabwe, Malawi, and Zambia. The crisis was brought on by governance problems, weather conditions, and longer-term trends, particularly the HIV/AIDS epidemic, long-term economic recession, and generally declining livelihood security at the household level throughout the region. Women and female-headed households were especially hard hit, as they must often cope with labor shortages and lost sources of income.

An emergency food aid intervention was required in the short term, but it was clear from the outset that the southern African food crisis was not just an acute emergency – it reflected chronic vulnerability and deteriorating livelihoods. Therefore, the response had to go beyond simply providing emergency assistance – much of the response had to be addressed to the need to protect against further asset losses, and to enable to rebuild sustainable livelihoods.

The C-SAFE Program (Consortium for the Southern Africa Food Security Emergency) was developed to address this set of problems. The C-SAFE consortium was comprised of three international NGOs (Catholic Relief Services, World Vision, and CARE International). The program operates in the three hardest-hit countries to address not only immediate food requirements, but also to use food aid and complementary cash resources to address the chronic vulnerability that helped to bring about the crisis. The objective of the program is to improve and protect health and nutrition status while improving productive asset holdings at the household level and community resilience to future shocks.

C-SAFE introduced health and nutrition education and crop diversification efforts to support the longer-term food security and nutritional status of the vulnerable groups receiving food, as over-reliance on a single crop (maize) appears to be part of the problem. The program also focuses on greater agricultural production and profitability (for example, soil and water conservation, irrigation, and conservation farming methods), since farming is the mainstay of rural livelihoods in all three countries. Most of these activities are being implemented using a food for work design. The program also aims to strengthen local systems to prepare for, predict, and respond to future food shortages. Important activities include improving roads and trade infrastructure, development of village grain and seed banks, savings-led village micro-finance groups, and livelihood diversification.

C-SAFE is managed in each country by one of the members of the consortium, with overall management responsibility based in the Regional Program Unit, located in Johannesburg, South Africa. The budget is an estimated 160,000 metric tons of food aid per year, complemented by cash resources.

Note:
1   Drawn from C-SAFE Consortium, *A Developmental Relief Proposal for the First 24 Months of a 5-Year Strategy.* Johannesburg: CARE, CRS, World Vision, 2002.

Shocks pose problems not just when they happen, but also because of their mere prospect, people go to great lengths to avoid potentially calamitous downside risk. The key points to take away from the economic literature on risk[6] are (1) households that are risk-averse in any fashion are willing to pay a premium (in the form of foregone average income) to reduce risk, and (2) not all households will be equally willing to pay to avoid identical risks. In particular, poorer households will likely be willing to pay relatively more than richer households to avoid a risk of identical magnitude when faced with the same opportunities. They may even be willing to pay more to avoid a risk of a given proportion of income (i.e., pay more to avoid lower absolute risk). The risk of being excluded from safety nets increases households' perceived downside risk, encouraging them to take costly risk-avoidance strategies themselves, for example, eschewing higher-return, higher-risk livelihood strategies that might enable them to grow their way out of poverty and food insecurity. Thus, the guarantee of timely provision of safety nets which at least meet minimal nutritional criteria necessary to preserve valuable human capital are of critical importance both to the protection of livelihoods in chronically vulnerable areas and to underpinning household strategies for livelihood improvements.[7] Food *insecurity* – and especially improving the capacity of poor households to manage risk and vulnerability – has become a major focus of interventions over the past five or six years with a greater emphasis on social protection and mitigation of shocks, rather than a straightforward emphasis on long-term improvements in income or productivity.[8]

One of the increasingly important roles of social safety nets, especially in Sub-Saharan Africa, relates to mitigating the impact of the HIV/AIDS pandemic. HIV/AIDS is qualitatively different from many other kinds of shocks that threaten food security. It may be hidden in a shroud of stigma and silence. It undermines some of the known coping strategies for dealing with other kinds of shocks (for example, labor migration, a common response to famine in many chronically vulnerable parts of the world). And, it primarily kills people in the sexually active age bracket, which is also of course the most economically active demographic group. Communities that have been hit hard by the AIDS pandemic tend to be left with households disproportionately heavy with very elderly and very young members, i.e., with a high dependency ratio.[9] While sometimes directly infected through mother-to-child transmission, the lives of nearly all these children are devastated by the death of the economically active members of their households. AIDS has thus become a major cause of increasing chronic poverty and food insecurity.[10] Robust and long-term social safety nets are required to prevent the slide of the surviving members of HIV/AIDS affected households into chronic poverty and remaining trapped there.

The southern African food crisis of 2002–3 highlighted the complex interaction between food security and HIV/AIDS, and the role of both short-term and longer-term interventions using food aid. For a number of years, the main emphasis of intervention in the HIV/AIDS pandemic was on awareness and prevention, and on interventions to assist infected individuals. More recently, the broader impacts of the pandemic have been recognized, as has been the need for a broader set of interventions focusing on both the infected and affected population, and at the levels of the prevention and care of people living with AIDS and mitigation of its broader effects. The AIDS pandemic is now seen by many observers as representing a new and completely different kind of emergency, one requiring new approaches and thinking to both humanitarian response and mitigation. One noted authority on famine, Alex de Waal, and his co-author Alan Whiteside, see the AIDS crisis as a completely new variant of famine, one in which there is little expectation of a post-crisis return to either sustainable livelihoods or a demographic equilibrium.[11]

Food aid has come to comprise a major component of safety nets to mitigate the impact of the HIV/AIDS pandemic in important cases in Sub-Saharan Africa.[12] But there are major obstacles around issues of targeting, stigma, and other causes of poverty in the same communities[13] not to mention concerns about guaranteeing the sustainable provision of safety nets that rely on food aid which, at best, are tied to 3–5 year funding cycles, whereas AIDS-affected orphans may require some form of support from infancy to adulthood. The other concern about safety nets for AIDS-affected families and children is that beyond providing for consumption requirements (which in any case are far broader than just food), such safety nets must include education and other inputs if children are to have any chance of avoiding a life of chronic poverty.

The preceding discussion of HIV/AIDS and food aid underscores a critical point about food-based safety nets in general: they really only protect food security and nutritional status (or other assets) in the short term. Food-based safety nets are therefore insufficient for those who were already chronically food insecure or who inevitably become so because of the shock(s) they experience. Safety nets are intended first and foremost to provide insurance in order to permit those threatened or impacted by a shock to recover and maintain an adequate quality of life. By so doing, safety nets can induce effective and appropriate, if somewhat risky, investment by poor households. But safety nets are not investments themselves in households. Many shocks inevitably carry long-term consequences, most notably mortality shocks to working-age adults, whether due to HIV/AIDS, malaria, tuberculosis, other diseases, violence, or accidents. Such shocks may push people well past the threshold dividing the transitorily poor from the chronically poor. These people need more intensive programmatic assistance – the "cargo nets" described in Chapter 6. The same is true of those who were chronically poor and food insecure even before a shock hit. A safety net may guard against further permanent decline in their situation, but it will not lift them beyond the threshold point at which they can begin climbing out of poverty on their own. The literature on social protection highlights the need to enable the poor to invest in higher return livelihood activities that, over time, make them less vulnerable to shocks.[14] This approach allows people to move out of poverty, while still providing support for those in most severe need.

Although anecdotal evidence abounds, hard data on the impact of food aid used for safety net purposes are difficult to collect. Safety net activities comprise an important element of the new strategies of both WFP and USAID/Food for Peace – especially in chronically famine-prone countries – underlining the importance of these activities to the protection of human nutritional status and livelihood assets. Food aid is an important component of safety nets in periods and places of insufficient food availability by providing insurance against the violation of basic human rights and the loss of human capital due to undernutrition and by pre-empting households' rational divestiture of productive physical assets in order to protect their nutrition and health.[15] There are many other essential elements in safety net programs, including curative and therapeutic health care, sanitation, infrastructure rehabilitation, emergency shelter services, and keeping children in school. But protecting human nutritional status and physical assets are fundamental and thus so is insurance of adequate food availability and access.

Food aid for development

The conceptual distinction between safety nets – which keep people from falling into poverty traps – and cargo nets – which lift or enable people to climb out of poverty traps – reflects the difference between food aid for asset protection, which we just discussed, and food aid for asset accumulation, more commonly referred to as "developmental food aid" or "food aid for development." Whether provided free or in exchange for recipients' commitment of time to a public works project, schooling, or some other initiative, food aid is commonly programmed as a development resource to try to facilitate asset accumulation and to reduce vulnerability to the shocks that traditionally induce food insecurity. This is a major component of the new strategy developed by the USAID Office of Food for Peace, the world's largest food aid donor.[16]

The nature of the manner in which food aid is currently programmed and targeted – from assessment of requirements to donor appeals, delivery and distribution – all make food aid at best a clumsy tool for dealing with chronic poverty and vulnerability. The food aid procurement and distribution process still tends to be based on the presumption that famine or acute food insecurity is an event, not the outcome of a process of destitution.[17] As a result, food aid is probably overused as a tool for development, although there are some roles in which food aid can be a useful resource to support development efforts.

Food aid is currently used in a variety of ways often labeled "development." The World Food Programme, for example, explicitly ties a number of its programmatic activities to the Millennium Development Goals.[18] These interventions, briefly described below, justifiably receive widespread support as instruments of development policy, although there remain legitimate questions as to whether this justifies food aid as the means to support cargo net interventions of these sorts, as we discuss below.

Maternal and child health supplemental feeding

Chronic malnutrition among vulnerable groups such as women and young children is a problem that often goes unnoticed, to the permanent detriment of those affected by it. Food aid is often used directly to supplement the diets of young children and pregnant and lactating mothers. Protection of the health and nutritional status of vulnerable groups is thus correctly viewed as a long-term investment in human capital accumulation, recognizing that the effects of malnutrition are cumulative, that they pose a major risk factor in child and maternal morbidity and mortality, and that the most crucial period of cognitive and physical development is that from conception through a child's second birthday. Prenatal and early childhood interventions are especially important in preventing low birthweight and various micronutrient deficiencies (most notably iron-deficiency anemia, iodine and vitamin A deficiency) and in improving infant and child growth, and supplemental maternal and child feeding programs have been repeatedly shown to be highly effective means of improving child nutrition.[19]

The use of micronutrient fortified foods is a particularly important input in these programs. This links directly to the provision of food since fortified foods are not commonly available at affordable prices through commercial channels in poor communities. Provision of fortified foods to malnourished individuals in areas of high HIV prevalence is also thought to be an important means of slowing the impact of AIDS.[20] Nutrition and health education is often an important complement to direct food supplementation in maternal and child health programs. In many instances, food distribution is assumed to provide an added incentive for women to visit health centers, especially with their children, thereby giving them access to health services perhaps more valuable than the food they receive.

Maternal and child nutrition has become a higher priority for both the largest operational agency – the World Food Programme – and the largest donor – USAID.[21] A recent program evaluation of USAID/Food for Peace Title II programs showed a decline in the prevalence of stunting (low height for age, a measure of chronic malnutrition) of 2.4 percent per year among targeted participants of programs, albeit with considerable variance, implying important program management issues. In three-quarters of the programs examined, this level of nutritional improvement was better than national averages, suggesting that the Title II programs contributed significantly to the positive impact.[22]

Food for education

The provision of food to schoolchildren in poor communities can serve three high priority purposes: (1) to protect the nutritional status of these children; (2) to enhance learning and cognitive development; and (3) to create and maintain parental incentives for children to attend school and not to drop out in times of stress. Like supplemental feeding through MCH projects, school feeding programs are justifiably considered valuable long-term investments in human capital. The traditional school feeding programs target children in school and are an attractive incentive to students from poor families to enroll (or remain) in school. They have been shown to help alleviate short-term hunger and to improve micronutrient status in children in a variety of programs in low- and middle-income countries.[23] School feeding programs have been shown to be a particularly effective incentive under some circumstances for parents to keep children, perhaps especially girls, in school,[24] thus enhancing opportunities for improved education of children from poorer households, in particular girls, a major international development objective. A newer kind of program, "food for schooling" also provides a family ration of food, based on the school attendance of school-aged children. Many food for education programs often also have a governance component as well, working with Parent–Teacher Associations or other mechanisms that enhance community relations with and supervision of education institutions. The WFP has long been a strong advocate of food for education programs based on food aid, and the US Congress launched a significant new food for education program in 2002. A recent study by the International Food Policy Research Institute noted that a food for education program in Bangladesh improved primary school enrollment and attendance (particularly among girls) and improved caloric intake at the household level.[25] Important questions remain about the efficacy of school feeding programs in advancing educational attainment because school feeding may not always address the limiting factors, especially the quality of education. There are also questions about whether food is the appropriate resource. Similar cash-based programs in Latin America have achieved the same goals, with recipients expressing a preference for cash over food resources.[26] Nevertheless, well-targeted food for education programs are generally desirable, if not always of the highest priority.

Food for work

Food for work (FFW) projects can be used to harness the one major asset virtually all poor people control – their labor – to feed their families, while in the process building or maintaining important physical assets to stimulate productivity and thus local development through public employment guarantee schemes. In the abstract, public goods such as roads, irrigation infrastructure, schools and clinics, soil and water conservation structures, and reforestation are unambiguously good. There is a danger, however, that FFW programs can crowd out or distort private investment, thereby generating little, or even negative, net change in future productivity. And while there is evidence of lots of public infrastructure developed with FFW as the input, there is scant hard evidence of favorable nutritional impacts of FFW programs.[27]

FFW efforts are perhaps the paradigmatic example of efforts to link safety net and cargo net interventions, in this case bundling them up together. When well-managed employment-based safety nets are integrated into developmental objectives, food for work programs have tremendous potential to contribute to infrastructure. A recent study in Ethiopia estimates that if the Employment Generation Scheme was actually run according to policy guidelines and linked to well-designed programs, it would generate an average of over 230 million person-days of labor per year. That could be harnessed as a tremendous resource for irrigation development, rural road construction, and other infrastructure investment and rehabilitation to begin to address some of the structural constraints to rural development in Ethiopia.[28]

The catch is that food aid alone cannot achieve any of these outcomes. The "developmental" component often comes through the complementary activities and investments. And fears about free distributions of food aid leading to dependency can lead to activities being implemented under food for work programs that are damaging or simply "make-work."[29] Monetization sometimes generates the complementary cash resources required, but in many cases, FFW is a stand-alone activity that simply falls short of safety net (asset-protecting) or cargo net (asset-building) objectives.

Moreover, there may be crucial FFW design trade-offs between short-term safety net and longer-term cargo net goals. Indeed, the empirical evidence on FFW's efficacy in advancing development objectives is quite mixed.[30] The determinants of where and when FFW seems able to contribute to investment and long-term productivity growth and livelihoods improvement appear complex; although it can clearly be effective, FFW is nowhere near the magic bullet suggested by some of its proponents.

Food for participation

Just as food can be used to induce children's school attendance or adults' work in public employment schemes, so can food be used more generally as an incentive to participation in other activities, such as training, agricultural activities, or microfinance. The important point here is that other activities are the real objective; food aid merely adds an incentive to participation. There are important cases in which prospective participants face high entry costs to participation in beneficial activities and where the provision of food can mitigate that short-term cost sufficiently to make it worth their while to invest time in initiatives that will pay handsome long-term dividends, though few cases have been well documented which fit this description.[31] However, such inducements necessarily complicate effective evaluation of the efficacy of the underlying activities they are meant to encourage, increasing the likelihood of excessive investment in projects whose true relative rate of return would otherwise cause them to be closed down. We would like to see a careful assessment as to how these two opposing effects play out in actual food for participation initiatives – as well as the sustainability of any resulting behavioral change. At this stage, it is effectively impossible to form an empirically validated assessment of such efforts.

No matter how commendable the policy instrument, two key questions arise surrounding the use of food aid in support of maternal and child health care, supplemental or school feeding, food for work, food for participation or other such initiatives. The first is whether the international transfer of food is appropriate as the procurement mechanism. Nations can and do run effective programs without receiving food aid, for example, the highly successful school feeding or Special Supplemental Program for Women, Infants and Children (WIC) in the United States, between them serving an estimated 36 million individuals in 2002,[32] or at the similarly successful employment guarantee schemes implemented in Argentina and in India's Maharashtra state with negligible-to-no food aid support. Nonetheless, it is also true that food aid appears to have made notable contributions to food assistance programs in various countries around the world, perhaps especially in South Asia.[33] The appropriate question here is not only whether food assistance and public employment guarantee programs are effective. Their efficacy is a necessary but not sufficient condition to justify the use of food aid for these purposes.

The second, equally essential question is whether food aid is a relatively effective resource for achieving these objectives. The answer to this question turns fundamentally on three distinct subquestions: (1) are any other resources available? If food aid is truly the only way to fund such programs, then it may well be the "least bad" resource because it is the only resource available. If other resources are or could be made available (albeit perhaps requiring some political advocacy), then (2) is food aid as efficient as alternative resources at turning appropriations into supplemental food consumption? Targeted balance of payments assistance in the form of finance for the procurement of food on local markets (including perhaps commercial imports) for distribution through such programs will typically be far easier to defend than will expensive transoceanic shipment of bulk grains. We return to this issue of resource transfer efficiency in Chapter 8. Finally, (3) insofar as host country government commitment to such programs is essential for meeting citizens' right to food, does basing supplemental or school feeding programs on foreign food aid donations contribute to governments' abdication of responsibility to meet their citizens' right to food? If food aid undermines local "ownership" of valuable development initiatives, it can prove highly counterproductive. The availability of food aid is by no means sufficient to ensure the efficacy of food assistance interventions.

The extent to which food aid is truly developmental is therefore a highly contingent question, one without any clear answers outside of a given context and a given situation. The answer depends on where the food assistance is coming from, who benefits from the modalities by which it is purchased and delivered, the sustainability of the activity, its effects on other behaviors and thus its impact net of any displaced efforts along the same lines, and the extent to which underlying causes of poverty, vulnerability, and food insecurity are being addressed, rather than their symptoms. Unfortunately, little evaluation of this type is available for existing food aid programs. Sometimes an emphasis on food aid competes with the longer-term perspective required for overcoming the basic causes of food insecurity. The noted development economist Jeffrey Sachs, commenting on the balance of international assistance to Ethiopia during the crisis of 2002–3, noted:

> Things will not get better here unless there is a dramatic change in how the donors perform. [This] year, the United States generously gave US $500 million of food aid but at the same time only US $4 million help in raising agricultural activity. This is treating the emergency but not treating the underlying conditions, and that will never solve the problem.[34]

This case of US assistance to Ethiopia is just one example of how poverty traps can lead donors into relief traps.

Monetization

The preceding discussion focused on the distribution of food aid in support of development interventions. Much food aid, however, has historically been used merely as a form of general budgetary support, either to recipient country governments, in the case of program food aid, or to local or international NGOs, in the case of project or some emergency food aid. As Chapter 5 detailed, much food aid is monetized, meaning it is sold to commercial traders on the open market, with the proceeds from the sale then used for other purposes, not directly related to the provision of food to hungry people (though Title II development projects are intended to have food security objectives). Among US food aid programs, all Title I PL 480 flows are monetized, while about 70 percent of Title II development resources are monetized and 40 percent of flows under Section 416(b) and the Food for Progress program.[35] Very little monetization occurs with Title II emergency food aid.[36]

In some cases, monetization may be done in such a way as to encourage local market development by promoting private sector development. For example, food aid sold not through large commercial grain merchants, but rather through small, village-based processors and traders can help to stimulate the emergence of a competitive food distribution channel.[37] Of particular note is the Indian experience with Operation Flood, 1970–95, which was instrumental in helping establish milk producers' cooperatives and promote adoption of modern dairy production and processing technologies in villages in rural India. The first phase of Operation Flood was financed by the sale within India of skimmed milk powder and butter oil donated by the European Community via the World Food Programme. Initially, the program aimed at linking India's 18 best milksheds with the milk markets of the four main cities: Delhi, Mumbai, Calcutta, and Madras. By 1985 it had expanded to 136 milksheds linked to more than 290 urban markets and had created a self-sustaining system of 43,000 village cooperatives covering 4.25 million milk producers.[38] The European Community food aid thus promoted enhanced value-added in upstream production, processing and direct marketing by smallholder producers, increasing their share of the profits from retail milk sales in India.

While monetization proceeds are sometimes used to cover distribution costs of non-emergency food aid, in many cases the motivation behind monetization is simply recipient agencies' demand for cash, rather than food, as an input to programming and the perception that resources transferred in the form of food aid are partly or wholly additional to resource otherwise available as cash. Donated food then becomes merely an instrument to access cash. A study of monetization carried out in the late 1990s noted, "The reality is that, with diminishing cash resources for development activities, monetization can provide much-needed local currency to enhance the impact of food distribution and other development activities."[39] This was the tradition of program food aid that shipped disposable surpluses generated by donor farm policies to developing country governments needing balance of payments and fiscal budgetary support. That tradition continues today in the form of monetized project food aid handled by NGOs, which in terms of the food aid effects, is indistinguishable from program food aid received by governments.

We observe an analogous preference for cash over food transfers even at the micro-level of individual recipients. A recent study based on a nationally representative sample of more than 3,200 households reveals that even food-insecure rural Ethiopians would generally prefer cash to food. This is evident in how the wage rates at which they indicate they would be willing to participate in public employment projects varies by the form of payment they receive. Voluntary labor supply proved far greater and more responsive to modest wage increases, even at very low levels, in programs offering cash payments rather than wages paid as maize or wheat.

This can be seen in Figure 7.1. The two solid lines in Figure 7.1 depict the labor supply curves for payments in white wheat and cash (expressed in equivalent kilograms of white wheat, based on prevailing buyer and seller prices). Notice that the labor supply for (equal value) payments in cash is always greater than the labor

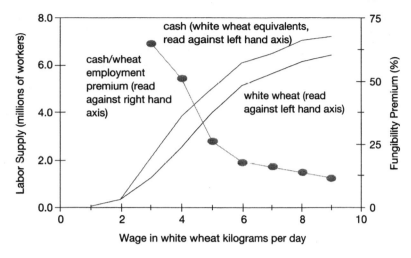

Figure 7.1 Estimated aggregate FFW labor supply

Source: Adapted from Barrett and Clay (2003)

supply when participants are paid in food. The gap between the two curves reflects a cash premium participants place on receiving cash rather than commodities because cash is more fungible than food. This "fungibility premium" is plotted in the line marked with dots (which should be read against the graph's right-hand axis). The premium ranges from 12 to 65 percent, with the cash premium highest for the poorest peoples working at the lowest wages.[40] Even very poor people lacking adequate diets typically put higher value on receiving cash – which they can more easily use for health care, to repay loans, or for other essential outlays – than food.

Although Ethiopian households prefer cash to food, an overwhelming majority of them have participated in food for work programs or are willing to participate at prevailing (food) wage rates. This situation is perfectly analogous to that of NGOs who would far rather have cash than commodities in most circumstances, even were they not to receive as much cash, but who accept commodities because that is the only form in which resources are offered. Just as there can often be significant efficiency gains from moving from food for work to cash for work programs, so can there be substantial improvements from substituting cash for food aid where it is used purely for monetization

European donors and the World Food Program have mostly stopped providing food aid for monetization and have largely discontinued program food aid that recipient governments would monetize. Title II PL 480 allocations by USAID's Food for Peace and Section 416(b) and Food for Progress shipments by USDA provide virtually the only remaining source of food aid for monetization by NGOs, while Title I PL 480 shipments account for the overwhelming majority of food aid cashed out in markets by government recipients. Therefore, food aid monetization is almost exclusively associated with US food aid now and US-based NGOs are the prime practitioners and advocates for the practice, as we explained in Chapter 5.

Supporters of monetization (US-based NGOs and others) argue that, in the absence of direct cash funding from donors, monetization proceeds can be used in a wide variety of activities widely viewed as important complements to the provision of food: development of basic health services, agricultural development, education, and local capacity building. In addition, a small proportion of monetization projects use the actual process of monetization to achieve developmental objectives, most frequently market development. These are typically achieved by using auction mechanisms to increase the participation of local wholesalers in imported food distribution, subsidizing start-up costs for producer marketing cooperatives, reducing the minimum size of trader sales, thereby facilitating small-scale trader access to commodity markets and improving market competitiveness, at least in the short term.[41]

NGOs have often made good use of funds provided by monetization. A 2002 evaluation of the results of PL 480 Title II development activities – depending mostly on monetization proceeds – demonstrates that these activities have had important food security and nutrition impacts. Some of these impacts were noted above under maternal and child nutrition. The evaluations claim that important achievements were made in other areas that directly affect food security, particularly enhancing agricultural production. And the report makes it clear that major strides have been made in program analysis, design, monitoring, and evaluation.[42] But this is more a testimony to the programming abilities of the organizations that rely on monetization for proceeds than it is an argument for monetization *per se*. Nevertheless, monetization provided much of the funding for both the programs and the capacity-building efforts that led to the improvements in programming.

At face value, local monetization of food aid is thus a more flexible way of making use of food aid resources, recognizing that food alone is an insufficient input to address food insecurity in all its complexity. Nevertheless, all the old concerns about monetization of program food aid by recipient country governments – market displacement effects, the inefficiency of the form of the transfer, etc. – apply equally to NGO monetization of project and emergency food aid. We discuss these issues in greater detail in Chapter 9.

In addition, monetization is a very inefficient means for making cash resources available for development programming. Procurement and shipping costs still eat up budgets because the food aid is shipped to the country in which programs supported by monetization are implemented, and then sold there. Few NGOs get full market value for monetized food – the 2002 Farm Bill eliminated the former 80 percent of value minimum on monetization proceeds – and most incur added expenses (for staff, storage, credit, etc.) for undertaking monetization. Cost efficiency concerns have been noted with regard to NGO monetization for nearly as long as it has been practiced.[43]

While monetization practices have improved in recent years, the cumulative effect of procurement and transport costs and below-market prices, received for monetized food aid typically result in only a fraction of foreign assistance dollars actually reaching the programs that monetized food aid supports. Moreover, because NGOs commonly settle for below-market prices they often undersell local commercial traders, disrupting long-term relationships in recipient country commodity markets. We have heard several complaints about this from traders in different countries, not so much about facing competition from NGOs monetizing food aid, as about the adverse effects on the commercial marketing channel of inept competition. These traders range from local representatives of international agribusinesses, to small local traders of precisely the sort food aid monetization for market development is meant to help. The problem is not that the monetization limits are set too low. The problem is that international NGOs do not have any comparative advantage in grain trading and thus are of their nature noncompetitive in this activity, unless they significantly change the nature of staff skills and competencies in order to attend more effectively to food aid monetization. NGOs then have to hire and retain additional personnel with expertise in commodity marketing, commercial contracting, finance, and logistics. Monetized proceeds must be deposited into special accounts that are handled separately from other resources. While a few private sector-oriented NGOs such as Africare and Technoserve do not seem to find this problematic, many others indicate that monetization detracts from institutional focus on humanitarian or development goals and is at best inconvenient. Some of these problems get resolved in places where several NGOs all receive and monetize food aid, enabling them to work cooperatively, enjoying some economies of scale with a single NGO – presumably with local comparative advantage in commercial commodity operations – taking a lead in such "umbrella monetization."

Furthermore, other problems beset development programs dependent on monetization. While program funds tend to be needed on an on-going basis, monetization can only be done at certain times and with certain commodities in order to avoid negatively affecting local markets. This often means that program expenses out-pace resource acquisition, and the implementing agency has to borrow money to finance program operations pending receipt of monetization proceeds, thereby adding to program costs, or slow down or stop program implementation, thereby reducing program effectiveness. And of course the price for the commodity to be monetized fluctuates on local markets, subjecting program budgets to sudden changes that may require drastic changes in the nature of the program itself.

A recent comprehensive study of food aid monetization recommends monetization as the "first-best" option for programming only when (1) a country has a chronic food and balance of payments deficit; (2) the commodity available for monetization is appropriate to local conditions; and (3) agencies working in the country can achieve local market development goals *more efficiently* through the monetization of food aid commodities than through the use of cash resources – a very restrictive set of circumstances.[44] The authors of that study recommend that cash resources should gradually replace food aid in all USAID Title II non-emergency programs where these conditions do not hold, with the exception of monetization during an acute food crisis to make food available in urban markets and enable policymakers to exert some control over food prices that might otherwise spike in the face of short-term supply shortfalls and speculative behavior by private traders.

Conclusion

The preceding considerations suggest that food aid can indeed effectively meet recipient requirement for adequate food in humanitarian emergencies; in social protection and safety nets, as insurance against difficult-to-reverse loss of crucial productive assets, especially human health; and sometimes in support of more general development efforts. But for food aid to address food insecurity effectively, it must be incorporated into an overall analysis of the underlying causes of chronic poverty and vulnerability, integrated into well thought-out community-based preparedness and mitigation plans, and linked to other programmatic inputs that can enable chronically poor and food insecure people to lift themselves out of poverty. The foregoing analysis raises serious questions as to when food is an appropriate resource for development activities, whether monetized or distributed directly. It is clear that improvements in human nutritional status, asset protection, school attendance, and a variety of other areas have been made using food aid. Questions linger nonetheless as to whether the same improvements could have been made much more efficiently using resources other than food aid. We develop the prescriptive implications of this analysis more fully in Chapter 10. Now we turn our attention to the management of food aid in addressing food insecurity and the consequences of poor food aid management.

8　The management of food aid in addressing food insecurity

Even with a more explicitly recipient-driven approach to food aid, numerous operational issues arise that limit its effectiveness and make food aid, even in the best of circumstances, a cumbersome resource for programming. In particular, questions abound regarding targeting, timeliness, information systems for early warning, procurement, and supply chain management. Many useful lessons have been learned in recent years. Continued improved practice in food aid management will go a long way toward allaying concerns that the availability of a resource as a byproduct of donor country farm support programs, rather than good contextual analysis of recipient needs and constraints, drives food aid decision-making. This section briefly reviews these issues and ties back to the more macro-oriented concerns discussed in earlier chapters.

Targeting[1]

Targeting is essential if food aid is to succeed in its core humanitarian purpose of providing temporary relief to acutely food-insecure people. Broadly speaking, the issue of "targeting" concerns the who, the where, the when, the how, the what, and the how much questions surrounding transfers. Does food aid reach people who need it (and does not flow to people who do not need it), when and where they need it, in appropriate form, in appropriate quantities, and through effective modalities? There has been considerable research in recent years on targeting transfers generally, much of it motivated by the search for effective targeting mechanisms that do not require costly administrative screening.[2] Targeting is of special importance in food aid for four basic reasons. Virtually all recognized experts on food aid and operational agencies recognize and endorse these objectives and their importance.[3]

First, like any resource, food aid is scarce. Each food aid dollar goes further and has greater impact the more effectively limited resources are targeted at those places and individuals for whom it will register the greatest positive impact. This is the logic underpinning all targeting issues in economics. The other three reasons for targeting's importance are more specific to food as a resource.

Second, in so far as food aid is meant to satisfy food-insecure people's right to food, its efficacy is measurable purely in terms of whether there are targeting errors of omission, that is, whether food-insecure people receive at least enough food to bring them up to agreed nutritional minima. Given the Sphere standard of 2,100 kilocalories/day per person, this is a tall order requiring (unrealistically?) effective targeting.

Third, food is a critical resource. People who go without enough and appropriate food for even a relatively short period of time can suffer irreversible health effects of undernutrition and related diseases. Therefore, reaching people who would otherwise suffer undernutrition, in a timely manner, and in an appropriate form is especially important for the effectiveness of food transfers. And if done corrrectly, food transfers can be fundamental to an effective development strategy, by safe-guarding the most valuable asset of the poor: the human capital embodied in their health, their skills and education, and most crucially, their ability to work and earn a living.

Fourth, the key alleged set of problems surrounding food aid – displaced inter-national trade, depressed producer prices in recipient countries, labor supply disincentives, delivery delays, misuse by intermediaries, diversion to resale or feeding livestock or alcohol brewing, dependency, inattention to beneficiaries' micronutrient needs, etc. – all revolve ultimately around questions of targeting, as broadly defined above. If the targeting of food aid is done correctly, it would improve the effectiveness of food aid in accomplishing its primary purpose, and reduce many of the errors that sometimes make food aid controversial, ineffective, or both.

A limited amount of descriptive research has explored *ex post* whether food aid has reached intended beneficiaries, and has found considerable targeting errors of inclusion (providing aid to people who don't need the assistance) and exclusion (failure to reach those who genuinely do) at both macro and micro levels. There have also been considerable efforts at improving *ex ante* food aid targeting through the development and refinement of early warning systems, vulnerability mapping, as well as supply chain innovations, so that aid might reach needy people in a more reliable and timely fashion. We discuss those complementary interventions in the next subsection. Here we focus exclusively on targeting issues, but these issues really are inextricable from one another.

In theory, the targeting issue is easy to understand: some countries – or some regions of a particular country, some households within a given community, or even some individuals within a household – do not have access to enough food to be able to meet their nutritional requirements. Targeting is simply the practice of ensuring that those (countries, regions, households, individuals) that require food actually receive it, and that those who do not require it do not get it (whether instead of or in addition to the intended beneficiaries). In practice, few tasks are operation-ally more difficult than ensuring that those with a genuine need get food assistance while those who do not are excluded.

Targeting: the "where?" and "who?" questions

The targeting of groups to receive food aid is a three-step process: defining *who* should be targeted; deciding *how to identify* that group; and ensuring that the assistance *actually reaches* that group.[4] Table 8.1 illustrates the first task of targeting – the question of "who?" The task of a recipient-driven approach to food aid is to target genuinely food-insecure communities, households or individuals, while excluding those who are food-secure. Thus, for example, reaching a genuinely food-insecure household (Cell 1) would be considered a success in targeting terms, as would not providing a food aid transfer to a genuinely food-secure household (Cell 4). In contrast, food aid provided to a food-secure household (Cell 2) would be considered an inclusion error or *leakage* error, while a food-insecure household that received nothing would be labeled an exclusion or *undercoverage* error. Both types of errors have serious consequences. Inclusion errors waste resources and lie at the heart of claims of food aid dependency, and disruption of markets and local producer incentives (see Chapter 9). Exclusion errors, on the other hand, come at a high humanitarian cost because households that cannot produce or purchase enough food do not receive food, or do not receive an adequate amount. Note that while Table 8.1 appears to be about specific groups of food-insecure people, it can apply at any level, national and regional, as well as households or even individuals.

All real-world transfer programs suffer targeting errors for the simple reasons that (1) information is costly to collect and process because it is impossible to have perfect information about all people at all times (i.e., to know who does and does not require assistance); and (2) actual allocations are made for multiple reasons, only one of which is objectively measurable need. Food aid targeting is arguably made especially difficult by the facts that (3) food insecurity is inherently unobservable and thus agencies must use imperfect indicators to try to distinguish between those who need food assistance and those who do not; (4) agricultural prices and surpluses in donor countries significantly affect food aid flows yet are themselves heavily affected by massive domestic farm support programs driven by local political considerations in donor countries; and (5) food moves relatively slowly and expensively (as compared to finance, for example), creating logistical challenges that can bring on targeting errors in space and time.

Because a program without targeting errors is practically impossible, there exists a difficult tradeoff between wasteful and distortionary errors of inclusion and

Table 8.1 Targeting: inclusion and exclusion of groups

	Food-insecure	*Food-secure*
Receives food aid	1. Successful targeting	2. Inclusion error (Leakage)
Does not receive food aid	3. Exclusion error (Under-coverage)	4. Successful targeting

Source: Adapted from Hoddinott (1999)

potentially damaging errors of exclusion that violate the basic human right to food. There is no clearly superior direction in which to err. The difficulty of this tradeoff makes minimization of targeting errors essential.

So what does the empirical record on food aid targeting look like? At the national level, quite a few studies have found at best weak relationships between various indicators of nonconcessional food availability in recipient countries and the food aid volumes they receive.[5] One reason is that food aid is multiply targeted, first to a recipient country with a particular bundle of commodities, and then to a region within the country, and finally to a particular group within that region through a particular form of food assistance. Targeting errors occur at all these levels.

The first reaction of many food aid practitioners is to attribute historical targeting errors in international food aid allocations to a fading emphasis on program food aid, which has always been heavily oriented towards donor objectives rather than recipient need. As noted in earlier chapters, however, although program food aid has shrunk rapidly in recent years, and humanitarian or emergency food aid has now become the principal type of food aid flow, food aid remains heavily donor-oriented at the macro-level for myriad reasons. As a consequence, statistical analysis finds that PL 480 Title II humanitarian food aid performs no better than PL 480 Titles I and III program and Title II non-emergency project food aid, nor has there been any improvement over time, in stabilizing food availability in recipient economies despite the shifting of focus to humanitarian assistance.[6]

At the macro-level, the empirical evidence shows that both bilateral and multi-lateral food aid allocation is modestly progressive, meaning that relatively more goes to those countries with the largest food deficits. Food aid today is mainly directed toward low-income food-deficit countries and recipients' average food aid inflows modestly increase as their per capita nonconcessional supplies from domestic production and commercial imports fall.[7] But the relationship between need, as reflected in various food security or nutrition indicators, and food aid inflows is weak and the average response of food aid flows to each unit (e.g., kilocalorie per day per person) increase in need is quite small.[8] This progressivity is not necessarily fine-tuned by year and country, sometimes just by region, which would be consistent with concerted response to cross-border movement of displaced persons, although the available data cannot establish whether this is indeed the appropriate explanation for the observed relationship. It is also clear that food aid needs assessment methodologies vary widely, making cross-country comparisons of food aid requirements difficult.[9]

It should come as no surprise that micro-level evidence yields similar findings. Several detailed recent studies from the Horn of Africa have found that food aid flows as frequently to the richest, most food-secure districts and households as it does to the poorest, most food-insecure ones, and that food aid flows typically do not respond to shocks to individual household income or productivity.[10] The inclusion/exclusion method of assessing targeting efficacy can be justifiably criticized on the grounds that it too often treats exclusion of people just below a poverty line the same as exclusion of those far below the line, whose omission presumably poses graver human and moral consequences, just as it penalizes inclusion of those only barely and temporarily above the poverty line as much as it does local elites. More recent regression-based assessments of food aid targeting nonetheless similarly find that food aid receipts respond weakly, if at all, to recipient income, assets or other measures of current well-being.[11] A range of studies from rural Africa find frequent targeting errors at community and household level, although the overall pattern is one of quite imperfectly progressive distribution.[12] Under some circumstances, particularly complex emergencies in which post-distribution monitoring is difficult or impossible, some experts suggest that the only way to ensure that targeted groups receive food assistance is to provide it in cooked form and enable recipients to actually eat it at the distribution site.[13]

Myth 8 Food aid reliably reaches hungry people and only hungry people

Ensuring that food aid reaches hungry people – and few or no non-hungry people – is the single most difficult task in managing food aid. Abundant evidence suggests that food aid does not always reach people who are acutely food-insecure (undermining the humanitarian objectives of food aid), and that it often ends up in the hands of people who are not acutely food-insecure (undermining international trade and incentives to local farmers and thus undermining some development objectives).

Targeting: the "how?" question

A variety of methods are used to target food aid at the micro-level. Each has its strengths and weaknesses. In the field, real programs therefore often combine more than one targeting method in an attempt to come up with an effective blend that will prove more effective.[14]

Administrative targeting based on screening of individual applications for assistance – a process used heavily in food assistance programs in Europe and North America – is generally too costly, time-consuming and information-demanding to prove feasible in most low-income regions. It is rarely used in targeting food aid distribution.

Operational agencies frequently practice "indicator" targeting, distributing food aid to subpopulations readily identifiable by age, gender, or location because in aggregate those cohorts are perceived as worse off than other broad, identifiable groups. The indicators used make enacting the restriction (e.g., to feed only children below a certain age at a center, to deliver food just to a region that has suffered severe drought) relatively simple. Types of indicator vary, but include physiological measures of vulnerability (nutritional or health status), demographic measures (women or women-headed households, the elderly), economic measure (asset ownership, wealth ranking) or measures of political vulnerability (displaced or minority groups). While many of these variables correlate broadly with food security status, no direct measure of food security exists, so one must necessarily use imperfect indicators.[15] Even where good information exists about the relation between these indicators and food security status, targeting on the basis of only a subset of such indicators will, by definition, incur errors of both inclusion and exclusion.

A major concern, however, is that indicator targeting relies on proxy measures that often entail substantial leakage within the targeted subpopulation, thereby weakening the safety net and pitting the transfer system against the commercial production and distribution system that otherwise serves consumers of sufficient means. Furthermore, if the indicator is not directly related to food insecurity, then the indicators employed may create significant targeting errors. For example, many targeting errors in rural Ethiopia have been associated with the use of gender and age indicators for targeting, resulting in a disproportionate number of female and aged heads of households receiving food aid even though their food needs did not differ significantly from those of the general population.[16]

The most popular current targeting methods are now "self-targeting" and "community-based targeting." Self-targeting transfers have no administrative restrictions on participation. In principle, the characteristics of the transfer are designed so that only those within a target beneficiary group self-select into participating, thereby obviating the need for costly administrative screening and minimizing leakage to the non-needy. Common self-targeting features of transfers include the (low) quality of a subsidized foodstuff, queuing to receive transfers, or a work requirement that carries a high opportunity cost of time for the relatively better-off. The cost (benefit) of participation is made an increasing (decreasing) function of one's pre-participation income or wealth, so that only the truly poor or acutely food-insecure people would find project participation attractive. Self-targeting methods have been used by government-run programs for a long time[17] but have become especially prominent in the past decade. The government of Ethiopia, for example, has a policy of committing 80 percent of food aid resources to food for work (FFW) programs based on the principle of self-targeting, although in practice this varies considerably, particularly in emergencies and in pastoral areas.[18]

Yet even self-targeting approaches, such as food for work and provision of only inferior foods typically eaten solely by the poorest peoples, suffer significant targeting errors. While much of the empirical evidence supports the claim that FFW – and self-targeting employment schemes more broadly – effectively reaches intended beneficiaries, several recent studies have found evidence that many nonpoor participate in FFW schemes, calling into question the efficacy of the self-targeting feature.[19] The most common explanation is that the FFW wages were set too high, inducing substitution of money wage work in the local labor market for FFW work, and thereby limiting the additionality of the FFW transfer since it largely substitutes for other income that would have been earned in the project's absence. Moreover, when wages are set too high, project managers commonly face excess labor supply – particularly from labor-surplus households – and have to ration participation in some fashion. There are good reasons to believe local elites enjoy a higher probability of selection for participation than do minorities or other marginalized groups. In addition to there commonly being unintended beneficiaries, many intended recipients get missed by FFW programs. In some cases this is because participating elites crowd them out; in other cases, it is simply not having the labor to enable participation.

In some cases, FFW wages are set too low to enable the truly food-insecure to meet their food requirements. Extremely vulnerable individuals (usually women household heads) may opt into food for work programs, when in fact the size of their families, the amount of work required, and the wage received (in kind) actually result in a net *loss* of calories for the program participant.[20] This is a different, and too-often-overlooked, kind of "undercoverage" targeting error. The point is that the wage rate can at once be too high for labor-surplus households – which encourages some unintended participation – and too low for labor-deficit households – meaning that intended participants get left out. The self-targeting feature of FFW schemes is too often naïvely assumed to eliminate difficult targeting challenges for program administrators.

At other times, finite transfer resources limit the geographic reach of the program to a few administratively selected locations. In programs such as FFW that are trying to couple long-term development benefits with the short-term safety net function of the transfer, programs are often placed where the expected return on investment is great rather than where need for assistance is greatest, trading off targeting errors for investment efficacy. Imperfect or missing local labor, land and finance markets can likewise distort incentives, leading the poor to opt out of FFW programs and the relatively well-off to self-select into them. For all of these reasons, self-targeting is a relatively blunt instrument, and many food for work programs in practice combine self-targeting with some kind of administrative or indicator targeting, both for inclusion in the food for work program and for those who require a supplementary component of food to protect against undernutrition.

In community-based targeting, donors and operational agencies wholly delegate responsibility and authority for household- or individual-level targeting to local leaders. The theory is that geographic indicator targeting – i.e., targeting of a region based purely on geographic indicators, such as rainfall, prevailing food prices, or regional average rates of child anthropometric measures such as wasting (reflected in a child's very low weight for height ratio) – can quickly, inexpensively and accurately identify food insecure areas, within which local leaders have better information with which to identify which households or individuals should receive food aid and how much. Letting the community do the targeting exploits local information advantages and has been shown to be effective in, for example, Albania or Tanzania, as described in Box 8.1.[21] Of course, in communities where there exist significant cleavages (e.g., along religious, ethnic, or caste lines), or in which there live significant numbers of recent immigrants not yet well assimilated into the community, or whose leadership is corrupt or venal, provision of a significant, discretionary resource can reinforce preexisting social problems. A recent review of case studies and the theory of community involvement in beneficiary selection and transfers delivery points out that elite capture, strategic targeting by local communities, and local preferences that are not pro-poor can all undermine the efficacy of community-based targeting.[22] It can equally prove politically difficult to offer anything other than a uniform distribution of food to everyone within a community, as has been the prevailing practice among community-based food aid targeting in much of northern Kenya in recent years or Ethiopia.[23] There may be substantial cultural differences in the perception and understanding of vulnerability between community leaders and external food aid managers. For all these reasons, community-based targeting can fail in spite of its informational advantages, just as self-targeting can fail in spite of its theoretically superior incentive structures.

Box 8.1 Community-based targeting in Tanzania[1]

Given the difficulties with administrative methods of targeting, many agencies began experimenting with more community-based methods of selecting food aid recipients in the 1990s. Not only is administrative targeting expensive, in both financial and informational terms, but external criteria of who is vulnerable and who is not are often very different from localized perceptions. Increased control over targeting has become one method of empowering local communities to take responsibility for disaster management, linked to other community-based emergency preparedness activities.

For example, a drought in central Tanzania in 1998–99 required a major food aid response. Save the Children (UK) and the Tanzania Christian Refugee Service implemented a program in which local communities supervised targeting and distribution. Decisions were made by a local committee that had to include at least one man and one woman from each sub-village in the location. External facilitators helped these committees think through the criteria for receiving food aid, and ensured delivery, but not with decisions about both the criteria and the actual distribution lists and household allocations. Village selection lists were read out in public meetings, and were subject to community discussions. While the system required a substantially greater amount of time and effort by community members, the evaluation showed a much greater level of appreciation for the food aid response than in more standard programs. The program was seen to be transparent and fair. And once the system was up and running, it actually required less time at distribution sites, because there were fewer administrative checks to carry out.

The evaluation of the program indicated that community-based targeting works very well under some circumstances, including: (a) a well-established village government with a tradition of public meetings; (b) consistent national policies on the right of participation; (c) peace and cohesion in local communities; (d) absence of intra-communal divisions (for example, no marginalized ethnic minorities); (e) no excessive stress (not a famine in which people are already starving); and (f) availability of agency staff with facilitation skills (rather than just logistical or accounting skills). Subsequent experience has shown that community-based targeting can work even in the absence of some of these conditions, but may require some additional administrative oversight – particularly ensuring that some minority groups aren't left out in situations where multiple ethnic communities share the same locations.

Note:
[1]   Based on Shoham (1999a) and Rideout (1999).

The general conclusion in much of the practical literature is that there is not a single correct means of targeting food aid. How one implements the targeting seems to matter as much as, if not more than, the choice of targeting method. But prevailing wisdom based on much accumulated experience over the past couple of decades suggests focusing first on getting geographic targeting right. Get food aid to the most food-deficit areas quickly, and worry relatively less about inclusion errors at a localized level. Given the increasing importance of rights-based approaches, many operational agencies place increasing emphasis on community participation in and control over local targeting practices, but monitor to ensure that minority or other groups are not excluded. But this sometimes results in blanket distribution of food aid at levels much below assessed requirements for targeted groups, and corresponding overprovision of food aid to groups assessed to need little or no assistance.[24] This underscores a fundamental question of whose criteria should underpin assessment: communities' views of vulnerability commonly differ from those of external evaluators.[25] So one major remaining unresolved issue is aligning assessment practices with targeting practices. All the issues surrounding the theory and practice of targeting revolve on the question of good information, a topic taken up below.

Targeting: the "what?" question

Targeting concerns not only the identity of recipients or the timing of transfers; the form of transfers matters as well. Historically, food aid has been the form most convenient to the donor rather than most beneficial to recipients. Too often, this means that the appropriateness of any given response is not seriously reviewed, and a request for food aid goes out as soon as a food security problem is assessed. Or food aid may be rapidly forthcoming in an emergency, but complementary forms of assistance may not be forthcoming, or may lag far behind, thereby undermining the benefits of the food aid intervention.[26] In recent years, a few European donors have made significant shifts in their food aid strategies, away from domestic farm support and export promotion and in favor of attending to recipient nutritional needs at minimum cost (see Chapter 3). Unfortunately, this remains largely the exception rather than the rule.

Sometimes what poor or emergency-affected groups most need to ensure their food security is not food – or at least not the type of food being provided through food aid distribution – but rather health care, clothing, shelter, or other essential goods and services. Recall our earlier discussion (in Chapter 7) about the "fungibility premium" on cash wage payments over wages paid in food in public employment schemes in rural Ethiopia. The existence of a substantial cash premium suggests significant mistargeting at the resource level. This observation reinforces the point that the justification for transfers in kind turns on the need to resolve a local supply problem for the foodstuff in question since the transfers become more expensive per recipient to achieve the same desired end of support.[27]

The controversy over the inclusion of genetically modified foods in food aid shipments (see Chapter 4) similarly reflects important questions surrounding targeting of the form of a transfer. In the 2002 Zambia case, considerable expense, time and political goodwill were wasted due to the provision of food aid in a form that, while arguably safe for human consumption, nonetheless proved politically unacceptable and perhaps environmentally inappropriate. The Food Aid Convention commits donors to providing foods that are culturally appropriate for the recipients, but that injunction is not always heeded carefully.[28]

The issue of what type of food to provide concerns not just commodities or varieties, but also the question of whether to provide raw or processed product. Outside of supplemental feeding programs – whether in development projects or acute humanitarian emergencies – and the more recent controversies surrounding genetically modified food aid, donors are typically loathe to incur milling costs for donated grains. The distribution of whole grain instead of flour can affect the impact of food aid. For example, cooking trials showed that granular maize distributed to pastoralists in north central Kenya in response to drought in 2000–1 took significantly longer to cook than flour, requiring more fuelwood and demanding more of women's time for cooking and firewood collection. The pastoralists receiving the grain had neither access to mills – little maize is grown in the region – nor a tradition of grinding maize meal themselves. So they would eat the cooked granular maize. A recent study shows that there would be significant gains to both the natural environment – by reducing fuelwood demand – and to local women – due to time savings – from hiring women or small businesses locally to mill the bulk grain, which would have the additional benefit of stimulating local employment and the regional food processing subsector.[29]

While food requirements in acute emergencies are most frequently thought of in terms of calories, **micronutrient** deficiencies pose an increasing concern, particularly given improvements in nutritionists' understanding of the role of micronutrients in the general maintenance of good health.[30] In addition, micronutrient malnutrition may be widely prevalent in populations even before an acute emergency occurs. Some 2 billion people worldwide are believed to have chronic deficiencies in one or more micronutrients.[31] Fortification of food aid is a relatively cheap and effective means of supplementing micronutrient intake, particularly for people heavily reliant on food aid and who do not have access to other food-based sources. Providing fortified foods to such groups is now part of World Food

Programme policy. However, such foods must be processed at least to some extent. Vegetable oil, for example, is the usual food fortified with vitamin A. Milled cereal or blended foods can be fortified with multiple vitamins and minerals, while whole grain cereal cannot easily be fortified. Nonfat dried milk powder is sometimes fortified with vitamin D to prevent rickets. Insofar as a large share of such processed foods must inevitably come from the world's main food aid donor – the United States – and US policy places severe restrictions on who may undertake such processing and where, the cost, availability and timeliness of processed food aid delivery all become compromised by donor country commercial interests.[32]

Targeting: the "when?" question

An oft-overlooked feature of targeting relates to timing. There are at least two dimensions to the timing question. First, food aid can be targeted for moments in time when intended recipients' vulnerability proves especially damaging, as when they are at heightened risk for malnutrition-related disease in emergencies or when seasonal food insecurity distorts production and investment behavior, as during the planting season for many poor rural farming households. Properly timed food aid delivery can remedy vulnerable households' problems of access to adequate food, protecting their productive assets and sometimes even crowding-in investment (see Box 9.2 in the next chapter for one example). Second, at the more macro-level, food aid in relatively large volumes could be used to stabilize prices and food availability if donors adjust food aid flows in response to (positive and negative) shocks to food output, world market prices, and foreign exchange availability in recipient countries. In this way, food aid could provide a counter-cyclical transfer – meaning it increases when nonconcessional food availability decreases – so as to help reduce food insecurity. If food aid is to respond effectively to short-term shocks to recipient country food availability, donors need to identify emerging needs early and deliver the food quickly. In fact, bilateral food aid tends to flow pro-cyclically – increasing when food available from own production and commercial imports increases, contrary to the rhetoric and intention of food aid – for multiple reasons.[33]

First, the complex logistics of procuring and transporting food causes much food aid – especially program food aid – to suffer extraordinarily long lags between the time of commitment and delivery. Lags of up to two years in flows from the European Union are not uncommon.[34] Data on PL 480 flows show similarly long lags. In 1994, the US General Accounting Office reported that USAID did not at that time have a system to expedite the approval of emergency food requests. As a consequence, it took nearly three months on average to approve requests from the WFP and submit them to USDA to initiate commodity procurement operations. Ultimately, United States donations to WFP emergency operations took, on average, nearly eight months to reach the destination, ranging from 43 to 345 days.

The timeliness of USAID emergency response has improved somewhat over time, but delays remain considerable. Even emergency shipments faced a median lag of 139 days (almost five months) in 1999–2000 between the **call forward** date (the date of formal procurement, which follows the initiation of a request, often by

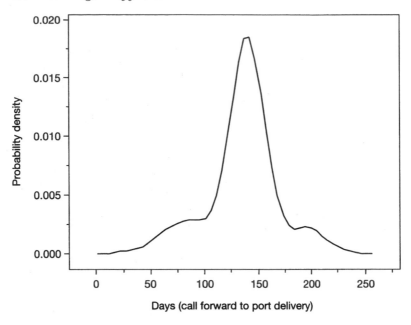

Figure 8.1 US Title II emergency shipments delivery lags

months) and the date of delivery to port (which precedes delivery to individual recipients by weeks or months), as shown in Figure 8.1.[35] Note that these delivery lag figures are for emergency shipments for which timeliness is crucial, not for programmed non-emergency shipments for which lags can be planned without complication. These lags arise due to inevitable bureaucratic delays compounded by heavy reliance on domestic procurement of both food and sea-freight shipping services. International food aid shipments based on donor country government procurement mechanisms are just inherently slow. Estimates of the resource transfer inefficiency of food aid shipped from donor countries (see below) inevitably omit this crucial but very real cost of transoceanic food shipments. This increases the importance of timely and accurate early warning and needs assessment systems and of inter-donor coordination so as to ensure that food aid does not arrive too late to address acute humanitarian emergencies. Ultimately, however, these situations are subject to political determinants that can disrupt deliveries to even long-anticipated emergencies in places where food aid distribution operations have become reasonably efficient through considerable practice, as the Ethiopia crisis of 2000 clearly showed.[36]

Delayed deliveries can also pose problems for NGOs running programs that depend on monetized food aid. Beyond the obvious problem that shipment delays can interrupt the flow of monetization proceeds, another serious problem arises when PL 480 Title II shipments approved for monetization arrive into port at the same time as PL 480 Title I food aid or commercial food shipments. Then the NGO has to find storage for the shipment – on short notice and often at high rental rates – because the **Bellmon Amendment** prohibits it from monetizing the shipment in direct competition with US commercial exporters.

Second, because donors budget food aid on a monetary basis, food aid flow volumes generally covary negatively with international market prices and donor country food inventories.[37] In other words, aggregate food aid from donors is most readily available when prices of food are low. Of course, this does not mean that food aid supplied to a particular recipient varies with global food prices, although there is in general clear, positive co-movement of shipments to individual countries with aggregate food aid donations. As a consequence, food aid volumes are far more volatile than are food production or trade volumes. Available food aid volumes tend to shrink precisely when importing countries most need concessional food flows – when food prices rise – causing both food import volumes and food import unit costs to increase. Program food aid disbursement patterns may thereby destabilize food availability and prices in recipient nations.

The third and final reason for the procyclicality of food aid flows is inertia. This is manifest in statistical findings across multiple data sets that last year's food aid receipt volume is the single best predictor of this year's food aid flows.[38] Administrative inertia and chronic need lead to considerable momentum in food aid flows. Figure 8.2[39] shows that the probability of future PL 480 receipt – in either one unbroken spell of annual deliveries or in a sequence of spells subject to interruption – is at least 70 percent for a country that has already received PL 480, no matter the number of years the country has already received food aid. The WFP's extensive use of supplemental resources raised through emergency appeals seems to reduce inter-annual inertia in food aid shipments to any given country relative to analogous parameter estimates found with respect to PL 480.[40] Inertia commonly leads to targeting errors, however. There exists strong empirical evidence of food aid inertia, both at multinational level in WFP food distribution, wherein aid flows to regions based on generalized need without regard to year or country-specific

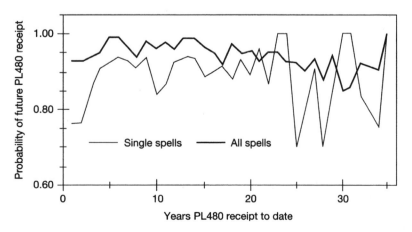

Figure 8.2 Persistent food aid flows

Source: Barrett (1998)

food availability, as well as intra-national regional inertia in food aid distribution within Ethiopia.[41]

This raises a corollary to the "when?" question: "for how long?" or "when to stop?" These questions apply in emergencies as well as in longer-term programs that use food aid.[42] For all the discussion about exit strategies, there are few firm conclusions in the literature or in operational agency practice. There remains a distinct need for monitoring capacity and indicators that inform humanitarian managers when it is time to move out of a response to an acute emergency, and make specific suggestions for the information sources needed and the programmatic alternative to be considered.[43] Building or strengthening local institutional capacities is an important component.[44] The consequences of failing to transition out of providing food aid are similar to other targeting failures. Planning on transition and exit strategies from the beginning is critical in development programs using food aid.[45]

Myth 9 Food aid reliably arrives when it is needed

Food aid purchased in North America or Europe takes a long time to reach locations in Sub-Saharan Africa and South Asia, averaging almost five months even for emergency shipments of Title II PL 480 food aid from the United States. Early warning systems and strategic food reserves have helped to ensure that food aid is available when needed. But food aid still frequently arrives too late to help avert malnutrition or distress sales of key productive assets, and in some especially tragic cases, too late even to avert the loss of life.

Targeting: the "how much?" question

The "what? " and "how much?" questions are often labeled "assessment" rather than "targeting" questions. But in the overall scheme of attempting to provide food assistance to people who urgently require it (from both a needs perspective and a rights perspective), the issue of how much food to provide becomes inextricable from the classical targeting questions of "who," "where," and "when?" Huge disparities in the quantity of humanitarian response (both of food aid and other forms of international transfers) have been widely documented in cross-national comparisons, both on a per-capita basis, and on the basis of the ratio between assessed requirements and the collective response.[46]

The determination of needs can be exceedingly difficult, and multiple methods have been employed by various actors in attempting to identify and plan for food aid needs.[47] As a 1989 gold standard review by the US National Research Council emphasized, the variation among projections at relevant scales of analysis – individual countries or sub-national regions – has historically been considerable and each assessment method's estimates have generally proved highly unreliable as a predictor of either actual shortfalls or food aid flows.[48] This should not be terribly surprising because (1) the availability of reliable data on which to base accurate yield, demand and price forecasts tends to be weak in the poor countries most in need of food assistance; (2) much need is based on humanitarian emergencies that are typically difficult to predict far in advance; and (3) needs assessments are politically sensitive exercises for all involved. All needs assessment methods are inherently contestable for these reasons.

Nonetheless, some of the guesswork in food aid needs assessment has been substantially reduced over the past decade or so. At the macro-level of long-lead, country-level needs assessments, the USDA – which has a Congressional mandate to produce annual food security assessments that ostensibly inform food aid allocations – has continued to refine its assessment methods. More importantly, the rise of the FAO's Global Information and Early Warning System (GIEWS),[49] launched in 1975 following the world food crisis of 1973–74, has created a generally accepted set of needs estimates that are continuously updated based on satellite imagery and new information from a variety of sources. At more micro-levels of analysis and with nearer-term horizons, the widespread adoption of methods such as the household food economy approach developed by Save the Children have likewise improved the apparent reliability of needs assessments for food aid programming.[50]

Despite these improvements, rapid and accurate assessment of the food requirements of a population and their own ability to provide for those requirements (to arrive at a quantitative estimate of the gap that defines food aid requirements) remains an enormous and difficult task. Needs assessment necessarily involves reliance on a variety of assumptions, including the statistical representativeness of very small samples; the truthfulness of respondents facing clear strategic incentives to overstate their needs; the ability of external analysts to quickly come to grips with local realities, etc. Conflict significantly compounds these analytical difficulties, as does the existence of significant numbers of displaced persons and strong patterns of intra-community discrimination. Food aid needs estimation remains as much an art as a science. Because the human costs of poor information are high and pressures to act quickly are equally great, informed guesswork is a staple of the trade. All of these factors make delivering the right amount to the right people at the right time an exceedingly complex operational task. The costs of delivering too little can be substantial, however, as highlighted in Box 8.2 on Ethiopia. In Chapter 9 we will likewise discuss the problems of delivering too much food.

Box 8.2 Under-response: explaining the rapid onset of a "slow-onset disaster"

In July and August 2002, it rapidly became clear that a major drought emergency was shaping up once again in Ethiopia, particularly hitting the zones of East and West Hararghe, in the eastern highlands and surrounding lowland areas. While drought is classically considered to be a "slow-onset" emergency, this crisis hit with stunning speed, with the change from a relatively "normal" situation to a full-blown emergency response in a matter of two months. What explains this rapid deterioration? While there are many reasons, one of the major ones was that the coping capacity of local households had been so undermined by repeated emergencies in these two zones that a shock of any magnitude quickly sent them over the edge of survival. One of the reasons for this exhausted coping capacity was the failure of the food safety net in Ethiopia over a period of years. Figure 8.4 depicts Ethiopia's assessed food aid requirements for the eight years prior to the onset of the 2002/2003 crisis, and the actual amounts of food aid distributed.

The pattern of "under-response" is quite clear. On average roughly only two-thirds of assessed requirements are met. In fact, the proportion of assessed need that was actually met is higher during acute crisis years (2000) than in "good" years (1998). Given general knowledge about how people cope with food insecurity, it should not be surprising that over time, circumstances have forced the poorest Ethiopians to steadily sell off assets in order to survive in the short term, making them increasingly vulnerable to even relatively minor shocks. The intensity and speed with which the 2002/2003 crisis hit testify less to the magnitude of the shock that hit the area than to the exhausted capacity of the most vulnerable groups to cope with any kind of shock.

The same pattern noted in East and West Hararghe in 2002 was repeated all over the country as the crisis spread in 2003 (and in 2003, the proportion

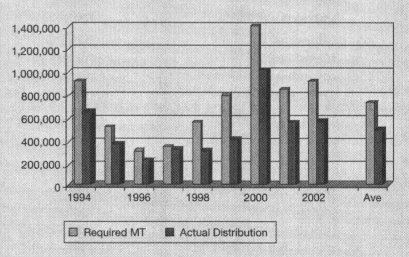

Figure 8.3 Food aid requirements and deliveries, Ethiopia 1994–2002

Source: WFP Ethiopia

of distribution to assessed need was again much higher than average). While meeting a high proportion of assessed need in crisis years is a laudable achievement, these data underscore the need for a safety net to mitigate the impact of fluctuations in the weather and other shocks in "non-crisis" years. The use of food aid in humanitarian response is considerably less controversial than is the use of food aid in safety nets – fears about food aid usage in the latter leading to dependency and undermining market incentives are widespread. But in situations of chronic vulnerability, the protection and improvement of assets – human as well as physical, natural and economic – are critical components of reducing both poverty and vulnerability to disasters. Providing assistance, including food aid, in the right amount in "good" years as well as "bad" years is critical, a point made repeatedly in the literature on famines in Ethiopia as well as elsewhere.[1]

Note:
[1]   Hammond and Maxwell (2002), Lautze *et al.* (2003), Devereux (2002a).

Summarizing the targeting issues

Effective targeting is the key to a recipient-oriented food aid system. It involves getting the right kind of food in the right quantity to the right people in the right place at the right time, and then getting it only to those people who actually need it to make up the difference between what they are able to provide for themselves and the amount they require to meet minimum standards for consumption. Over the past few decades, operational agencies and donors have invested a great deal in trying to refine and improve targeting systems in each of these dimensions. Targeting errors are inevitable because it is impossible to get perfect, timely information. But continued significant reduction in targeting errors appears feasible and likely as improvements continue in information systems and in targeting methods.

Different constituencies within the food aid community have different concerns about the impact of poor targeting. Agricultural producers (in both donor and recipient countries) worry mainly about targeting errors that may displace commercial sales of food and cause market prices to fall. Their concern therefore revolves around errors of inclusion related to food aid reaching unintended beneficiaries. Humanitarian agencies tend to be concerned primarily about exclusion errors, about malnourished women, children, or elderly, who are "missed" in the system of selecting the "right" people, the "right" place, or the "right" time. These errors undermine the right to food and leave people in a weakened, malnourished condition (or worse), and squander the most precious asset of poor or vulnerable people everywhere: their own labor. However, most operational agencies involved in distributing food aid also engage in development programming, and thus harbor concerns for the incentive effects of poor targeting associated with errors of inclusion as well. If these errors undermine the development of self-reliant production and marketing systems in areas receiving food aid – in effect, also squandering the labor of poor people – then they may predispose these areas to requiring food aid in subsequent years. Development agencies are thus concerned that the use of food aid as a safety net not contribute to perpetuating chronic poverty and food insecurity. Finally, food aid recipient communities' perceptions of "need" and appropriate intra-community targeting of external assistance often differ substantially from those of the donors and agencies that provide food aid. The maintenance of traditional social norms of sharing and equity and of established power relationships and social differentiation often matters a great deal to recipient communities and their leaders. True community-based food aid management of food aid is, in itself, a major task, quite apart from managing the rest of the supply chain.

In sum, targeting issues are legion and complex in food aid and the variety of interests held by different stakeholder groups implies the absence of a universal prescription as to how best to target food aid. In practice, the emphasis in recent years has been on geographic targeting, on getting food aid to the hardest hit areas or the most food deficit countries. There is much to commend in this minimalist approach. But clearly if food aid is to serve both a humanitarian purpose in protecting the right to food of vulnerable people while not undermining longer-term objectives of encouraging sustainable and self-reliant food production/marketing and consumer access systems, the targeting of food aid must improve substantially. This will require far better information than has been available to food aid managers in the past.

Information systems and sources[51]

In order to improve targeting, detailed information about food security status is required, in "real time," by food aid managers. The systems that collect, synthesize and disseminate information are therefore of critical importance to the overall functioning of a food aid management system. The humanitarian and development industries now largely accept that famines (or less severe food security crises) are not one-off events; they are the logical outcomes of underlying processes. If these processes are understood, monitored, and analyzed, it should then be possible to predict with some accuracy the onset of crises and who is likely to be affected by them. This is largely the premise underlying the whole idea of food security early warning systems, and indeed improvements in early warning have been a major achievement in recipient-oriented food aid systems. However, despite improvements, there remain major challenges in providing the kind of information needed to make intelligent policy and operational decisions regarding the management of food aid. This section briefly reviews the information systems required and the major information challenges remaining.

Over the years, the information available to managers has improved markedly, and in general, improved information systems are widely regarded as one of the success stories of the global fight against hunger.[52] Since the Sahelian droughts of the 1970s, and particularly since the catastrophic famines in the Horn of Africa in the 1980s, a broad consensus has emerged that much better advance notice is required about impending hazards and their potential to result in humanitarian disasters, and much progress has been made.

Major global or regional early warning systems now exist to monitor basic information related to food crises and the genesis of famine, including the FAO-Global Information Early Warning System (GIEWS) and the USAID-funded Famine Early Warning System Network (FEWSNET). The WFP's Vulnerability Assessment and Mapping (VAM) Unit synthesizes information from various sources into both global and national monitoring systems to track food insecurity. At the national level, many countries have invested substantially in improved information collection and analysis capacity. The rapid response to major food crises in both Southern Africa (2001–2) and the Horn of Africa (2002–3) can be attributed in large measure to the timely provision of information about impending crop failures and their interaction with underlying processes of destitution, as well as about the HIV/AIDS crisis.[53]

However, major challenges remain. As will be clear from the preceding section, while simply predicting the onset of a food crisis is useful in mobilizing a response – whether of food aid or of a more holistic nature – predicting a crisis is not sufficient for providing the detailed kind of information required to answer all the questions inherent to accurate targeting of food aid or other interventions. To be effective, these information systems must take into account much more than just food deficits and access problems, and they must inform many more constituencies than just food aid donors and managers.

Often the kind of information required to make good programmatic decisions may simply not be available, or the available information is of poor quality, methodologically *ad hoc* and spotty in terms of coverage.[54] The line between acute crises and chronic vulnerability has blurred considerably, requiring an integrated analysis of current trends and underlying causes. And the information requirements are much broader than just food crises, and certainly much broader than just food aid requirements.[55] This includes an analysis of livelihoods and the vulnerabilities that livelihood systems face; an analysis of underlying poverty trends and causes; an assessment of current needs, not only for food, but for health care, water, physical protection, and other human rights concerns as well. Information systems may be well tailored to one agro-ecological region or livelihood system, but completely fail in another. For example, the 1999–2000 crisis in Ethiopia was worst in lowland pastoral areas while Ethiopia's early warning system was designed for the highland agricultural areas, partially resulting in a slow and inadequate response.[56] Information systems therefore constitute a major element of effective response to acute emergencies, chronic vulnerability and to sustainable development issues related to food security.

Existing information systems suffer a number of problems: many were originally designed to do nothing more than predict drought or estimate food aid requirements, but now are called upon for a much broader set of applications.[51] They are commonly expected to provide all the kinds of information required for targeting (and for a much broader range of inputs than just food) as well as to monitor underlying poverty trends. In general, early warning systems were designed with drought or other natural disasters in mind, and are poorly equipped to analyse political causes of crises. A major criticism of information systems is that, even when generating good information, they are often poorly linked with response planning, thereby delaying intervention or otherwise making it difficult to meet even the most basic objectives of saving human lives, or protecting livelihoods and assets.[58]

Existing monitoring systems have often focused on supply chain management and commodity tracking, specifically of food aid flows, even though it is well known that most, if not all, humanitarian emergencies require a broader response than just food aid. While avoiding acute human suffering has been the objective of humanitarian interventions, most now also implicitly or explicitly embrace poverty reduction objectives as well. However, information systems can quickly become tasked to cover so much that they cannot cover any of it especially well or quickly. Coherent humanitarian information systems are comprised of a number of components, and the absence of any one of these may lead to a failure in humanitarian response, or may cause humanitarian and development efforts to be at cross purposes with each other.[59]

The typical components of existing food security information systems include early warning and response monitoring. These provide information necessary to predict the onset of a food crisis and provide some information about where the response needs to be. Emphasis on accurate assessment of needs has led to increased efforts to include this kind of information into existing systems, and has led to standardized, accepted methods such as the Food Economy Approach,[60] but also a variety of other methods, some of which incorporate both food security and nutritional assessment.[61] More in-depth approaches consider both an assessment of current status and an analysis of causal factors with a focus on both immediate life-saving interventions, and interventions that protect livelihoods and assets.

Procurement, supply chain management, and reserves

Along with changes in information systems that permit more responsive targeting of the appropriate intervention to the right groups of people at the right time, innovations in the way food is procured, transported, and stored have improved the ability of food aid managers to target food aid deliveries. In general, these innovations have improved the ability of food aid managers to provide assistance on a more timely basis.

Triangular transactions and local purchases

The targeting and information systems questions just discussed focus on the destination side of food aid flows: who should receive it, when, how to get it to them, etc. The source of the food provided as food aid matters as well to the effective use of food aid. Food given internationally as aid can be purchased in and sent from one or more donor countries in Australia, Europe, or North America,[62] or it can be purchased in the recipient country – so-called "local purchases" – or in a third country that neighbors the recipient country – what are known as "triangular transactions." A variation on the triangular transactions theme involved "swaps" or "commodity exchanges" – sometimes also referred to as "trilateral transactions" – wherein a donor ships food to a supplier country in exchange for (presumably more culturally appropriate) foods available in the supplier country which are then sent to the recipient. The terms of these barters can be wholly commercial, in which case the entire grant element of the donor's aid goes to the recipient country, or they can be concessional, meaning that the supplier country receives donor commodities worth more than the food it provides in exchange, reaping a *de facto* transfer in kind. The United States has been the primary practitioner of such trilateral transactions, largely because its food aid has historically been driven by farm surplus disposal objectives and trilateral exchanges enable surplus disposal; they do not require cash appropriations for procurement overseas.

The use of local purchases and triangular transactions is a product of the past 25 years, beginning in the late 1970s, most notably the 1979–83 relief operation on the Thai-Kampuchean border and the 1981–83 Zimbabwe Maize Train operation, the first large-scale coordinated donor efforts employing triangular transactions.[63] The Maize Train, funded by 20 donors and led by the World Food Programme, distributed Zimbabwean maize to 18 African countries until Zimbabwe suffered a drought and domestic shortages itself in 1984. Almost all the food aid donated by Sweden, the Netherlands, and Germany now comes in the form of local purchases or triangular transactions. The same is true for about three-quarters of the food aid provided by Switzerland, the United Kingdom, Norway, and Belgium.

Although local purchases and triangular transactions have become popular in rhetoric, their use remains limited in practice. By 1992, local purchases had reached about 500,000 metric tons annually, and have remained remarkably stable around that level ever since (Figure 8.4). Until the dawn of the twenty-first century, triangular transactions had been utilized more extensively than local purchases, accounting for more than 1.5 million metric tons annually, on average, 1992–95, before falling back below 1 million tons in 2001, to essentially the same volume as local purchases. Together, local purchases and triangular transactions peaked at nearly one-quarter of global food aid flows in 1997, before falling back to 10–17 percent annually 1999–2002.

The location of food aid procurement matters for multiple reasons. First, the method of food aid procurement affects the "when" and "what" dimensions of targeting. The delays between procurement and delivery are typically thought to be much shorter for local purchases and triangular transactions than they are for transoceanic food aid shipments, although there is no systematic data with which to make direct comparisons, and the limited available evidence is somewhat mixed.[64] Recall that the median lag between the call forward date and delivery to port was nearly five months for Title II PL 480 emergency shipments. In principle, these lags can be shortened dramatically by procuring food in nearby surplus regions for shipment to regions facing food availability deficits. Actual performance,

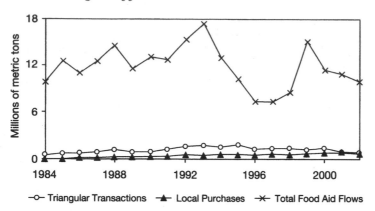

Figure 8.4 Local purchases and triangular transactions

Source: WFP INTERFAIS

however, depends on donor and operational agency efficiency and on local infrastructure. Moreover, there are places where logistical bottlenecks are so severe that local purchases provide food no faster (or even slower) than transoceanic shipments suffering below-average-to-average shipment delays.

Procurement location also matters to the appropriateness of the commodity distributed, in particular, whether it is suited to local tastes and dietary habits. Because food aid flows largely from temperate agroecosystems in Europe and North America to tropical agroecosystems in Africa, Asia, and Latin America, the foods grown in recipient and donor countries commonly differ. A classic example of the questionable suitability of the form of food aid involves massive American, Canadian, and European shipments of wheat to the Sahelian countries of West Africa in the emergencies of the mid-1970s and mid-1980s. Wheat is not native to these regions and is not commonly consumed, especially in rural areas, where millet and sorghum are the staples in the arid and semi-arid areas and rice is a staple in the river basins.[65] Food aid donors were excoriated by many observers for dumping inappropriate commodities into the region or even for following a Trojan Horse strategy, entering the local market surreptitiously through a gift in order to take over future commercial markets by changing consumer tastes.

The commodity appropriateness issue concerns varieties of foods, as well, such as the crucial distinction between white and yellow maize. White maize is the staple food in much of east and southern Africa. Yet northern donor countries grow little white maize. They produce mainly the yellow variety, commonly called "corn." The two commodities are imperfect substitutes to African consumers,[66] but are often treated as if they were the same thing by donor country officials. Donors have become far more sensitized to this issue over time, but it remains nonetheless and inevitably so due to the basic geography of global agricultural production.

Third, the source location matters in so far as it channels whatever demand stimulus may result from food aid procurement to producers and processors in the source market. As we discuss in greater detail in Chapter 9, the market price effects of food aid distribution have long been a prominent concern because food aid deliveries, by expanding local supply will, all else held equal, decrease the price local producers receive for their produce, thereby depressing the incentives they face. A widespread argument in favor of local purchase has been its potential to create an offsetting demand expansion in the recipient country – albeit typically in a different, food surplus region of the country, not precisely where food aid is to be distributed – that could improve local farmers' incentives to grow food. The argument in favor of triangular transactions is similar, that food procurement in one developing country for distribution in a neighboring country can have stimulative effects on the source country agricultural sector while providing emergency relief to the destination country. The donor can supposedly thereby get more bang for the food aid buck, although the actual impact of either local purchases or triangular transactions on market prices and producer incentives has not yet been established through careful empirical analysis. As we discussed in Chapters 2 and 3, the source-market price effects of food aid procurement in donor countries – as distinct from the price premia enjoyed by successful, registered suppliers to government procurement agents – are negligible. But given weaker demand and poorer market integration in developing countries, it remains an open question as to what effect local purchases and triangular transactions have on farmgate prices there. Market demand stimuli tend to have greater price effects in markets that are less well integrated with global markets because supply is more price inelastic.

Livestock destocking projects seem to offer a good example of weakly integrated markets where local food aid procurement can make a difference. Livestock markets appear poorly integrated across space in most of rural Africa – at least outside the peri-urban regions with easy access to metropolitan markets – and when drought hits, livestock prices collapse.[67] Poor pastoralists have trouble finding buyers for weakened animals that may not survive until the next rains. Destocking projects buy up animals in remote parts of drought-stricken rangelands, providing poor families with desperately needed cash. Purchased animals can then be inspected, slaughtered and the meat distributed (either fresh or dried) to provide inexpensive protein, calories and valuable micronutrients to local schools, hospitals and relief food distribution programs, benefiting poor consumers as well as supplier pastoralists. Livestock offtake linked to local distribution of meat offers an excellent example of a local purchase that provides culturally appropriate and nutritionally valuable food to food-insecure subpopulations while also benefiting food-insecure producers and without disrupting broader markets.

The perception that food aid procurement affects local market prices influences the political support for food aid by farm lobbies in donor countries. Food aid administrators have a tougher time selling local purchases and triangular trans-actions to legislators more concerned about domestic constituencies than they are about small farmers or hungry peoples abroad. The success of many European donors in moving to more progressive food aid procurement modalities nonetheless proves that the case can be made effectively, even in the presence of powerful domestic farm lobbies.

The appropriateness of local purchases or triangular transactions as a food aid procurement method turns fundamentally on two necessary conditions: (1) poor market integration of destination markets with nearby source markets; and (2) the existence of exportable food near areas of significant food availability deficits. If markets are well integrated within a food aid recipient country and between countries within a region, then the injection of financial resources into the distribution location with which operational agencies can purchase food, should suffice to elicit commercial flows into that market. Then there is no need for food aid donors to spend time and money on transport and other logistical issues, especially since they are generally unlikely to handle the logistics of shipments more efficiently than commercial traders. This is the essence of the "aid for food" instead of food aid argument championed by Shlomo Reutlinger, a longtime observer and thoughtful critic of conventional food aid,[68] hence the necessity of poor market integration to justify food aid, a point to which we return in Chapters 10 and 11.

The empirical evidence on food market integration in developing countries suggests that prices indeed covary and commodities flow between spatially distinct markets in response to demand or supply shocks in one or the other. Market integration is imperfect, to be sure, and there are significant areas where high marketing costs effectively create spatially segmented markets. But the empirical evidence to date suggests that commercial food market integration in low-income countries is generally better than most commentators acknowledge.[69]

The second necessary condition concerns the availability of exportable foods in markets near the intended site of food aid distribution. In statistical terms, this is a matter of the degree to which market food availability – defined as local production plus commercial imports – covaries positively across locations. A common (albeit often implicit) claim one hears in support of intercontinental, transoceanic food aid shipments is that regional drought, pest infestation, war or other supply shocks cause significant positive correlation in production or market availability across neighboring markets. The 2002–3 crisis in southern Africa is a recent example where both climatic (drought) and economic/health (HIV/AIDS) shocks in several countries at once created huge regional food availability deficits that required (most, if not all) food aid deliveries to be sourced from considerable distance.[70] There seems to be a latent, although not explicit, belief in some quarters that such cases are the norm, that food availability rises and falls together across countries in a region. Of course, this assumption harkens back to the old "food availability deficit" conceptualization of food aid that was effectively discredited a quarter century ago by Sen and others.

In fact, the conventional wisdom is wrong. The claim that transoceanic food aid shipments are necessary because food availability crises occur mainly due to regional drought, floods, war or other covariate biophysical or sociopolitical shocks finds little support in the data. We computed the statistical correlation between nations' annual per capita production of cereals and then calculated the average correlation of each nation's per capita cereals production with that of its neighbors. The results are displayed in the map in Figure 8.5.

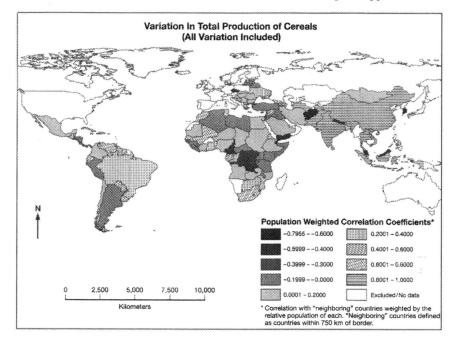

Figure 8.5 Country-specific correlations with neighbors in cereals production

The more horizontally striped the country on the map, the stronger the positive correlation of its food production with its neighbors. In other words, the more likely it becomes that a country's neighbors do not have an exportable surplus from which donors could source food through triangular transactions when the subject country faces a serious availability deficit. Conversely, the more darkly shaded, the stronger the negative correlation. In such cases, triangular transactions will commonly be feasible as means to fill in country-specific shortfalls. Lighter shading or more vertical striping reflect very weak correlations, negative or positive, respectively. Strong positive correlations are less common on the map than strong negative correlations if one just counts up countries. But contemporary food aid flows are modest into countries with positive correlation statistics – Eritrea, Indonesia, Pakistan, and Zimbabwe are notable exceptions – while cereals production in many of the biggest food aid recipient countries – e.g., Afghanistan, Bangladesh, the Democratic Republic of Congo, Haiti, Kenya, Nepal, Uganda – is reasonably strongly negatively correlated with that of their neighbors. The correlation is near zero (specifically, between –0.05 and 0.05) for many other major food aid recipients, such as Angola, Egypt, Ethiopia, Malawi, Mozambique, Nicaragua, Peru, Somalia, and Sudan. In general, the common assumption of positive food availability correlation between food aid recipients and neighbors that could prospectively serve as nearby procurement sites proves false when confronted with the data. This implies that in most years and for most major food aid recipient countries, the potential for expanding triangular transactions as a procurement modality seems considerable. Finally, these results do not seem an artifact of our statistical methods, because we tried a range of different techniques and consistently got the same pattern.[71]

Myth 10 Food availability shocks covary across countries within a region

Just as most income shocks are specific to particular households rather than experienced generally within whole communities, so are most food availability shocks relatively local. If food production shortfalls hit all countries in a region simultaneously, the need for transoceanic shipments of food would be self-evident. In very few countries, however, is food availability strongly and positively correlated with that of their neighbors. There seems considerable untapped potential to exploit surpluses in one country to meet short-term deficits in a neighboring one.

In spite of the prospective benefits and the feasibility of local purchases and triangular transactions, these procurement modalities can prove problematic, for at least three distinct reasons. First, food surpluses are not always reliable in developing countries heavily dependent on rainfed agriculture. Orders placed under a triangular transaction may get cancelled or postponed if source market supplies come in under target, as happened in 1984–85 with grains ordered from Zimbabwe for delivery to neighboring countries.

Second, the underdeveloped marketing systems responsible for the poor market integration necessary for food aid to be an appropriate transfer to ameliorate food insecurity can also cause significant quality control and throughput management problems in triangular transactions and local purchases. This problem emerged when the European Community procured 10,000 tons of white maize from Malawi in 1984 for distribution in Tanzania, following the earlier-mentioned deferment of purchases from Zimbabwe. Acquisition and logistics problems delayed the first shipment out of Malawi until March 1986 and the full delivery had not been made by the time Malawi suffered a poor 1987 harvest while Tanzania experienced its second bumper harvest in a row.[72]

A range of other problems can emerge as well. Contract enforcement is notoriously difficult in rural markets in the least developed countries and processing and transport capacity limits in local markets can severely constrain procurement and packaging. Quality and sanitary standards can also prove substandard in some source countries. In the 1996 local purchase program in Ethiopia sponsored by the European Union, fixed lot size tenders beyond the reach of most traders, segmentation of the tender/auction process by region, and potential collusion among the few large traders able to participate credibly in the bidding process drove up costs to the point that average procurement costs were, on average, only negligibly less than the landed import cost of comparable quality grain.[73] As a consequence, bulk food aid procurement can sometimes prove risky in developing country source markets. As food markets mature and become more reliable and efficient in low- and middle-income countries, they can be relied upon more as sources of food aid for intraregional distribution.

The other potential problem caused by local purchases and triangular transactions relates to their prospective impact on food buyers in the source market or in markets that typically import food from the source market. This issue reflects the other side of the producer incentives coin. If one believes that food aid procurement stimulates demand and thereby increases the prices fetched by producers and processors, then it necessarily follows that food aid procurement likewise increases the prices paid by consumers in the source market and by those who import the same commodity from the source market. Put differently, in so far as food aid procurement through local purchases and triangular transactions benefits net sellers of food in the source market, it also has the potential to hurt net buyers in that same market. Since a large share of the farming population and all of the nonfarming population in low-income countries are net food buyers, local purchases and triangular transactions may exacerbate chronic food insecurity among the poor in source markets even while potentially providing more efficient transfers to reduce food insecurity in destination locations. When the European Community and the United States undertook significant triangular and trilateral transactions involving Zimbabwe in the 1980s, they commonly purchased one-third to one-half of Zimbabwe's total maize exports, driving up prices for Zimbabwean white maize in regional markets.[74] When triangular transactions have significant price effects, they can impose costs in excess of their benefits, proving a terribly inefficient means of transferring resources to developing countries. We have seen no systematic empirical evidence on this question of the distributional effects of local purchases and triangular transactions. Such analysis will need to be done prior to any concerted expansion in use of these modalities, their considerable promise notwithstanding.

Efficiency of resources transfer

Ultimately, food aid reflects an international transfer of resources from a donor country to one or more recipient countries. The donation takes the form of food, but the end use is not always as food – i.e., much food is monetized by governments or NGOs, with the proceeds used for food security interventions that are often distinctly different from food distribution – nor does the food transferred to individual recipients necessarily have to be shipped internationally. It could instead be procured nearer to final distribution points. Put differently, the use of food as a medium for making international transfers raises serious questions as to the efficiency of these transactions.

This resource transfer efficiency question has long been a source of concern in reviews of food aid programs. The Nobel Laureate T.W. Schultz objected that the counterpart funds generated by the sales of program food aid by recipient governments in the 1950s amounted to only about one-third of the total outlays made by the US government at the time.[75] Ed Clay and his colleagues, in their thorough review of program food aid flows from the European Union[76] – both coordinated actions by the European Union and separate shipments by individual member states – similarly found relatively low counterpart funds generation efficiency. By their estimates, the value of the counterpart funds generated by EU food aid was 23 percent less than the cost to EU donors. These analyses essentially ask how much money is generated for recipients per dollar spent on food aid by a donor. In Schultz's case, he arrived at an answer of 30–35 cents, while Clay *et al.* – looking at different programs, a quarter century later, from different donors – arrived at an answer of 75–80 cents. In the analysis below on US Section 416(b) and Food for Progress shipments, we come up with estimates closer to Schultz's than to those of Clay *et al.*

Of course, there are a variety of different ways one can try to attack the resource transfer efficiency question. Food is necessarily a more efficient form of transfer when recipients ultimately want food because recipients do not incur costs to cash in food aid. One approach to estimating the efficiency of food aid would be to compare food aid against alternative mechanisms for ensuring stable food supplies in food-insecure countries. Toward that end, import insurance and grain stocking programs might be significantly more cost-effective in some settings.[77]

Looking instead at the value of the delivered commodity relative to the cost of getting it to recipients, Clay *et al.* found reasonably good resource transfer efficiency for European Community shipments. They appeared to be only 10 percent greater than the reference cost for landed commodities of comparable quality. However, they found individual EU member states' food aid costs were typically 71 percent higher than the value of the delivered shipment. We find that the equivalent figure for the excess costs of American food aid deliveries to be, on average, 113 percent, relative to the open market costs of equivalent commodities delivered in the recipient country port.

Computation of the true costs of food aid is exceedingly difficult. The range of commodities, source and destination markets and the frequent absence of parallel commercial transactions to use as a benchmark – plus the general dearth of good price data series in many food aid recipient countries – necessarily limit the precision with which such comparisons can be made. Nonetheless, it is important to have some data-driven estimates of these costs so as to know how serious is the leakage of appropriated food aid funds en route to the beneficiaries they are intended to help.

Toward this end, we used publicly available USDA data on specific corn and wheat food aid shipments, 1999–2000, to identify the costs per ton for procurement and freight of 84 distinct Section 416(b) and Food for Progress food aid shipments. We then used other USDA data to establish the open market price for the same commodity in the month and location the food aid procurement took place. By comparing the open market procurement price and the price on the successfully tendered food aid contract, we can estimate the average procurement premium accruing to US grain suppliers. We then took USDA data on freight costs on foreign flag carriers hauling the same commodity between the same ports in the same three-month period to establish a benchmark open market transport cost for food aid shipments. Comparison of that benchmark figure against the actual transport costs paid US-flag carriers for food aid shipments yields an estimated average shipping premium accruing to the few shipping lines with restricted access to US food aid freight forwarding contracts. Finally, we obtained open market prices for the same commodity in destination country port market from Foreign Agricultural Service attaché reports posted from various US embassies around the world and from price series generously made available to us by colleagues at the International Food Policy Research Institute, Michigan State University and the World Bank. This local market price establishes the value of the delivered food aid, the price at which it could have been procured locally instead.

When one puts all of those figures together, the estimated value of delivered food aid – the destination market cost – comes to just 47 percent of total expenditures, as shown in Figure 8.6. This implies that it costs 113 percent more to deliver food through these US food aid programs than it would cost to buy the same food in the recipient country market. Why? Part of the reason is the cost of shipping low value-to-bulk commodities across long distances.[78] An estimated 27 percent of the total costs of the food aid program covers the open market costs of trans-oceanic food aid shipments. But that still leaves more than one-quarter of the cost of American food aid unaccounted for. The remaining 26 percent of total food aid appropriations flow as rents to successful vendors under the food and freight procurement systems operated by the US government, 5 percent of it to US agribusinesses and 21 percent – 80 percent of the economic rents attributable to restricted competition in procurement – to shippers. These seem handsome returns for the privileged few who win food aid tendering contracts.

By our estimates, more than half of the dollars appropriated for food aid in the United States leaks out in delivering food to poor and hungry people abroad. This is a conservative estimate because it does not include ground transport and handling

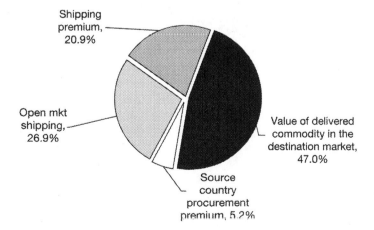

Shipping premium, 20.9%

Open mkt shipping, 26.9%

Value of delivered commodity in the destination market, 47.0%

Source country procurement premium, 5.2%

Figure 8.6 Value shares of US food aid deliveries

costs between port and final destination points nor any of the administrative costs incurred by either donor or recipient agencies, and it puts no value on any delays associated with longer-distance procurement and shipment. Time is money, and in emergencies, slow delivery can be terribly costly in both economic and human terms. Savings in delivery lags can be vitally important, but terribly difficult to quantify in monetary terms, so we make no effort to do so here.

Our estimates also assume away problems of quality control, which can be significant in transoceanic shipment of food. Voyages from western hemisphere ports to Sub-Saharan Africa and South Asia commonly take one to two months at sea. Such a period creates significant opportunities for food to get wet and spoil, rendering it useless. We were unable to find any systematic statistics on food aid spoilage. But few practitioners doubt that spoilage rates of food procured in donor countries and shipped internationally are less than the equivalent rates for food procured in recipient countries. Other issues, such as security and the liability of the distributing agency also arise. Although these pose financial risks for agencies, they are difficult to assess in dollar terms.

We also neglect the potential costs borne by third parties. Any price changes induced by food aid deliveries have spillover effects, as we cover in greater detail in Chapter 9. For example, local purchases in markets with relatively price-inelastic supply drive up the prices paid by food buyers in the source country.[79] Similarly, poorly targeted food aid distribution – including monetization by government or NGOs – outside of periods of acute food shortage will tend to lower food prices, imposing real costs on net food sellers (both farmers and traders) in the recipient economy. These real economic costs necessarily vary markedly by program, destination market, and period, but need to be borne in mind.

In sum, we offer relatively conservative estimates of the inefficiencies associated with American food aid as currently practiced. Taking into account only the cash outlays required to deliver food to port in a recipient country, the United States appears to spend more than twice the value of the food. This inefficiency becomes all the more pronounced when the delivered food is then only a medium through which governments or NGOs generate cash.

Monetization trades ground transport costs and losses due to spoilage and theft between port and final destination points for losses associated with below-market prices typically fetched for monetized food and the variable and fixed costs (e.g., staff time, agent commissions) of monetization. The apparent inefficiency of food aid monetization as a means for funding food security activities by development and humanitarian agencies prompted the US Office of Management and Budget to recommend a 50 percent reduction in USAID-approved monetization rates as part of the Fiscal Year 2003 budget review process.

So why does such inefficiency persist? The core answer seems to be the parochial donor interests that lead to what is commonly referred to as "aid tying."[80] Aid tying refers to transfers that are somehow restricted in form; they are not unconditional gifts of cash. These restrictions reflect efforts by influential interest groups to siphon off overseas development assistance funds justified to the American population – and many legislators – on the basis of helping combat poverty and hunger abroad.

Myth 11 A dollar spent on food aid is a dollar consumed by hungry people

Because food aid represents an in-kind income transfer and even very poor people do not spend all of an extra dollar of income on food, a dollar spent on food aid does not increase food consumption by a dollar. Moreover, given food aid procurement, shipping and handling costs and monetization losses, the cost of delivered food is typically at least twice as much as the value of the food in recipient markets. At the upper end of the cost scale (e.g., if airlifts have to be used), the value of the food may represent as little as one-tenth the cost of the delivered food aid.

The funds are still available for the ostensible purposes, but the fine print of the authorizing legislation obligates expenditures on particular activities or goods provided by a restricted set of providers. This generates profits for those who can manipulate the aid system, while making aid unnecessarily inefficient. Aid tying has become a prominent subject of discussion with the OECD in recent years, at least as regards capital goods. The tying of food aid has only very recently begun to draw significant attention.

In the case of food aid, transfers are typically doubly tied. First, they are provided in the form of a specific commodity. Second, that commodity typically is often sourced from the donor country because it is provided in kind. The recipient essentially faces a take-it-or-leave-it offer of particular foods from particular sources, regardless of the highest return use for the next dollar available for discretionary spending.[81]

Since tied food aid represents a small share of total food exports from donor countries and because food aid has negligible apparent price effects in donor markets, the aggregate economic gains generated by it for donor country producers are trivial. The politics are, however, powerful. There are small subcommunities of producer groups – suppliers of nonfat dried milk or dehydrated potatoes in the initial years of the twenty-first century, for example, or Californian raisin producers who successfully lobbied to add raisins to US food aid procurement programs when a glut emerged on the market in 2003 – for whom the impact of food aid can be significant. The few large agribusinesses that sell repeatedly to US food aid programs earn a slight premium over prevailing open market prices. Add to these scattered but motivated groups of commodity suppliers the half a dozen or so freight forwarders who earn astronomical premia from cargo preference restrictions on international food aid transport and the dozen or so US-based NGOs who have preferential access to resources provided in the form of food, and a powerful political coalition emerges to defend the provision of aid in the form of food. Mancur Olson's theory of collective action seems to apply well in explaining the persistence of food aid that appears terribly inefficient overall as a means for transferring resources to food-insecure peoples in the developing world.[82]

Defenders of present practice commonly offer one of two arguments. First, they argue, corrupt officials can more easily divert cash aid than they can food aid. Intuitively, this seems probable, although no empirical evidence on the issue seems to exist (for obvious reasons). Second, defenders of food aid claim that cash aid is commonly no less tied than food aid. The tying of cash aid – to the procurement of goods and services from donor country contractors – is just less visible than the tying of food aid. This argument once had considerable merit. Jepma reports a range of instances around the world of aid tying and concluded that "an average of 15 to 30 per cent seems to serve as the best aggregate estimate" of the cost of tying to recipients over the 1970s and early 1980s.[83] He also found that over the 1970–80 period, 63 percent of total aid flows were tied.

The OECD has made a strong push over the past quarter century to reduce aid tying,and many donors have responded to this push. Belgium, Ireland, Japan, Luxembourg, the Netherlands, Norway, Sweden, Switzerland, and the United Kingdom, in particular, have untied all or very large shares of their aid programs in response to this new thinking on development cooperation and the European Union has introduced new provisions supporting further aid untying. The United States is the only major donor that has not moved significantly in the direction of untying overseas development assistance. Internal OECD data indicate that the share of total ODA that is untied has increased from around 45 percent, 1980–83, to better than 80 percent, 1998–2001.[84] This would suggest that the inefficiency associated with the tying of foreign aid more broadly is appreciably lower than that associated with food aid, although a more direct and precise comparison of the inefficiencies associated with each would be helpful information for current negotiations of the World Trade Organization's Doha Round and of renewal of the Food Aid Convention.

Supply chain management and strategic reserves

One of the fundamental problems of food economics – and indeed human survival – concerns the mismatch between highly seasonal food production and relatively constant food consumption needs within any single location. Variation across space and time in food production gives rise to commercial trade between spatially distinct markets and to commodity storage by private traders. Once food aid has been procured, it too enters a supply chain through which food is transported, stored, or both before it is ultimately distributed or monetized. In recent years, a number of improvements have been made in the management of the supply chain for food aid, both in the timeliness of logistics and in commodity accounting.

Transportation of food aid from its point of entry to final distribution has long been a constraint to timely delivery. The World Food Programme has devoted considerable energy and resources to expanding logistical capacity and improving the efficiency of its operations in recent years, often with very good results. For example, recent (2000 and 2003) crises in land-locked Ethiopia have had to rely on relatively limited port facilities in Djibouti as a transit point for well over a million metric tons of food aid in each year (in addition to all other imports and exports). In both cases, the upgrading of port facilities and careful management of logistics prevented major delays in shipments. But results in other locations (for example, Angola in 2002) have not been so successful. Other innovations in food aid transportation remain possible and some have been piloted, for example, the role/potential of backhaul capacity from food aid deliveries for enabling sales (e.g., livestock offtake during drought). This was attempted on a limited scale in Kenya in the 2000 drought, seemingly with positive effect on pastoralists' sales of animals that would likely have perished otherwise.[85] But much broader scope exists to scale up such creative interventions in resolving transport bottlenecks associated with food aid.

Food storage has long been of interest to policymakers concerned about food insecurity. Many countries have maintained, at various times, some type of grain reserve aimed at stabilizing (interseasonally or interannually) domestic food prices faced by consumers, farmers, or both, or at providing a publicly-held strategic stockpile for distribution in times of crisis.[86] Variously called strategic food security reserves, buffer stocks, famine reserves, or strategic stockpiles, publicly managed food storage has declined significantly in the wake of grain market liberalization over the past twenty years in Africa, Asia, and Latin America. The primary reasons for this decline have been a perceived tendency for publicly-held stocks to crowd out private storage, general ineffectiveness in meeting price targets, and high fiscal costs to resource-constrained governments.[87]

This decline has been somewhat controversial. For example, the failure of the Malawi Strategic Grain Reserve (MSGR) in 2002, and particularly its decision to sell off substantial stocks of grain in 2001, were major factors contributing to the food security crisis that gripped Malawi in 2002–3.[88] While the lessons from that particular experience are very relevant to the management of strategic reserves, we do not analyze the Malawian case in detail because, like many grain reserves, the MSGR operated on a commercial basis, having bought domestic surpluses in previous years for inter-annual storage. Food aid *per se* played no role in the Malawi Strategic Grain Reserve and its failure. By contrast, government stockpiles of rice and wheat appear to have helped stabilize markets and food prices in Bangladesh during the 1998 floods, stemming the sorts of private hoarding and price increases in response to trader expectations of post-harvest price spikes that contributed significantly to excess mortality during the 1974–75 crisis in that country.[89] While trade liberalization and increased availability of foreign exchange to private traders have improved timely access to affordable imported foods and rural infrastructure improvements have increased the efficiency of domestic food distribution – both factors reducing the need for large government food security reserves – the favorable experience in Bangladesh seems to underscore the prospective value of such reserves.

In theory, food aid could be used to make up short-term deficits in any strategic grain reserve, no matter its purpose or management regime. In recent years, how-ever, food aid has played a major role only in the development and provisioning of strategic famine relief stocks, primarily in countries that are prone to production shocks, such as Bangladesh, Ethiopia, Mali, and Tanzania.[90] The major role of such stocks is to provide a bridge to commercial food imports or food aid inflows at the outset of an emergency, enabling rapid response while mobilizing a longer-term response that necessarily involves time-consuming donor-pledging processes, international and domestic transportation, internal logistical bottlenecks, etc., and to provide some insurance against interruptions to the flow of commercial imports and food aid during emergencies. That is why it is important to have stocks on hand, especially in places routinely subject to serious food availability shocks and populated by many nutritionally vulnerable people.

It has nonetheless proved difficult to build up the stock of strategic reserves, and even more problematic to maintain both adequate stock levels and appropriate turnover rates, as commonly stipulated by donors.[91] In countries with a high level of food aid utilization every year, sufficient turnover to prevent excessive spoilage has been less difficult. But where turnover rates are adequate to prevent grain spoilage, countries often find themselves at the beginning of a crisis with an inadequate stock of food in the reserve because of inadequate replenishment rates. The case of the 1999–2000 Ethiopia crisis offers a classic example (see Box 8.3). It should be noted, however, that the functioning of the Ethiopian Emergency Food Security Reserve (EFSR) was much smoother and more reliable during the crisis of 2002–3, an indication that the lessons from 1999–2000 were capably taken on board both by the Government of Ethiopia that manages the reserve, and the donors that had long-outstanding debts to the EFSR in 1999–2000.

Box 8.3 The emergency Food Security Reserve and the timing of food aid delivery in Ethiopia, 1999–2000[1]

During 1999–2000, Ethiopia suffered a major humanitarian disaster, with some 10 million people estimated to need food assistance at the height of the crisis. While excess mortality figures are not known precisely, the best estimate for the hardest hit location was about 20,000 malnutrition-related deaths,[2] but the crisis was widespread beyond this particular location, with the prevalence of global acute malnutrition (low weight for height) reported above 30 percent of children under the age of five in many areas of the country. Nationwide, well over a million metric tons of food aid was required from sources outside Ethiopia to avert a major humanitarian disaster. A repeat of the catastrophic famine of 1984–85 was avoided, but food aid from abroad was very slow in arriving.

Both the Government of Ethiopia and donors had invested substantially in improved early warning and the Ethiopia Food Security Reserve (EFSR). But in spite of these and of the existence of the EFSR, the lag in the arrival of food aid to Ethiopia from donors, resulted in a substantial shortfall in distribution of food aid at the height of the crisis (Figure 8.3). The Reserve, already in a depleted state when the crisis of 1999–2000 began, was not able to bridge the shortfall. For several months in late 1999 and early 2000, the requirements of food for distribution to acutely food-insecure populations were substantially greater than the cumulative amount of food available from the EFSR and the direct food aid pipeline.

As depicted in Figure 8.7, the cumulative deficit in food available for distribution over a five-month period between October 1999 and April 2000 – the critical period of the emergency – was over 280,000 metric tons. The EFSR held about 60,000 metric tons in October 1999, and over the ensuing six months had a net replenishment of about 85,000 metric tons – far less than the requirements for distribution. But the replenishment to the EFSR also came at the expense of direct distribution, so the total figure in the Reserve at the outset of the crisis was the critical one. When the crisis hit with the failure of the *belg* rains in mid-1999, the EFSR held about one-quarter of the grain it was designed to hold. The precise impact of both the pipeline problems and the delays in repayment to the EFSR was a very contested issue at the time. Had the EFSR been fully stocked at the outset of the crisis, and had the rate of payment been faster, it is clear that the humanitarian disaster would have been less critical, though a shortfall still would have occurred.

The reasons for the delay in the arrival of food aid – as well as the reasons why the EFSR was only partially stocked at the outset of the crisis – are many: multiple crises elsewhere in the world requiring attention; tension between the Government of Ethiopia and the donors over Ethiopia's war with Eritrea;

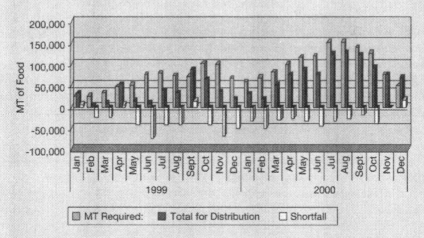

Figure 8.7 Shortfall in food distributions in Ethiopia in 1999/2000 (metric tons)

Source: DPPC Fortnightly Bulletins, WFP; FEWSNet/CARE, 2000

Note: Figures are combined from several sources; for any given month they might not be precisely correct due to differences in the way monthly totals were calculated by different sources. Overall, they do present an accurate picture.

and some level of doubt about information and estimation of needs. Nevertheless, what is clear is that, even with a relatively good early warning system and a reasonably functioning strategic reserve, the timing of food aid delivery lagged badly behind assessed, time-bound requirements for food assistance from outside the country.

Notes:
1   Drawn from Hammond and Maxwell (2002).
2   Salama *et al.* (2001).

While the advantages of maintaining a strategic food security reserve in chronically food insecure countries may be self-evident and reserves are an important innovation in famine prevention and the management of acute humanitarian emergencies, many problems have dogged the operations of reserves. For example, establishing the optimal size of reserves has proved problematic, and many of the assumptions on which such calculations are made do not pan out in the event of a major crisis. The costs of storage, including spoilage and theft, and the transactions costs involved in turnover to prevent spoilage can be substantial. Many countries are now planning strategic cash reserves or open lines of credit that can quickly be used to mount a rapid response to shocks, rather than maintaining relatively more complex and expensive strategic food reserves.[92]

Conclusion

Most of the main problems associated with food aid are directly related to the management of food aid in the field, particularly the question of targeting. Targeting involves not only ensuring that food aid reaches the right people at the right place (and does not end up in the hands of other people), but also involves the timeliness of delivery, the appropriate quantity and quality, and the availability of key complementary inputs. A variety of targeting methods have been devised, but none guarantees accurate targeting. Poor targeting inevitably undermines either the humanitarian goal of food aid or the developmental goals associated with food security. Without a clear preference for one type of undesirable error over the other, agencies need to emphasize minimizing targeting errors of all sorts.

Good information is absolutely critical for good targeting. While many improvements have been made in food security information systems over the past two decades, there remains an urgent need to improve these systems, to integrate them better with mitigation and response mechanisms, and to broaden them so as to enable a greater range of responses than just food aid. Good information and, where necessary, well-managed strategic reserves, can greatly mitigate the humanitarian and economic impact of shocks.

There is much greater scope for local purchase and triangular transactions in food aid procurement in developing countries than is commonly believed or practiced. This kind of procurement has the potential to speed up deliveries of food aid, to reduce the cost of food aid (dramatically, in some cases), and to have developmental knock-on effects in the countries from which such food is purchased. However, local purchases and triangular transactions are not always and everywhere appropriate or feasible. And just as the selling of food aid in small markets requires good information, so to does the purchase of food, in order to prevent price rises that would be harmful to low-income, net food-purchasing households. Enabling local purchase or triangular transactions would also significantly "untie" food aid, a practice the OECD has been promoting in recent years. Bad management of food aid, resulting from poor practices in any of these dimensions, leads directly to harmful consequences for the intended recipients, to which we now turn.

9   Consequences of poor food aid management

As we mentioned previously, most of the highly controversial issues surrounding food aid arise due to targeting errors and other forms of mismanagement of food aid, for example, poorly executed monetization or stocks management. In this chapter, we look at the consequences of these management problems. We divide these into two basic classes of effects: humanitarian impacts associated with health and nutrition – which is broadly associated with undercoverage errors (of exclusion) – and economic impacts related to disincentives, induced distortions or possible dependency created leakage errors (of inclusion). As noted in Chapters 7 and 8, many positive results have been achieved using food aid when it is well managed. In this chapter, we address the effects of poorly managed food aid.

Humanitarian impacts: nutrition and health

The greatest risk in poor management of food aid is of failure to protect human nutritional status. As discussed in Chapter 8, this kind of failure is usually associated with some kind of undercoverage error. Firm evidence on the nutritional impacts of food aid is strikingly scarce. The issue is not the absence of good evidence of favorable effects of food assistance programs more generally – food stamps, food subsidies, public employment schemes, school feeding programs, supplementary feeding programs, etc. – on participant food consumption, health or nutritional status, for there is abundant, clear, evidence that food assistance improves nutritional status.[1] Rather, the issue is the absence of any significant body of empirical evidence that food donated from abroad – food aid – in particular accounts for the difference in the nutritional or health status of individual food aid recipients. And this is unfortunately the case whether one is talking about humanitarian assistance in an emergency or other kinds of food aid uses.[2]

The problem arises from two main sources. First, formidable methodological obstacles make it difficult to establish conclusively the nutritional impact of food aid. Even under the best of circumstances, it is difficult to measure nutrient intake accurately. Much survey-based evidence relies on imperfect recall data. It is especially tricky to disentangle the effects of food consumption from other factors that affect nutritional status in purely observational (i.e., non-experimental) data. And given the circumstances under which food aid is sometimes administered, collection of *any* information – let alone the detailed information required by a dietary intake survey – is fraught with difficulty. And for obvious ethical reasons, randomized, controlled trials of the provision of food aid to nutritionally threatened peoples cannot be run.

Second, insofar as food aid flows to chosen communities, there can be an important program placement effect in measurement. For example, if food aid is delivered mainly to communities with greater *ex ante* nutritional deficiencies, then there will be a negative correlation between food aid receipt and anthropometric measures of nutritional status reflecting the effects of the latter on targeting rather than the effects of food aid on nutritional status.[3] Third, and of more immediate relevance, the considerable targeting errors that have historically pervaded food aid programs necessarily dampen the latent nutritional effects of well-targeted food aid. Inclusion in the treatment population of many people whose need for, and thus response to, food aid are modest to negligible, and tardy delivery of food to needy people after the period when it would have had the greatest effect both dampen the observable nutritional or health response to food aid receipt.

In theory, a good system of monitoring and evaluation would track where food aid actually goes, who receives and consumes it, and an indication of the extent to which the food aid improves food security, nutritional, health or economic status. Such information would provide valuable feedback to the assessment and targeting process. In reality, however, the emphasis in monitoring has classically been on accounting for the commodities up to the point of distribution, with post-distribution monitoring of end-use lagging far behind, and impact measurement almost non-existent in humanitarian emergencies. Anthropometric assessment is increasingly used to track emergency-affected populations, but this alone cannot account for the impact of any food assistance provided, especially without adequate controls for other factors affecting subjects' heights and weights. This is often rationalized, especially in acute emergencies, by the need to get food distributed, rather than monitoring who gets it or who eats it, much less the actual impact on the food security or nutritional status of groups targeted to receive it.

Part of the problem of uncertain health and nutritional impacts arises because the humanitarian community relies on nutritional status as its main impact indicator. This is appropriate in that nutritional status – as reflected in anthropometric measures such as height/age, weight/height, and body mass index ratios – offers one of the best available indicators of physical well-being, at least in young children, and where humanitarian operations are concerned, monitoring an overall measure is critical. Nonetheless, many factors other than dietary intake affect nutritional status, and food aid in itself can only improve dietary intake, and has often improved only caloric intake, not intake of protein or micronutrients, although improvements in the latter are now high on the agenda for emergency response.[4] Examples abound of situations in which malnutrition remains stubbornly high despite large-scale food aid inputs over a substantial period of time.[5] In some of these circumstances, poor access to primary health care or clean water may have been the limiting factor in restoring nutritional status in an emergency as diarrhea and infectious disease (e.g., measles, cholera) overwhelm the effects of increased caloric intake from food aid. This implies the need for a monitoring system that can separate out the impact of food aid on nutritional status, and highlight whether or not other necessary inputs to adequate nutritional status are being addressed. Work on approaches to measure the effects of food consumption – tied to food aid receipts – have been piloted in a number of countries, but are too new to have been adopted broadly thus far.[6] Even in relatively tightly defined activities such as maternal/child health or food for education programs, the impact of food aid is difficult to demonstrate because it proves so tricky to disentangle the effects of modestly expanded dietary intake from the constellation of other factors influencing anthropometric status.[7]

Provision of food aid with appropriate micronutrient content has also been a longstanding concern in the nutrition community. Far more people suffer from micronutrient deficiencies (e.g., of iron, iodine, vitamins A or D) that affect health than from protein-energy malnutrition.[8] But because food aid has traditionally been driven by donors' desire to dispose of surplus exportable cereals, food aid has generally failed to contribute much to the nutritional variety necessary to ensure a balanced diet providing all the essential vitamins and minerals needed for a healthy, active life. Concerns about this fostered the rise of blended food products over the past twenty years, especially in direct feeding programs, particularly for children.[9] Blended foods are expensive products, however, limiting their reach to the billions of people suffering micronutrient deficiencies worldwide. Moreover, until the early 2000 introduction of the USDA Total Quality Systems Audit, the micronutrient levels even in fortified and blended foods were unreliable because of poor quality control standards in processing since processors were not required to meet the same standards mandated in the domestic US food market.[10] A related targeting error in the form of the transfer (the "what?" as distinct from the "who?" or "when?" questions of targeting) concerns complementary inputs to the maintenance of good health. Good nutrition is only one crucial input into good health and in many settings is not the limiting factor in improving or protecting the health of vulnerable populations.[11] In spite of its scarcity, in many situations, food is not the form of aid most needed by populations at health or nutritional risk. If the objective of aid is improving targeted recipients' health and nutritional status, then assistance often also needs to flow in the form of cash for nonfood interventions. A common mistake made by the general public, but even by a number of donors, is to assume poor nutritional indicators are necessarily best addressed through increased food consumption. Improved targeting in the commodity composition of food aid transfers, as well as in their timing, in the identity of recipients, and in the allocation of assistance between food and nonfood forms, could significantly improve the difficult-to-measure nutritional impact of food aid. But better monitoring of both end-use and impact is also necessary. The absence of clear evidence in support of the hypothesis that food aid improves recipients' health and nutritional status proves problematic for agencies and individuals trying to build or sustain political will among donors to respond to periods of particularly acute need – as during recent crises across several different parts of Africa – with significantly increased food aid supplies.

Distortions, disincentives, and dependency

Food aid dependency?

Webster's defines "dependency" as a "condition of receiving assistance from . . . others," or as a "state of inability to exist or sustain oneself without assistance or direction from another." Recipients' "dependency" on food aid is taken almost as an article of faith in some quarters within development agencies and recipient country governments, although "dependency" can mean a variety of things. However, there has been surprisingly little serious research on the topic, and few empirical findings on which to base policy. As best we can tell, much of the assumed dependence on food aid follows from assertions made by Lappé and Collins, although they offer nothing more than a few anecdotes and seem mainly to have been casually invoking a term popular at the time among progressive development scholars and practitioners.[12]

Outside of the most severe cases of acute humanitarian crises or refugees or internally displaced persons resettled temporarily into camps, food aid rarely represents more than a small proportion of recipients' total food consumption or overall expenditures.[13] Consider the evidence from one of the more extreme circumstances outside of refugee feeding situations: food aid among pastoralists in the Horn of Africa during and immediately following the severe 2000–1 drought.[14] Detailed quarterly data from 330 pastoralist households in the drylands of northern Kenya and southern Ethiopia show that half the Ethiopian households received no food aid during this period. Coverage was far broader in neighboring areas of Kenya, where nearly every household in the sample received food aid at some point during the 21 months to December 2001, due to geographic targeting of the area and the inclusiveness of community-based targeting. Nonetheless, the amounts received were relatively small. Food aid comprised 11 percent or less of income for half the Kenyan households during this crisis, and only represented half or more of income for 17 and 7 percent of Kenyan and Ethiopian households, respectively. Only about one in ten southern Ethiopian pastoralist households derived more than one-quarter of their income from food aid, as did only 30 percent of Kenyan pastoralist households. Keeping in mind that severe drought among pastoralists is among the paradigmatic cases in which critics decry "food aid dependency," these amounts seem modest. Indeed, we find no qualitative or quantitative evidence that the meager amounts of food aid they received had an appreciable effect on their capacity to become self-reliant. Recent longitudinal survey work in South Wollo, one of Ethiopia's most food-insecure areas, emphasizes that uncertainty surrounding the amount and timing of food aid delivery have taught residents not to depend on it.[15] Evidence from the 1998 floods in Bangladesh similarly find that food aid – while effectively targeted in that case – was quite small, relative to households' needs and to other coping mechanisms. For example, household borrowing was six to eight times the value of all transfers to poor flood-exposed households.[16]

A classic example of claimed "food aid dependency" is described by a program officer for an international NGO, based on experience in northern Kenya:[17]

These people become permanently destitute . . . dependent [forever] on hand-outs. Many [local] people participated in the food for work program. Although well intentioned, this program was poorly targeted both in terms of the actual work done and the people involved in it. Many of the workers were by no means from the truly destitute population, but opportunistic pastoralists using this as an opportunity to gain an additional income. The work undertaken had little meaning for them. Building earthen walls to retard rainwater in concept sounded a good idea, but the [local people] are nomadic herders and this work was completely foreign to them. They undertook it without any belief or stake in it, and what was constructed was of poor quality and had little value. Similar assistance in small-scale irrigation too was poorly undertaken. At one point in my experience [local] "farmers" were demanding food payment to plant the sorghum seeds they had been given for free in their own farms that they had been paid to prepare and cultivate!

Note, however, that little that is described here about food would be accurately described as "dependency" and most of the concerns stem directly from poor targeting of food aid. The undesirable effects noted here stem directly from poor management of food aid and would be best described as creating incentives that distort behavior rather than breed dependency.

To be sure, people do become chronically poor and food-insecure, thereby needing assistance for a prolonged period of time – as in the case of pastoralists who lose their herds due to drought, disease or cattle rustling – so long as only safety nets, not cargo net-type assistance (e.g., skills training, herd restocking) are provided. Our claim is that sustained reliance on food aid, in the relatively rare instances in which it occurs at household or individual level, reflects less dependency than behavioral change caused by a loss of livelihood options, which leaves people with chronically inadequate access to food. Put differently, claims of dependency seem to have the direction of causality wrong. Shocks cause behavioral change that may necessitate various types of safety nets, including food aid. But food aid volumes transferred are, in almost all cases, simply too modest to make people dependent upon them, although they can help keep them alive and they can surely change the incentives that affect the behavioral choices they make, as the ensuing subsections describe.

Myth 12 Food aid creates dependency

Poorly managed food aid distorts production and trade incentives in local economies, and sometimes distorts collective action in local communities, even policies at the national level. But generally speaking, the amount of food aid that individual households receive represents only a small percentage of their consumption or income, and food aid represents only a drop in the ocean of recipient countries' overall food supply. In the rare instances where people are genuinely dependent on food aid, it is usually because their livelihoods have been destroyed and their survival hangs in the balance . . . hardly an occasion to worry about abstract concerns such as "dependency." But it is rarely food aid itself that destroys livelihoods. Dependency seems badly overblown as a concern about food aid.

Labor supply disincentives

Perhaps the most pervasive – and we believe, misguided – claim is that food aid somehow makes people lazy. It is certainly true that microeconomic theory suggests that because transfers increase recipients' welfare, they generate income effects that will tend to reduce labor supply simply because even hard-working people prefer more leisure to less.[18] The economic reality that any transfer – whether in the form of food or not – discourages recipients from working, everything else held constant, undermines much popular support for transfers, as heated debates over the past decade about domestic welfare programs in Europe and North America have vividly demonstrated. The empirical evidence also shows, however, that labor supply becomes more responsive to changes in income as people grow wealthier. The implication is that targeting errors of inclusion magnify the labor market disincentive effects inherent to food aid (or any other form of transfer) by providing benefits to those who are most able and willing to turn transfers into leisure instead of increased food consumption. The distortionary effects of food aid on labor supply will be minimal when food aid is appropriately targeted to intended recipients. Put differently, when one encounters an apparent labor disincentive problem, this typically signals poor targeting as the root problem, not a poor work ethic among recipients.

There has been relatively little direct empirical research on the effects of food aid on labor supply in practice and the extant evidence is mixed.[19] To date, there has been no explicit research as to what effect targeting errors have had on the labor market disincentives associated with food aid. The predictions of theory are clear on this point: targeting errors of inclusion will increase the disincentives to work that worry many people about food aid programs and the alleged dependency of recipients on hand-outs. But the magnitude of such effects need not be large in well-targeted distribution programs.[20]

Induced change in consumption patterns

Part of the donor-oriented rationale for food aid has long been export promotion. Since the exports from temperate zone donors are commonly different from the staple crops grown in tropical recipient countries, the logic of export promotion necessarily entails some effort to change consumers' preferences, to introduce them to new foods and thereby endogenously stimulate demand for foods with which they were previously unfamiliar or which had formerly represented only a minor share of their diet. As we showed in Chapter 4, trade promotion objectives have generally proved unsuccessful. Food aid has been an extremely inefficient means of promoting exports for donors.

However, food aid that is relatively inappropriate to local uses can and does distort consumption patterns. Massive shipments of wheat and rice into the West African Sahel during the food crises of the mid-1970s and mid-1980s were widely believed to stimulate a shift in consumer demand from indigenous coarse grains (mainly millet and sorghum) to more western crops, notably wheat.[21] Similarly, food aid deliveries into pastoral areas in the Horn of Africa over the past decade have been repeatedly described to us by pastoralists as having changed dietary patterns. Peoples traditionally reliant on animal products suddenly begin to consume grains (primarily maize) in unprecedented quantities. Shifting from a protein-heavy to a carbohydrate-heavy diet can have unintended physiological consequences for pastoral populations.[22]

A perhaps more subtle but damaging induced consumption change occurs when culturally inappropriate foods – e.g., maize to pastoralists with a strong preference for milk, meat, and tea – are not consumed but instead processed into home-brewed alcohol. During the 2000 drought in northern Kenya, the price of *changaa* (a locally distilled alcohol) fell significantly and our own casual observations as well as reports from many local observers suggest that consumption increased significantly, all because grain food aid inflows increased the availability of low-cost inputs to the extant, town-based informal distilling industry. While food aid certainly does not cause the emergence of local brewing nor of excessive alcohol consumption, the point is that excessive shipments of foods most recipients don't especially care to eat can have adverse, unintended consequences. Once again, poor targeting is the root source of such effects.

Distorted patterns of natural resource exploitation

Recent research suggests that patterns of food aid distribution may have an impact on the natural environment, as well, by changing consumption patterns and by inducing locational change in grazing and other activities. A pair of studies in northern Kenya find that food aid distribution seems to induce greater spatial concentration of livestock around distribution points, causing localized rangeland degradation, and that food aid provided as whole grain requires more cooking, and thus more fuelwood, stimulating local deforestation. The form of the food aid affects fuelwood demand, with granular maize requiring more cooking than maize meal and thus adding to the pressure on the natural resource base.[23]

Distorting community norms

In terms of the operational implications of food aid, perhaps the strongest argument to be made regarding dependency is at the level of the community, where the use of food aid as a wage may distort previously existing behavioral norms of collective action. Detailed econometric research in recent years suggests that a considerable share of asset and income shocks are idiosyncratic rather than covariate, meaning that they tend to be specific to particular individuals and households rather than universally experienced within communities or regions.[24] The implication of significant idiosyncratic risk is that informal insurance, social reciprocity arrangements and altruistic transfers within communities and kinship networks should be able to address many temporary shortfalls. The need for injections of outside resources to cope with **idiosyncratic shocks** – as distinct from chronic shortage and **covariate shocks** commonly associated with natural disasters and warfare – may be limited in most places and times. This raises a concern as to the effects of direct food aid distribution. To what extent does it merely displace – or "crowd out" – private transfers that otherwise would occur?

A small literature within development economics finds mixed evidence on the hypothesis that public transfers crowd out private transfers. When such effects are found, the estimated magnitudes of displaced private assistance are typically rather small, while other studies find no such statistically significant effect.[25] While some observers argue that public transfers from the outside too often replace or undermine customary social networks, but with less dependable resources that are almost certainly going to be available for a shorter period of time,[26] there has been precious little careful empirical research on these effects. These effects can have broader impacts as well, for example, shifting the incentives for pastoralists to remain migratory.[27]

A nice anecdotal example of the disruption of community decision-making and collective activity was provided to us by another international NGO:[28]

> [In this example] folks had been paid food aid (food for work) for maintaining water catchments during the drought years of 1998–2001. This year doesn't happen to be a year when food aid is required in this particular location, but local leaders told us that people would not be willing to maintain water sources without food aid. If that meant waiting for another drought – so be it (which is of course illogical in terms of having access to water because the water catchments need to be maintained during good rainfall years, not after the rains fail). Now admittedly, it is very difficult to explain precisely the impact of food aid on this kind of behavior, but this is in an area where people are reputed to be fiercely self-reliant, and our own staff say that in the early 1990s, this would not have been an issue. Maybe "dependency" isn't the best description, but it is certainly an instance of humanitarian aid-induced behavioral change – and change for the worse in terms of it having undermined voluntary collective self-reliance.

Such distorted incentives for community solidarity appear disturbingly common where food aid – or any sort of assistance – has been mismanaged. There is nothing intrinsic to food aid that necessitates such an outcome. Rather, adverse impacts result from project mismanagement, both in terms of targeting and in terms of attempting to address too many objectives with a single resource.

Market price effects: production and marketing incentives to local agriculture

Perhaps the most widespread concern about targeting errors of inclusion relates to their food market price effects. When food aid leaks out to unintended recipients, they (partially) substitute free food for purchased food. The supply increase associated with food aid reduces residual demand for locally produced food, with the effect more pronounced the poorer the targeting of the transfer.

Insofar as poorly managed food aid causes prices to fall in destination markets, it may undermine agricultural production in recipient countries, perpetuating food availability problems that may ultimately precipitate a need for food aid flows. A longstanding literature in agricultural and development economics, dating from the early 1960s,[29] explores the possible adverse effects of food aid flows on recipient country farmers. Figure 9.1 captures the simple analytics of food aid's effects on food prices – and thus on producer incentives – in recipient country markets. In the left-hand panel of the figure, we array households according to their willingness to pay for food – roughly, according to wealth – with the least food-insecure at the upper left end of the demand curve, D, in the figure and the most food-insecure on the lower right. Commercial supply – from production on households' own farms plus marketed food supply – is reflected in the curve labeled CS. The equilibrium market price emerges where D and CS cross, at price P, associated with food consumption level C.

When food aid enters the system but is poorly targeted, it shifts out the entire demand curve, to SD, by providing consumers with additional income (in kind). But it has an even greater effect on supply expansion – because people do not consume an extra dollar of food when they receive an extra dollar of income and here all the transfers are in the form of food. This is reflected in the increase from commercial supply, CS, to total supply, TS. The resulting post-food aid equilibrium price, P*, is necessarily lower than P. Although food consumption has increased from C to TC (total consumption), total sales, TS < C, are lower than they were without poorly targeted food aid. This is the sense in which food aid can hurt

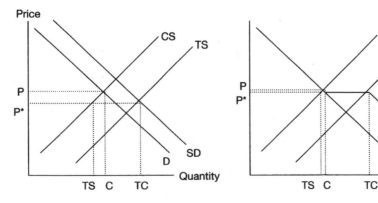

Figure 9.1 Market price effects of food aid

producer incentives. It can lower local market prices, thereby reducing local sales and production.

The right-hand panel presents the case where food aid is well targeted, reaching only those poorer households who would otherwise be rationed out of the market. Because the income elasticity of demand for food is higher among the poor, the demand curve shifts out further, but it becomes kinked, with the expansion occurring only among the households on the lower tail of the demand curve. The aggregate food supply expansion from CS to TS is exactly the same. But the effect of better targeting on demand patterns results in a far more modest decrease in prices and, assuming no difference in factor markets (for labor, finance, and other inputs), in total sales of locally produced foods. Because the same volume of food aid displaces less local sales, well-targeted food aid also increases total consumption more than does untargeted or poorly targeted food aid. So the food price effects and resulting supply-side incentives due to the product market impacts of food aid distribution turn fundamentally on the efficacy of food aid targeting.

The problem of poor targeting is not confined to errors of inclusion of recipients who are not food-insecure. Mistiming of deliveries often reveals itself through downward price adjustments on local food markets as well. For example, large shipments of food aid to Russia in the 1990s seem to have caused prices to fall well below *ex ante* market prices, while large shipments of yellow maize to Mozambique caused both white and yellow maize market prices to fall sharply.[30] If food aid shipments are unstable and large relative to demand, market prices may become unstable since prices are then determined by the variable quantity of food aid in the market. These effects can be large and may spill over into neighboring countries, as shown in Box 9.1, which describes Somalia's experience in 2000 in the wake of a surge in food aid deliveries into the neighboring Somali Region of Ethiopia.

Box 9.1 Spillover into Somalia in 2000

In mid-2000, at the height of the famine affecting the pastoral areas of eastern Ethiopia, sorghum prices collapsed in a number of market towns across the border in southern Somalia (Figure 9.2). At the time, there was much anecdotal evidence of food aid moving across the border, but at the time, there was no evidence on the extent of the flow. However, more detailed analysis reveals a distinct link both in the timing and availability of food aid in Ethiopia (much of which was sorghum), and the collapse of sorghum markets in southern Somalia.

The crisis in Somali Region in eastern Ethiopia came to the attention of authorities in early 1999, and steadily worsened as the year progressed. But the Ethiopian early warning system was adapted primarily to the chronically vulnerable rainfed highlands, and was largely not functional in the pastoral areas. As a result, the crisis got out of hand before good information was available. Even when information was available, a variety of factors delayed

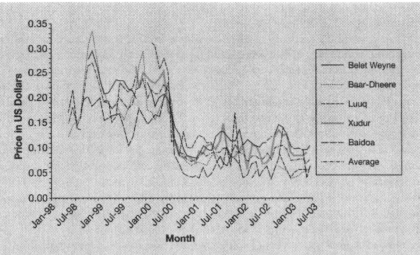

Figure 9.2 Real ($) sorghum prices, southern Somalia, 1998–2003

Source: Somalia Food Security Assessment Unit (FSAU)

a substantial response until well into 2000, by which time the media focus on Somali Region, and Gode zone in particular, was intensive, and aid agencies were under pressure to respond rapidly.

Figure 9.3 depicts food aid deliveries in Ethiopia's Somali Region from mid-1999 through the end of 2000, as well as the actual response in terms of food aid distributions. While estimates of assessed need vary substantially, food aid distribution clearly climbed rapidly in early 2000, and correspond almost exactly with the collapse of sorghum prices in southern Somalia. Given that food aid was by far the major donor response to the crisis, and that affected communities had urgent requirements for much more than just grain at that point (a substantial measles epidemic was underway incurring major health care costs, among other things), it is not surprising that much of the available food aid found its way back onto the market. Food aid cashed in by recipients in Somali Region of Ethiopia naturally flowed to the main available outlet, across the border in Somalia.

This coincided with the harvest in Somalia, and while prices generally fall during the immediate post-harvest period, the collapse of farmgate prices in 2000 was dramatic, far more so than had been seen previously in southern Somalia. Factors other than just food aid were surely involved in the collapse, as reflected in the fact that prices have still not returned to their pre-2000 levels in real terms. A better than average 2000 Gu season, the introduction of new currency notes and exchange rate manipulation by unregulated traders operating from Mogadishu, and dampened urban demand elsewhere in Somalia are probably also implicated in the collapse of prices. But the

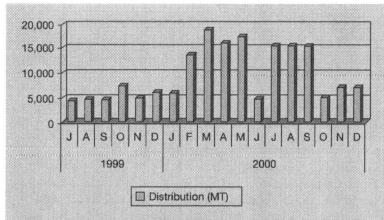

Figure 9.3 Distribution of food aid in Somali Region, Ethiopia (in metric tons)
Source: FEWSNET Ethiopia

impact of rushing to catch up with lagging food aid deliveries in Ethiopia clearly seems to have played a significant role in triggering the collapse in sorghum prices, and the impact of the low prices is still felt in the agricultural areas of southern Somalia, itself a desperately poor region.

Producer incentives turn not only on the prices they receive for their output, however, but also on the prices they pay for their inputs and the constraints they face in making production and investment decisions. Although food market prices will almost always fall – although the extent of the drop depends on targeting efficacy – the question of net producer incentives ultimately turns on how potentially favorable factor market effects on purchased (especially imported) inputs, capital, and labor balance out against the inevitable adverse product market effects manifest in lower food prices.[31] In spite of lower food prices, food aid can stimulate local production through any of several pathways.

First, it can relieve short-term borrowing constraints that otherwise force small farmers to forego buying fertilizer, seed, livestock feed, or other productivity-enhancing inputs because they must buy food for their families. Box 9.2 describes a specific case from north central Kenya where these effects seem to have been important.[32]

Box 9.2 The stimulating effects of food aid in Baringo District, Kenya[1]

Lower Baringo District, in north central Kenya, is a semi-arid region populated by agro-pastoralists. A series of survey-based studies there found that households that received food aid – almost entirely through food-for-work projects – were able to reduce distress sales of livestock, to increase use of improved agricultural inputs such as fertilizer, irrigation, and hybrid seed, and investment in remunerative, nonfarm enterprises such as village stores or bicycle transport services, and to help farmers with optimally time cultivation tasks such as land clearing, planting, and weeding by relieving them of the need to be off working for others in order to earn cash wages with which to buy food for their families. These benefits seem to have been relatively concentrated on the lower end of the wealth distribution.

In each case, food aid appears to have relieved the short-term financing problems faced by some poor people who lack access to formal credit or insurance. In the case of those suffering severe stress, food aid thereby obviated somewhat their need to either liquidate a scarce and valuable asset (livestock), providing a safety net against decline into greater destitution, or to divert labor from their own farm to others in order to earn wages needed to meet immediate needs. In other cases, food aid provided a form of quasi-credit, permitting investment in new businesses and inputs to crop production that increased household productivity, farm output, and income. The Baringo case demonstrates how food aid not only can be effective in protecting households against temporary deprivation, but in so far as it affects factor markets – in this case effectively providing credit in kind – it can even have a favorable impact on local food production, rather than the adverse effect many commentators think inevitable. These effects could in theory be achieved through cash transfers as well, but sometimes food is the only form in which resources are available to provide poor households with high-return transfers.

Note:
[1]   Based on Bezuneh *et al.* (1988) and Barrett *et al.* (2001).

Second, because food aid reduces a country's need to import food, it frees up scarce hard currency for importing other key inputs – farming and transport equipment, fuel, chemical fertilizers, etc. – that affect agricultural output, both in the same year and with a lag.[33] Third, by providing a safety net in times of stress, well-targeted food aid can prevent irreversible health problems due to under-nutrition-related illness. Maintaining a healthy labor force is central to agrarian nations' agricultural productivity and food aid can contribute vitally to this goal. Fourth, by providing a safety net, food aid can encourage producers to take on a bit more risk, such as that associated with experimenting with a new crop variety or production method that promises higher yields once one has properly learned the method. Fifth, in so far as food aid deliveries into remote communities have the potential to increase transport capacity – through backhaul on trucks or planes – for shipping local output to distant national, regional or global markets, food aid can help relieve an important bottleneck to commercialization of agricultural output, thereby stimulating greater production. All of these salutary effects likewise depend, however, on the good management of food aid.

The net outcome of these conflicting factor and product market effects is analytically ambiguous. Recipient country farmers could either benefit or lose from food aid shipments into their local market. The empirical evidence remains quite inconclusive, consistent with the notion that food aid has countervailing positive (factor market) and negative (product market) effects on farmer incentives in recipient countries.[34] There certainly does not seem to be strong evidence in support of the hypothesis that food aid significantly displaces domestically produced food on recipient country markets. Indeed, the most methodologically rigorous empirical study of this topic to date finds that food aid inflows cause, on average, slightly increased food production per capita in Sub-Saharan African agriculture for the three subsequent years.[35] This surely reflects not the desirability of food as a commodity for transfer to small farmers but instead that even a highly imperfect instrument can be beneficial in these resource-starved situations. As a result, most of any losses resulting from food aid shipments seem to be distributed among foreign commercial suppliers. This is precisely why food aid is contentious in trade circles.

Myth 13 Food aid necessarily hurts recipient country producer incentives

Because food aid adds to food supplies in recipient countries, it tends to reduce food market prices, although the extent of induced price reductions depends heavily on the efficacy of targeting. While the induced product price effects of food aid tend to diminish farmers' production incentives, food aid can also affect factor markets for seasonal finance, labor, and purchased inputs. Where food aid relieves small farmers of the burden of buying food during the lean season, it can enable them to purchase high-yielding inputs, to invest in on-farm improvements, and to allocate their labor to on-farm operations according to optimal agronomic practices, not according to when they have free time between unskilled jobs to earn wages. The net farm production incentives created by food aid's product and factor market effects are analytically ambiguous. On a global scale, they seem largely to cancel each other out. But in especially resource-starved areas like Sub-Saharan Africa, food aid can prove stimulative to agricultural production in spite of adverse food price effects.

Food aid is most likely to affect local food markets negatively when it is monetized, whether by recipient country governments monetizing program food aid to generate counterpart funds for fiscal operations or by NGOs cashing out food aid to use in development projects. While the receipts of monetization are used in targeted programs, there is rarely any effort to target the final consumption of the food aid itself, which increases the risks of trade and producer-price disincentive effects of food aid. Precisely because much of the market displacement effect is borne by commercial exporters into the recipient country market, farm lobbies in most food aid donor countries object strenuously to food aid monetization.

In the past few years, one of the issues concerning the prospective market price effects of food aid has revolved around monetization, whether by governments receiving program food aid or by NGOs taking delivery of project or emergency food aid. An influential report on program food aid by the European Union offered a careful and quite condemning assessment of the effect of program food aid on the food security of poor households.[36] It cited vast evidence of serious leakage to unintended beneficiaries and lack of any particularly effective pro-poor targeting in the use of counterpart funds generated by the sale of program food aid shipments. These targeting errors imply minimal demand expansion coupled to the supply expansion associated with food aid receipts, leading inevitably to decreased local food prices. Hence the great interest in the adverse producer price incentive effects of food aid in the days when program food aid overwhelmingly dominated aggregate flows. With sharp rollback of program food aid over the past decade, monetization has increasingly become the domain of NGOs trying to use the proceeds to benefit poor target populations. Yet the same issues remain with respect to market price effects due to the lack of any effort at targeting the distribution of food once it is dumped in local markets in order to obtain operating funds.

In order to prevent or minimize the interference of food aid monetization on the agricultural economy of the recipient country, recipient agencies are required to conduct a **Bellmon Analysis**, named after the sponsor of the covering legislation, the former Senator Henry Bellmon.[37] A Bellmon Analysis determines the adequacy of storage facilities in the recipient country to prevent the spoilage or waste of commodities being monetized; and determines whether the importation and monetization of food aid will lead to a substantial disincentive to domestic production or interfere with agricultural marketing in that country. The Bellmon Analysis must be undertaken for every commodity monetized for each year of a program.[38]

The onus for undertaking the Bellmon Analysis is with the "cooperating sponsor," usually the NGO undertaking to monetize the food aid in order to operate programs. The completed analysis is submitted to USAID as part of the process of estimating annual requirements for food aid. The process of recipient agencies conducting the market analysis on behalf of the donor, to determine the potential negative impacts of the resource upon which they both depend to fund other food security programs, has been criticized as lacking in the necessary checks and balances needed to ensure that monetization does not have deleterious effects on host country production or marketing systems. Recently, a senior US government official remarked privately that "Bellmon Analyses are sheer fraud . . . no one believes them." While some such analyses are undoubtedly accurate and helpful, the core point is that their quality is variable, and the general utility of these assessments remains limited at best.

Moreover, while monetization frees up substantial funding for food security programs that do not directly distribute food aid, it can also exacerbate some of the risks of food aid mismanagement. In particular, because monetized food aid is not targeted to food-insecure people, it tends to aggravate targeting programs, with all of the adverse consequences discussed previously: production disincentives effects, import displacement, etc. This can undermine any benefits from the programs being funded by monetization proceeds.

The extensive literature on food aid's effects on market prices has implicitly focused heavily on prospective errors of inclusion, or leakage effects that depress producer incentives. Of potentially greater humanitarian consequence are errors of exclusion at both the macro- and micro-level, when food aid fails to reach groups, regions or countries that suffer significant food availability shortfalls. Prices of food commodities are characterized by regular spikes as local stocks become exhausted.[39] Price stabilization policies, often underpinned by buffer stocks supplied by food aid, have attempted to curb food price spikes, which have been shown to have at least as great an effect on hunger and excess mortality as crop failures.[40] Over the past twenty years, such schemes have been rolled back around the world following the argument that stocks prove overly expensive to maintain and are often managed according to political rather than humanitarian or economic objectives. This places a greater premium, however, on timely delivery of food aid to places experiencing shortfalls in food availability that could otherwise lead to "stock-outs," a situation in which physical, carry-over stocks are fully depleted so that there are no longer any stored reserves available. Stock-outs are strongly associated with price spikes in storable commodities.[41] When errors of exclusion are minimal, the likelihood of stock-outs becomes negligible, which dampens speculative bubbles in storable food prices.

Distorting government and NGO incentives

When poorly managed, food aid can likewise enable recipient country governments to postpone inevitable and important policy reforms. Food aid can be a crutch for governments practicing policies that discriminate against domestic agriculture, causing regular shortfalls in availability that then have to be plugged with food aid. Not only can food aid fail to induce needed policy reforms, it can foster the continuation of bad policies. Perhaps the best example is the enormously wasteful Egyptian wheat subsidy program that was underpinned by American food aid shipments for many years. If food aid provides the key resource necessary to maintain an ill-conceived policy, curtailing deliveries – rather than providing food aid – may hasten necessary reforms.

Conditionalities tied to food aid distribution sometimes help provide an impetus to reform policies, especially where short-term transition costs might otherwise dissuade governments from summoning up the courage to reform failed policies. The use of conditional food aid for pushing policy reforms depends fundamentally, however, on tangible results of the proposed reforms, and a credible exit strategy from the food aid intervention. As discussed previously, such cases are rare and the experience of using food aid for extracting useful policy reforms from recipient country governments has generally been a failure.

Conclusion

As showed in Chapters 2–5, food aid programs have traditionally been driven primarily by the availability of the resource rather than by a grounded analysis of food insecurity. Food aid has been moving slowly towards a more recipient-oriented approach over the past two decades, thanks in large measure to an improved conceptualization of the challenge of reducing poverty and acute food insecurity, an increased emphasis on protecting nutritional status, and especially, operational improvements by agencies that handle food aid. Yet in many ways, the global food aid regime remains tied to objectives that are often only tangentially related to the needs or rights of food-insecure people. And at the outset of the twenty-first century, food insecurity and famine continue to threaten close to a billion people. Food aid must be made more appropriate to address this threat, although as a small and specialized resource it can only address *some* of the problems of food security.

In recipient-oriented systems, food aid has been used for a variety of applications. These include: (1) direct humanitarian response to emergencies, whether resulting from "natural" or "man-made" causes; (2) "developmental" uses of food aid in programs such as maternal/child health care, food for education, and food for other kinds of incentives, and the increasingly widespread practice of monetization, practiced mainly by American donors and NGOs; and (3) the middle ranges of the so-called "relief/development" spectrum – uses in mitigation, safety nets for asset protection, and "developmental relief."

While there is relatively little controversy about the use of food aid in genuine humanitarian emergencies, its deployment in support of development programs remains more contentious and more closely tied to donor considerations than it is to the real resource requirements for programs that address the fundamental causes of poverty and food insecurity. Food aid clearly can play an important role in safety nets, but in order to have any lasting impact, it must be tied to other programmatic inputs. Food aid provides the means for the protection of poor people's most valuable assets in the short term – most notably, their own and their children's health – but only rarely can food aid itself enable people to lift themselves out of poverty or chronic vulnerability, and even to protect human health and livelihood assets, food aid is rarely sufficient on its own.

The management of food aid remains subject to several major operational constraints. Most of these revolve around the broad issue of targeting. Targeting involves deciding the answers to a long list of questions, including *who* should receive food aid and *how* best to identify them; *where* these groups are found; *what kind* of intervention is required (both food and non-food, and what kinds of food); *when* and for *how long* it is needed (and how to know when to stop); and *how much* is needed. Getting the answers wrong to any of these questions, or more problematically, failing to address these issues in the field, almost invariably results in targeting errors – either "under-coverage" errors of exclusion – meaning that food-insecure people do not receive the food assistance they urgently require; or "leakage" errors of inclusion – meaning that people who do not urgently require food receive it needlessly.

Innovations in the management of food aid supply chains and specifically in the development of strategic food reserves have helped to reduce time lags, and to improve on the "when" of food aid targeting. Improved early warning and assessment practices have helped to improve on the "who," the "where," the "what," and the "how much" questions. But these all remain heavily dependent on having high quality and timely information about both current vulnerability and baseline patterns of livelihoods and food security. Resources available for technical support to food aid distribution remain astonishingly meager. Technical support to emergency food aid programs amounts to only about $1 for every $1000 of food shipped.[42] The information available to food aid donors and managers has improved dramatically in the past two decades, but major information constraints still exist. These informational constraints make the problem of accurate targeting more difficult. While information systems have mostly focused on drought-related emergencies and predicting other types of "natural" disasters, information constraints are much more serious in conflicts and complex political emergencies and in responding to the HIV/AIDS pandemic. The production of reliable information can also be expensive, which increases the costs of food aid as an intervention. But poor information or a total lack of information increases the likelihood of poor management of food aid programs. It is generally more wasteful and dangerous to try to do development or humanitarian programming on the cheap than to spend scarce funds on careful assessments, targeting and management systems.

Both "undercoverage" and "leakage" errors undermine the recipient-oriented objectives of food aid. The former undermines the obvious humanitarian objective of food aid programs. The latter type of error creates problems that are variously described as forms of "dependency" – a term we think is misused and overused with respect to food aid – but that generally refers to interfering with either production incentives or markets for food and labor. However, there is no clear policy preference as to which type of error operational agencies ought to minimize. Inevitably, attempts to minimize one kind of error increase the likelihood of the other kind. Targeting therefore remains a major constraint on effective food aid management. For food aid to play a constructive role in either humanitarian response or safety nets, significant structural reforms must be undertaken. This is a central topic to which we now turn.

10 Recasting food aid's role

The general strategy

Food aid can, under clearly defined circumstances and when properly managed, be an important instrument in an overall strategy for addressing both acute food insecurity and chronic poverty. However, it can also be detrimental to those objectives if not properly managed, or if the humanitarian or poverty-reducing goals of food aid are subservient to other policy objectives. A central part of the challenge of recasting food aid so as to realize its potential as an instrument for satisfying basic human rights and advancing human and economic development lies in exploding many of the popular myths that pervade contemporary policy debates. Having challenged the most important of these myths in the preceding chapters, our task now becomes to articulate a sensible, evidence-based role for food aid in international development and humanitarian policy. This chapter lays out the general strategy we envision for food aid. Chapter 11 then closes by addressing both the imperative of food aid reform and some of the key details of such a strategy and the politics of fruitfully recasting food aid's role.

It is critical to note from the outset that our aim is not to develop a "food aid strategy" *per se*. For far too long, the response to food insecurity in low-income or disaster-affected countries has been resource-driven, with donated food commodities as the resource. Rather, the humanitarian and development community must develop a coherent strategy for reducing acute food insecurity and poverty, and then, based on that broader strategy, demonstrate when and where food aid is an appropriate tool with which to implement (part of) such a strategy, and when it is not. The natural objectives of such a strategy are to fulfill and protect basic human rights to life, health, and food and the reduction of chronic poverty and acute food insecurity. In such a strategy, food aid must be seen as *one* resource, not *the* resource.

Our aim in these final two chapters is therefore to build on the analysis presented thus far to spell out the circumstances and applications to which food aid is well suited to advancing a coherent strategy for reducing acute food insecurity and poverty, and those to which it is not. In this chapter, we sketch out the main points of such a strategy before turning to the core question of how food aid fits into such an overall strategy.

In brief, we conclude that food aid is most effective and necessary in addressing acute humanitarian emergencies, with some limited applications in safety nets in support of anti-poverty interventions and even more limited support of cargo net interventions in situations where effectively no other resources are available. Food as a resource can advance food security and poverty reduction objectives effectively by ensuring adequate availability of and access to necessary nutrients, and by pre-empting distress sales of productive assets – or the cessation of investment in children's education – that might imperil future well-being. As we will emphasize repeatedly in these final two chapters, this preferred use underscores the importance of linking food aid directly to conditions of insufficient local food supply and imperfect food markets. In other situations, alternative instruments are more effective than food aid in meeting poverty reduction and humanitarian objectives. Other policy objectives that have traditionally been associated with food aid (surplus disposal, export market development, maintaining a maritime fleet, etc.) are likewise best achieved with policy instruments other than food aid.

In recasting food aid's role in support of development and humanitarian objectives, policymakers and implementing agencies must therefore consistently ask two core questions: (1) Is food aid *an effective resource* with which a particular problem can be addressed?; (2) Is food aid *the most effective resource* with which to address the problem? The first question establishes a necessary condition for the use of food aid. If the answer is not "yes," then food aid is clearly an inappropriate tool and should not play a role (even if it is currently used, due to policy objectives other than reduction of poverty and food insecurity). The second question establishes a sufficient condition to justify the use of food aid. When and where the honest answer is "yes," food aid is a critical resource for combating food insecurity and poverty. More nuanced criteria will be required where the first question can be answered "yes," and the second question answered "no." Under such circumstances, there may be operational reforms that can improve the performance of food aid, enabling a "yes" answer to the second question. We discuss such changes later in this chapter and in Chapter 11. The tricky cases emerge where food aid is a "second-best" resource. Does and should it play a limited role, perhaps balanced with other resources? If so, what are of those other resources and the politics of their allocation? Much of the political tussle over food aid, especially in the United States, concerns this grey area.

A strategy for reducing poverty, food insecurity, and undernutrition

Traditional food aid programs were based on the assumption that declines in food availability cause food insecurity, including its most acute form: famine. Theoretical and empirical advances in the 1970s and 1980s demonstrated that while an inadequate overall food supply necessarily meant that some people would go hungry, an adequate overall food supply did not, in itself, guarantee that all people would have access to food sufficient for an active, healthy life. Thus, the theory of entitlements to food, and particularly entitlement failures of certain groups of people, has justifiably dominated food security analysis for much of the past two decades. Yet food aid as a key instrument used to address problems of hunger and food insecurity still tends to be based on the assumption that the lack of food itself is the problem.

Indeed, food aid can be used directly for what Sen called "transfer entitlements," the direct provision of food by some external party. Within the normative framework of human rights, food aid can help to fulfill the right to food. Yet implicit in a rights-based approach is the obligation not only to deal with the literal fulfillment of rights in the short term, but also to create the enduring circumstances in which rights will continue to be respected, protected, and fulfilled. In other words, a rights-based approach obligates states and the international community to deal not only with acute food insecurity but also with the chronic poverty that causes people to be acutely hungry for long periods of time. Food-based interventions that fail to attend to the underlying causes of persistent poverty and food insecurity may keep people alive while failing to prevent recurrent or intensifying problems. This must change if food insecurity and poverty are to be overcome in the twenty-first century, and if food aid is to be a useful tool in addressing these issues.

While this book is not the place to try to articulate all the details of a broader strategy for reducing poverty and vulnerability, a central thesis of this book is that the efficacy of food aid as an instrument for reducing food insecurity depends directly on how well food resources support more general poverty alleviation policies. Our claim is that effective strategies for reducing poverty and vulnerability must focus in particular on *chronic* poverty and vulnerability, on those whose standard of living is persistently low or who are merely one adverse shock away from semi-permanent poverty – subpopulations who simply "can't get ahead for falling behind."[1] As we emphasized in Chapter 6, an effective strategy to reduce poverty and vulnerability, and thus acute hunger and food insecurity, must address the structural causes of poverty traps.

This way of framing the discussion reveals a fundamental complementarity between the rights-based approach to development and humanitarian assistance and one based on the economics of poverty traps. The rights-based approach emphasizes individuals' right to an adequate long-term standard of living, reflected in a variety of dimensions, as well as a corresponding obligation on the part of national governments, including donors. This perspective gives rise to a natural emphasis on rights to food, health care, education, and shelter, all fundamental to human labor productivity.

Poverty traps – the condition in which people are not expected to naturally grow their way out of poverty over time[2] – arise due to the existence of critical asset thresholds at which the dynamics of accumulation and standards of living tend to bifurcate, with one path leading to lower level equilibria below an appropriately defined poverty line and the other to a more desirable standard of living above the poverty line. In order for an individual to avoid poverty not only today but for the indefinite future, he or she must control enough assets to surpass the critical asset threshold and to be able to stay at or naturally grow towards a higher-level dynamic equilibrium.[3] The economics of poverty traps thus emphasize the potential for external intervention to keep people from falling below critical asset thresholds, including (but not limited to) those based on physiological need for food. The economics of poverty traps likewise relates directly to asset-based approaches that enjoy increasingly widespread acceptance as the cornerstone of anti-poverty programs, both domestically within the OECD economies and internationally within low- and middle-income countries.[4]

While the rights-based and poverty traps approaches are by no means perfect substitutes, they are nonetheless highly congruent. On either approach, there emerge three key strategies to combating chronic food insecurity, poverty, and vulnerability.

First, donors and governments must be prepared to act quickly and substantively to address humanitarian emergencies where and when they occur. The necessity of emergency response quite obviously supports a short-term rights-based approach in that those with authority and resources incur an obligation to protect basic human rights to food, health, education, etc. when emergencies threaten the capacity of individuals, households, and communities to provide for themselves adequately. It also forms a critical piece of a poverty traps approach. The most extreme cases of micro-scale poverty traps involve essentially irreversible human capital loss or human development failures due to childhood undernutrition, illness, injury, and lack of education. Not only are basic human rights most intuitive at this scale and setting, but the most compelling models of poverty traps emerge at this micro scale as well. Undernutrition, morbidity, and a lack of education early in life can lead to permanent reductions in physical stature, health status, and cognitive development associated with sharply increased risk of involuntary unemployment and lower incomes in adulthood, thereby propagating poverty across generations.[5]

Second, both a rights-based approach and the economics of poverty traps point toward the importance of safety nets for the protection of critical assets, including human capital. If productive assets underpin long-term well-being, then combating chronic poverty and hunger demands keeping those who are not currently chronically poor or acutely food insecure from losing assets to the point that they fall below a critical threshold and collapse into a poverty trap. The aim is to promote households' resilience in the face of various shocks.[6] By similar logic, safety nets are necessary to ensure the protection of basic human rights when people confront adverse shocks to their living conditions. The threat of uninsured asset loss and the possibility that unforeseen events can knock people into lower-level livelihood strategies underscore the extremely valuable role safety nets can play in mitigating asset risk, in keeping short-term shocks from leading to chronic poverty and acute food insecurity through endogenous asset decumulation or low-return production and portfolio strategies. Put more vividly, safety nets keep people from falling into a vicious cycle of deepening, long-term destitution. While the experience with targeted safety net schemes has been mixed, many seem to work well when designed and implemented properly, perhaps especially those based on public employment guarantees, including food for work programs.[7]

Third, those who are already in a poverty trap need assistance in building up productive assets to or beyond the critical threshold at which accumulation dynamics bifurcate. This is the domain of "cargo nets," to use the terminology of Chapter 6 – interventions expressly aimed at helping the destitute exit chronic poverty by building up the stock and productivity of financial, human, natural, physical, and social capital at their disposal. This is essentially a familiar investment strategy, typically founded especially on advancing the labor productivity of the chronically poor through education, health and nutrition, and physical asset-building interventions.

Whether approached from a rights-based perspective or one following the economics of poverty traps, these three pillars – emergency humanitarian assistance, safety nets, and cargo nets – form the foundation of a sensible strategy for reducing chronic poverty and acute food insecurity. But these pillars extend well beyond food as a resource. So where does food aid fit into an overall strategy for reducing poverty and food insecurity?

The roles of food aid in an overall food security strategy

Food aid plays a key role mainly in a few well-defined circumstances, including the protection of human life and livelihoods in emergencies, in situations of chronic poverty or vulnerability. But the use of food aid must always be in support of – not instead of – other longer-term strategies and investments to reduce chronic poverty and vulnerability. And food aid must be utilized in ways that complement – not undermine – these strategies. Applicability should be reviewed on a case-by-case basis. Food aid delivery should be governed by adequate international mechanisms and triggered by accurate information about both the nature of food crises, and the magnitude of food requirements, together with requirements for other necessary interventions.[8]

Acute humanitarian emergencies

Emergencies can be caused by economic shocks (e.g., the East Asian financial crisis of 1997–98), natural disasters (e.g., cyclones, drought, earthquakes, floods, hurricanes, and typhoons), disease epidemics, and, especially in the past ten or twenty years, militarized conflict or shocks brought about by the failure of governance, or some combination of these factors. One early consequence of many shocks is the collapse of food production and distribution systems, accompanied by deterioration in people's ability to access adequate and appropriate food. Food aid is often a necessary component of humanitarian response in such emergencies. For example, populations caught in a conflict are often unable to pursue their usual livelihood strategies and then they become either refugees or internally displaced persons lacking both food and the cash necessary to procure it. In the short term, food aid is often the only option for the protection of the human right to food for such groups.

However, food aid can have serious unintended consequences incompatible with the objectives of reducing chronic poverty or protecting basic human rights. Any food aid programming must directly guard against such adverse effects. For example, as described in detail in Chapter 9, food aid and other forms of humanitarian assistance have too often been used as a weapon in conflict, or manipulated for the military purposes of one or more parties to the conflict, from outright looting of food shipments or "taxing" local populations for protection, to clearing human populations out of certain areas by only granting humanitarian agencies access to displaced populations somewhere else nearby, to hiding armed combatants among refugee populations from whom fighters receive (voluntary or involuntary) assistance. Such abuses are not so much an argument against the use of food aid as one in favor of the careful use of all forms of assistance in conflict, especially conflict in which civilians are targets of military objectives, as is frequently the case in contemporary warfare.[9] The politicization of food aid and the confusing overlap of humanitarian, strategic, and political objectives (often referred to as "coherence") have become a real concern, as has security of NGO, UN, and donor agency staff.[10]

More fundamentally, food aid is not always and everywhere an appropriate response to acute humanitarian emergencies. While food assistance may often be a necessary component of response to emergencies that involve a collapse of production systems or entitlements (or both), it is very rarely, in itself, a sufficient response. It is essential to identify the key contexts in which direct delivery of food – whether sourced locally or internationally – makes sense, as well as to identify complementary responses in, for example, human and animal health care, conflict resolution, or provision of shelter, water, and sanitation services.

As a basic rule of thumb, food aid, in the form of physical delivery of commodities, is an essential resource for responding to acute humanitarian emergencies that are underpinned by both:

- a significant food availability deficit and
- a market failure.

When faced with an outright deficit of food in a given location, whether at the scale of a local community or a nation-state, the food necessary to meet human consumption requirements has to come from somewhere else. When coupled with market failure – due, for example, to conflict or to natural disaster that has destroyed roads and other essential marketing infrastructure, or to powerful social networks that effectively exert market power by forcibly excluding entry by credible competitors – then even increased availability of cash in the hands of food-insecure people does not stimulate sufficient commercial inflows from surplus areas to meet local needs. Instead, it often drives up local prices, making cash-strapped households even more vulnerable to food insecurity. The set of circumstances characterized by a significant food availability deficit and a market failure may be thought of as the "first-best" use of food aid. And although such circumstances are arguably becoming less frequent worldwide, they remain distressingly common.

The emergency that affected large areas of Ethiopia in 2002–3 could be broadly described as precisely this kind of situation. There were cases of localized surpluses, but the crisis was triggered by large-scale crop failure throughout much of the country, notably in areas very poorly served by roads and other market infrastructure. In the context of a rural peasant economy characterized by poor market integration, the harvest failure represented both a collapse of production *and* a collapse of entitlements. Chronic poverty also underpinned the Ethiopian crisis of 2002–3, and food aid, while an important humanitarian response, was not an adequate tool with which to address the underlying chronic poverty issue, at least not by itself. This raises the issues of safety nets and cargo nets (see the next two sections), rather than viewing all cases of widespread and acute human suffering in classic humanitarian response terms.

In emergencies underpinned by just one of these two criteria (food deficits or market failures), food aid is only sometimes appropriate and following only some modalities. Where food is available within the country but markets have failed, food aid remains a logical option. But local purchase of food commodities, even if funded from abroad, is often a faster, cheaper, and more effective procurement method than international shipment of food. These situations were more common in a past era when governments heavily regulated markets, setting prices and maintaining parastatals' legal monopsony[11] over grain purchases. But to the extent that poor infrastructure, weak commercial finance and contract enforcement systems, and physical insecurity continue to impede strong food market integration in many low-income regions, market failures continue to necessitate direct food deliveries into emergency-affected areas.

In emergencies underpinned by food market failures, the appropriate mix between international food shipments and food aid commodities sourced more locally, whether in other regions of the affected country (local purchases) or in nearby countries (triangular transactions), depends fundamentally on the quantity, cost and accessibility of local surpluses relative to donor country commodities. In many smaller-scale emergencies, nearby food availability is adequate and at sufficiently low cost to meet most delivery needs. In larger-scale emergencies, transoceanic shipments typically must play a larger role.

By contrast, where adequate food is available and affordable through markets that remain accessible to disaster-affected people, food aid is clearly *not* necessary. Indeed, it is typically not an appropriate resource for emergency response under these circumstances. This is most commonly the case in urban crises, where a strong network of traders continues to operate and food insecurity typically reflects unemployment or extremely low wages best addressed through means other than food aid. Cash transfers – whether directly through disaster payments, public employment schemes or other transfer systems – are generally the response of choice in such settings when operational agencies can reasonably effectively target vulnerable households because local private sector traders can typically move food in more quickly and cheaply than international agencies, who can themselves deliver cash more quickly than food. The trick is obviously making cash available from donors, a topic to which we turn in Chapter 11. The one notable exception comes when targeting is difficult and food aid monetization can help stabilize food prices in an urban area with many food-insecure residents.

Bangladesh's recent experience in the wake of the most serious floods in a generation, reported in Box 10.1, offers a useful illustration of how effective food marketing systems obviate the need for food aid deliveries. Food aid, whether sourced locally or in donor countries, is unnecessary when markets function well. This method reinforces, rather than undermines, local marketing systems, facilitating the emergence of adaptive local systems that improve medium-to-long term responsiveness to both demand- and supply-side shocks.

Box 10.1 Food markets and a disaster avoided: the Bangladesh floods of 1998–99[1]

From July to November 1998, Bangladesh experienced its most disastrous flooding in modern history. At the flood's peak in mid-September, water inundated 66 percent of the nation's land. Although the country is regularly affected by floods from overflowing rivers and coastal tidal rises, this flood substantially exceeded previous ones in 1954, 1974, and 1988. Crop losses were extensive. In the fall of 1998, the country faced a 22 percent shortfall between food production and national consumption, while 20 million people were made homeless. The magnitude and duration of the flooding raised the grim prospect of famine, as occurred in 1974–75, when 30,000–100,000 people died in the wake of more modest flooding.

In spite of the magnitude of the flood and the associated production losses, interruptions to transport and displacement of households, no major food crisis emerged. The primary reason is that massive private sector imports, made possible by market and trade liberalization earlier in the 1990s and by government investment in marketing infrastructure, stabilized rice markets, enabling government and international NGOs to focus effectively on reaching the 4 or so million most desperate households with direct food transfers. The *aman* rice harvest in November/December 1997 had also been poor, so stocks were relatively low, prices rose and the private sector responded by importing nearly 900,000 tons of rice from India in the first five months of 1998. As the floods began, private sector imports resumed, and at an accelerated pace. The Government of Bangladesh removed rice import tariffs and facilitated speedy trans-shipment and movement of grains into and across the country. Prices of food grains that escalated just before the floods remained relatively steady during and after the floods, rising only 7.0 percent August–November over the May–July period. In contrast, in 1974–75 rice prices jumped 58.2 percent over the same period and most famine mortality arose because staple foods were priced beyond the reach of the poor. The 1974 price spike cannot be explained by production shortfalls – which ultimately proved less than in 1998 – but were instead the consequence of poorly functioning domestic food markets. The timely availability of food was undoubtedly helped by the immediate food aid pledge of 650,000 tons when government finally sought international assistance in late August. But ultimately the government distributed less than one sixth as much rice as the private sector, and households relied far more heavily on private borrowing than on government or NGO transfers to cope with the flooding. The key to averting a humanitarian disaster was the quick response of the private sector – actively encouraged and facilitated by government – which effectively stabilized rice prices during the crisis, thereby protecting many poor households' food security through the worst of the flooding.

Note:
[1]   This example draws on Ravallion (1987), Khan (1999), and Del Ninno *et al.* (2001).

Figure 10.1 reflects these market functioning and local food availability criteria for the use of food aid in emergency response in a decision tree framework. The first question one ought to ask in an emergency setting is whether local food markets continue to function well. If so, the best intervention is to make use of local markets rather than wasting precious time and resources in trying to replicate them through food deliveries. If local food markets are incapable of sourcing and distributing adequate quantities of appropriate foods, then food aid deliveries are indeed necessary. The question then arises as to where to source this food. The most appropriate answer to that logically subsequent question turns on local food availability. To the extent that surpluses exist nearby and can be mobilized quickly and cost-effectively, local sourcing is most appropriate. Unfortunately, these questions are not often confronted explicitly, much less in the logical sequence, in emergency response operations (in which all too often, food aid, sourced from abroad, is the default option for response).

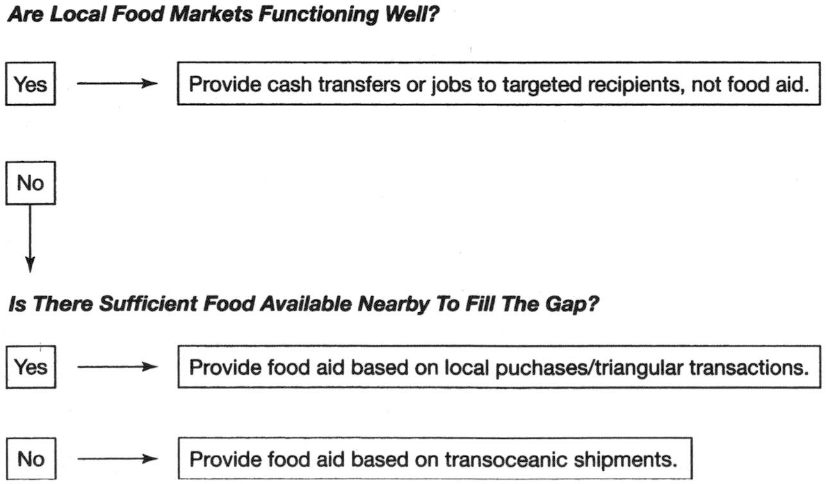

Are Local Food Markets Functioning Well?

| Yes | ⟶ | Provide cash transfers or jobs to targeted recipients, not food aid. |

| No |

Is There Sufficient Food Available Nearby To Fill The Gap?

| Yes | ⟶ | Provide food aid based on local puchases/triangular transactions. |

| No | ⟶ | Provide food aid based on transoceanic shipments. |

Figure 10.1 Decision tree for appropriate food aid response

This decision tree approach brings into stark relief the fact that transoceanic shipment of food aid procured in donor countries really is the last option, albeit one that frequently remains necessary. Yet transoceanic food aid shipment continues to account for nearly 90 percent of global food aid flows, even within the sphere of emergency shipments. This underscores the importance of increasing the flexibility with which operating agencies can respond to emergencies, both in terms of where food aid shipments are procured and whether resources should be made available in the form of food at all.

The criteria laid out in Figure 10.1 carry obvious implications for early warning systems (EWS) that track climatic, economic, and political indicators of prospective emergencies. Not only must EWS incorporate the traditional indicators – rainfall, crop and livestock production information, market prices, child anthropometric status – they must begin to incorporate more sophisticated market information. Analysts within decision-support systems must be able to determine whether local markets (not just prices) are functioning or collapsing, the availability of food and other commodities in national and regional markets, and, critically, the prospective impact of large-scale food procurements in such markets on food prices, quality and availability, including the cost of transport and any required processing (e.g., milling or micronutrient fortification). No systems currently in place come close to doing this. Significant enhancements of EWS are therefore necessary.

This book is not the place to go into great detail on the operational management of food in emergencies. Clear minimum standards have been developed to guide early warning and assessment requirements as well as the targeting and delivery of food aid in emergencies. Major improvements are nonetheless still needed in the timing and targeting of food aid and in monitoring not only the delivery and usage of food aid, but particularly its humanitarian impact. These improvements will require more integrated information systems not only to provide adequate early warning for emergencies, but also to provide adequate monitoring and evaluation of food aid's impacts, including whether post-emergency transition programs begin on as timely a basis as emergency programs. Most critically, information systems must move away from predicting purely expected food deficits to include a broader range of humanitarian requirements and a broader range of causal factors.[12] The Sphere guidelines and other extant codes of conduct already align the use of food aid with both respect for the human right to food and the humanitarian imperative to protect life in emergencies. Nonetheless, much work remains to be done to operationalize these guidelines and codes of conduct more precisely, and to get various parties – donors, national governments, belligerent parties in war, and operational agencies – to live up to their obligations under these codes of conduct.

Where emergencies are underpinned by an outright food deficit and the failure of markets – a distressingly common feature of emergencies resulting from conflict, as well as by climatic and environmental shocks combined with chronic poverty – food aid is not only an acceptable resource for dealing with crisis, it is a necessary resource. Decisions regarding where to source this food – from surplus areas within the same country, in commercial markets of nearby countries, or from overseas donor markets – require context-specific analysis.

Regardless of source, ensuring the nutritional appropriateness of this food is a constant concern.[13] WFP has recently made significant, appropriate efforts to mainstream nutritional quality concerns, such as the timely provision of small-but-critical amounts of fat, micronutrients, and protein from foods such as iodized salt, fortified blended foods, ready-to-use therapeutic foods, and vegetable oil.[14] Recent advances in the medical and nutritional sciences, and increasing application of those advances in the field, have reduced excess mortality in emergencies even as the number and scale of disasters have increased, not least of which because of significant improvements in the nutritional quality of much food aid.[15] Nonetheless, where food aid remains driven primarily by special interests in donor countries, ensuring nutritional appropriateness remains a challenge.

Moreover, it must be remembered that food alone is rarely sufficient to address acute humanitarian emergencies. Access to adequate health care, shelter and clean water, in particular, are essential complements to food in order to ensure protect human lives. Nevertheless, for the foreseeable future, food aid will remain a necessary instrument for protecting human rights and human life in emergencies.

Safety nets for vulnerability reduction and asset protection

The World Food Program's strategic plan for 2004–7 notes

> the inability of hungry people to manage risks is a danger to the very process of development. Hungry people often resort to activities that are potentially harmful to their future, such as stripping forests of timber to sell as fuel wood, selling farm implements, or engaging in commercial or survival sex and so increasing the risk of HIV transmission.[17]

Safety nets aim to protect people against severe shocks, or at least from having to respond to shocks in such as way that threatens their longer-term well-being, so that they can recover from shocks on their own. The objective of safety nets is to enhance households' resilience to adverse shocks.

The major considerations of safety nets are to ensure "asset smoothing" and recovery capacity. Asset smoothing[17] refers to the preservation of productive asset stocks so that one does not fall below the critical thresholds at which households or individuals switch from a pathway of expected recovery to one of expected decline into destitution. The purpose of safety nets is to enable people to cope with vulnerability without depleting their stock of productive assets and thereby forsaking their capacity to recover from shocks.

People face threats to their productive asset stock continuously and many such threats are household- or individual-specific (i.e., "idiosyncratic risk") rather than common to whole communities, regions or countries (i.e., "covariate risk").[18] Therefore, in order to be effective, safety nets must function continuously, with levels of activity responding to fluctuating requirements. Because of this need for continuous coverage to insure against idiosyncratic risk, credible and effective safety nets can be expensive, and thus they are often absent in low-income countries. As safety nets become less effective, however, the need for humanitarian response systems activated under extreme circumstances becomes greater and more frequent. But incorporating the asset protection function of safety nets into humanitarian response systems almost inevitably involves delays that undermine the fundamental purpose for which safety nets exist. So humanitarian response and safety nets are best viewed as complements rather than substitutes for one another.

The circumstances under which food aid-based safety nets make sense are similar to those for food aid for humanitarian assistance. When and where an overall food availability shortfall combines with markets that do not function well enough to support an effective cash-based transfer system, the provision of food as a transfer can spare recipients from having to liquidate productive assets (e.g., livestock, land, a small business) in order to purchase foods essential for maintaining adequate nutrition and health.

However, food itself is rarely sufficient to define the critical asset thresholds that a safety net must defend. Therefore, food aid works in support of safety nets only where it reduces participants' vulnerability to adverse shocks and protects their broader portfolio of productive assets and their recovery capacity when they suffer shocks. Moreover, food aid-based safety nets almost always require other, complementary inputs or activities to protect the productive assets of vulnerable peoples. As a result, the role of food aid in establishing and maintaining safety nets is more limited than its role in acute humanitarian emergencies, where the objective is more simply to protect human life.

It must also be borne in mind that safety nets' role is less to help move recipients out of chronic poverty than to prevent decline into destitution. Properly conceptualized and designed, safety nets are not intended for those who are *already* destitute. Rather, they provide a means to prevent people from *becoming* destitute – to keep transitory poverty or food insecurity from becoming chronic – and to provide the insurance needed to encourage vulnerable populations to choose higher-risk, higher-reward livelihood strategies that can lower the critical asset threshold a bit, enabling some of them to climb out of chronic poverty with the passage of time through steady accumulation and improved productivity of productive assets.

The classic safety net activities involving food aid are employment guarantee schemes, typically food for work (FFW) programs. FFW schemes span a wide range of activities. Most aim at creating or maintaining community assets – e.g., reforestation, road maintenance, water resource protection – but an increasing proportion focus on more individually held assets – e.g., on-farm soil and water conservation or job skills training. In this sense, there is not always a clear distinction between safety nets and cargo nets. The difference really comes down to the balance between insurance (safety net) versus asset building (cargo net) objectives, which cannot always be effectively differentiated or reconciled.[19] It therefore becomes essential to be very clear as to the primary objective of a public works program: is it intended mainly to serve as a safety net to protect vulnerable individuals and households against calamitous asset loss or as a means of building up assets for poor individuals or communities? The Tinbergen rule – that one typically needs one separate policy instrument for each policy objective – applies here as much as it does to food aid more generally.

Other operational considerations arise with safety nets based on food for work. FFW purports to have an attractive "self-targeting" feature, meaning households self-select into the pool of participants and the poor are typically thought more likely than better off households to avail a member to work in such schemes. However, as noted in Chapter 7, it has been well established that not only do labor-surplus households take advantage of additional income in the form of food even if it is not particularly needed, the most vulnerable households are often defined by a shortfall in available labor, and therefore are unable to participate in food for work schemes even if the income is urgently required.[20] Under such circumstances, food for work must be both proactively targeted and very flexible, in effect paying the most vulnerable households to do things they might need to do on their own if they had the labor to be able to do so.[21] Critical issues regarding the timing of activities arise as well, particularly with employment guarantee scheme activities at critical times of the year in the local agricultural cycle. For example, activities that take people off their own land holdings necessarily conflict with on-farm labor requirements, so off-season safety nets should provide adequate support to cover times of the year when people need to be working on their own holdings, otherwise this work on their own holdings should be directly supported.

As with food aid for emergency response, where markets remain accessible to food-insecure groups so long as they get cash with which to buy food, cash-based transfers are typically a less expensive, more effective and more timely means of providing a safety net. For example, public employee schemes based on cash wages have often proved more effective than food for work schemes and are almost always less expensive to run.[22] But cash for work schemes obviously require cash resources, which may be feasible in middle-income countries, as in Argentina's highly successful Trabajar program,[23] but are rarely available in low-income countries that depend on donors who continue to provide much of their assistance in the form of food commodities rather than cash.

Just as the distinction between cargo net and safety net activities is often blurred in FFW activities, so is the distinction between humanitarian response and safety net operations similarly subtle. Moreover, the two must often be linked in practice. Emergency response operations aim to protect human life, while safety nets aim more broadly at protecting the broader array of productive assets that underpin target populations' sustainable livelihoods and their capacity to recover and grow. Where humanitarian assistance focuses on protecting a minimally acceptable standard of living and fulfilling basic human rights, regardless of recipients' capacity for subsequently lifting themselves up by their bootstraps, safety nets encompass a broader range of assets, not just human capital, but also the land, livestock, trees, social networks, businesses and other non-human assets necessary for households to be able to make subsequent progress in improving standards of living and accumulating wealth.[24] In rural areas where sustainable livelihoods depend on more than just human capital, the distinction between humanitarian response and safety nets becomes important. In places with active labor markets – typically towns and cities – where wage or salary employment suffices to keep people out of poverty and food insecurity, human capital (good health, nutrition, education, and the capacity to work) may be the primary relevant asset and thus the distinction between humanitarian response and safety nets virtually vanishes.

The protection of productive assets reduces the need for humanitarian response. Humanitarian response systems must be activated when safety net systems are either overwhelmed by a covariate shock (e.g., a massive drought, floods, or civil war), or are ineffective or non-existent. Safety nets and humanitarian response are thus nested interventions, both in conceptual and practical terms, particularly where vulnerability results primarily from climatic, environmental, or economic shocks. Because safety nets require the reliable presence and functioning of government or NGO providers, however, they are typically not viable where vulnerability results from conflict or poor governance associated with a failed state. Safety nets function best in insuring against climatic, economic, environmental, and health shocks.

In our experience, the subtle but important distinction between safety nets and emergency response is often lost, with many programs misclassified as safety nets although they would more appropriately be labeled humanitarian response programs, some of which may be the result of absent or dysfunctional safety nets. For example, the recent crises in Ethiopia and southern Africa were classified officially as drought emergencies. However, both were underpinned by an accelerating downward spiral of poverty and vulnerability that necessitated a massive humanitarian response to a moderate climatic shock. Had functioning safety nets been in place, the combined effects of chronic poverty, HIV/AIDS, and a climatic shock might well have been contained before the situation deteriorated into an acute humanitarian emergency. But in the absence of a flexible and ready safety net, the response had to be funneled through the classic humanitarian response system of early warning alerts, assessments and consolidated appeals. Paradoxically, emergency response is inevitably slower than safety nets because the former is a response to a particular event or confluence of events while the latter should involve a continuous presence activated as needed for threatened subpopulations.

The role food aid can play in addressing the HIV/AIDS crisis, especially in Sub-Saharan Africa, deserves special mention. Food aid can clearly play a humanitarian role in the care of people infected with the disease and their families. Although there is not yet any clear, peer-reviewed evidence as to if or how food aid affects the course of HIV/AIDS, adequate nutrition slows the onset and progression of full-blown AIDS, at least when complemented with anti-retroviral treatment. Nutrient-rich supplementary foods have been shown to slow the progression of the disease, although not necessarily the kind of foods routinely made available in food aid programs.[25] Most critically, HIV/AIDS progressively weakens people, making them less able to work, and poor nutrition puts infected people at greater risk of secondary infections which are often both an additional expense to the household caring for infected persons, and ultimately the cause of death. Additionally, HIV/AIDS commonly leaves the affected households and communities poorer (because of health care and funeral costs); with a declining labor pool (because of the death of economically active people and increased labor devoted to care of infected persons), and in some cases with a drastically depleted physical resource base (particularly in the case of widows losing land rights or other assets of deceased husbands). While all these concerns require much broader forms of intervention, all call for an increasingly effective safety net in the short to medium term to mitigate some of the most harmful impacts of the pandemic. Unless and until there is widespread accessibility to curative treatments, little can be done about death and the resulting grief and loss of household labor supply for survivors. But safety nets can reduce the loss of other productive assets by infected and surviving households.

However, food aid is plainly not a first-best response; direct prevention and treatment campaigns are the most appropriate way to attack the HIV/AIDS pandemic. Moreover, the use of food aid as a response to the HIV/AIDS crisis is fraught with operational difficulties. First, targeting becomes very difficult with regard to a disease status that remains highly stigmatized. Second, the most commonly used self-targeting mechanism (food for work) is largely inapplicable because affected households are almost by definition labor-deficient because of the disease. Third, wide-scale, untargeted use of food in response to HIV/AIDS can undermine other community-based approaches, for many of the same reasons as we discussed in Chapter 9. Innovative approaches to using food as a resource have been developed,[26] and food aid can be a part of a safety net for dealing with both the immediate and secondary effects of the HIV/AIDS pandemic. But the problems noted above require a different approach than do other risk factors. And to restate the obvious, food is only one (small) part of the resources needed to effectively address HIV/AIDS.

Safety nets commonly get overwhelmed in low-income countries where risk mitigation policies are thin or non-existent and shocks increasingly lead to destitution, necessitating the use of formal and informal social safety nets as coping mechanisms to protect the assets of vulnerable peoples. Risk mitigation – *ex ante* measures to reduce the likelihood of suffering a shock – is typically less costly and more effective than coping mechanisms – *ex post* responses to reduce the adverse impacts of a shock.[27] One needs to be very careful, therefore, that resources devoted to safety net interventions in no way substitute for resources devoted to preventive measures to mitigate against the suffering of adverse shocks. For example, diversion of scarce development resources from investment in, say, developing drought-tolerant cereals cultivars that might limit the impact of unavoidable climate fluctuations to fund instead immediate needs for food aid and other forms of emergency response to drought may only reinforce the problem.[28]

The distinguishing feature of safety nets is their objective, not the particular activities undertaken. Similar activities, particularly those involving food aid, may be undertaken with either humanitarian response or with cargo net programming. The key distinguishing feature is that safety nets proactively protect the assets of poor and vulnerable people in the face of known vulnerability, and not just vulnerability to broad-scale shocks, but also to important idiosyncratic shocks (e.g., crop loss to pests or wildlife, illness, injury, or unemployment).

Determining which assets or asset categories are most at risk in the face of either an acute shock or a chronic condition is logically the first task of safety net programming. Livelihood assets typically include at least five categories: (1) natural assets (land, water, and forest resources, etc.); (2) physical assets (tools, livestock, consumer durables, etc.); (3) financial assets (cash, bank deposits, etc.); (4) social assets (group membership, informal reciprocal relationships); (5) and human assets (health, nutritional status, education and skills, and the ability to work). Once the crucial asset(s) have been identified, the second crucial question concerns the best means of protecting these assets.

For example, in the widespread drought emergency that affected pastoral areas of the Horn of Africa in 2000, the biggest category of asset losses that were associated with (and to some extent preceded) the humanitarian crisis was livestock death. Rapid intervention to protect livestock assets – or to enable pastoralists to hold assets in some durable, alternative form – likely could have mitigated both the immediate (humanitarian) and longer-term (asset destruction) consequences of the drought. Logically, the issue of resource appropriateness would have arisen at the stage of determining suitable interventions to protect assets. Donors did support some limited livestock-oriented interventions during the 2000 drought emergency, but they were tiny in comparison to the food aid response, and happened so late in the crisis that they saved few assets.[29] Food aid was evidently the default resource for a drought emergency response. Beginning with the assumption that food aid is the resource and food for work is the implied activity of safety net programming not only puts the cart before the horse, it also risks driving the cart backwards. To be effective, safety nets have to be on-going and supported by a reliable stream of resources, and not just food.

Cargo nets for asset building among the chronically poor

As explained in more detail in Chapter 6, where the emphasis with safety nets is on protecting previous investments and currently held assets, to prevent a descent into destitution and to build resilience to shocks, the emphasis with cargo nets is to increase the stock and productivity of chronically poor people's productive assets so as to enable them to climb out of chronic poverty and vulnerability.

While we do not want to dwell excessively on definitions, it is nonetheless important to keep concepts and terms straight for conceptual and programmatic clarity. It therefore seems necessary to digress for a moment to explain the mapping among our three classes of intervention – humanitarian response to emergencies, safety nets and cargo nets – and some other terms in play within the broader development and humanitarian communities. The World Bank refers to "productive safety nets," USAID talks of "resilience safety nets," some analysts talk of "trampolines" (i.e., a safety net that bounces people right back to where they were), and others use the term "developmental relief."[30] All these labels describe a mix of humanitarian response, safety nets, and cargo nets. As we have emphasized throughout this book, it is important to keep the primary objective of a policy clearly in mind (the Tinbergen Principle). Actual activities may look similar – for example, food for work schemes can be intended for asset building in communities, as a safety net to insure unemployed or underemployed persons against asset loss, or even as a means of humanitarian assistance among disaster-affected people – but the intended outcomes and design details differ according to program objectives. The concepts are necessarily nested in that the objective of protecting assets necessarily includes the objective of protecting life, while effective asset building necessarily requires protecting assets.

Cargo nets span a wide variety of activities intended to build public and private assets – such as roads or schools on the public side, and livestock, soil and water conservation structures, or education on the private side – or to improve the productivity of existing assets – for example, job skills training or diffusion of improved agricultural production technologies. However, food aid is typically not the most effective instrument for providing cargo nets and is often not even appropriate. The notable (but currently common) exceptions are cases where cash resources are simply unavailable and food enables recipients to invest – either their savings from reduced food purchases, in the case of direct distribution, or the proceeds from monetization – in acquiring other productive assets, including equipment, skills or livestock without doing harm to non-recipients. Such cases are relatively less common than the cases where food aid is appropriate and effective in humanitarian response and support for safety nets.

The second critical point with regard to all these programs is that food alone can rarely achieve the objective of building assets. Yet the necessary, complementary cash resources are often not made available by donors. This undermines the developmental aspect of the program *and* exacerbates the negative impacts of the food aid, since it basically forces people to sell, rather than consume, food aid received as part of a wage or benefit package. Food aid for cargo nets, like food aid for safety nets or for humanitarian response, only makes sense where there are food deficits, but the missing ingredient for effective programming – regardless of the kind of activity – is often the complementary cash resources. Donors need to address this basic design flaw in contemporary overseas development assistance in support of an overall strategy for reducing poverty and acute food insecurity.

In addition to food for work efforts that aim to create public or private assets, the main three other current uses of food aid for cargo net programming are: (1) direct nutritional support to vulnerable groups – particularly mothers and young children; (2) school feeding programs to support nutritional objectives, school participation, or both, among older, school-aged children; and (3) monetization of food aid to raise funds with which to finance a wide range of interventions intended to build assets or increase the productivity of intended beneficiaries' existing asset stock. We address the first two issues here, but leave monetization to the next section because food aid monetization can also be in support of humanitarian response or safety net operations.

Nutritional support programs are important for protecting vulnerable children in the first 24–36 months of life. Prenatal and childhood undernutrition can result in permanent health problems. Therefore efforts to prevent childhood undernutrition are a crucial investment in life-long health. Since adult health and physical stature are among the strongest and most important correlates of adult labor productivity and earnings,[31] prenatal and early childhood nutritional support programs are among the most fundamental "asset building" interventions any agency can undertake.

While operational methods for using food aid in support of maternal and child health programs have improved steadily over time, perhaps especially with recent advances in community-based approaches,[32] food aid is generally an expensive way to support such programs. Much programming in this area has been driven by resource availability and, as is the case with emergency response and safety net programs, non-food requirements for this kind of support are often funded at much lower levels.

School feeding programs likewise are valuable investments in building durable human capital for lifelong productivity and reduced future vulnerability to shocks. School feeding has been shown to increase school attendance (particularly of groups that often are not in school, such as girls); to improve school performance (where hunger and malnutrition were the constraint to performance – school feeding alone cannot address education quality issues); and is increasingly attached to other incentives such as "take-home" rations that are contingent on child participation in school – the "food for schooling" programs described in Chapter 7.[33] It remains an open question, however, whether school feeding programs are the best use of either scarce development resources or food aid, or whether food aid is the most effective means of enhancing school attendance or children's cognitive or physical development.[34]

One last issue relates again to the multiple roles any given food aid-based activity can play. Agencies that are charged with responding to food emergencies in chronically vulnerable countries must always remain prepared for the "next" emergency. However, because agency budgets at the country office level are often determined by the tonnage of food aid moved, institutional incentives favor continuing food aid programming even under circumstances when food aid is not required for humanitarian assistance, or is required only in limited areas and specific seasons. Under these circumstances, other programs such as school feeding and other "development" activities are sometimes required to keep staff employed, pipelines open, and key information systems operational. An important latent benefit of such programs – beyond any direct cargo net role – arises from their contribution to emergency preparedness. The cargo net programming can be dropped quickly in the event of another acute humanitarian emergency, with the staff, equipment and administrative systems already in place to handle the crisis. While this obviously helps with emergency preparedness, it may also undermine the efficacy of the cargo net programming. The demonstrable inertia in food aid distribution[35] surely reflects this reality. Again, the problem is not food aid *per se*, but the way in which resources are allocated to agencies – in this case, providing staff and information systems resources in proportion to the tonnage of food moved, not in proportion not to the requirement for emergency preparedness. The objectives of programs, not the availability of resources, should drive the choice and design of activities.

Monetization

The resource-driven use of food aid has perhaps grown most obvious and egregious in the case of food aid monetization. As documented in Chapter 5, monetization of non-emergency food aid shipments from the United States has skyrocketed over the past decade as NGOs have come to rely increasingly on this mechanism to generate cash resources needed for activities intended to advance food security objectives, but not through the direct distribution of food.[36]

Monetization has nonetheless increasingly come under question for its inefficiency as a means of providing cash resources for development interventions and for possible competition with US food exporters, most notably by the US Office of Management and Budget (OMB). Monetization's defenders within NGOs and the US government commonly argue that while monetization is imperfect, under present foreign assistance policy, monetization remains the only reliable, longer-term source of cash resources for moving beyond the distribution of food to addressing other causes of food insecurity and that even a flawed resource can be valuable when no other resources are available.

Both sides are right in this argument. Food aid monetization is a poor means of transferring cash abroad and one that often distorts recipient country food markets. But in resource-starved settings such as much of Sub-Saharan Africa, in the absence of cash for development programming, monetization is often better than nothing. And in the case of USAID resources, Title II non-emergency programs are the major resources targeted specifically towards poor and vulnerable groups. The argument over food aid monetization is thus largely a misplaced argument over the form and level of development assistance funding provided to operational agencies by donor countries.

There are certainly situations in which monetization can play a useful role. Food aid monetization can underpin cargo net interventions serving a market development objective when food is an intrinsically important resource, particularly by working with small vendors to develop local markets in places where markets are functioning poorly or with small producers to develop downstream food processing and marketing capacity, as was done quite successfully in India under Operation Flood.[37] Monetization of food aid can also support safety nets or humanitarian response by helping to control food price spikes in food security emergencies underpinned by a sharp drop in aggregate supply or by hoarding based on traders' speculation of an impending supply shortfall.[38] Such use can protect the real wages of workers and net food-buying small farmer households. For example, release of rice food aid stocks held in Madagascar helped reduce and stabilize not only rice prices, but also the prices of other staples during the volatile period of food market liberalization and exchange rate devaluation there in the late 1980s.[39] By no means should monetization be completely dismissed; it can play a useful role in supporting an overall strategy to reduce chronic poverty and acute food insecurity where food itself provides clear benefits.

Nonetheless, monetization has simply become an alternative source of cash resources for agencies to use in programming. This practice must change, as the OMB rightly emphasizes. The necessary reform, obviously, is to make more cash available for development programming, even at the cost of reducing food aid flows, and even, if necessary, at the cost of very modest reductions in already meager development assistance budgets.

The reasons for promoting a different approach regarding monetization are several. First, food aid is a hugely inefficient mechanism for generating cash resources for development programming. Second, monetization itself commonly diverts operational agency staff attention from core programmatic activities more directly related to poverty reduction and food security objectives.

Third, where monetization income lags behind program expenditure requirements, implementing agencies must either absorb the cost of borrowed capital, delay programs, or, in extreme cases, lay off staff, all of which reduce the developmental impact of programming. While it is impossible to put a dollar figure on the sum of these costs because they are so highly variable depending on context, monetization is at best a clumsy and inefficient mechanism for generating cash resources for projects addressing food security objectives.

Fourth, food aid monetization recreates many of the problems generated by widely disparaged program food aid: displacement of commercial trade, the undermining of production incentives, and the distortion of labor markets. These result largely because monetized food aid is dumped in recipient country food markets rather than targeted to vulnerable groups with a higher propensity to consume the additional food.[40] As we emphasized in Chapters 8 and 9, poor targeting (or in this case, the absence of any attempt to target food aid shipments) lies at the root of most of the problems food aid causes.

Food aid alone will never be sufficient to address key underlying causes of food insecurity and poverty in developing countries. The main problem is that there are few sources of cash resources for addressing key underlying problems. In the long term, the solution is to allocate funds for development programming through a mechanism completely different from food aid, and to use food aid monetization as a mechanism only where it serves consumption and market development goals, or when it helps to control extreme price spikes during emergencies. This will improve NGOs' efficiency, simplify some of their staffing and management problems, and reduce competition with donor nation (and other nations') exporters, as well as with recipient country producers and merchants. But it will also require the support of a somewhat different political constituency from the one that currently supports food aid, as we discuss in Chapter 11. In the near term, at a minimum, addressing this problem requires additional analysis to identify and mitigate potentially harmful impacts of monetization, and also requires that agencies begin developing exit strategies from monetization.[41]

Local purchases and triangular transactions

When local food availability (and/or processing capacity) in the vicinity of a target group are adequate, the efficiency and timeliness of food aid delivery can commonly be enhanced by procuring (and/or processing) commodities within the food aid recipient country or in neighboring nations. In Chapter 8, we showed that this is commonly feasible, although it is by no means always the case. These efficiency and timeliness considerations alone would seem to support an expanded role for local purchases and triangular transactions in global food aid procurement.

The prospectively stimulative effects of local purchases and triangular transactions on source country agriculture typically reinforce this conclusion in favor of expanded local purchases and triangular transactions. These effects must, however, be balanced against the prospective adverse impacts of local purchases and triangular transactions on food consumers in source markets. Research has repeatedly shown that one of the most vulnerable groups in any country are net food-purchasing households: low income urban households and resource-poor rural households.[42] The effects, if any, on producers and consumers in source countries results from food market conditions. Where local markets are well integrated into regional and global food systems, food aid procurement will typically have little, if any, impact on prices and thus on either farmer incentives or consumer welfare. This is why food aid programs generate no measurable price benefits for farmers in major donor countries such as Australia, Canada, and the United States. Precisely because developing country markets do not always function as efficiently and throughput capacity is often limited, food aid procurement in low-income country markets must be preceded by careful market analysis of the likely effects of such purchases.[43] In the absence of such analyses, the "developmental" impact of local or triangular transactions could largely be undermined.

Program food aid

As detailed in Chapters 2 and 3, program food aid has declined steadily for years, first in Canada, then in Europe and the United States. The reasons for this vary from donor to donor. In the main food aid donor country, the United States, the primary reason has been the decline in government-held surplus stocks and the relative ineffectiveness of food aid in promoting commercial exports, especially relative to alternative export enhancement programs. There is little reason to believe these conditions will change appreciably in the future.

Indeed, program food aid is especially difficult to defend. It is an extremely inefficient means of resource transfer and as an untargeted, monetized resource maximizes the distortionary effects of food aid on markets. In the form of concessional exports, as practiced by the United States under PL 480 Title I, it looks a great deal like a subsidized export, in contravention of international trade accords, thereby inviting trade disputes. Moreover, program food aid adds significantly to the administrative costs of food aid to the United States since it requires separate administration within the US Department of Agriculture, parallel to the emergency and project food aid managed by the US Agency for International Development. Ending program food aid once and for all would also help to focus the instrument a bit more on the one major policy objective for which food aid has proved itself effective: helping to reduce acute food insecurity.

Figure 10.2 summarizes our perspective on the broad changes needed in the global food aid system. Program food aid would be eliminated entirely, acute

Global Food Aid Regime Over Past Decade

Type of Food Aid		Humanitarian	Project	Program
Share of total flows	Percentage	~45%	~20%	~35%
Sources	Local/Triangular	10–20%	~5–10%	Very little
	Donor nation markets or stocks	80–90%	90–95%	Almost all
Mode of distribution	Direct distribution	Almost all	~50%	Almost none
	Monetization	Almost none	~50%	Almost all

A More Effective Global Food Aid Regime

Type of Food Aid		Humanitarian (Life-protecting)	Safety Nets (Asset-protecting)	Cargo Nets (Asset-building)
Share of total flows	Percentage	65–75%	10–20%	5–10%
Sources	Local/Triangular	Where market analysis indicates appropriate	Where market analysis indicates appropriate	Where market analysis indicates appropriate
	Donor nation markets or stocks	When local purchase/triangular transactions are inappropriate	When local purchase/triangular transactions are inappropriate	When local purchase/triangular transactions are inappropriate
Mode of distribution	Direct distribution	Almost all	Almost all	Almost all
	Monetization	Only in rare cases (price spike control)	Limited: only in support of market development goals	Limited: only in support of market development goals

Figure 10.2 Recasting food aid sources: modes of distribution and uses

humanitarian emergencies would receive a greater share of aggregate food aid flows, less food aid would be monetized, and the sourcing of food aid would depend not on the use of the resource but, rather, on what local market analysis would indicate is the capacity of local markets to supply sufficient quantity and quality food on a timely basis without significant adverse local effects on net food buyers. Aggregate food aid volumes would vary with need in recipient economies, rather than with global food prices and donor country political cycles. On average, food aid volumes would fall and a reasonable portion of the current value of the average annual reduction in food aid flows would be added to untied overseas development assistance flows in the form of cash, capital goods, and technical assistance. The level of resource availability would be driven far more by careful analysis of requirements in low-income, food-deficit countries than is presently the case.

We acknowledge that this represents a relatively radical reform of the existing global food aid system, and that such changes will not happen overnight. In order to achieve long-term change, interim or transitional strategies will be necessary. But we believe it is not only imperative from the point of view of protecting the right to food for all the reasons detailed thus far, but also politically feasible, as we explain in Chapter 11. Such a recasting of food aid will necessarily imply some revision of roles and policies of key actors in the food aid system.

The roles of the main food aid actors

There are three main categories of organizations involved in food aid – donor governments, recipient country actors (national and local governments, and local communities), and the operational agencies that dominate food aid distribution. Each has a role to play in improving the way in which food aid is used as a resource to address overall food security concerns.

Donors

The biggest changes necessary for improving the use of food aid in support of an overall strategy for reducing poverty and acute food insecurity must occur in donor country governments because the greatest distortions of and inefficiencies in food aid today are a direct result of the continued donor-orientation of food aid, especially (but not solely) in the United States. In general, donors must recognize that:

1   Food aid is a resource that has an important but limited application to the policy objective of reducing food insecurity and poverty.
2   Food aid has proved ineffective at advancing other donor government policy objectives – domestic farm price support, agricultural export promotion, foreign policy leverage, maintenance of a strategic maritime fleet – toward which it is commonly directed.

3   The inappropriate use of food aid in pursuit of these latter objectives impedes realization of the erstwhile objectives of either the appropriate use of food aid, or the objective of reducing food insecurity and malnutrition generally.

These have been core themes throughout this book.

Recognition of these three key points implies several general directions for bilateral donor policy. First, and most importantly, it implies delinking development assistance in general, and food aid in particular, from domestic farm policy. This means reducing aid tying, as has been the general trend in recent years among most bilateral donors. It implies ensuring sufficient cash resources to make a concerted effort at achieving the most basic of the Millenium Development Goals – notably, halving poverty and hunger by 2015 – including through international procurement of food, processing, and transport services, instead of merely dumping domestically produced commodities abroad and labeling it "aid." It suggests the need for some creative thinking about how best to credibly commit donors to provide food as it is needed, counter-cyclically with non-concessional availability in low-income food deficit countries, rather than pro-cyclically, as has been the case for the past half-century. Finally, it implies desisting from unnecessarily dragging trans-Atlantic trade disputes over genetically modified foods and related questions into humanitarian crises.

The European Union, most of its member states, and several of the European national donors outside of the EU have uncoupled food aid policy from domestic farm policy, trade, and maritime objectives. Australia, Canada, and Japan have all made significant progress in this direction. There nevertheless remains significant room for improvement in the food aid programs of each of these donors. Australian and Canadian aid remains excessively tied to domestic sourcing of commodities. European food aid response remains frustratingly slow. Japanese food aid continues to be driven by its import obligations under multilateral trade accords. And lavish subsidization of domestic farmers in Europe, Japan, and the United States continues to distort the global agricultural economy far more than even the most mismanaged food aid programs ever could, given the stark difference in scales.

The main laggard among the donors, however, is the biggest food aid provider: the United States. Although changing rhetoric and the rise of NGOs in American food aid programming have brought about some improvements, American food aid continues to underperform, to ignite trade disputes with other donors, and to distort development activities due to: (1) the continued use of concessional exports through Title I of PL 480; (2) restrictions on procurement or processing outside the United States and on using non-US flag carriers for ocean freight; (3) an excessive emphasis on food over cash, as manifest in heavy monetization of non-emergency Title II PL 480 resources; (4) divided administration of food aid programs between two Cabinet-level agencies – a clear signal of the lack of clarity over the effective role of food aid and of unnecessarily costly bureaucratic oversight of an array of overlapping American food aid programs; and (5) the tangled web of regulatory restrictions designed to yield significant, but generally unnoticed windfall profits for a small number of well-connected commercial players. Reforming the global food aid system depends most fundamentally on reforming American food aid programs.

The new draft USAID Food for Peace strategy is a step in the right direction. It stresses reducing vulnerability and risk, "protecting lives and smoothing consumption" and enhancing community and household resilience, showing real progress in conceptualization of the challenge of reducing poverty and acute food insecurity and how food aid fits into that broader program.[44] This strategy, while admirable, will fail without changes in the resource mix USAID gets from the Congress, which remains overwhelmingly based on food commodities. The most egregious current example is probably food aid to Ethiopia, to which the United States committed half a billion dollars during the humanitarian emergency of 2003 (including cash transportation and distribution costs), but less than $5 million during the same time period in cash resources for programs that address agricultural factors underlying Ethiopia's chronic poverty and food deficits.

The problem with American food aid is not FFP policy, which generally makes sense. The problem originates with the enabling legislation, the division of executive authority over food aid between USDA and USAID, and the coalition of interests that supports a very unwieldy constellation of policy objectives that food aid is meant – but is unable – to address. In Chapter 11 we propose an approach for making substantive changes in American policy that will be necessary to recast food aid as an effective instrument in a broader strategy to reduce poverty and food insecurity worldwide.

An important first step in recasting food aid as an effective instrument for humanitarian and development policy will be to renew and strengthen international coordination of food aid so as to increase the coherence of bilateral and multilateral food aid programs and the efficacy of disciplines to reduce trade-related disputes over food aid. The Food Aid Convention (FAC) has expired and is widely viewed as irrelevant by signatory countries, while the FAO's Consultative Sub-Committee on Surplus Disposal (CSSD) has become ineffective in its role in overseeing compliance with nonsensical usual marketing requirements. The Berlin Statement, issued in September 2003, calls for scrapping the FAC, and replacing it with a new international agreement that could enforce strictures against trade distorting food aid, increase the coherence of bilateral and multilateral aid flows, and advance a global code of conduct for governments and operational agencies alike.[45]

Perhaps most fundamentally, donors need to reverse steady declines in real funding for development. As we detail in Chapter 11, while global development assistance funding has largely recovered in recent years from the sharp cuts experienced in the 1990s, a rapidly increasing share of that funding goes to emergencies, squeezing out funding for bread-and-butter investments in building poor people's assets and improving their productivity. Funding for emergencies must come on top of, rather than as replacement for, core development investments or else donors undercut the base for long-term recovery, leading to poverty traps in recipient countries and relief traps for donors.[46]

Recipient country governments and communities

Local and national governments play a central role in food aid operations: organizing and operating national and local information systems that feed into and draw upon donors' and operational agencies' early warning systems, negotiating appeals and terms of shipments, managing strategic food reserves, providing security for donor and operational agency staff, and, in some cases, distributing food to communities, families and individuals (and where not directly carrying out the distribution function, providing the necessary coordination of the operational agencies that do carry out the distribution). Yet most countries with low-income, food-deficit economies have limited technical capacity to support food aid operations or even to coordinate effectively with and among donors and operational agencies. Where capacity has been developed, it is too often diverted for patronage politics, as was tragically evident in Zimbabwe in the 2002–3 southern African food crisis. And in most cases, limited capacity exists to efficiently manage strategic grain reserves or other elements of a food aid procurement and distribution system.[47]

Although they were once almost totally marginalized in discussions of development strategies and particularly of emergency response, community-based organizations and the communities they represent and serve are increasingly recognized as important intermediaries, not simply passive recipients of external aid.[48] This is perhaps especially the case with regard to community management of such activities as targeting and distribution, but is increasingly the case in terms of community-based emergency preparedness and early warning/monitoring, as well as managing many community mitigation and response mechanisms. Often such activities stand in clear contradistinction to – not a part of – a food aid-based response, and therefore lie somewhat outside the scope of this book. But it is increasingly recognized that improving communities' capacity both to manage idiosyncratic risk internally and to monitor and manage external response to covariate shocks, is strategically important for effective poverty reduction and disaster management. Food aid may be part of that response, but the prime issue here is about empowering community management and community response.[49]

Operational agencies: the World Food Programme and NGOs

The main operational agencies responsible for the distribution of food aid for either emergency response or in support of safety net or cargo net interventions are the World Food Programme of the United Nations (WFP) and NGOs, often although not exclusively international NGOs. Most of the advances observed in the conceptualization and practice of food aid over the past decade or so have originated in these operational agencies. While there remains room for improvement in NGO and WFP performance with respect to food aid, many of their shortcomings result primarily from constraints imposed by donor (especially United States) policy.

Since its founding in 1963, WFP has been the main multilateral intermediary for food aid delivery. Its role expanded dramatically in the aftermath of the 1973–74 world food crisis, and more recently, its programs have shifted dramatically from project food aid toward humanitarian shipments, with non-emergency flows through the WFP declining from $500 million to $200 million, 1989–2002, while emergency shipments increased from $258 million to $1.3 billion. The WFP is now the largest of the United Nations agencies. And particularly in emergency appeals, it enjoys by far the highest proportion of assessed requirements met by donors. At the same time, its multilateral mandate has been diminished somewhat as it has become increasingly dependent on a single donor, the United States.[50] Few of these changes are the result of WFP's own policy: it is the only UN agency with both humanitarian and developmental mandates but essentially a single resource: food.

WFP has recently developed a new four-year strategic plan,[51] which includes many points in common with the strategy outlined above. The new strategy emphasizes saving lives among the most acutely affected groups in emergencies, on reducing vulnerability, and on reducing malnutrition, particularly of women and children. It also notes that chronic hunger continues to make a mockery of the Millennium Development Goals. There is also a heavy emphasis on addressing HIV/AIDS and on working within the broader context of national poverty reduction strategies, as articulated in Poverty Reduction Strategy Papers (PRSPs) prepared by national governments in consultation with the World Bank and the International Monetary Fund. In this sense, the new WFP strategy is fairly closely aligned with our recommendations.

Yet there is little doubt in the strategic plan that food will remain the agency's primary resource. Were the United States to place greater emphasis in using its food aid contributions for humanitarian response, redirecting non-emergency resources to forms other than food, WFP's role in food aid would almost certainly expand, although so would its dependence on American contributions.

Ed Clay suggests that the WFP should become the lead UN agency on all emergency response, rather than being simply a food aid agency. This, he argues, would enable it to provide a better basis for determining when food aid is the appropriate response and for accessing other resources when food is not appropriate. Such an approach would not, however, be capable of addressing the critical safety/cargo net issues raised here, as it is not clear where the dividing line would be drawn between the increasingly fuzzy notions of "emergency" and "development." Established partnerships, staff, and pipelines all enable a more rapid response when WFP is called upon to lead in food emergencies, and Clay's recommendations do not address how these would be maintained were the WFP to metamorphose into a more general purpose emergency response agency. In any case, altering the mandate of UN agencies is outside the scope of this book.

WFP's current mandate and strategic focus on food as the resource will likely continue, but its policy and advocacy work should extend well beyond the role of food aid *per se*, as it has recently begun to do. WFP's current strategy does acknowledge (at least implicitly) that the agency is put in an awkward position by having multiple mandates, but essentially only one arena of intervention, and an admittedly inadequate one for addressing some of the mandated developmental or protection goals.

Almost by definition, NGOs are hard to classify. The range of international NGOs involved in food aid operations has always been relatively limited. Today there are probably less than 30 engaged in large-scale food aid operations. But these have numerous local partner organizations. Some local partners are national and local government agencies. The majority are also non-governmental, but indigenous to the recipient country. Nearly all these NGOs – local, national, and international – would claim multiple mandates (developmental, emergency, public education and advocacy, and a host of more specialized areas). Some have exclusively humanitarian mandates, but only a very few (for example, the Canadian Food Grains Bank) have an exclusive focus on food aid. NGOs operate both as implementing partners of WFP and also as direct distributors of food aid from donors. Increasingly in humanitarian emergencies, NGOs are mandated by national governments to lead responses in geographically delimited areas, and therefore in some cases, channel national government resources as well.

A major debate in the humanitarian community is on the independence and neutrality of NGOs in the provision of humanitarian assistance in conflict, particularly when dependent on donors that are belligerent parties in the conflict (with Iraq and Afghanistan as the prime current examples). This debate pertains to all humanitarian assistance, not food aid only, and lies beyond the scope of this book.

Given their greater flexibility, NGOs are well placed to utilize food aid where it is an appropriate resource, but to tailor an approach that matches the resource to the task. However, the strategy outlined above will require substantially greater effort on the part of some NGOs to advocate with donors for the appropriate resources, and to turn down potential funding when it is not appropriate. Many NGOs, including some of the largest, are rightfully accused of simply being instruments of donor interests. A study by Tufts University in 2000 among major food aid actors in the US NGO community noted a resigned acceptance that continued reliance on food as the source of resources for programming was not going to enable an appropriate kind of programming in many instances, but revealed little enthusiasm to "rock the boat" in terms of the complex legislative alliances that support the allocation of these resources. "Best practice" in this case, meant only marginal tinkering with modalities.[52]

Several approaches will prove important to NGOs adopting the strategy outlined here. NGOs must make it clear when they will and when they will not use food aid as a resource. This in turn means developing and maintaining the analytical capacity and the self-discipline to determine when food is not the appropriate resource. This includes a critical judgment about monetization as the means of acquiring cash resources where US-funded NGOs are concerned, a topic many NGOs are loathe to tackle. The Tufts study clearly noted that food aid is perceived as a suboptimal resource (referred to above as a "least bad" resource), but often the only available source of multi-year program funding available from US donors – particularly where food security outcomes constitute the programmatic objectives. Changing this situation will undoubtedly require engaging the legislative processes that allocate resources.

Codes of conduct relating to food aid already exist, but more effort needs to go into the self-enforcement of these codes of conduct, including critically, the space for operational agencies to hold each other accountable in the field. The Berlin Statement calls for reforms at both international and at national level, including an international code of conduct that would strengthen accountability, effectiveness, fairness, and transparency, and that would be monitored by an independent body under the Global Food Aid Compact.[53] The contents of a new code of conduct would be the subject of negotiations among the range of stakeholders, including representatives of recipient countries and communities, but the issues raised here should be part of those negotiations. Eligibility to handle food aid provided by any signatory donor country or the WFP would require that the intermediary agency endorse and abide by the GFAC code of conduct.

Operational changes are called for as well. Better information systems are required to support improved situation analysis, both in terms of accuracy and timeliness. Longer-term planning in crisis-prone countries or regions needs to incorporate risk management and vulnerability reduction (whether or not the long-term interventions have anything to do with food aid). And approaches to improve the capacity of local and national partner organizations in all the above will be critical for long-term sustainability of reducing food insecurity and malnutrition, i.e., in creating appropriate exit options in the longer term.

Because they are increasingly important as local partners of both international NGOs and WFP, local (and community-based) NGOs are in many ways better placed than international agencies to deal with the nitty-gritty details of understanding local problems, perceptions of vulnerability, and their implications for assessment and targeting. Local organizations are winning broader recognition as perhaps the most capable agencies for dealing with many of sensitive issues that surround the HIV/AIDS crises, particularly as regards HIV prevention and education programs, addressing the problem of stigmatization, and providing long-term support to affected communities. International agencies can play an important capacity-building role. Food aid can necessarily play only a small role in an effective overall strategy to deal with HIV/AIDS.

Many NGOs embrace the right to food, but have not addressed the thorny questions that arise about the implied obligations to respect, protect and fulfill rights. Most observers agree that primary responsibility lies with states, and that the international community and non-state actors play a supporting role where states either cannot or will not fulfill their obligations. But rights-based approaches also emphasize addressing the underlying causes of hunger and food insecurity, which requires going beyond simply meeting individuals' right to food in the short-term. This underlines a central point of this volume: food aid plays a role in addressing the right to food and in reducing poverty and acute food insecurity, but only a partial role.

Conclusion

Food aid has been commonly misused over the past fifty years, too often causing problems for recipient country producers and third country exporters and coming up well short of its potential as a policy instrument to be used in support of a strategy to reduce poverty and acute food insecurity. A recasting of food aid's role – and of the roles played by the main stakeholders in the contemporary food aid system – can nonetheless substantially reduce the negative effects of food aid and contribute substantively to development and humanitarian policy objectives.

Both operational and policy issues need attention. At the operational level, the most fundamental change needed is to change from a resource-driven to a problem-driven perspective on the use of food aid. Just because donor governments are willing to provide commodities – too often due to misguided efforts to advance donor domestic farm, foreign, or trade policy objectives – does not mean that food is the most appropriate resource with which to attack a food insecurity problem. Food aid is often not even *an* appropriate resource, especially when adequate food is available locally or commercial food marketing channels can move food at least as quickly and cheaply to poor people if their purchasing power can be boosted to create effective market demand. Operational agencies need to resist the short-term temptation to use whatever resources might be offered while advocating for longer-term reform in the overseas development assistance programs of major donor countries, especially the United States.

In this chapter, we argued in detail that a problem-driven perspective based on assessment of the appropriateness of food aid for a given context will likely lead to a far greater focus of food aid shipments on humanitarian emergencies underpinned by both a food availability shortfall and local food market failures. Moreover, a problem-driven approach will put increased emphasis on rapid response based on improved procurement and delivery modalities, and on more integrated information systems to provide not only adequate early warning of emerging emergencies, but also improved targeting and timing of food shipments and satisfactory monitoring and evaluation of food aid's impacts. Although transoceanic bureaucratic food aid flows really ought to be a last-ditch option, it presently accounts for nearly 90 percent of global food aid flows, including emergency shipments. Although local purchases and triangular transactions suffer their own problems associated with quality, availability, and timeliness (and sometimes cost) of deliveries, there needs to be increased flexibility for operating agencies to respond to emergencies by procuring, processing and transporting food quickly and cheaply from source markets outside donor countries.

Similarly, there is a critical need for increased flexibility to be able to use cash and policy inducements rather than commodity resources to work in partnership with, rather than against, local commercial interests in places where food markets function sufficiently well that the private sector can fill the food availability shortfall if there is external support for local purchasing power. Much can be learned from Bangladesh's success in avoiding famine following the devastating 1998 floods, largely thanks to commercial food market response encouraged and assisted by government and NGO actors (see Box 10.1).

Food commodities are less commonly appropriate in support of safety net or cargo net interventions intended to protect or build assets among vulnerable populations. Food rarely suffices to define and protect the critical asset thresholds necessary to prevent a descent into destitution and chronic food insecurity after an adverse shock. By emphasizing that food aid is better suited for humanitarian emergency operations than for safety net and cargo net interventions, we in no way de-emphasize the importance of policies to protect or build assets. Rather, emergency feeding and food distribution operations are plainly just short-term responses to longer-term, structural problems associated with poverty and vulnerability. Asset protection and creation programs based on cash appropriations for development assistance are fundamental to addressing those deeper structural problems so as to achieve sustainable reduction in chronic poverty and food insecurity. Food can sometimes play an important role as a complementary input into, for example, efforts to promote early childhood health, primary and secondary education, provide public employment guarantees, and other safety net or cargo net interventions. But food aid has too often been taken as the primary or only resource with which to support such efforts. That is typically a recipe for failure.

The resource-driven approach to food aid has perhaps grown most obvious and egregious in the form of monetization, an inefficient – and sometimes highly distortionary – means of transferring resources abroad that, in the absence of more flexible cash resources for problem-driven programming, is often seen as better than nothing. Contemporary arguments about US food aid monetization largely reflect (1) misplaced policy debates over the appropriate form and level of development and humanitarian assistance funding provided to operational agencies by donor country legislatures and executives; and (2) the persistence and power of myths about food aid's efficacy in advancing more parochial donor objectives, such as domestic farm price support, agricultural export promotion foreign policy leverage, or maintenance of a national maritime industry in the interests of national security.

The global constellation of agencies and actors engaged in food aid programming has been insufficiently proactive in engaging these debates so as to bring about the sorts of reforms that could render food aid a far more effective and less controversial instrument of development and humanitarian policy. In the next (and final) chapter, we outline some key details of this strategy, and discuss how one might set about building the political support necessary to successfully recast food aid as an effective instrument for humanitarian and development policy for the twenty-first century.

11 Recasting food aid's role

The particulars and the politics

There is no such thing as an apolitical food problem.

(Amartya Sen 1981)

The preceding chapter explained the general direction in which food aid needs to be recast and why. In this chapter, we focus on particular reforms that are necessary. Most of our specific recommendations are reasonably independent of time-bound events, such as recommendations with respect to improved targeting by operational agencies and the need for a global food aid agreement encompassing not just donors but also recipient countries and operational agencies.

Other specific recommendations, however, necessarily relate to impending events of great near-term importance to the structure, conduct, and performance of food aid globally, such as the negotiation of the WTO Doha Round and of the next Farm Bill in the US Congress. We acknowledge that some of the discussion that follows will therefore necessarily be dated in another few years. We include those issues nonetheless, both because of their importance to the design of food aid and to underscore the unusual opportunity available at this particular moment in history. Fifty years after the beginning of modern food aid, several key domestic and international policy processes are converging in such a way as to afford a rare opportunity to recast food aid so as to markedly enhance its effectiveness in serving humanitarian and development objectives. We aim to advance that effort.

Following the general structure of the second half of Chapter 10, we begin with policy changes in the international arena, focusing in particular on essential elements of a new Global Food Aid Compact and the importance of restoring global development assistance flows more generally. We then turn to discuss the policy changes necessary within donor programs, starting with and focusing primarily on the United States, the world's largest and most influential program and, arguably, the one most desperately in need of significant reforms. We then we address some of the changes necessary in recipient countries and communities and key changes necessary at operational levels by agencies working with food aid in the field.

Of course, reforms occur not due solely to their internal logic or their moral imperative, but because they win political support. Therefore, in the second half of this chapter we explore the political economy of effecting such changes. With strong legislative leadership from elected representatives and with cooperation among operational agencies, reform is feasible, even likely. Although farm price support, export promotion, surplus disposal, geopolitical and humanitarian assistance motives have all provided political support for food aid as a general phenomenon, these objectives almost inevitably conflict over the specifics of food aid policy. And the devil is in the details. A sensible strategy of reform can attend to the interests of all parties, and, by reducing the waste in a system serving too many political masters at once, make food aid a more effective tool for advancing development and humanitarian objectives.

International policy changes needed

Reforming the global food aid system will require concerted multilateral efforts in at least two key domains. First, donors must renew and strengthen international coordination and disciplines to reduce trade-related disputes over food aid and to increase the coherence of bilateral and multilateral food aid programs. Second, donor countries must restore real overseas development assistance financing after a decade of steady, sharp decline. The absence of funds with which to undertake proper development programming induces operational agencies to use whatever remaining resources they can lay their hands on – commonly food commodities – irrespective of the resource's inefficiency or distortionary effects. The right resources must be made available for the job.

Recommendation 1 Negotiate a new Global Food Aid Compact to replace the Food Aid Convention

The Food Aid Convention (FAC) was an agreement among donor countries only to ensure a minimum volume of food aid that, under the FAO's Principles of Surplus Disposal, would not disrupt commercial trade. Lacking monitoring or enforcement capacity – Chapter 4 detailed how ineffective the FAO's Consultative Sub-Committee on Surplus Disposal (CSSD) has become in overseeing compliance – the FAC languished. This has fed into concerns over the tying of food aid as member states of the OECD's Development Assistance Committee (OECD/DAC) have gradually adopted a convention of reduced tying of bilateral assistance flows of all sorts. Food aid has been a slow arena for the untying of aid, and the United States has been among the slowest donors to untie aid.[1] The multiple, largely ineffective international mechanisms for coordinating global food aid flows have brought increasing calls for reform and streamlining of the international governance of food aid.[2] A new Global Food Aid Compact (GFAC) must be negotiated to replace the FAC.

The GFAC must make several important breaks from the FAC. First, it should include recipient country governments and agencies that distribute food aid as well as donor countries. So long as international governance of food aid remains a donors-only club, downstream distributors and recipients of food aid will feel little ownership of and responsibility for the food aid system. Furthermore, the GFAC can then give signatories explicit responsibilities under an international code of conduct that can strengthen accountability, effectiveness, fairness, and transparency. A GFAC encompassing all parties to food aid shipments will improve the coherence of bilateral and multilateral food aid programs.

The commitments by recipient country governments would include the following:

- to safeguard the physical security of all donated commodities and the staff of all operational agencies;
- to renounce the use of food as an instrument of political oppression or war, and to reaffirm their commitment to international humanitarian law;
- to allow donor and operational agencies random, wholly independent monitoring of food aid distribution in any location, using local or foreign employees of the agencies' choosing;[3]
- to cooperate with international efforts to conduct nationally representative nutritional, health and socio-economic surveys to establish which populations are most at risk so as to improve targeting efficacy and the monitoring and evaluation of food aid-assisted interventions.

For their part, operational agencies (e.g., NGOs, WFP) would likewise commit themselves:

- to agree on and abide by a code of conduct, such as those discussed in Chapter 6;
- to work cooperatively with donor organizations, recipient country governments and other national institutions on improving early warning and monitoring and evaluation systems, including livelihood monitoring systems to help identify emerging crises and to target the neediest households effectively.

Second, the GFAC would commit donor countries not only to traditional tonnage minima, but also to provision of adequate complementary financial resources and to some flexibility in the rules mandating donor-country procurement, processing and shipping services. The GFAC could thereby help humanitarian and development agencies bring appropriate resources to bear in any given context, and in an economical and timely fashion. Minimum tonnage commitments remain necessary. One obvious reason is that food will always be needed in emergencies. But physical volume commitments are also needed because food aid programs based entirely on monetary commitments can lead to dangerous shortfalls in food aid availability at times when global food stocks are tight and prices high, as was tragically evident during the 1972–74 world food crisis. Minimum annual tonnage commitments under the GFAC should be set at a substantial fraction – three-quarters is an arbitrary but reasonable level – of projected global emergency needs and updated annually by the GFAC based on analysis by the GFAC Secretariat of recent and emerging emergencies. In years when minimum tonnage requirements exceed needs – an exceedingly rare event, but a contingency for which there must be explicit preparation – then surplus volumes should be stored for addressing emergencies in subsequent years through the International Emergency Food Reserve (IEFR) or by competently managed strategic food reserves in countries chronically vulnerable to food crises and to which international deliveries can be slow.[4] The GFAC should also formalize the original intent of the IEFR when it was first crafted in 1975, that all contributions be unrestricted, so that the WFP and cooperating operational agencies can use those resources to respond to emergencies anywhere, not just in emergencies attracting high-level media and political attention.[5]

Physical tonnage commitments are not enough, however. Cash is essential because acute food insecurity and hunger occur most commonly when individuals and households simply lack the purchasing power necessary to procure adequate food. When there is food in the system and commercial marketing channels can and will deliver it to those who can afford to buy it, transfers of cash can more quickly address this type of food insecurity than moving food into the region. Therefore, the GFAC should include donor minimum financial contributions to the World Food Programme and to NGO signatories to the GFAC at a significant scale, say, equal in value[6] to signatories' physical volume commitments. These financial commitments would not be tied to any source market for the commodities, any shipping, processing, bagging, etc., allowing for flexible response to address food insecurity emergencies.

The key distinctions between these financial resources and existing food-related financing facilities, most notably the International Monetary Fund's Compensatory Finance Facility (CFF) and Emergency Assistance Facility (EAF), which provide quick-disbursing loans to developing country governments,[7] are that (1) these resources could be deployed where governments are ineffective or non-existent (e.g., Somalia in its peak crisis years in the 1990s); and (2) these would be pure grants, not loans. Various proposals for an international food financing facility have been floated for a number of years, most recently by a group of 16 food-deficit developing countries in the context of WTO negotiations over the Doha Round and by the Executive Director of the WFP, James Morris. Morris called for a $300 million African Food Emergency Fund to act as an immediate response account for use at the onset of a food crisis to buy food locally, hire transport, set up communications and monitoring systems, and to tide vulnerable populations over until a reliable transoceanic pipeline is established. A WTO panel appointed to evaluate existing and prospective means of providing multilateral financial assistance to meet commercial food import requirements concluded in 2002 that a new fund would be unlikely to address these problems effectively, but that some modifications to existing IMF programs would be advisable.[8] Given the problems with the IMF's existing emergency food financing mechanisms – its Compensatory Finance Facility has not been used once since access rules were tightened in 2000 and the IMF is seriously considering eliminating it altogether – we do not see IMF programs as a viable response. Rather, a commitment to funding channeled through established operational agencies in compliance with the GFAC code of conduct – rather than yet-another multilateral bureaucracy – would be simpler and more effective.

Third, by linking GFAC to the next WTO agreement – a move endorsed by international experts in the September 2003 Berlin Statement[9] – there could finally be effective disciplines to reduce trade-related disputes over food aid. This would give the GFAC some teeth in enforcing strictures against trade-distorting food aid practices by donors. While there remains widespread reticence within recipient countries and many NGOs about the WTO, there is merit to exploiting the WTO's established and relatively effective dispute resolution process so as to enforce disciplines regarding food aid. As Chapter 4 explained in great detail, an irrefutable mass of empirical evidence and theoretical logic underscore that non-emergency food aid – and even some emergency food aid – almost inevitably displaces some commercial agricultural trade. Of course, that is an indefensible argument for ending food aid, as more extreme observers sometimes suggest. However, because international trade is essential to economic development, the inevitability of trade displacement underscores the need to pay close attention to the trade-offs inherent to food aid, between short-term humanitarian and longer-term development objectives. Regulations to reduce excessive or inappropriate uses of food aid-US food aid shipments to Russia in 1998–99 offer perhaps the most egregious recent example – should be welcomed by those who believe that food aid can be effective precisely because such regulations would limit the misuse of food aid. The WTO is the only mechanism that has effective means of enforcing trade-related disciplines. Therefore, food aid must be included within the WTO Doha Round Agreement, appropriately the so-called Development Round.

Note that we are not recommending that the WTO exercise global oversight on food aid operations, merely that its proven trade-related disciplines and dispute resolution mechanisms be made available within the realm of food aid. We favor establishing a GFAC Secretariat within the World Food Programme, co-chaired by the WFP, the WTO, and by the OECD/DAC. This body would bear responsibility for ensuring accurate and timely reporting of aid flows by donors, including the extent to which such aid comes with donor-mandated restrictions on procurement, bagging, processing or shipping (i.e., the "tying status" of food aid). This configuration would explicitly recognize the interlinkages between food aid, global agricultural trade, and overseas development assistance more generally, matters in which the three co-chairs play lead roles in international coordination. The GFAC would absorb within it the regular consultations among donor countries that presently take place within the CSSD, rendering that body unnecessary. Indeed, it could improve upon the CSSD by subjecting food aid to WTO disciplines. Moreover, moving the GFAC out of the International Grains Council, where the FAC has been based since its founding in 1967, will signal clearly that food aid is no longer viewed as a trade promotion tool.

These enhancements to the existing Food Aid Convention would contribute significantly to improvements in the timeliness and efficiency of food aid delivery, to a heightened sense of ownership by low-income, food-deficit states over food aid as a component of broader poverty reduction strategies, and to reduced distortions and disputes in the global agricultural economy over food aid.

Recommendation 2 Restore real global development assistance flows – not just emergency assistance

The second area requiring concerted donor attention revolves around broader patterns of overseas development assistance.[10] Food aid will ultimately prove ineffective without restoration of necessary volumes of foreign aid. Indeed, we are increasingly witnessing the emergence of a "relief trap" in which the insufficiency of donors' foreign assistance budgets leads directly to emergency spending crowding out development spending, which means that subsequent emergencies become more likely, exacerbating the effect until donors are trapped in an almost perpetual and complete relief mode. This hypothesis is consistent with the numbers on overseas development assistance.

Aid to low-income countries has dropped sharply over the past ten years. OECD/DAC data show that after growing sharply through the 1980s, real global aid flows to developing countries – depicted by the solid line measured against the right-hand axis in Figure 11.1 – fell rapidly through the mid-1990s before recovering over the past half dozen years (due largely to conflict-related aid flows to Afghanistan and the Balkans). In 2001 dollars, real aid flows peaked at $57.2 billion in 1992, fell to $44.1 billion in 1997, and nearly recovered to $56.1 billion by 2002. However, this recent recovery is attributable to sharp increases in emergency spending, continuing the trend toward an increasing concentration of foreign assistance on establishing refugee camps, emergency feeding programs, and other responses to humanitarian emergencies. The share of global aid flows spent on structural development – economic infrastructure, agriculture, industry, and other productive sectors – fell from 47 percent in 1993 to merely 21 percent in 2002,

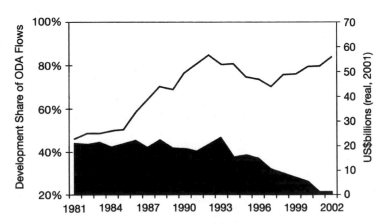

Figure 11.1 Overseas development assistance flows from OECD countries

Source: OECD/DAC, updated from Barrett and Carter (2002)

as shown in the solid portion of Figure 11.1, which should be read against the left-hand vertical axis. The 24 OECD countries[11] contributed, on average, only 0.39 percent of GDP in 1999, far below the United Nations target contribution rate of 0.70 percent, with the United States last in the group at 0.10 percent.

The multilateral development agencies – the World Bank, the regional development banks and UN agencies such as IFAD, FAO, and UNDP – have not picked up the slack. Given that chronic poverty and acute food insecurity remain most concentrated in rural areas where people depend disproportionately on agriculture, development assistance targeted at agricultural and rural development remains especially important to any coherent strategy to reduce poverty and food insecurity. Yet, total agricultural development lending by the World Bank, for example, fell by more than 70 percent in real terms, from $4.7 billion in 1990 to $1.4 billion in 2000, both measured in 2003 dollars.[12] Food aid can only succeed as part of a broader strategy to combat poverty and food insecurity. Such a strategy requires resources and renewed commitment on the part of bilateral and multilateral donors to finance safety net and cargo net interventions that do not require food commodities.

United States policy changes needed

The fiftieth anniversary of PL 480 elicited many tributes to American food aid programs, capped by a grand celebration in Washington on July 21, 2004, eleven days after the anniversary itself. Many testified to the beneficial effects of food aid and the usefulness of the private–public partnership among businesses, NGOs, and government. The event celebrated the humanitarian and development goals and accomplishments of US programs, the instrumental role of food aid during emergencies and the constructive use to which many agencies have put food aid for development projects. Yet there were also signals that day that key players in the US food aid community recognize that while American food aid has undeniably done good, it could be improved considerably with a few substantive reforms. Perhaps most notably, CARE USA President Peter Bell emphasized in his keynote address that "we must push ourselves to identify policy and operational changes to make food aid a more effective tool for reducing poverty and hunger. We must not shy away from those changes."

While there have been important improvements over time – notably with the 1990 Farm Bill and subsequent adjustments in Food for Peace policy – American food aid programs remain relics of earlier domestic farm and export support policies. Current food aid programs were designed by policymakers and politicians who believed that food aid could be an effective means for surplus disposal at a time when generous farm price support programs generated massive government food stockpiles that were expensive to maintain. Those price support programs, and the government surpluses they produced, have largely vanished. US food aid programs were also predicated on two then-untested hypotheses. First, food aid was considered a potentially effective tool for promoting commercial agricultural exports. Second, it was believed that food aid was important to advancing

American geopolitical interests. The historical record has proved both of these hypotheses false. The sole objective for which food aid has proved partly successful is as development and humanitarian assistance. It is high time to focus food aid programs on the one objective for which they remain relevant and effective.

Recommendation 3 Negotiate reductions in outdated forms of food aid in exchange for reductions in EU export subsidies that harm both US and developing country farmers

Because food aid based on surplus disposal or export promotion objectives tends to displace commercial trade, food aid has become a bitter point of contention in multilateral trade negotiations. Following up on progress initiated with the Uruguay Round Agreement on Agriculture (URAA) concluded in 1994, the WTO's current Doha Round negotiations have emphasized agricultural trade liberalization heavily, for good reason. Although agricultural products comprise less than 10 percent of all global trade, agriculture is by far the most heavily protected sector in the global economy today, so much so that two-thirds or more of the economic gains to be enjoyed from complete liberalization of merchandise trade globally would come from agriculture.[13]

Nearly 40 percent of all government subsidies worldwide support the agricultural sector.[14] According to the OECD, farm support programs in the European Union alone exceeded $100 billion in 2002, more than $260/year per EU resident, roughly equivalent to annual per capita income in the world's poorest countries. Japanese outlays on domestic farm support, although less than half that of the EU in absolute terms, averaged more than $300/year per resident. US farm subsidies were a bit less than Japan's in absolute terms, about $125/resident in per capita terms, given the much larger US population. These support programs are a heavy tax on European, Japanese, and American food consumers and taxpayers – nearly $1000 and $650/household annually in Japan and Europe, respectively. Since 98 percent of their own populations who are food consumers, rather than food producers, the overwhelming majority of these nations' population would benefit from reducing these implicit taxes. Even the pro-business publication *The Economist* editorializes that, "Rich-country farm subsidies and tariffs are outrageous by any rational measure. . . . America and the EU have put far too little effort into making concessions."[15] Yet powerful domestic farm lobbies in each country protect a lucky few firms and invoke populist favor for things rural, thus far succeeding in impeding sensible reforms.

In recent years virtually every international economic or development research organization has documented the damage OECD nations' farm support programs cause in low-income countries. For example, the World Bank estimates that ending trade-distorting farm subsidies and tariffs would increase global wealth by more than $800 billion and lift more than 150 million people out of poverty by 2015, with most of those gains accruing to developing countries.[16] Removing farm subsidies would allow Least Developed Country (LDC) producers to compete with OECD producers in many agricultural sub-sectors. The lowest credible estimates we can find of the welfare costs to developing countries of OECD agricultural subsidies and market access barriers is on the order of US$10 billion annually.[17] The damage done by farm programs in the OECD countries dwarfs any damage from even the most mismanaged food aid program. Indeed, it far exceeds total global food aid flows. Eliminating such harmful distortions must be a priority for those concerned about poverty and hunger worldwide.

Food aid is an important bargaining chip in efforts to reduce harmful agricultural price supports. Food aid was addressed in the Uruguay Round Agreement on Agriculture of the WTO, and since concerted negotiations on the WTO Doha Round began in 2001 there have been several proposals floated for further disciplines on food aid. The EC, supported by a range of Latin American governments and the Cairns Group,[18] originally proposed subjecting all concessional export programs to WTO disciplines on export subsidies. This proposal would effectively restrict all food aid to wholly grant form, ending Title I concessional export programs. The USA initially opposed this proposal, but in August 2003 agreed to subject food aid to WTO disciplines aimed at reducing disruption of commercial international food shipments. Then, in the spring of 2004, the EU signaled a willingness to negotiate the end of all direct farm export subsidies. There thus seems to be slow but steady progress toward reducing agricultural export subsidies of all forms, but this will almost surely have to include food aid based on concessional export credits.

Sacrificing a portion of non-emergency food aid – in particular, concessional exports under Title I of PL 480 – and accepting limits on monetization[19] of food aid in exchange for significant concessions from the EU on agricultural export subsidies is a good deal. The US General Accounting Office has twice recommended that Congress consider eliminating the Title I and Section 416(b) programs altogether, even without any EU trade concessions in return, simply due to their historic failure to achieve measurable impact on sustainable economic development or on commercial agricultural export market development.[20] The Bush Administration has already announced its intent to curtail use of Section 416(b) food aid due to the problems it creates in commercial markets and the waste and inefficiency historically associated with its use. It therefore seems wise to seize the opportunity to trade away programs of negligible value for concessions of real value both to American agriculture and to developing countries. This would more tightly focus food aid on the one major policy objective for which food aid has sometimes proved effective: helping to reduce acute hunger and food insecurity.

Recommendation 4 Focus on quicker and more flexible emergency response

Food aid's most important impacts are saving lives and preempting liquidation of hungry people's crucial productive assets during emergencies and in post-crisis recoveries. This is particularly true in situations characterized by an outright shortfall in food availability and poorly functioning food markets. But shipping food across oceans is expensive and slow, especially with the range of congressional mandates presently imposed on US food aid shipments with respect to bagging, procurement, processing, and shipping.

In order to improve the efficacy of US food aid, the Congress should give the USAID Administrator authority to deploy food aid in the early stages of emergencies without the encumbrance of the usual mandates on domestic procurement, processing, bagging and US-flag carrier shipment. If USAID could purchase food in developing countries,[21] it could reduce emergency response time from the current average of five months and cut costs from the current average of more than 40 percent of total food aid costs. It is indefensible to continue to impede humanitarian response with obscure but highly restrictive regulations that benefit only a few American firms.

Congress first needs to end the internal inconsistencies in US food aid laws that make food aid administration costly and difficult. This will require clarifying food aid's primary objective and making the resources and constraints consistent with that objective. Cargo preference restrictions, 50 percent bagging minima for whole grains, prohibitions against procurement, bagging, fortification or processing overseas, etc., all add to costs and slow response time, without any broad benefit to the agricultural or maritime sectors. Our argument is simple: humanitarian food aid should serve humanitarian objectives. The US government doubtless has other objectives, but these can and should be met more cost-effectively with separate policy instruments, not all piled onto one instrument.

Congress should more generally convert into direct subsidies the mandates that currently impede food aid programming. Chief among these are maritime subsidies. Currently, US shipping lines double dip routinely, as described in Chapter 5, collecting Maritime Security Program (MSP) subsidy payments while also enjoying lavish implicit subsidies – a 70 to 80 percent premium over free market freight rates – from Cargo Preference Act restrictions that obstruct competitive bidding for food aid shipping contracts. Since the US government already runs a maritime subsidy scheme with the same objective – to maintain a viable US maritime industry – as cargo preference, why not fold the implicit subsidies from cargo preference into the explicit subsidies under MSP? This would have the added benefit of eliminating the complex and costly inter-agency reimbursement schemes that have caused tension between – and consumed tremendous bureaucratic resources within – the Maritime Administration in the Department of Transportation, the Department of Agriculture, and USAID. The current MSP authorization expires in October 2006, so the impending renewal of the program provides a natural opportunity to restore the MSP to funding levels on the order of the old Operating Differential Subsidy program it essentially replaced, at the same time liberating US food aid programs from the expensive shackles of cargo preference restrictions.

Just as competition is good for shipping food aid, so too is it desirable in distribution. Although there have been some recent proposals to channel all emergency food aid through multilateral organizations, primarily WFP, we favor maintaining the healthy competition that comes from using NGOs as well as UN agencies (chiefly, WFP) to receive and distribute emergency and project food aid. Such competition plainly does not preclude cooperation among operational agencies.

Just as lack of competition in procurement, processing, and shipping impedes effective use of scarce food aid resources to attend to emergencies and to foster sustainable development, so would lack of competition between operational agencies retard progress.

Recommendation 5 Eliminate unnecessary bureaucratic duplication

The *President's Management Agenda* of 2002 begins with the words "To reform government, we must rethink government."[22] It then focuses on food aid programs as one of fourteen key areas in need of substantial reform, rightly noting that food aid's "humanitarian purpose is being eroded by other uses having little to do with food."[23] By consolidating the federal government's six different food aid programs now run through two different agencies (USAID and USDA) into a single program, as OMB has proposed, a more streamlined food aid system would emerge that would be less costly and less wracked by conflicting objectives and institutional incentives that impede effective use of food aid resources.

American food aid programs would most logically fall under the control of USAID, which presently administers most US food aid resources with the aim of reducing poverty and hunger, the only objective for which food aid has proved reasonably effective. USDA would continue to handle domestic food procurement and coordinate the match of commodity and shipping vendors through its Farm Service Agency, a task it currently performs for domestic food assistance programs (e.g., school feeding) quite competently. International programming, however, should revert to a single agency, USAID.

The dispersal of responsibility for food aid across multiple cabinet-level agencies belies a more general lack of seriousness in proactively confronting global-scale problems until they have reached crisis proportions. Consolidating responsibility for food aid in one agency, focusing its use on strategic objectives related to humanitarian assistance and economic development worldwide, and recognizing food aid as just one tool among several for combating poverty and hunger – rather than as an end in itself – would not only save money by reducing bureaucratic duplication of effort, but would also make the system more effective.

Since issuing its guiding Food Aid and Food Security Policy Paper in 1995, USAID has increased development food aid and focused these resources more on the most food-insecure countries and regions and on improving agricultural productivity and household nutrition.[24] There have been simultaneous and related advances by operational agencies in program design and targeting. USAID programs remain hampered by both operational problems – such as continued general weakness of monitoring and evaluation systems – and, especially, by the dearth of non-food resources to run programs for which food is an inherently inappropriate resource. USAID, like many development agencies around the world, also needs reinvigoration of technical expertise and stature in helping set foreign policy.[25] The USAID programs nonetheless shine in comparison with the USDA food aid programs, which have been routinely excoriated in GAO studies for inefficiency, lack of accountability, and limited effectiveness in advancing food security objectives.

The two main USDA programs outside Title I – Food for Progress and the International Food for Education and Child Nutrition (IFECN) programs – could readily be absorbed into USAID without requiring any new bureaucratic structures or significant increase in personnel or associated administration costs. USAID has greater technical expertise in the relevant topics and more of a field presence in developing countries with which to facilitate project evaluation and monitoring. Food for Progress could be absorbed directly into USAID's existing programming for market-based agricultural development. As the GAO emphasized, the general design of the McGovern–Dole program merits some revisiting to incorporate the lessons of an earlier generation of school feeding programs that the WFP ran with quite mixed results,[26] and the overwhelming evidence of the nutrition and health literature that early childhood nutritional interventions, during a woman's pregnancy and during the first 24–36 months of life, have a far greater effect on children's long-term cognitive and physical development than do feeding programs later in life. Since early childhood interventions are grossly underfunded worldwide today, it would seem prudent to tinker with the targeting of resources appropriately aimed at helping poor children globally. USAID is in a far better position to undertake such a strategic review and redesign exercise than is USDA.

If Title I concessional exports and Section 416(b) programs are terminated (see Recommendation 3), the only remaining USDA program to be transferred to USAID would be the Bill Emerson Humanitarian Trust. USAID's Office of Food for Peace would be the natural manager of a strategic food reserve for use in emergencies. However, the Emerson Trust is expensive to maintain and rarely used because of the cumbersome nature of its replenishment requirements. Further, agribusiness opposes its use because commercial providers lose storage fees when food in the Trust is dispersed. The Emerson Trust is a relic of the Carter–Reagan era that has been maintained because it is a lucrative source of steady payments for a small number of companies holding the grain on contract for the federal government (see Chapter 5). It would be preferable to replace it with an emergency funding facility, such as the proposed fast-disbursing US$200 million Famine Fund, to be managed by USAID's Office of Foreign Disaster Assistance (OFDA) in response to impending humanitarian crises or the recently proposed $100 million Emergency Fund for Complex Foreign Crises.

Recommendation 6 Within current budgets, adapt the resource to fit the application

The public–private partnership of government, agribusiness, and private voluntary organizations operates a variety of humanitarian and development efforts using essentially just one resource: food commodities. Yet over the years, as we have repeatedly stressed in this book, it has become clear that while direct distribution of food can address acute hunger in emergencies, it is not sufficient to address the causes of hunger. Almost 60 percent of all PL 480 resources are not for emergencies.

To increase the flexibility of food aid, the US government has permitted mone-tization. Monetized food has been a valuable, flexible resource that many NGOs have put to good use in combating poverty and hunger.

But because it is bulky and expensive to ship, food is a terribly inefficient way to generate cash resources for programs that fight global poverty. Additionally, monetization increases the risks that food aid will displace commercial imports by recipient countries or will discourage food production by farmers in the recipient country. And, because it is sold on the open market and thus not at all targeted at food-insecure subpopulations, it often fails to reach the most vulnerable people that taxpayers aim to help.

Converting about 35–40 percent of the current total PL 480 budget – in other words, a bit more than half the non-emergency budget – into direct cash grants to supplement the poverty reduction and hunger alleviation work of non-profit development agencies around the world would encourage more sustainable programming. As discussed in Chapter 10 (see Figure 10.2 and the accompanying text), such a reallocation leaves space for appropriate levels of monetization and for cargo net and safety net interventions for which food is an intrinsically important resource. In converting food to cash resources, it will be essential to retain the emphasis on the Food for Peace strategy of focusing these resources on populations most vulnerable to food insecurity. A significant recasting of the food aid and poverty reduction budget would also help eliminate some of the unintended consequences of food aid that hurt food-exporting countries, domestic agricultural producers in recipient countries, or both.

For far too long, American policy has focused on the use of food aid, rather than on the objective of reducing hunger and poverty. We need to focus more on food security and less on food as a resource. Not only have USAID and operational agencies recognized that it would be beneficial to convert food resources to cash for development and humanitarian programming, so has the OMB, the White House, USDA and commercial exporter lobbies in the United States.[27] Development interventions could become more effective and there would be an increased role for commercial markets in promoting food security. The focus needs to shift to developing and employing efficient, competitive commercial markets rather than trying to work around them through NGO-mediated food monetization.

Development practitioners have long been calling for Congress to increase cash resources for development programming by NGOs. This should not be tied to food commodities, as in **Section 202(e)** funding or direct funding of internal trans-port, storage and handling expenses associated with direct food aid distribution. Operational agencies require cash for programming, especially for multi-year development interventions to preempt emergencies. It is far cheaper to prevent crises than to respond to them.

Strong political will is required to generate the necessary resources. While many organizations and people support monetization because they believe no other resources would be forthcoming were food aid to be trimmed back, we have yet to meet anyone who favors food over cash as a resource for programming. When food is absolutely the only form in which development assistance is available, thoughtful people try to figure out how to use it for programming in spite of its many obvious inefficiencies. Our argument is that reducing the inefficiencies in the system will create opportunities to meet the objectives of all stakeholders, achieve some modest budgetary savings, and still have at least as much in the way of ultimate cash resources for NGO programming as result from monetization. This is achievable.

The trick is coordination, especially among NGOs, because no single agency can afford to break with current policy while many others practice business as usual. The most sensible approach would be to make multi-year cash grants available under the food security objectives articulated in the 1990 Farm Bill to enhance the poverty reduction and food security work of current Title II partners.

These reforms of US food aid policy would reinforce improvements made over the past decade in USAID Title II programming, focus American food aid more tightly on the one objective for which it has proved reasonably effective – saving and improving lives – and put a lid on the inefficiencies and excesses of a suite of dispersed and poorly coordinated programs. Many of the changes we advocate have been under consideration for some time. It is, however, time to accelerate reforms to their logical conclusion. Title I has fallen by 90 percent in real terms since 1980. It is time to close it down entirely. OMB and GAO have been pushing for the consolidation of food aid programs across agencies, for an end to Section 416(b) and Title I programs, for reduced monetization, and for rolling back cargo preference premia or at least consolidating maritime subsidies under a single vehicle. USAID has won approval to procure, process and bag foods locally in the Iraq emergency. Low-level variants of these proposed changes are thus under way already anyway. The time has come to nudge them into fruition.

Other bilateral donor policy changes needed

It is not only the United States that needs to open up its food aid procurement system, permitting more local purchases and triangular transactions. Other bilateral donors need to make food aid policy changes as well. However, we offer limited precise recommendations in this section because (1) there is considerable variation between bilateral donors as to the most desirable reforms – we discuss the full range in this section; (2), as indicated in the Introduction, our expertise lies more with the United States than on other donor countries; and (3) because of American dominance of food aid flows, there will be no significant reform of the global food aid system without substantial movement in the United States. Thus, we focus more on the specifics of reforming US policy, but not because there is no need for policy change in other donor countries.

Only about 10 percent of global food aid is procured in developing countries, typically at lower cost and greater timeliness in deliveries. Australia, Canada, France, and Japan could likewise all improve the efficacy of their food aid programs by moving further in this direction. Local purchases and triangular transactions are by no means a cure-all. But they are currently significantly under-utilized relative to their potential to more effectively manage scarce resources for food delivery.

Several donors – notably Japan – likewise need to mainstream food aid within development assistance and reduce the influence of food aid by ministries of agriculture, state trading enterprises and commodity boards. The Canadian case is instructive. Food aid now comes from a central aid budget in Canada, making the trade-offs between food and cash clear to senior decision-makers. Food has to meet a cost-effectiveness criterion to justify its use. Mainstreaming food aid within donors' general development assistance budgets can help to reinforce the objective of food aid and to concentrate its use where it is needed.

Finally, several of the major donors, perhaps most especially the EU, need to work at expediting their approval and disbursement processes. The EU has earned a reputation among NGOs for often being slower to deliver resources than the USA, in spite of the EU's more flexible and frequent use of local purchases, triangular transactions and complementary cash resources. Part of the problem originates in a culture of bureaucracy. Part reflects free-riding problems inherent to the consolidated appeals process commonly used to elicit food aid, especially in emergencies. By delaying response, a donor can often induce other donors to pick up a greater share of the collective burden of support. Of course, with all donors playing the same game, the end result is commonly just delayed resource deliveries and unnecessary suffering by vulnerable or emergency-affected populations.

Recipient country government and community policy changes needed

Recipient country governments and communities often stand accused of "dependency" on food aid. While we tried to debunk the myth of widespread food aid dependency in Chapter 9 and one needs to take care not to blame the victims of food insecurity and poverty, the accusation of recipient government inattention (unfortunately) has merit in many places. The general empirical finding that aid flows have a positive macro-level effect only in the presence of good policy applies to food aid as much as to other forms of overseas development assistance.[28] Local and national governments need to become more pro-active in food assistance programs to combat food insecurity and persistent poverty. This requires both direct government action and increased cooperation with operational agencies and donors on several fronts. The specific policy changes needed vary markedly from country to country. In some places, the problems largely concern preparedness for frequent emergencies. In others, the problems relate more to improving cooperation and coordination with international donors. In still other countries, the issues pertain to political marginalization of particular subpopulations. In the interests of brevity, we avoid country-specific issues here, focusing on policies relevant to many countries worldwide.

Recipient countries that find themselves chronically vulnerable to food crises need well-managed food security reserves and pre-arranged letters of credit for food imports in order to provide an adequate initial pipeline during the early onset of emergencies. As early warning and procurement systems become more efficient and response lags in food aid or commercial imports become shorter, food security reserves can shrink. Holding reserves is expensive, so one needs to guard against excessive stockpiling and ensure adequate management accountability systems are in place to guard against gross inefficiencies that have too often plagued government-run food reserves.[29] But as Malawi's experience during the 2002 drought underscores, it can be disastrous to be caught in a rapidly advancing emergency without any reserves in a place not quickly and easily provisioned by international channels. Well-managed reserves should combine actual food stocks with cash reserves for rapid purchase of grain as well. The cost of unpreparedness dwarfs the expense of maintaining modest precautionary food security reserves.

There are important lessons to be learned from developing countries such as Bangladesh and India that have used food aid to help spark domestic agricultural research and market development to improve productivity. As one former senior Indian government official recently noted privately, "we used food aid to get rid of food aid" by investing in the nation's public and private seed development and distribution systems, small farmer cooperatives, and state-funded safety nets based on reasonably effective beneficiary targeting (e.g., the successful Maharashtra Employment Guarantee Scheme). We repeat one of the central messages of Chapter 10: food aid can only succeed as a (small) element of a sensible, broader strategy for economic development and the fulfillment and protection of human rights. Ultimately, this is the responsibility of recipient country governments and communities. Donors and operational agencies can merely play a valuable supporting role.

Operational agency policy and programming changes needed

Along with policy changes by donor and recipient governments, operational procedures must be improved by the various implementing agencies in the field, particularly NGOs and WFP.

Recommendation 7 Improve the targeting of food aid

The major operational improvement needed is to continue to improve targeting, the root of most operational problems associated with food aid. This includes not only the questions of who should receive food aid, but where such groups are located, what kind of assistance they need and when it is needed. As explained in Chapter 8, good targeting means ensuring that food aid reaches those who are genuinely food-insecure and do not have adequate money to purchase food, and ensuring that, to the extent feasible, it does not go to other groups. When food aid fails to reach truly food-insecure groups it will not have the intended positive impacts. Providing food to relatively food-secure groups displaces trade, hurts production incentives, or both. Food aid agencies – NGOs and WFP – have developed adequate mechanisms to get food distributed to the designated recipients with reasonable efficiency and accuracy. The key targeting questions revolve mainly around identifying the appropriate recipients and timing and the right form of transfer.

Effective targeting requires good information. There is little argument about the need to continue to improve the information systems used to identify where and when food insecurity is developing, who is affected, and how badly and how long they will be affected. In addition, food-insecure households may be in need of non-food assistance. Food alone is rarely the only requirement of disaster-affected groups, and is equally rarely effective as a stand-alone intervention. Information systems have classically been operated on the basis of early warning and commodity-management components, with an emergency needs assessment component becoming increasingly important during the 1990s. Information is expensive to acquire, perhaps especially in complex emergencies, but both the human and the financial costs of bad or no information are far higher.[30] Improved information systems are important to operational agencies for targeting and food aid management purposes and to donors for prioritizing scarce resources and for planning. Information system budgets must not be tied to the current food aid pipeline, which inevitably results in slow responses to rapid onset emergencies.

Operational agencies increasingly have a difficult time retaining experienced food distribution staff. This will become more difficult still if food aid distribution becomes more focused on humanitarian emergencies. The costs of maintaining staff who are capable of responsibly managing food aid – not just distributing it, but also generating and analyzing accurate information for good targeting, monitoring and evaluation – must be viewed by donors as part of the cost of doing business in emergencies.

Recommendation 8 Use food aid only where it is appropriate

Food aid has been used as a resource not only to address acute hunger, but also to improve agricultural production, develop infrastructure, improve health and education, and pursue a variety of other desirable goals. Yet experience shows time and again that there is one major role for which food aid is ideally suited: addressing acute food insecurity in humanitarian emergencies that are underpinned by both an outright shortage of food and the failure of markets to respond to demand stimuli (e.g., through cash from public employment schemes). While food aid's use in other applications is understandable – it is often the only available resource – this inevitably increases the risk of the harmful side effects of which food aid is often accused. Figure 10.1 in the preceding chapter illustrated an appropriate decision tree for establishing whether or not to use food aid in a given context.

One implication of the need to put greater emphasis on emergency food aid is the need to pay more attention to the nutrient content of food aid transfers. Emergency food rations constitute an investment in long-term human capital, especially through protection of children vulnerable to long-term health problems as a direct result of temporary nutritional deprivation.[31] WFP is making significant strides in this direction, as reflected in their recent five-year strategy and efforts to mainstream nutrition within food aid programming.[32] Bilateral food aid programs could be improved, as could many operational agencies' attention to nutritional issues.

Food aid also has a limited role as one part of social safety nets, under the same set of circumstances as described in the figure above. This can include, for example, government-to-government provision of food aid, for example, to underpin limited food security reserves. Reserves are necessary to fund food-for-work programs which act as safety nets to help protect households against shocks.

Getting there from here: the politics of reform

The reforms we propose imply a significant recasting of food aid programs, especially those of the United States. In this section, we outline why we believe such reforms are not only imperative, but also politically feasible if leadership for reform emerges at the right levels within governments, donor agencies, and operational agencies. Because US food aid programs drive the entire global system and are most in need of reform, we focus here on the politics of reforming American food aid.

Several impending policy decisions create an opportunity to reconsider and recast food aid programs. Ongoing WTO negotiations of the Doha Round Agreement will continue to focus on agriculture and food aid will remain one of a host of key issues. It is highly unlikely that the EU and other food exporting counries will drop their objections to America's concessional exports program and it is almost as unlikely that the US farm lobby will put maintaining Title I PL 480 ahead of other objectives in the WTO negotiations. There will thus naturally be pressure for our Recommendation 3 (*Negotiate reductions in outdated forms of food aid in exchange for reductions in EU export subsidies that harm both US and developing country farmers*) over the coming few years. On top of the WTO negotiations, two impending legislative actions create an opportunity for reform of the US food aid program: the necessary reauthorization of the decade-old Maritime Security Program, a centerpiece of federal government support to the maritime industry, and the negotiation of a new Farm Bill. Both are needed by mid-2006, and debates on both issues will build in intensity during 2005.

There is latent support among American voters for reforms. Polls consistently show Americans believe the foreign aid budget to be something on the order of 20 percent of federal government spending, although it's actually less than 1 percent. When informed of the actual amount spent on foreign aid, Americans overwhelmingly support sharp increases in foreign aid. Indeed, it appears that the USA is falling behind with respect to foreign aid. In total dollar terms, Japanese foreign assistance is larger than the USA, with the EU rapidly closing on the USA. Unfortunately, although the majority of American voters believe foreign aid to be an important and worthwhile expenditure, food aid – indeed international foreign assistance more generally – is not an issue that decides elections. Thus, changing food aid policy requires more than an appeal to the conscience or common sense of American voters. It also requires structuring the reforms in a way that will win over those with established interests in current US food aid programs.

As discussed in Chapter 5, the main beneficiaries of current American food aid policy are the "iron triangle" of select NGOs, the maritime industry concerns, and agribusinesses. The political economy of changing US food aid policy therefore necessarily involves making reforms at least reasonably palatable to each of the vested interests. Reform is possible by alleviating current inefficiencies in the system and by acknowledging and addressing the internationally and domestically contested aspects of current food aid policy.

Convincing the NGOs

NGOs have been a major political force in Washington for food aid for some time and are among its staunchest defenders. They were key behind-the-scenes players at the creation of PL 480 in 1954 and their prominence has increased markedly since the landmark 1990 Farm Bill, which made food security objectives prominent. And of course, NGOs have gained prominence as the main purveyors of American food aid.

However, NGOs are caught in a dilemma regarding food aid. While all Title II partner NGOs defend food aid, many of them at least privately question its current application. All would argue that under current circumstances, it is a critical resource. Most, however, would also add (if only privately) that on its own, food aid is an inadequate and terribly inefficient resource. With respect to applications outside of humanitarian crises, virtually all would say that cash, not food, is the resource of choice, but that given the current donor priorities, such resources are unlikely to be made available. Addressing NGO concerns that there might not be new cash resources to adequately replace foregone non-emergency food aid, and convincing the NGOs to take a leadership role in reshaping donor priorities, will be essential to any serious attempt to reform food aid.

The locus of NGO lobbying for food aid is the Coalition for Food Aid, a consortium of fourteen NGOs established in 1985.[33] The Coalition has championed food aid monetization and worked tirelessly to try to get the US government to undertake multi-year food aid commitments. The Coalition also mounted a spirited attack on the early 2003 Harbinson draft of the Doha Round agreement on agriculture, which had proposed limiting in-kind food donations and ending all non-emergency food aid distribution through governments and NGOs, requiring it to be channeled instead through multilateral organizations such as WFP.

Most US NGOs have a mixed mandate: they are both humanitarian agencies, providing emergency assistance to disaster-affected populations, and development agencies, working to reduce long-term poverty. NGOs got into the food aid business initially in pursuit of their humanitarian goals, and their reliance on food aid for development or poverty reduction came about largely as a result of resource availability, not as the result of an analysis of underlying causes of poverty. Given greater opportunities to use food aid for development purposes since the changes brought about in the 1990 Farm Bill and relatively easier access to food than to cash resources, NGOs have become very proficient at using food aid as the "least bad" resource for development programming. Monetization and the Development Assistance Programs (DAPs) they support enable NGOs to use food aid for non-emergency programming that otherwise could not be directly addressed using distributed food (e.g., improving agricultural production and non-farm rural livelihoods, improving access to potable water, micro-credit, education, etc.). But monetization is terribly inefficient and raises the risks of unintended negative effects of food aid, as we have extensively demonstrated (see Chapters 8 and 9).

This highlights the dilemma in which the NGOs find themselves. NGOs defend food aid and depend on it heavily. Yet few field managers defend their reliance on food aid for long-term development programming – as quite distinct from emergency relief operations – on the basis of anything other than the lack of any alternative available resource to address long-term food security problems. The Europeans, the White House and commercial agricultural exporters all want to eliminate or sharply reduce food aid monetization by US NGOs. They therefore need to work with the NGOs and Congress to make new sources of funding available for poverty reduction programming, especially in places most vulnerable to food insecurity, where Title II programs are mostly targeted.

NGOs' reliance on food aid – and on Title II in particular,[34] as described in Chapter 5 – makes most of them fearful that changes in food aid programs will directly and negatively affect their budgets and therefore their ability to fulfill their laudable mission. Food aid budgets contribute directly not only to the cost of the delivery of food commodities themselves, but also to the budgets of field offices, recurrent staff costs, and other operational costs related to project management, so-called "shared project costs." Furthermore, food aid can also be used to leverage other, non-food (cash) resources. For example, a large Title II DAP will often successfully attract companion funds from a donor for achieving complementary results.

As discussed in Chapter 5, some NGOs also fear that a drop in food aid receipts would adversely affect private donations they receive because of a widespread – but unsubstantiated – belief that NGO private fundraising performance depends in part on the ratio of program expenditure to overall expenditure as an indicator of managerial efficiency. Having a large food aid budget helps keep that ratio high because the marginal management costs of additional food aid are low: 100,000 tons of food aid can be handled with roughly the same headquarters management costs as 10,000 tons.

These factors have generally fed NGO fears that if food aid were reformed, they would suffer financially, leading to a widespread "don't-rock-the-boat" attitude. Nevertheless, NGOs will have to show some courage and break from their short-term, income statement dependence on food as a resource.

First, NGO leaders need to recognize the imperative of food aid reform in order to be able to achieve their own stated goals. If overcoming hunger requires overcoming poverty, then NGOs' chief strategy must be to fight poverty. Food aid is at best a flawed and insufficiently flexible instrument in much of that fight, although there are critical applications where food is crucial. As the main (or only) advocates for the poor among the primary beneficiaries of US food aid programs, NGOs must exercise leadership in reforming food aid. In particular, the NGOs must ensure not only that food aid remains available when and where it is needed in emergencies, but also that food aid is not misdirected to applications and locations where it is inappropriate. Some leading NGOs have begun moving in this direction. OXFAM, for example, has called attention to the misuse of food aid while clearly supporting its application in poverty reduction efforts.[35] A number of major international humanitarian agencies have long eschewed food aid. Many of the larger Title II partners are currently questioning the appropriate role for food aid.

Second, NGOs' and food aid's primary role in humanitarian emergencies must be more broadly recognized and valued, not least within the NGOs themselves. Outside of major, headline-making emergencies, the humanitarian role of both the operational agencies and the resource (food aid) are both generally under-valued and under-emphasized. Staff promotions and careers are rarely built on effective emergency programming activities, at least in part because emergencies are viewed as being short-lived and having short-term goals. To retain the staff who can handle the operational requirements of humanitarian emergencies, agencies almost by definition need to have long-term programs employing these staff between emergencies, and to keep pipelines primed with resources, even if the resource is poorly matched to the activity. This is equally the case with some WFP programs. But poorly resourced development programs do not serve their ostensible poverty reduction objectives very well, nor do they serve their less readily obvious emergency preparedness functions. NGOs and the development community must begin valuing and clearly stating these two objectives, and appropriately resourcing each.

Third, NGOs must begin to take advantage of latent public support for greater allocation of resources to development and poverty reduction, taking a lead role in mobilizing public support for private and public funding of programs for poverty and hunger reduction at home and abroad. As we noted earlier, Americans tend to believe the USA spends much more on poverty reduction and humanitarian assistance than it does – and are supportive of spending more on international development assistance, perhaps especially hunger eradication. While one shouldn't read too much into such survey results, they do reflect support for poverty reduction and hunger eradication that has yet to be realized in budgetary allocations, in large measure because of the nature of interest group politics in Washington. As the economist Jeffrey Sachs has argued, "We must have leaders who recognize that the problems of the poor aren't trifles to leave to do-gooders, but are vital strategic issues. . . . In the case of a superpower, ignorance is not bliss; it is a threat to Americans and to humanity."[36]

Fourth, NGOs need to revisit some of their fears about the financial repercus-sions of reforming food aid. As an example, Box 11.1 breaks down the expenditures of CARE USA – one of the largest Title II partner organizations – to examine the possible effects of changes in either general food aid distribution or monetization on the ratio of administrative and fundraising costs to total expenditure. This example underscores that the financial risks associated with a prospective cut-back in inappropriate uses of food aid may be less serious than some NGO observers seem to believe.

Box 11.1 NGO budgets and program/ administration ratios: how real are the fears?

As noted in Chapter 5, US NGOs are major beneficiaries of the food aid status quo. One of the largest of these, CARE, relied on food aid for over 50 percent of its total budget less than ten years ago. Figure 11.2 shows that this proportion has dropped over recent years. Slightly more than one-quarter of CARE's budget now comes from food aid. There has been a general decline in the use of food resources in kind, although this has stabilized since 2001. Over the same period, monetization increased dramatically before dropping off slightly since 2001.

CARE's record demonstrates that declining levels food aid do not, in themselves, affect the ability of an organization to attract alternative sources of funding, particularly from institutional donors. Indeed, one can calculate the ratio of administrative and fundraising expenditures to total expenditures for FY04: 8.4 percent, a very good figure by industry standards that consider anything below about 10 percent excellent. But note that even if all monetization of food aid were to end immediately (and the resource was not replaced), that ratio would increase to only about 9.3 percent, an effectively

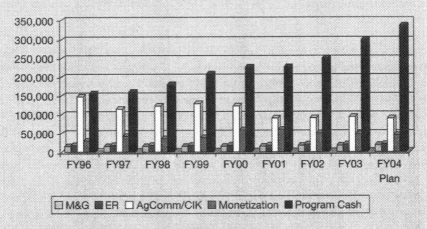

Figure 11.2 CARE-USA expenditure, financial years 1996–2004

Notes: ER: External Relations (Fundraising/Public Information)
M&G = Management & General (Finance and Business Services, Information Technology, Human Resources, Internal Audit, President's Office, Legal, Corporate Management, Depreciation, Taxes) AgComm/CIK = Agricultural Commodities/Contributions in Kind (food aid for distribution)

imperceptible change. Even a substantial decrease in food aid in kind would not increase the ratio above 10 percent. And these back-of-the-envelope estimates reflect worst-case scenarios. The reforms we advocate with regard to both monetization call for resource substitution, not simply the cessation of monetization, and no one is calling for a large-scale reduction in the use of food as a resource to address emergencies.

Fifth, rational change processes will require transitional strategies. An instrument that has evolved only slowly over fifty years will not change sharply overnight. NGOs can take the lead by making adaptations to their food aid operations which push the process of change in the right direction, demonstrating a credible long-term vision without jeopardizing essential ongoing operations. Several prototype transitional strategies exist, where food aid is targeted to uses where food itself is the necessary resource and cash is leveraged to address other, poverty programming.

One such example arose from the renegotiation of the Title II Development Assistance Programs in Ethiopia in 2002. Numerous problems had emerged with relying on monetization for cash requirements. And in a country such as Ethiopia – with chronic food insecurity, overall food deficits in most years, and poorly integrated rural markets – there clearly were useful applications for food aid in both humanitarian and safety net programs. The 2002 Title II non-emergency programs in Ethiopia were negotiated to reduce levels of monetization, while food aid was targeted to appropriate safety net programs.[37] In the process, additional cash resources were leveraged from other USAID sources to support the non-food requirements for complementary programs addressing other aspects of rural poverty. While the overall reform of US food aid that we advocate here would ultimately require more substantive changes, the 2002 recasting of DAPs in Ethiopia clearly represented a significant step in the right direction, suggesting the kind of transitional strategy that both operational agencies (Title II partner NGOs) and donors (USAID/Food for Peace and USAID/Ethiopia) need to develop en route to more substantive changes.

NGOs and other operational agencies are clearly doing some excellent and important work in spite of being starved of first-best cash resources. If NGOs can do good things even with poor resources, they could do even better with more flexible resources, even if there was less of it in aggregate in the system. The evidence presented throughout this book indicates that such reforms are not only necessary but feasible. But NGOs must cooperate on this. No single NGO has much incentive to change its food aid operations without the cooperation of other NGOs. If, however, they can move as a bloc to push for real reform of food aid and development assistance more generally, they will be a potent force for a reallocation of resources that would enhance, not constrain, the resource base for fighting poverty. Yet many NGOs continue to push food aid aggressively, seeing monetization as the best short-term route for greater cash resources for development, even while acknowledging the questionable economic returns on monetization. NGO staff too often argue that the lobby supporting the status quo in food aid is far too powerful to change, perhaps not recognizing the extent to which they themselves are a substantial part of that lobby. In order for real reform to take place, the NGOs must wield their influence to bring about overdue reform of food aid programs.

Addressing maritime interests

If NGOs are the key constituency that must move in order for food aid to be recast sensibly in support of more general development and humanitarian assistance strategies, the maritime industry is perhaps the key constituency that must be moved in order to achieve significant reforms. This is apparent from even the most cursory review of food aid costs. Whether one looks at the aggregate federal food aid budget – roughly 40 percent of which goes toward shipping costs in any given year – or at shipments-level data (e.g., Figure 8.7) that suggest a slightly higher share spent on shipping (roughly 47 percent), transport is the biggest expenditure that does not directly benefit food aid recipients.[38]

For fifty years, US shippers have been extraordinarily successful in lobbying for food aid and in twisting the program to suit their own interests. The Seafarers International Union, the Transport Institute and the Maritime Research and Development Institute have been vigorous contributors to the campaign coffers of key Congressional supporters and very effective in championing cargo preference restrictions. In perhaps their clearest demonstration of political strength, in 1985 the maritime industry strong-armed the farm lobby into expanding the share of food aid shipments subject to cargo preference restrictions from 50 percent – the level applying to all other non-military government-impelled cargo – to 75 percent in exchange for exemption of agricultural export promotion programs, such as the Export Enhancement Program, from cargo preference provisions.[39] The 50 percent growth in the cargo preference program resulting from the maritime industry's lobbying efforts increased shipping costs, diverting resources away from procuring and distributing aid. In other words, the farm lobby and the shippers directly gained at the expense of the NGOs and poor people in whose name the agricultural and maritime interests promote food aid. Food aid is a clumsy means by which to advance either the maritime industry's financial interests or national security concerns over the viability of national sealift capacity in time of war.

As mentioned in our discussion of Recommendation 4 (*Focus on quicker and more flexible emergency response*) above, one sensible approach to reform would be to consolidate explicit and implicit subsidies of the US maritime industry under a single program managed by the Department of Transportation or the Department of Defense. Advocates for food aid reforms should therefore support a significant enhancement of shipper subsidies under the Maritime Security Program (MSP) in exchange for termination of the cargo preference provisions that routinely drain 40 percent or more from US food aid budgets. The maritime industry may well welcome support for an expanded and secure program of its own in place of a threatened, hidden subsidy within the food aid budget. Cargo preference has been under increasingly effective attack for a number of years. Much of the defense establishment is concerned that existing programs do not adequately address military concerns about sealift readiness. And some key legislators express concern that freight lines "double dip," drawing roughly $6,500/day per vessel in MSP subsidies while also reaping handsome cargo preference premia on food aid cargo.[40] The Maritime Security Program comes up for review on roughly the same schedule as the Farm Bill, creating a prime opportunity to reallocate maritime support from the fine print of the Farm Bill into appropriations under the Maritime Security Act.[41] US shipping lines could retain preferential access to competitively bid freight contracts on US government funded food aid shipments, whether from the United States or from a source location in a developing country. But the enormous hidden subsidies benefitting a very small number of US shipping lines should be eliminated or rolled into the extant, direct maritime subsidy program.

Those favoring food aid reform could likewise support the maritime industry's efforts to curtail the use of flags of convenience: ship registration in places such as Liberia, Panama, and the Bahamas where the absence of regulation and strong secrecy laws permit low-cost freight operations. Curtailing flags of convenience would reduce low-cost competition for US shipping lines, improving their commercial competitiveness and reducing the need for implicit subsidies such as those embodied in cargo preference restrictions on food aid. Those wishing to engineer a useful recasting of food aid programs will inevitably be obliged to support the US maritime industry's quest for alternative – and more effective – ways to maintain its viability.

Satisfying donor country agricultural interests

Real reform of American food aid is possible in part because the strange coalition of bedfellows that has coalesced around food aid is more fragile than many people appreciate. Perhaps especially within the agricultural sector, there are few real beneficiaries from current food aid programs. As we document in Chapters 3 and 5, the $1–2 billion annually spent on food aid is a tiny fraction of agricultural sales, considering that US agricultural exports are $55–60 billion and annual food expenditures in the United States are more than $900 billion. Food aid simply doesn't significantly affect farmgate price. Nor does it effectively promote future commercial exports. A few small producer groups and specialized processors depend heavily on food aid, but the vast majority of American agriculture reaps little if any economic benefit. As a result, much of the American farm lobby can be convinced that they no longer have a major stake in food aid, as happened in Canada and Europe.

Moreover, the farm lobby has far greater concerns than protecting food aid sales. It wants to protect direct federal subsidies to farmers, which averaged $21.7 billion annually, 1999–2001.[42] And it wants improved access to protected markets in Europe, Japan and other countries. The stronger commodity groups – especially those that have never participated significantly in food aid, such as beef, cotton, peanuts, pork, poultry, and sugar – should be prepared to sacrifice Title I and Section 416(b) food aid in exchange for reduced EU agricultural export subsidies.

Similarly, relaxing some of the various restrictions that make international food assistance expensive and slow will effectively cost American agriculture nothing while greatly increasing the flexibility and effectiveness with which food aid can be deployed for development and humanitarian causes that are in American agriculture's medium-to-long-term interests. Many American agribusiness and farmers recognize that their long-term future is tied not to short-term, small-scale demand stimuli such as food aid, but to longer-term demand growth on a far larger scale through economic development and liberalized commercial trade around the world.

Furthermore, the once-united farm lobby is increasingly fractured as small farmers are parting company with large corporate farms, and as both break with processors on key policy issues in Washington. Farm state legislators are battling each other on key elements of US farm policy. One example is the ongoing debate concerning federal farm support payments to large farms. Many Midwestern farm state legislators support caps on payments to large farms, a proposal fervently opposed by legislators from big corporate farming states in the South and West.

It is plausible, even likely, that as farmers become informed as to the failure of food aid to match agricultural objectives, they will stop offering blanket advocacy for food aid programs that do not benefit them financially, especially for those programs that offer only inefficient and sometimes ineffective means of helping poor people abroad. There is a precedent in Canada, where farmers several years ago supported rolling food aid into the general development assistance budget because they recognized there were no significant material benefits to them from food aid.[43] Canadian farmers – who are as vocal and politically influential in Ottawa as American farmers are in Washington – mainly wanted to see food shared with the hungry, appreciating its symbolic value but not overselling its effectiveness at reducing hunger. American farmers can likewise be convinced of the symbolic, humanitarian and long-term commercial benefits of recasting food aid.

The various farm lobbies, perhaps especially the North American Export Grain Association, which represents the nation's largest grain traders, already favor capping monetization because they rightly view it as disruptive to their overseas markets. These groups face domestic opposition from NGOs that rely heavily on food aid monetization for programming resources. Of course, this creates an opportunity for a mutually beneficial compromise: the farm lobby supports converting some non-emergency food resources into cash for development programming in exchange for the NGO lobby conceding the need to limit food aid monetization.

Under our recommendations, the farm lobby would have to make some concessions with respect to relaxing domestic procurement, processing and bagging restrictions for cash commitments under the GFAC and for emergency food aid provided in the initial stages of emergencies. But the more than $200 million spent on the overseas procurement, bagging, and processing of food aid for Iraq in 2003–4 has already established the precedent for such a change.

Winning support from non-traditional allies

While the parties engaged in one aspect or another of the current food aid regime are the major players in any reform, we have found a number of allies for reform in other walks of public life, and their support for reform could be helpful if food aid is to be recast so that it more efficiently and reliably serves humanitarian and development objectives. At least three main groups would have some overlapping interests: (1) the foreign policy community; (2) the international financial community; and (3) groups advocating greater fiscal responsibility in government budgets. While few from within these communities have engaged food aid policy discussions in the past, and while their incentives to do so remain limited, these groups have objectives consistent with the reform of food aid and thus may offer a latent, non-traditional source of support.

Organizations and individuals concerned about foreign policy and national security have concerns that overlap with the food aid policy reforms we recommend. First, since the terrorist attacks of September 11, 2001, and the subsequent US-led wars in Afghanistan and Iraq, there has been increased awareness that national security interests are inextricable from global poverty reduction efforts.[44] While food aid reform alone will not address the global problem of poverty reduction, it is one important step toward this end. Thus foreign policy interest groups are a natural source of support for food aid reforms, perhaps especially for restoring real development assistance flows (see Recommendation 2 above).

A second concern within the foreign policy community revolves around lessons learned about sealift capacity from recent conflicts, raising questions about government subsidization and control of the US maritime industry under the Department of Defense. This could well imply replacing complicating mandates, such as those associated with cargo preference provisions for food aid, with more direct subsidies from the Pentagon. The reauthorization of the Maritime Security Program will be a prime occasion to explore the possibilities for such restructuring.

The third foreign policy constituency offering potential support for a recasting of US food aid programs harbors concerns about the strength of the North Atlantic alliance. Many foreign policy specialists appear troubled by the tensions created by trade rifts, growing US unilateralism, and relations generally between the USA and Europe. Through the late 1980s, the Soviet threat induced Euro-American cooperation through such tensions. No such commonly perceived threat holds the North Atlantic alliance together today. A substantial portion of the foreign policy community therefore favors small US concessions on relatively minor matters like aid tying and trade disputes over Title I food aid or food aid monetization because of the larger, indirect gains to be enjoyed from closer cooperation with the Europeans and Canadians (and, analogously in the Pacific, with the Australians and Japanese) on other matters.

The international finance community is another prospective source of support for food aid policy reform. They stand to benefit directly from reallocation of development assistance from food to cash resources because this helps both to stimulate demand for financial services by operational agencies, and to reduce commercial trade disruptions, thereby further stimulating demand for export credit and related financial services. Increasingly cash-based development and safety net programming could help stimulate demand for such products from insurance and re-insurance companies around the world. The insurance industry could benefit from rapid growth in interest in insurance products to provide coverage against natural disasters (drought, flood, earthquakes, typhoons, etc.) for NGOs and even small businesses and farmers in developing countries. Prototype insurance products have drawn considerable interest within the development community in the last few years.[45]

Advocates for greater fiscal responsibility provide the final prospective constituency that might support an effort to recast food aid. The obvious, longstanding inefficiencies in the current system invite attention from those dedicated to reducing government waste. Our recommendations to eliminate unnecessary bureaucratic duplication in federal food aid programs and to focus on cheaper means of accomplishing the same development and humanitarian objectives should find favor with those concerned about federal deficits.

Our recommendations could yield budgetary savings of nearly 20 percent on the total US food aid budget. The gains would be realized by eliminating Title I PL 480, folding the remaining USDA-managed food aid programs into existing USAID operations – with associated downsizing of duplicative bureaucracy – reduced freight costs from authorizing procurement of commodities overseas, at least in the early stages of emergencies, and modest (e.g., 10 percent) reduction of program budgets in converting from food to cash for most non-emergency programming by USAID/Food for Peace. Combined, these changes would yield estimated annual savings to the US government of better than $300 million, or about 18.9 percent of average spending on food aid over the past three years.[46] These savings do not include extra-budgetary expenditures on Section 416(b) programs, which the Bush Administration proposes to wind down. Because food aid programs are small by federal government standards anyway, the budgetary savings available from recasting US food aid programs are modest. But they are real nonetheless. Furthermore, these estimates do not include prospective savings on freight costs to be gained by reducing the tied nature of procurement of not only commodities but also shipping and processing services could simultaneously expand the real value of food and cash available for emergency assistance and poverty reduction programming overseas.

Conclusion

Food aid provided by a range of donors and channeled through scores of operational agencies worldwide has improved or saved the lives of millions of poor and food-insecure people worldwide over the past fifty years, since US PL 480 was passed in 1954. This anniversary offers an appropriate opportunity to reflect on the modern history of global food aid and to analyze its past performance with an eye toward advancing an evidence-based agenda for reform. In doing so, we have tried to dispel some longstanding myths about the effectiveness of food aid in advancing donor country objectives other than those associated with development and humanitarian goals. We have also tried to highlight how food aid could – and, when properly used, does – contribute directly to economic development and to the protection of basic human rights.

The global food aid system seriously underperforms its potential, due primarily to misguided policies among donors compounded by policy errors by recipient country governments and by the operational agencies that handle food aid. The good news, however, is that a relatively few significant policy and operational changes could make existing food aid far more effective in reducing poverty and hunger.

Such changes are feasible. Strong legislative leadership and cooperation among key advocates for food aid for humanitarian and development purposes can shift the present, precarious political economy of food aid in the United States, where reforms are not only most needed but where they can also have the greatest impact on global poverty and food insecurity. A widening circle of key players are beginning to recognize the possibilities of recasting food aid for the next fifty years. It is time to seize the opportunity to turn an underperforming and largely misused resource into an integral part of a strategy to reduce poverty and hunger.

Glossary

Additionality: the extent to which food provided to a recipient adds to total food consumption.

Bellmon Amendment: an amendment to Section 401(b) of United States Public Law 480, passed in 1977, meant to address concerns over the potential disincentive effects of food aid on local agricultural production and marketing.

Bellmon Analysis: an analysis to determine the adequacy of storage facilities in recipient countries and whether the importation and monetization of food aid will negatively affect domestic production. See Bellmon Amendment.

Bilateral aid: aid granted and distributed government-to-government.

Bill Emerson Humanitarian Trust: a reserve of grain purchased by the USDA's Commodity Credit Corporation for distribution to meet emergency humanitarian food needs in developing countries. Until 1998, this was known as the Food Security Commodity Reserve.

Blended or fortified foods: foods that have been processed to mix different commodities (e.g., corn-soya blend, soy-fortified bulgur), or to which micronutrients have been added so as to create a more nutritious ration for distribution to targeted, vulnerable groups in an at-risk population.

Call forward: a formal request initiated by a field agency to a donor for delivery of a specified amount of a particular food commodity for use over a specified period of time. The donor subsequently initiates the procurement and delivery process, soliciting bids, and arranging procurement and shipping.

Cargo nets: development interventions intended to build up the productive asset stock of, or improve the productivity of existing assets held by, the chronically poor. Examples include investments in education, technology transfer, and land transfers or improvements.

Chronic poverty: the condition of falling below the poverty line for an extended period of time, sometimes also referred to as "persistent poverty."

Commodity Credit Corporation (CCC): a part of the US Department of Agriculture that manages export credits, surplus stocks, and acquisition of commodities for PL 480 and Section 416(b) purposes.

Complex humanitarian emergencies (CHEs) or complex political

emergencies (CPEs): involves multiple causes, both man-made (i.e., conflict) and natural factors (e.g., drought, flood, hurricanes).

Conditionality: conditions on the provision of program food aid. Conditions can take any of a wide variety of forms, from agreeing to negotiate on military and diplomatic matters, to placing the proceeds from the sale of food aid into a "counterpart fund" to be used for particular sorts of development interventions, to changing macroeconomic, trade or agricultural policies.

Consultative Sub-Committee on Surplus Disposal (CSSD): the international regulatory body established to oversee global food aid flows.

Cost, insurance, and freight: the price of imports including costs of goods, insurance, and transport to the importing nation.

Counterpart funds: the monetary resources generated by the sale (monetization) of donated foods.

Covariate shocks: unexpected loss of income or assets common to many people in a region due to, for example, drought, floods, or civil war.

Daily caloric intake (minimum): total availability per person of 2,350 calories per person, as established by the FAO.

Developmental paradox: the observation that low- and middle-income countries with large agricultural sectors tend to tax agriculture, rather than support it as the rich countries tend to do.

Dumping: occurs when producers to sell products abroad for less than their cost of production at home. Dumping has long been outlawed by the WTO and its predecessor, the General Agreement on Tariffs and Trade (GATT).

Emergency food aid: aid in response to emergencies resulting from natural disasters, such as droughts, floods or hurricanes, economic shocks, or from civil strife or war.

Errors of inclusion and errors of exclusion: programs rarely reach only intended beneficiaries. Errors of inclusion relate to unintended beneficiaries, while errors of exclusion refer to non-participants who were intended beneficiaries.

Farm Bill (1996): Federal Agriculture Improvement and Reform Act.

Farm Services Agency (FSA): section of USDA that procures US food aid based on FAS and USAID FFP programmatic needs.

Farmgate prices: the value of a product purchased directly from farm producers (versus from a third party marketing intermediary).

Food access: ability of a household or individual to purchase or self-provision in food.

Food aid: the provision of food commodities for free or on highly concessional terms to individuals or institutions within one country by foreign donors.

Food Aid Convention (FAC): an international legal agreement that establishes food aid guidelines, originally created as part of the 1967 International Grains Agreement and renewed repeatedly since that time.

Food assistance programs (FAPs): transfers in cash or in kind intended to increase food intake and improve participants' nutritional status. Examples include school feeding, maternal and child health programs, food subsidies, food price stabilization, etc.

Food availability: the gross supply of food, comprising production, purchases, and carry-over stocks.

Food for education: the use of donated food commodities for school feeding projects.

Food for Peace (FFP): see PL 480; the general term applied to the food-donation program authorized by the Agricultural Trade Development and Assistance Act of 1954 (PL 480); also a specific bureau within the U.S. Agency for International Development (USAID) with primary responsibility for emergency and project food aid shipments from the United States.

Food for Progress: food aid program that allows the US Department of Agriculture's Commodity Credit Corporation to provide agricultural commodities to developing countries as food aid, either as grants or subsidized exports. The commodities come from Title I of Public Law 480 (PL 480) or Section 416(b) of the Agricultural Act of 1949.

Food for work (FFW): a compensation plan for workers who are paid in food rather than cash wages.

Food insecurity: the absence of food security, defined by the World Bank (1986) and the 1996 World Food Summit as "access by all people at all times to sufficient food for an active and healthy life."

Foreign Agricultural Service (FAS): section of USDA that promotes American agricultural exports and coordinates all USDA food aid programs.

Freight on board (FOB): the cost of a commodity shipment once loaded onto a vessel at the port of origin (i.e., the exporting country).

Grant element: effective discount relative to the open market cost.

Humanitarian food aid: see Emergency food aid.

Hunger: the physiological phenomenon defined by the United States Department of Agriculture as "an uneasy or painful sensation caused by a lack of food" (used in this book interchangeably with "undernutrition").

Idiosyncratic shocks: unexpected loss of income or assets specific to a particular individual or household and not strongly correlated with the income or asset realizations of others in the same group or region.

Income elasticity of demand: the percentage increase in demand for a good in response to a 1 percent increase in income.

Internal transport, storage, and handling (ITSH): costs associated with the internal transport, storage and handling of relief commodities from the seaport of entry to the distribution point.

Internally displaced persons (IDPs): persons who have fled their homes for another location in the same country.

Local purchases: purchases made in surplus regions of the countries in which the aid is ultimately distributed.

Malnutrition: poor anthropometric status; ill health due to a deficit, excess, or imbalance of nutrients consumed.

Marginal propensity to consume: the increase in consumption per unit increase in income.

Micronutrients: vitamins and minerals, as distinct from macronutrients such as calories, fats, and proteins.

Monetization: the sale of donated food in order to obtain currency for other expenses, which may or may not be related to food distribution.

Multilateral aid: aid distributed by an international organization such as the World Food Programme.

Need: in the context of this book, needs are the difference between that adequate amount of food and the ability of individuals, households, or communities to self-provision.

Nongovernmental organization (NGO): a not-for-profit, private organization established for the purpose of charitable or development assistance.

Overseas development assistance (ODA): international aid to low- and middle-income countries from a government (ODA does not include private contributions).

Private voluntary organization (PVO): see Nongovernmental organization.

Program food aid: foreign aid provided, in the form of food, directly on a government-to-government basis, typically for sale on local markets to meet balance of payments and budget support objectives.

Project food aid: food aid provided on a grant basis to a recipient government, its agent, or NGOs operating in the recipient country for use in development or food security projects.

Public Law 480 (PL 480): the Agricultural Trade Development Assistance Act. Originally passed in 1954, PL 480 is the law that established the primary food aid program of the United States.

Refugee: an individual temporarily uprooted from his or her home who has crossed an international border because of a well-founded fear of persecution.

Safety nets: development interventions intended to protect against permanent asset loss associated with a collapse into chronic poverty and destitution.

Section 202(e): the portion of the PL 480 legislation that provides funding to operating agencies to cover complementary cash costs of food aid programs in the field.

Section 416(b): a food aid program under the Agricultural Act of 1949 that provides for government procurement of food by the USDA's Commodity Credit Corporation for donation overseas.

Targeting: the act of attempting to direct transfers (e.g., food aid) to one or more specific group(s), at a specific time or place, or in a specific form.

Tinbergen rule: the principle advanced by the Nobel Laureate Jan Tinbergen that optimal policy requires one policy instrument for each objective.

Transitory poverty: the condition of falling below an appropriately defined poverty line for a limited period of time. Transitory poverty can be episodic (e.g., during an unemployment spell), periodic (e.g., every "lean season" before the harvest), regular but aperiodic (e.g., during droughts that recur routinely but not on a set schedule), or it can be associated with steady growth out of poverty from a low starting point.

Triangular transactions: food aid shipments paid for by one country (the donor), sourced in a second country (the supplier) for distribution in a third country (the recipient).

Undernutrition: Malnutrition caused by insufficient intake of nutrients and commonly accompanied by the sensation of hunger (used in this book interchangeably with "hunger").

United States Agency for International Development (USAID):   the arm of the US government, located within the Department of State, with the mandate for development and emergency assistance.

United States Department of Agriculture (USDA):   the arm of the US government whose mandate is to promote American agriculture.

Uruguay Round Agreement on Agriculture (URAA):   signed at Marrakesh, Morocco, in April 1994; under Article 10, World Trade Organization member countries that are international food aid donors are prohibited from tying food aid directly or indirectly to commercial exports of agricultural products to recipient countries.

Usual marketing requirements (UMR):   the average of the preceding five years' commercial imports for the particular recipient country and commodity in question of food aid; used to determine a "normal" level of commercial food imports in order that food aid not displace trade.

World Food Crisis of 1973–74:   unprecedentedly large-scale food shortages caused by drought, sharp oil price rises, and global economic downturn, which led to famine in the West African Sahel and in Ethiopia. The ensuing World Food Conference of 1974 subsequently set out to establish more effective means to address future fluctuations in world food supplies and food prices so as prevent further acute large-scale food shortages.

World Food Programme (WFP):   an agency of the United Nations, established in 1961, with primary responsibility for multilateral food aid flows.

World Food Summit: The November 1996 international conference hosted by the FAO at which countries made public commitments to halve hunger by 2015.

Notes

Introduction

1 Bold indicates that this term is defined in the Glossary at the end of the book.
2 Although typically couched in terms of "needs," this term here and throughout this book is derived from the basic human right to adequate food, where "needs" are the difference between that adequate amount of food and the ability of individuals, households or communities to self-provision. This right obliges a response by the state and is directly related to the origin of the humanitarian imperative for food aid as intrinsically important, as distinct from the economic logic of food aid as instrumentally important because of its role in building or maintaining productive human capital. We discuss the rights-based approach to food aid more in Chapter 6.
3 Rosegrant *et al.* (2001).

1 The basics of food aid

1 For example, the Berlin Statement on Food Aid for Sustainable Food Security, issued in September 2003 at an international workshop hosted by the German Ministry of Consumer Affairs and Agriculture, included a definition of food aid as "all food-supported interventions aimed at improving the food security of poor people in the short and long term, whether funded via international, national, public and [*sic*] private resources," which elicited objections after the workshop from several participants and an email exchange between Dr Edward Clay of the Overseas Development Institute, a leading authority on food aid, and Prof. Joachim von Braun, author of the Statement and Director General of the International Food Policy Research Institute. The World Food Programme proposed a similarly expansive definition of food aid in a background document to the 1996 World Food Summit, but prevailing expert use of the term falls more in line with definition we advance and similar, but less precise, definitions used by the Food and Agriculture Organization of the United Nations (FAO) and the Organization for Economic Co-operation and Development's Development Assistance Committee (DAC). The Berlin Statement, the Clay–von Braun email exchange and papers from the Berlin conference are available online at http://www. foodaid-berlin2003.de. Clay (2003a), available at that website, provides a detailed discussion of the history of contending definitions of food aid.
2 See Barrett (2002a) for a detailed explanation of food assistance programs.
3 We owe this example to Ed Clay.
4 The Organization for Economic Co-operation and Development's Development Assistance Committee (OECD/DAC) maintains the most reliable data on ODA flows. The earliest date for which comparable, comprehensive series are available on food aid as well as overall ODA is 1971, at which time food aid represented 13.5 percent of total ODA flows.

5   Data come from the FAOStat data base (http://apps.fao.org/default.htm) and refer to all primary food (not fiber) crops.

6   Analysts often use cereals figures only – for which aggregation across different food types is less problematic – and report the somewhat higher figures of 3 percent of trade and 0.5 percent of production. Because the Food Aid Convention restricts trade in many non-cereals, as we discuss in Chapter 4, using just figures for cereals necessarily creates some upward bias in food aid's role in the global food economy. Either way, however, the volume of food aid is plainly dwarfed by production and trade volumes. The extraordinarily attentive reader may note that global production has increased more slowly than per capita caloric availability, as reported in the Introduction. This is due to the changing composition of food production, in particular, and to increased production share of animal products and fats and oils that have a higher calorie content than basic grains, pulses and tubers.

7   Hoddinott *et al.* (2004).

8   This is not the place to go into detail on the technical differences between the concepts of hunger (the physiological phenomenon defined by the United States Department of Agriculture as "an uneasy or painful sensation caused by a lack of food"), undernutrition (insufficient nutrient intake), malnutrition, poor anthropometric status, and food insecurity (the absence of food security, defined by the World Bank (1986) and the 1996 World Food Summit as "access by all people at all times to sufficient food for an active and healthy life"). In this book, we emphasize food insecurity and will use the terms hunger and undernutrition interchangeably throughout, recognizing that the former is inherently unmeasurable while the latter can be measured directly.

9   Data from Food Balance Sheets, available from the Food and Agriculture Organization of the United Nations through FAOSTAT (http://apps.fao.org/).

10 FAO (2004). Recent research by Lisa Smith and her colleagues at the International Food Policy Research Institute calls these estimates into question. As Smith (1998) reports, the FAO estimates reflect national food availability and strong assumptions about intra-national food distribution. Those estimates thus fail to reflect disparities in access to food well. Using household expenditure survey data from eleven Sub-Saharan Africa countries, Smith and Aduayom (2004) find that the FAO method leads to considerable underestimation of food energy deficiency. In ten of the eleven countries, the FAO estimate was lower – in some cases less than half – than that derived from more comprehensive household data. The mean FAO estimate of food energy deficiency across these eleven countries was 40.4 percent, while that based on more reliable household expenditure survey data was 58.7 percent. One therefore ought to treat the 852 million ballpark figure as a lower bound estimate of the true number of undernourished people in the world.

11 Nord *et al.* (2002).

12 See Barrett (2002a) for a detailed review of domestic food assistance programs.

13 A standard of 2,350 kilocalories may appear high until one recognizes that this is total availability per person. Once one accounts for losses to brewing, seed, feed and waste and for unequal distribution across individuals, this is not a generous national nutritional standard, although a country's demographic profile – its mix of adults and children, men and women – and patterns of employment (e.g., how much energy is expended in physically taxing labor?) clearly matter to the details of aggregate food sufficiency. Project Sphere (2004) uses a lower minimum of 2,100 kilocalories/day.

14 These data are provided by national governments to the FAO and are very rough, sometimes based on questionable (or no) underlying survey data and using imperfectly comparable methods across countries and years. One should therefore exercise caution in interpreting these data. These are, however, the only data series available with which one can make such comparisons. We therefore emphasize the qualitative points rather than the precise quantitative estimates, which are fraught with measurement error.

15 The terms NGOs, private voluntary organizations (PVOs), humanitarian agencies and

registered charities are used by different commentators virtually interchangeably to identify nongovernmental, non-profit service organizations that handle food aid and that work to assist poor populations. We will tend to use the term NGO to refer to nongovernmental, not-for-profit actors. When referring more broadly to groups that receive, procure or distribute food aid in recipient countries, we will sometimes use the more encompassing term "operational agencies," which includes UN agencies such as the World Food Programme in addition to NGOs.

16 A considerable literature on hunger and famine addresses these issues in far greater detail than we can go into here. Chapter 4 returns to this issue in somewhat greater detail. The reader interested in much greater detail should consult Sen (1981a), Devereux (1993), Ravallion (1997), and Barrett (2002a).

17 The calorie minimum has been declared by the Food and Agriculture Organization of the United Nations (FAO). The protein minimum is less clearly defined, with this minimum at roughly the midpoint of the range of minima one finds in the relevant nutritional sciences literature.

18 As Chapters 2 and 3 emphasize, there are other, donor-oriented reasons why cereals have dominated food aid flows historically.

19 This figure and, unless otherwise noted, all the others presenting national or global-level data on food aid are based on statistics reported by the World Food Programme's International Food Aid Information System (INTERFAIS).

20 The distinction between "refugees" and "internally displaced persons" (IDPs) derives from location and sense of persecution. Refugees have fled their home country to another due to a well-founded fear of persecution in the country they flee. IDPs have fled their homes for another location in the same country, usually without any sense of persecution.

21 A combination of severe drought in several parts of the globe, the first oil price crisis, which drove up the price of fertilizers and transport, and wars in several areas of the developing world sparked a severe food production shortfall, plummeting food reserves, unprecedented food price spikes and pockets of famine around the world in 1973. This precipitated the calling of a high-level World Food Conference of 1974 at which significant attention turned to questions of improved food information and early warning systems so as to head off the recurrence of sudden, acute, large-scale food shortages. The International Fund for Agricultural Development (IFAD) and the World Food Council (WFC) were both established as a result of the World Food Conference of 1974, the international agricultural research system was expanded, and the WFP's role in addressing emergencies was sharply broadened as the world's major powers all agreed on the need for multilateral response to global problems.

22 After the USA and the European Commission, the leading WFP contributors were Japan, the Netherlands, Germany, Denmark, Canada, Norway, Italy, France, and Australia (data source: WFP website, http://www.wfp.org/appeals/donors_list/2001.html).

23 There have been periodic exceptions to this general rule. For example, in 2002–3, more than 20 percent of the United States' contributions to the WFP were in cash in support of operations in Afghanistan and Iraq.

24 In later chapters, we will contest the labeling of food aid as "development," but Charlton's point is an underappreciated one.

25 In some cases, blended and fortified foods are intended for young children who need greater nutrient density in a bulky diet or as therapeutic foods for persons who have suffered extreme nutrient deprivation and associated ill health.

2 Donor-oriented food aid: the United States of America

1 Ruttan (1993, 1995) and Charlton (1992) offer excellent, detailed studies of food aid programs, their histories and motivations in the United States and Canada, respectively.

2 Tinbergen (1956).
3 Repeated GAO studies have emphasized that competing objectives hamper the effectiveness of US food aid programs in meeting their stated objectives. See, for example, Yager (2002) and the many cited studies therein.
4 The "developmental paradox," as it is sometimes known in the literature on economic development, is that low- and middle-income countries with large agricultural sectors tend to tax agriculture, rather than to subsidize it as richer countries typically do.
5 The reader interested in a more detailed history should read Vern Ruttan's excellent volumes, *Why Food Aid?* (1993) and *United States Development Assistance Policy* (1995), on which we draw repeatedly in this section.
6 The USDA thus enjoys an authority unusual among executive agencies within the United States government: it can sign contractual agreements with foreign governments without the advice and consent of the US Senate.
7 Section 416(a) commodity donations go to domestic programs, such as school feeding.
8 Mustard (2003) offers an interesting history of the USDA Foreign Agricultural Service, including the rise of the "surplus disposal" group led by Gwynn Garnett, one of the chief architects of Public Law 480.
9 Ruttan (1993, p. 12).
10 Quoted in Ruttan (1993, p. 2).
11 Ruttan (1993).
12 Gardner (2002) offers a masterful history of American farm programs that describes these innovations in detail.
13 Young and Wescott (1996).
14 Chite (1999) reports that between 1988 and June 1999, the US Congress passed thirteen supplemental appropriations – farm disaster Acts – amounting to $17 billion in funding for USDA programs. Most went for direct disaster payments to US farmers, which has the effect of keeping farmers solvent and thereby increases supply in future periods. But the next biggest portion went for "market loss" payments to address low commodity prices by adding to market demand. There have been at least four further supplemental appropriations since that time. CCC purchases for Section 416(b) shipments average more than $600 million per year, 1999–2002.
15 In recognizing the 50th anniversary of PL 480 food aid, the US Senate passed Senate Resolution 402, submitted by Senators Cochran and Harkin, noted that

> the title I program has facilitated sales of agricultural commodities from the United States, totaling an estimated $30,000,000,000 to nearly 100 countries; . . . [and] a number of countries that were early beneficiaries of both [Title I and Title II] programs have emerged as democracies and strong commercial trading partners, including South Korea, Taiwan, the Philippines, Thailand, Malaysia, Singapore, Mexico, and Turkey, in part as a result of development projects and food distribution programs conducted using agricultural commodities from the United States.

This hopeful misinterpretation of a loose association for a causal relationship underscores the durability of an important myth: that food aid stimulates a donor's commercial exports.
16 For example, Diven (2001) finds a strong, positive relationship between carryover stocks and US food aid shipments once one controls for a variety of other explanatory variables in a multiple regression model.
17 Ruttan (1995).
18 "Soy growers want to help needy become food buyers," *AgJournal*, February 25, 2001.
19 US Grains Council, *Global Update*, January 31, 2003. Letter online at ⟨http://www. ncga.com/public_policy/PDF/Letter_EU_Moratorium.pdf⟩. See Chapter 4 for more detail on disputes regarding genetically modified foods in food aid.
20 Amy Ridenour, "Feed the World: Bush Challenges European Ban on Genetically-

Modified Foods," National Center for Public Policy Research, June 2, 2003. ⟨http://www.nationalcenter.org/TSR6203.html⟩.

21 Speaker Hastert: "American Agriculture Can Help Solve World Hunger Tells House Science Committee. Europeans Exacerbating Food Problems in Africa" ⟨http://speaker.house.gov/library/intrelations/030612ag.shtml⟩.

22 Consultative Sub-Committee on Surplus Disposal, *39th Report to the Committee on Commodity Problems*, March 2003 (http://www.fao.org/DOCREP/MEETING/005/Y8286e.HTM).

23 Concerns about the prospective negative effects of NFDM availability on mothers' incentives to breastfeed their infants did induce USAID to enact a policy in 2001 to restrict Title II monetization of nonfat dried milk (NFDM) powder. We thank Tom Marchione for calling this to our attention.

24 "Dumping" refers to the overseas sale of product for less than the domestic cost of production and has long been banned under international trade agreements enshrined in the General Agreement on Tariffs and Trade and its successor institution, the World Trade Organization.

25 Ruttan (1996) makes this argument, drawing on, among other sources, USDA ERS studies such as Grigsby and Dixit (1986) and Shapouri and Rosen (1987). Longen (1983) similarly finds no solid evidence that federal purchases of surplus commodities have any significant positive effect on producer prices. We thank Bruce Gardner for calling Longen's thesis to our attention.

26 *New York Times* editorial, "The Hypocrisy of Farm Subsidies," December 1, 2002.

27 Farm program figures come from the USDA website.

28 This section draws heavily on Ruttan (1993 and 1995).

29 According to the USAID Budget Office, actual appropriations for bilateral assistance in FY2002 were $11.5 billion, of which food aid comprised $959 million. There are other ways to do the accounting – e.g., adding multilateral spending and that coming from other Departments' budgets, such as Agriculture, Health and Human Services or Treasury – but the qualitative point of low and declining shares of American foreign assistance spending stands. Food aid's proportion of total ODA has always been much lower among other donors.

30 Autarky refers to national economic policies oriented toward self-sufficiency, commonly through the erection of trade barriers to keep out imports.

31 Quoted in Ruttan (1993, p. 2).

32 As quoted in Ruttan (1993).

33 The identification of the Kennedy administration with the birth of the World Food Programme is an irony of the first order, as a multilateral food aid agency was originally championed by Vice President Richard Nixon in his 1960 campaign against Kennedy and formally proposed by President Eisenhower that September (Ruttan 1993).

34 Ruttan (1993, p. 18).

35 As quoted by Ruttan (ibid., p. 87).

36 Barry Riley, personal communication.

37 Noland (2000), Table 5.3.

38 Barrett (2001a).

39 The Farm Security and Rural Investment Act of 2002.

40 USDA Economic Research Service analysis of provisions of the Farm Bill ⟨http://www.ers.usda.gov/Features/FarmBill/Analysis⟩.

41 WFP is also a major distributor of Title II and Section 416(b) shipments. But the WFP made a policy decision in the late 1990s not to monetize Title II and Section 416(b) resources, even though many of their country programs are hampered by inadequate flows of local currency resources needed for local capacity building, external audits and even local travel by in-country staff.

42 As quoted in Mutume (2003).

43 See Ruttan (1993), Ball and Johnson (1996), and Diven (2001).
44 Paarlberg (1985).
45 Ruttan (1995, p. 123).
46 US GAO (1995).

3 Multilateral and other bilateral donors

1 This section draws heavily on Charlton (1992), Shaw and Clay (1993), CIDA (2003) and personal communications with various Canadian agriculture experts.
2 Charlton (1992, p. 145).
3 Ibid., p. 26.
4 As a senior executive of the Canadian Foodgrains Bank told us, "Taking cash to buy food simply to convert it back into cash did not make sense, and was not consistent with the public purposes of the program. Also, the food exporters were also getting annoyed, as NGOs were starting to interfere in commercial trade."
5 One major reason why Canada ships almost exclusively bulk, containerized commodities rather than higher-value-added bagged or processed products – as has been the trend in the United States and several other donors – relates to port capacity. There is no capacity on the Great Lakes to handle bagged grain and only very limited capacity on the Pacific Coast, and that capacity is at a premium for commercial shipments.
6 By law, 90 percent of CIDA's food aid budget must be spent on Canadian goods and services. This is a higher rate of tying than prevails with regard to other Canadian overseas development assistance, which is pegged at a 50 percent rate for Sub-Saharan Africa and a 66 percent rate for the rest of the world. Until recently, the national Treasury Board determined the prices that ought to be paid. Now CIDA and the Canadian Wheat Board negotiate the price of food aid grains directly.
7 Note that the premium paid for food aid above prevailing export prices cannot be explained by the quality premium usually paid for Canadian grains since the premium is relative to other Canadian grains exports.
8 "Aid tying" refers to transfers that are somehow restricted in form; they are not unconditional gifts of cash. Aid tying has become a prominent subject of discussion with the OECD in recent years, at least as regards capital goods. The tying of food aid has only very recently begun to draw significant attention. We discuss food aid tying in more detail in Chapter 8.
9 The incremental integration of the member states and expanding membership has been accompanied by changing labels, as what was originally known as the European Economic Community has become known, most recently, as the European Union.
10 Cathie (1997) offers a detailed explanation of European food aid programs, while Shaw and Clay (1993) provide helpful descriptions of the EC, Dutch, German, and Swedish programs as of the early 1990s.
11 Cathie (1997), p. 121.
12 Japan once ran a relatively small concessional food exports program somewhat akin to the Title I PL 480 program in the United States. This facility closed in 1983 (Shaw and Clay 1993).
13 The reader interested in greater detail of the WFP is strongly encouraged to read John Shaw's (2001) excellent insider history of the organization.
14 Shaw (2001).
15 Clay (2003b).
16 WFP (2000).
17 Singer *et al.* (1987), Ballenger and Mabbs-Zeno (1992), Gabbert and Weikard (2000), and Shaw (2001).
18 In the 1980s, WFP had scaled back its school feeding programs, as documented by Shaw (2001) and helpfully pointed out to us by Ed Clay.
19 Barrett (2002a).

20 Legend has it that all parties had agreed to relocate the food for education initiative within USAID under the 2002 Farm Bill until Sen. Pat Roberts (R-Kansas) wrote a letter at the behest of his daughter, then an intern with WFP, insisting that the initiative remain within USDA. The letter was unprecedentedly signed by 99 or 100 of the nation's 100 Senators. (The figure depends on whose version of the story one believes; we were unable to obtain a copy of the letter to verify this directly.)

21 See Macrae (2002) for a good discussion of the broader issue of bilateralization of humanitarian response.

22 The Consolidated Appeals Process includes needs assessments, although the methodologies differ across countries for which appeals are mounted and are widely believed to be based in part on what operational agencies think the donor "market" can bear (Macrae 2002).

23 Barrett (1998) and Diven (2001).

24 Barrett and Heisey (2002).

25 Hoddinott *et al.* (2004).

26 Barrett and Heisey (2002).

27 Barrett *et al.* (1999) and Gabbert and Weikard (2000).

28 Shaw (2001).

29 As quoted by Ruttan (1993, p. 2).

4 International regulatory mechanisms and trade disputes

1 The Food Aid Convention was also renewed and updated in 1971, 1974, 1980, 1986 and 1995.

2 Furthermore, the 1999 revision permits cash contributions to transport and other delivery costs to be counted against the value of commitments, implying an even sharper reduction in food aid commitments than is implied by the tonnage targets.

3 The July 1999 revision to the Food Aid Convention expanded the list of authorized non-cereal commodities donors would provide, although contributions of milk powder, sugar and seed remain capped, most recently at 15 percent of total food aid shipments.

4 Benson (2000).

5 Need is estimated through any of several needs analysis exercises by UN agencies, especially the FAO, and food aid donors. USDA carries out this analysis for the United States.

6 UMR determination is part of the Bellmon Analysis required of NGOs receiving and monetizing PL 480 Title II food aid from the United States. We discuss Bellmon Analyses in greater depth in Chapter 7.

7 Committee on Commodity Problems (2003).

8 In early 2003, the members of the Cairns Group were Argentina, Australia, Bolivia, Brazil, Canada, Chile, Colombia, Costa Rica, Guatemala, Indonesia, Malaysia, New Zealand, Paraguay, the Philippines, South Africa, Thailand, and Uruguay.

9 See Barrett (2002a, 2002b) for more detailed and technical explanations of this phenomenon. For readers with a bit richer understanding of economics, the income elasticity of demand for food is commonly on the order of 0.3–0.6, higher for poorer populations than for richer ones. Such figures emerge from careful econometric studies of both household-level data within particular countries and from macroeconomic data related to the effect of food aid on commercial food imports.

10 See Barrett (2002b) and OECD (2003) for evidence on this point.

11 This subsection draws heavily on Barrett (2002b) and is perhaps a bit technical for readers with little or no background in economics.

12 Ruttan (1995).

13 "Dumping" occurs when government subsidies permit producers to sell products abroad for less than their cost of production at home. Dumping has long been

outlawed by the WTO and its predecessor, the General Agreement on Tariffs and Trade (GATT). Current WTO definitions, however, define dumping as selling in foreign markets at a price lower than that prevailing in one's domestic market, largely because prices are far easier to measure than costs of production (perhaps especially for field crops dependent on untraded inputs such as soil quality and rainfall). The distinction between domestic market prices and cost of production – which should be equal in long-term competitive market equilibrium – matters because of generous income support payments to farmers and other agricultural subsidies that do not involve mopping up excess supply and thereby propping up domestic market prices. Simply put, current subsidies allow domestic prices to fall below costs of production without forcing farmers out of the market, creating an important gray area in determining what constitutes "dumping" of agricultural products abroad.

14 Hanrahan (2002).
15 Much of the material on trade and food aid is relatively technical, relying heavily on econometric methods that may be unfamiliar to many readers. The interested reader is directed to Srinivasan (1989), who provides a clear treatment of the applied general equilibrium theory, and to Barrett (2002b), who provides a much more detailed review of the methodological issues surrounding the empirical analysis of food aid and commercial international trade in foodstuffs.
16 Abbott and McCarthy (1982), von Braun and Huddleston (1988), Fitzpatrick and Storey (1989), Nathan Associates (1990), Saran and Konandreas (1991), Clay *et al.* (1996), Barrett *et al.* (1999), and OECD (2003).
17 See, for example, Isenman and Singer (1977), Stevens (1979), Farzin (1991), or Shaw and Clay (1993).
18 Herrmann *et al.* (1992) generate these results by estimating a cereals import demand model for five countries (Peru, Botswana, Egypt, Sudan, and Morocco) using 1971–87 data.
19 Strauss and Thomas (1995), Deaton (1997), and Barrett (2002a).
20 Ruttan (1993), Ruttan (1995), Ball and Johnson (1996), Clay *et al.* (1996), Gabbert and Weikard (2000), Barrett (2001a), Diven (2001), and Barrett and Heisey (2002).
21 Pinstrup-Andersen (1988) and Hoffman *et al.* (1994).
22 There is also an increase in the average cost of delivered food due to the more complex procurement and distribution, as we discuss in the next section.
23 Barrett *et al.* (1999).
24 See Barrett (1998) and Barrett *et al.* (1999) for richer explanations and testing of this hypothesis. This paragraph and the next rely heavily on results from Barrett *et al.* (1999).
25 This effect emerges largely because of considerable persistence in food aid shipments and recipient demand for variety. See Barrett *et al.* (1999) for a more complete discussion of the estimation methods and findings.
26 As quoted in Ruttan (1993, p. 88).
27 Delgado and Miller (1985) argue that food aid has contributed to shifting consumer demand from rice to hard wheat in West Africa. Merbis and Nubé (2001) likewise argue that food aid can be an effective marketing tool. These claims are not, however, based on particularly rigorous empirical methods, so the extent to which such effects truly exist remains quite unclear.
28 Barrett (1997), Barrett *et al.* (1999), and Donovan *et al.* (1999).
29 One might imagine that coarse grains shipments could, for example, depress market demand for coarse grains in the recipient economy but stimulate demand for animal products, sugar and vegetable oils.
30 For example, see Behrman and Deolalikar (1989).
31 Put differently, given that food is being given away on highly (in the limit, fully) concessional terms, it is akin to dumping. Srinivasan (1989) explains the logic behind this phenomenon.

32 Leon and Soto (1995), Miljkovic (1999), Barrett (2001b), and Fackler and Goodwin (2002).

33 Food aid in the form of one commodity will also affect the price of other commodities in the same spatial market. Donovan *et al.* (1999) demonstrated this in showing that deliveries of yellow maize food aid to Mozambique depressed not only yellow maize prices in the Maputo market, with the effects dampening out after eight to ten week, but also white maize prices, albeit on a more modest scale.

34 This section draws significantly on Maxwell and Maunder (2003).

35 USDA-NASS (2002).

36 Clapp (2004) reports that GM products have been included in food aid shipments to Bolivia, Colombia, Ecuador, Guatemala, India, Nicaragua, Sudan, and Uganda. A small row erupted in September 2000 over a WFP delivery into Kenya of GM maize from the United States, as reported in the (Nairobi) *Daily Nation*, September 24, 2000.

37 Zimbabwe initially refused GM food aid in July 2002 before studying the issues further and then taking this position of qualified acceptance.

38 IRINNews.org story, "Zimbabwe: GM Maize By-products Dumped," June 26, 2003.

39 Interestingly enough, the Zambian government did allow distribution of GM food aid to 130,000 Angolan and Congolese refugees in camps on Zambian soil, but subsequently reversed its decision and ordered that all remaining GM food aid be taken away from the refugees (*Ag Biotech Reporter* 2002, pp. 2–3, and BBC News, September 11, 2002).

40 As quoted in IRIN News , "Zambia: GM Ban Will Complicate Relief Efforts, Aid Agencies," 29 October 2002.

41 European Union Press Release, "EU Clarifies Its Position on GMOs," Annex II of WFP, Policy Issues, Agenda Item 4. WFP Policy on Donations of Foods Derived from Biotechnology (GM/Biotech Foods). Rom, WFP/EB.3/2002/4-C.

42 Zeigler (2003, p. 8).

43 As reported by the United Nations Office for the Coordination of Humanitarian Affairs' IRINNew.org service on October 17, 2002, in a story headlined "Zambia: Villagers Loot GM Food Aid."

44 South Africa produces GM corn as well and to the best of our knowledge does not maintain segregated marketing channels for GM and non-GM grain, so it would not be a GM-free source in the region.

45 Quotes from "The Politics of Hunger," *Ag Biotech Reporter* (2002, pp. 1–2).

5 So who benefits? The "iron triangle"

1 The Coalition for Food Aid was established in 1985. Its members are: Adventist Development and Relief Agency International, ACDI/VOCA, Africare, American Red Cross, CARE, Catholic Relief Services, Counterpart International, Food for the Hungry International, International Orthodox Christian Charities, International Relief and Development, Mercy Corps, OIC International, Save the Children, and World Vision.

2 Bonnard *et al.* (2002).

3 Harinaryan *et al.* (2000).

4 Smith and Lee (1994) report USDA Economic Research Service findings that US food aid shipments of wheat were estimated to boost domestic wheat prices 1–5 percent in the mid-to-late 1980s. We could not identify the original source of these estimates. They seem to us implausibly high since (i) food aid shipments during that period still involved significant surplus disposal; and (ii) reputable USDA Economic Research Service estimates of the effects of larger, domestic food assistance programs are that they raise farmgate prices by less than 1 percent, on average (Martinez and Dixit 1992).

5 MacDonald *et al.* (1998, 2002).

6 Thurow and Kilman (2003).

7 US General Accounting Office (1984).

8 US General Accounting Office (1984, p. vi).

9 MacDonald *et al.* (1998, 2002).

10 The sample is small compared to the broader range of food aid shipped because we could not obtain (i) procurement prices for most US food aid shipments nor (ii) truly comparable open market prices for the same time period, purchase location and commodity for most shipments for which we had procurement prices. Furthermore, we ultimately want (in Chapter 8) to compare food aid procurement prices in donor countries with open market prices in destination countries so as to be able to analyze the difference between destination and source country markets into distinct types of leakage (e.g., due to procurement premia, shipping premia, shipping costs). This forced us to restrict attention to a subset of recipient countries for which we had good market price data on food aid commodities. A review of US market prices and food aid procurement prices for a broader range of commodities indicates that the basic pattern we report is far more general, not specific to these three destination markets. But given the small and nonrandom sample we are able to construct, we caution against attributing false precision to these estimates. We should also note that the corn price series we use were likely affected by the Star Link GM corn controversy in 2000.

11 These averages are weighted by procurement contract volume.

12 The Congress did mandate that the Department of Transportation's Maritime Administration reimburse USAID and USDA any extra costs associated with this change. Nonetheless, a recent audit by the USAID Inspector General uncovered significant problems with the reimbursement system and considerable unclaimed reimbursements, amounting to as much as $289 million over the period 1992–2000 (USAID 2001). Sources tell us that these arrears were apparently largely the result of billing errors, lack of documentation and other bureaucractic complications. Much of this was resolved in early 2004.

13 The Maritime Security Program was established in 1996 to help the US merchant marine fleet meet the higher costs of maintaining US citizen crews and meeting DoD standards for military readiness. In 2004, MSP subsidies were $2.1 million/ship annually. These subsidies are essentially call options that give DoD the legal right to use ships and crews for military operations when necessary. Some MSP vessels were employed in the military action against Iraq in 2003.

14 Bagged food aid – and most fortified or processed product is bagged rather than bulk – also uses container or roll-on/roll-off ships that are of greater commercial value to shippers than bulk vessels.

15 A few ports also depend heavily on food aid shipments. For example, the *Wall Street Journal* reports that food aid makes up one-third of the tonnage shipped from the Gulf of Mexico port at Lake Charles, Louisiana (Thurow and Kilman 2003).

16 Prior to the restriction imposed on freight forwarders, national governments contracting for Title I PL 480 imports would engage a freight forwarder that would subsequently contract with a shipping line. Because these freight forwarders sometimes doubled as brokers for shipping companies owned by – or owned ships on behalf of – elites in the importing country, these arrangements sometimes created at least the impression of impropriety.

17 Data come from USDA/FSA Export Operations FY 2001 416(b) and Food For Progress Agreement Reports (http://www.fsa.usda.gov/eob).

18 US General Accounting Office (1994b).

19 US General Accounting Office (1994b, p. 2) and US General Accounting Office (1990) for earlier estimates.

20 US General Accounting Office (1994b).

21 Ibid.

22 The weights are based on volume transported by ship type, given ship type-specific estimates of cost differences.

23 Ibid.

24 This includes shipments of wheat, corn, rice, vegetable oil, flour, cornmeal, and pork to Angola, Armenia, Bangladesh, Bosnia, Bulgaria, China, Côte d'Ivoire, D.R. Congo, Djibouti, Eritrea, Ethiopia, Guinea, Guinea Bissau, Honduras, Indonesia, Jordan, Kenya, Kyrgyzstan, Lebanon, Macedonia, Moldova, Mongolia, Morocco, D.P.R. Korea, Pakistan, the Philippines, Russia, Senegal, Sudan, Tajikistan, Tanzania, Yemen, and the former Yugoslavia.

25 American Maritime Congress website (http://www.us-flag.org/carprefcon.html).

26 UNCTAD (2003) and American Maritime Congress website (http://www.us-flag.org/background. html).

27 US General Accounting Office (1994b, p. 3).

28 US General Accounting Office (1994c).

29 We are deeply indebted to Jacqueline Murphy for her excellent and painstaking work in assembling these data from the financial statements available in NGOs' annual reports, USAID's annual *International Food Assistance Reports* (prior to 1997, the annual *US World Food Day Reports*), and USAID Food for Peace Information Services reports on approved monetization programs. This process was helped considerably by access to the valuable database and library at Food Aid Management and the helpful and well-informed staff there, particularly Trisha (Schmirler) Long, and by the gracious staff of these eight NGOs. We asked for similar information from most of the other NGOs that had received US food aid in recent years – ACDI/VOCA, CARITAS, Opportunities Industrialization Centers International, Projects in Agriculture, Rural Industry, Science and Medicine (PRIMSA), Relief Society of Tigray, Save the Children Federation, and World Share – as well, but the others ignored or refused our repeated requests.

30 Note that we are discussing the budgets and food aid volumes only of the US members of these organizations. CRS is a completely US-based organization; CARE and World Vision are global alliances with national members. The figures reported here relate only to CARE-USA and World Vision USA.

31 Unless otherwise noted, all weighted averages use weights based on 2001 gross revenues for each organization.

32 This is a classic "coordination failure" problem in economics. Each individual NGO would be better off if the United States were to reduce its use of food commodities in foreign assistance and to increase cash resources made available, even if the substitution of cash for food were significantly less than a dollar-for-dollar. But it is equally in each NGO's interest to let the other NGOs incur the costs and risks of pushing for such change, especially the risk that if it foregoes food aid that it will not receive any cash resources to replace the lost commodity resources. As a consequence, the system continues under suboptimal arrangements. One senior NGO executive remarked to us that the task of convincing fellow NGOs to advocate for significant reform of US food aid would be rather like asking them to "commit partial suicide."

33 Bonnard *et al.* (2002).

34 USAID data indicate that this is true as well of many of the NGOs that did not provide us with their own financial statements. For example, ACDI/VOCA, CARITAS, and PRISMA each monetized 83 to 86 percent of the food aid they received in 2000 and 2001.

35 The ensuing discussion has benefited considerably from the insights of Arthur Brooks of Syracuse University, an academic expert on the non-profit sector, and Jeff Brooks, the creative director of a marketing firm that handles fundraising for a range of nonprofit organizations, including international charities. We thank them for their generous guidance. See also Light (2000) for related discussion of the growing importance of efficiency indicators in non-profit sector management.

36 A bit more precisely, Guidestar (http://www.guidestar.org) provides descriptive statistics on every organization that qualifies for tax-exempt status under Section 501(c)(3) of the United States Internal Revenue Code. The Charity Navigator's website can be found at (http://www.charitynavigator.org/).

37 See Frumkin and Kim (2001) for strong statistical evidence and literature review on this point and Rose-Ackerman (1982) for a theoretical explanation.

6 Edging towards a recipient-oriented food aid system

1 This brief overview is not intended to be an exhaustive recount of the development of food security analysis and thinking. The reader interested in more detail should consult Devereux (1993) or Ravallion (1997), or Maxwell and Frankenberger (1992).
2 Sen (1981b), emphasis in original.
3 Sen (1981a, 1981b).
4 The concept of "utilization" refers to the uses to which food is put within the household: is it handled, prepared and distributed so as to ensure individual consumers enjoy the nutritional benefits of accessible food. "Utilization" also incorporates health and the ability of the individual to utilize the nutritional content of food consumed.
5 World Bank (1986).
6 Chambers and Conway (1992), as quoted and modified slightly by Carney (1998, p. 4).
7 Ellis (1998).
8 Barrett (2002a) and Webb and Rogers (2003).
9 De Waal (1989), de Waal (1997), Devereux (1993), and Lautze *et al.* (2003).
10 De Waal (1997).
11 Oshaug and Barthe-Eide (1997).
12 UN Economic and Social Council (1999) "The Right to Adequate Food (Art. 11)," E/C.12/1999/5,General Comment Number 12.
13 Kracht (1999) and Eide (1999).
14 The term "programming" reflects common NGO parlance for implementation strategies, including of classic projects. It can also include elements of policy analysis and advocacy.
15 See Anderson (1996) for the original perspective on the "do no harm" injunction, and CARE (2001) for an approach that explicitly demands recognition of potential harms resulting from interventions, how to monitor and mitigate their effects.
16 Rosset (2002).
17 Sphere Project (2004).
18 IFRC (1995).
19 "Access at all times, by all people, to enough food to lead active, healthy lives."
20 "NGO Code of Conduct on Food Aid and Food Security." Adopted in 1995 by Euronaid and the Liaison Committee of Development NGOs to the European Union.
21 Euron Aid (1995).
22 UNCHR, The International Code of Conduct on the Human Right to Adequate Food (p. 2).
23 UNCHR, The International Code of Conduct on the Human Right to Adequate Food (p. 7).
24 Windfuhr (n.d.).
25 Rieff (2002).
26 Maxwell (2001), Devereux (2002b), and Marchione (1996).
27 The critical point to grasp from a rights-based perspective is not the 2,100Kcal/day benchmark (which is in any case derived from empirical observation, not a normative mandate), it is rather the fact that the benchmark is a human right – and therefore an obligation of other parties to respect, protect, and fulfill (or at least create the environment in which individuals or households can fulfill).
28 This section draws heavily on Barrett and Carter (2002), Barrett (2003), Barrett and Swallow (2003) and Barrett and McPeak (forthcoming). Barrett and Swallow (2004) explain how a poverty traps perspective builds upon and strengthens the livelihoods approach.

29 Baulch and Hoddinott (2000) offer an especially good summary of and evidence on the differences between chronic and transitory poverty.
30 In more technical terms, for readers with more advanced training in economics, a poverty trap exists whenever a stable dynamic equilibrium income lies below the relevant poverty line. See Barrett (2003) for more detail.
31 Easterly (2001, p. 197).
32 See Cox and Jimenez (1992), Dercon and Krishnan (2003), Devereux (2002b), Albarran and Attanasio (2003) and Lentz and Barrett (2004) for empirical evidence on such "crowding out" effects. John Hoddinott (personal communication) raises the excellent point that transfers' "crowding out" effect need not be bad. Because people can commonly only go to others for help a limited number of times – and there is empirical evidence that net transfer receipts decline the greater an individual's past receipts (Lybbert *et al.* 2004; McPeak 2004) – then when individuals receive a public transfer, they may well choose not to request private transfers from others, instead "saving" this option for some future date when no public assistance is available. We know of no empirical studies that have controlled for such selection effects in estimating the degree to which public transfers crowd out private, informal flows.

7 The uses of food aid to address food insecurity

1 WFP (2003).
2 WFP (2004a).
3 Clay (2000), WFP (2003), and FFP (2003).
4 A "complex political emergency" involves multiple causes, both man-made (i.e., conflict) and natural factors (e.g., drought, flood, hurricanes).
5 CARE (2003) and Webb and Rogers (2003).
6 See especially Corbett (1988), Alderman and Paxson (1992), and Binswanger and Rosenzweig (1993), Payne and Lipton (1994), Morduch (1995), Deaton (1997) and CARE (2003).
7 Haddad and Frankenberger (2003) and Barrett and McPeak (forthcoming).
8 CARE (2003) and Webb and Rogers (2003).
9 UNAIDS (2000), UNAIDS/WHO (2002), and Haddad and Gillespie (2001).
10 FANTA (2002a) and Bonnard (2002).
11 de Waal and Whiteside (2003).
12 Harvey (2003) and FANTA (2002a).
13 WFP (2003).
14 Devereux (2002b) and World Bank (2002).
15 Bezuneh and Deaton (1997).
16 FFP (2003).
17 Raisin (2001).
18 WFP (2003). The Millennium Development Goals are consensus targets set by the United Nations member states for reducing human suffering early in the twenty-first century. They include reducing by half the proportion of people living on less than a dollar a day, and reducing by half the proportion of people who suffer from hunger.
19 See Beaton and Ghassemi (1982), Kielman *et al.* (1982), Martorell (1993), Allen and Gillespie (2001), Barrett (2002a), and WFP (2004c).
20 WFP (2003) and Piwoz (2004). It is almost impossible to conduct the research needed to support this conclusion, but nutrient requirements for people living with AIDS are higher.
21 WFP (2004b) and Swindale *et al.* (2004).
22 Swindale *et al.* (2004).
23 Del Rosso and Marek (1996) and Allen and Gillespie (2001).
24 Ahmed and del Ninno (2001), WFP (2001b), and Ahmed and Arends-Kuenning (2003).

25 Ahmed and Del Ninno (2001).
26 Dugger (2004).
27 Wijga (1983), Figa-Talamanca (1985), von Braun *et al.* (1999), and Barrett, Holden and Clay (forthcoming).
28 Neun (2000).
29 Rami (2002).
30 See Osmani and Chowdhury (1983), Clay (1986), von Braun (1995), von Braun *et al.* (1999), Devereux (1999), Ravallion (1999), Gebremedhin and Swinton (2000), Barrett *et al.* (2003) and Holden *et al.* (forthcoming) for evidence on FFW programs and broader workfare efforts intended to create valuable public goods.
31 One example is the WFP's Vulnerable Group Development project in Bangladesh. We are grateful to Allan Jury for calling this case to our attention.
32 This reflects USDA statistics on Fiscal Year 2002 participation rates: 28 million children participating in the National School Lunch Program and 2 million women, 2 million infants and 4 million pre-school age children in the Special Supplemental Nutrition Program for Women, Infants and Children (WIC). See Rush (1987) and Devaney *et al.* (1990) for detailed evidence on WIC performance. Barrett (2002a) provides a general review of such food assistance programs.
33 See World Food Programme (2001b) for a detailed treatment of food aid and its role in food assistance programs in seven South Asian countries.
34 As quoted by IRIN, July 28, 2003.
35 USDA FAS (2001).
36 Food aid is sometimes monetized in emergencies, perhaps most notably in the Somalia crisis in 1992–93, when food aid was monetized through small local traders in an effort to keep prices from spiking. When prices spike due to speculative stocking by traders or true supply shortages, food becomes even more inaccesible to poorer households, which are almost inevitably net food buyers. See Cekan *et al.* (1996) for further discussion of this role for food aid monetization.
37 Abdulai *et al.* (2003) and USDA/FAS (2001).
38 In the second phase of Operation Flood, the European Community decided to use a significant portion of its dairy surplus to support the project directly, rather than indirectly through the World Food Programme. Operation Flood II was therefore funded by the National Dairy Development Board (NDDB), the government of India, the World Bank, and the European Community through food aid, and the farmer-owners of the village dairy cooperative societies (Candler and Kumar, 1998). See also Doornbos *et al.* (1990).
39 Cekan *et al.* (1996).
40 Drèze and Sen (1989) discuss this issue extensively without providing specific estimates of the relevant premia for the form of payment. The reported estimates come from Barrett and Clay (2003), who compare labor supply curves for FFW programs in rural Ethiopia with payments in cash, maize, red wheat, and white wheat. These fungibility premium estimates ignore the additional costs of procurement, transport, storage, handling and loss of physical commodities, which only magnify the differences between food and cash distributions
41 Bremer-Fox *et al.* (1990), Abdulai *et al.* (2004a), and Tschirley and Howard (2003).
42 Bonnard *et al.* (2002).
43 Cekan *et al.* (1996), Mendez-England and Associates (1996), and Tschirley and Howard (2003).
44 Tschirley and Howard (2003), emphasis added.

8 The management of food aid in addressing food insecurity

1 This section draws heavily on Barrett (2002c).
2 See Barrett (2002a) for a review of targeting in the context of food assistance programs

and Besley and Kanbur (1990) for an excellent discussion of targeting questions more generally.

3 See, for example, WFP (2000), CARE (2003), and Sharp (2001).

4 See Sharp (2001) for an excellent discussion of these issues.

5 Ruttan (1993), Ruttan (1995), Ball and Johnson (1996), Clay *et al.* (1996), Gabbert and Weikard (2000), Barrett (2001a), Diven (2001), and Barrett and Heisey (2002).

6 See Barrett (2001a) for evidence on US PL 480 flows and Barrett and Heisey (2002) for evidence on WFP food aid shipments. Those studies explore whether food aid stabilizes nonconcessional food availability – defined as domestic production plus commercial imports – in recipient countries. Although stabilization of national-level food availability is certainly not an explicit goal of food aid programs, it is implied, not least by humanitarian goals that emphasize delivering food aid where there is a shortfall and reducing food aid inflows in places and at times when local harvests and commercial imports could prove sufficient to meet local needs if the poor were given adequate purchasing power. This merely reflects Sen's (1981a) observation that adequate food availability is a necessary – but not sufficient – condition to avoid famine and thus that food aid meant to address nutritional need therefore ought to covary negatively with food otherwise available in recipient countries. Put differently, if food aid is to serve as effective insurance against dangerous fluctuations in food supplies, it must covary negatively with nonconcessional food supplies, i.e., it must stabilize aggregate food availability.

7 Barrett (2001a), Merbis and Nubé (2001), Barrett and Heisey (2002), and Gupta *et al.* (2002).

8 Clay *et al.* (1996) and Merbis and Nubé (2001).

9 Darcy and Hofmann (2003).

10 Sharp (1998, 2001), Clay *et al.* (1999), Jayne *et al.* (2001, 2002), Dercon and Krishnan (2003), Yamano *et al.* (2003), and Lentz and Barrett (2004). Quisumbing (2003) finds evidence of somewhat better targeting in her study of Ethiopia.

11 Jayne *et al.* (2001, 2002), Dercon and Krishnan (2003), Yamano *et al.* (2003), and Lentz and Barrett (2004)

12 See von Braun *et al.* (1999) for a range of relevant studies.

13 Jaspars (2000).

14 Sharp (2001) and Jaspars and Shoham (1999).

15 The only direct indicator of food security would be to measure actual consumption – a tedious and time-consuming task even in basic research, and totally inapplicable to emergency assessment. However, a variety of behavioral indicators have been introduced recently that have proven to be a good proxy for consumption, but all are still at the pilot testing stage. See Maxwell *et al.* (2003).

16 Clay *et al.* (1999).

17 Drèze and Sen (1989).

18 Sandford and Habtu (2000).

19 See Ravallion (1991) or von Braun (1995) for surveys describing the general efficacy of FFW and other public employment schemes. Recent empirical studies that document targeting errors under FFW include Ravallion *et al.* (1993), Clay *et al.* (1999), Devereux (1999), Jayne *et al.* (2001, 2002), Teklu and Asefa (1999), Gebremedhin and Swinton (2000), Jalan and Ravallion (2000), Barrett *et al.* (2003), and Barrett and Clay (2003).

20 McCaston (1999).

21 See Alderman (2002) on Albania.

22 Conning and Kevane (2001). In other words, a clear judgment must be made that relying on local leadership to identify vulnerable groups will not result in resources being diverted to relatively better off groups with better political connections.

23 See McPeak and Barrett (2001) on northern Kenya, Mathys and Kebede (2000) on Ethiopia, and Lentz and Barrett (2004) on the two countries together.

24 Lautze *et al.* (2003), Mathys and Kebede (2000), and Jaspars and Shoham (1999).

25 There is, of course, a legitimate question as to whether there exists "a" unique community view or whether the parochial views of particular (usually elite) subgroups prevail. It becomes especially difficult to sort out the difference between the views of local communities and of local elites in emergency situations where time is of the essence and in conflict situations in which security concerns may prevent in-depth consultation.

26 Lautze *et al.* (2003).

27 Drèze and Sen (1989). See also Basu (1996) on the problem of adverse spillover effects on non-participants when local food supply conditions may result in increased food prices if program participation benefits are paid in cash rather than food.

28 Regulatory authorities in other countries, notably India, have recently closed down food aid programs that included genetically modified foods.

29 McPeak (2003).

30 Reed and Habicht (1998) offer an insightful, cautionary tale from refugee camps in Zaire, where food aid recipients routinely sold part of their rations in order to obtain other, more nutritionally appropriate foods. They find that "[f]ood sales improved the micronutrient content of diets but at the expense of energy lost from an already energy-deficient diet" (p. 128). Most alarmingly, operational agencies cut rations when they observed sales, mistakenly believing this indicated that recipients were receiving more than enough food.

31 WFP (2000).

32 See Marchione (2002) for some specific details.

33 See Taylor and Byerlee (1991), Barrett (1998, 2001a), and Diven (2001) for empirical evidence on this point.

34 Clay *et al.* (1996).

35 The figure presents a kernel smoothed nonparametric probability density plot based on data on 289 distinct shipments for which we could find call forward and port delivery data through the USDA Farm Services Administration website. These shipments included a wide range of commodities, from bulk wheat, corn, rice and sorghum to legumes, blended foods and vegetable oil. The shipments were destined for 31 different countries in Africa, Asia, and Europe. These figures necessarily understate delivery lags for two reasons. First, we use the call forward date to represent the date a request was initiated, although informal requests commonly begin weeks prior to the issuance of a call forward (but data on informal requests are not available systematically). Second, we can only establish the dates of port delivery, yet more than 35 percent of shipments docked at ports outside the recipient country, requiring further ground forwarding time to reach the recipient's port of entry.

36 Maxwell (2002) and Hammond and Maxwell (2002).

37 See von Braun and Huddleston (1988), Taylor and Byerlee (1991), Clay *et al.* (1996), Merbis and Nubé (2001), and Barrett (2002a) on this point. By contrast, because the EU food aid budget is fixed in volume terms rather than expenditure terms, there is no discernible correlation between world food prices and EU food aid flow volumes (Clay *et al.* 1996).

38 Barrett (1998), Barrett *et al.* (1999), Diven (2001), and Barrett and Heisey (2002).

39 Reproduced from Barrett (1998).

40 Barrett and Heisey (2002).

41 Barrett and Heisey (2002), Clay *et al.* (1999), Jayne *et al.* (2002), Yamano *et al.* (2003), and Lentz and Barrett (2004).

42 Maxwell and Watkins (2003), Harinaryan *et al.* (2000), and Rogers (2002).

43 Maxwell and Watkins (2003).

44 Harinaryan *et al.* (2000).

45 Rogers (2002).

46 Darcy and Hoffman (2003) and IFRCRCS (2003).

47 Detailed discussion of food aid needs assessment methods can be found in Devereux and Hoddinott (1999), Merbis and Nubé (2001), and Shapouri and Rosen (2003).

48 See NRC (1989).
49 FAO/GIEWS makes many of its products available on the web at http://geoweb.fao. org/.
50 Briefly, the Food Economy Approach is a rapid assessment method that examines total food intake and the relative proportions of household food consumption from different sources, including the various coping strategies that a household relies on, in order to calculate the total deficiency at the household level. When households are aggregated by wealth groups in a community, the method can provide an estimate of total food aid needs. The method has been widely adopted by the World Food Programme. See Boudreau (1998) and Save the Children-UK (2000) for more detail.
51 This section draws heavily on Maxwell and Watkins (2003).
52 Buchanan-Smith and Davies (1995).
53 Lautze *et al.* (2003) and Devereux (2002a).
54 Buchanan-Smith and Davies (1996) and Maxwell and Watkins (2003).
55 Macrae *et al.* (1997).
56 Sanford and Habtu (2002), Salama *et al.* (2001), and Hammond and Maxwell (2002).
57 Maxwell and Watkins (2003).
58 Buchanan-Smith and Davies (1996).
59 Maxwell and Watkins (2003).
60 Save the Children-UK (2000) and Boudreau (1998). See note 50 for a brief explanation.
61 FIVIMS (2002) and Young *et al.* (2001).
62 Donors may be in Africa, Asia, or South America, as well, although these three continents have cumulatively accounted for less than five percent of food aid donations every year for which data exist.
63 See Clay and Benson (1990) for a more detailed description of these two events.
64 The US call forward and port delivery date data used in Figure 8.1 are the only systematic source of information with which one can compute delivery lags, which makes direct comparisons among donors difficult. Moreover, since the United States rarely funds triangular transaction or local purchase operations – recent operations in Iraq and Afghanistan are notable exceptions – one cannot strictly compare delays in these mechanisms against direct shipments sourced in donor countries. Any observed differences in delivery lags would not be due solely to differences in procurement venue, since one would necessarily also be comparing different donors' administrative systems. RDI (1987) and Clay and Benson (1990) find that while most WFP triangular transactions appear to have been much quicker than comparable emergency shipments from donors, many EC triangular transactions were no more timely and sometimes faced extraordinary delays.
65 The French colonial influence created significant urban demand for wheat products.
66 There is also the fact that the quality of US yellow corn (often #2 or #3 by the time it reaches the recipients) often cannot compare with the average quality of locally-produced white varieties.
67 Barrett *et al.* (2003), Fafchamps and Gavian (1996), Kerven (1992), and Teka *et al.* (1999).
68 See especially Reutlinger and Bigman (1981), Hyden and Reutlinger (1992), and Reutlinger (1999).
69 The issue is by no means settled, as there remain significant concerns about the empirical methods used in most market integration studies (Barrett 1996; Fackler and Goodwin 2002; Barrett and Li 2002). Nonetheless, the extant literature from places such as Benin, Ethiopia, India, Indonesia, Madagascar, Mozambique, the Philippines, and Zimbabwe strongly suggests a reasonable degree of spatial market integration in developing country food markets. See Alexander and Wyeth (1994), Barrett (1995), Dercon (1995), Palasakas and Harriss-White (1993), Baulch (1997a, 1997b), Fackler and Goodwin (2002), and Mabaya (2003) for good examples.
70 We should note that there were huge commodity surpluses in East Africa in 2002, where

grain prices in Ethiopia and Kenya collapsed in the face of excess local supply of basic grains. The international community nonetheless did not procure any appreciable volume of food aid from East Africa to support emergency operations in southern Africa. The food aid overwhelmingly came from Europe and, especially, North America. There were at least 40,000 tons of maize local purchases by the World Food Programme in Kenya in 2002, but mainly for distribution to deficit regions in the north and south-east, as well as in Somalia and southern Sudan (IRIN Report, dated 27 June 2002).

71 We constructed the annual per capita cereals production series for 137 different food aid recipient countries over the period 1961–2000, based on data available from FAOSTAT, and computed the 9316 correlation coefficients among all pairs of countries. Figure 8.5 displays the average correlation coefficient for each country with all other countries within 750 kilometers of its borders, weighted by neighbors' populations (so as to reflect aggregate supply in absolute volumes). We recomputed these figures changing the definition of neighbors (using only bordering countries or only countries within either 500 or 1000 kilometers of the border), using market availability, defined as the sum of domestic food production and commercial imports of cereals, instead of production (i.e., including commercial cereals imports), and using only covariation among observations at least one standard deviation from the country-specific period mean, thereby capturing correlations only in periods of significant (positive or negative) supply shocks. The qualitative pattern remains exactly the same no matter which of these changes we make. The basic finding therefore seems quite robust to the particular statistical method one might choose.

72 Clay and Benson (1990) describe this incident.

73 Amha *et al.* (1997) provide a detailed evaluation of the 1996 Ethiopia local grain purchase program.

74 Martens (1990) discusses this case and the basic economics of triangular transactions.

75 Schultz (1960).

76 Clay *et al.* (1996).

77 Trueblood *et al.* (2001) find this to be true in southern Africa over the 1970–95 period.

78 Note that we are not factoring in the cost of shipping either locally procured or internationally sourced food from port to final inland destination for distribution. Those costs, which should apply equally to both locally or internationally sourced food aid, can be substantial. By leaving those out, we may overstate the share of total costs reflecting the value of food distributed.

79 Martens (1990) formally develops the welfare effects of triangular transactions under such circumstances in greater detail.

80 Jepma (1991) offers a detailed treatment of aid tying, albeit not applied to food aid. The 1987 Guiding Principles for Associated Financing and Tied and Partially Untied Official Development Assistance of the Development Assistance Committee of the Organisation for Economic Co-operation and Development (DAC/OECD) defines aid as tied if goods cannot be freely and fully procured from substantially all developing countries and from any OECD country.

81 This standard definition of aid tying differs from that sometimes implied by those who claim US food aid is not tied because recipients are not compelled to purchase commodities in addition to receiving free (or heavily discounted) aid shipments. In that unorthodox use of the term, no food aid is tied. In the more conventional (i.e., OECD) use of the term, US food aid is doubly tied, as explained in the text.

82 Olson (1965) famously argued that small groups with powerful individual interests are far more likely to band together successfully to advance their common goals than are much larger groups with weaker individual interests. As a result, small group interests will commonly prevail over the general interests of whole populations, often leading to distortion of policies and considerable economic inefficiency.

83 Jepma (1991, p. 58).

84 Frans Lammersen (OECD, personal communication).

85 McPeak (2004).
86 See Newbery and Stiglitz (1981), Newbery (1989), Williams and Wright (1990), Gilbert (1993), Conway (1998), NRI (1999), and Brennan (2003) for richer discussion about food storage and commodity price stabilization for addressing food insecurity concerns.
87 See Timmer (1989, 1996) and Gilbert (1993) for detailed discussions of these problems.
88 Devereux (2002a) discusses this episode in detail.
89 See Del Ninno *et al.* (2001) for a detailed description of the 1998 floods, including a positive assessment of the role played by government food security stocks. Ravallion (1987) describes the 1974–75 famine and the role played by food stockpiling and resulting price spikes based on forecasts of supply shortages that ultimately proved inaccurate.
90 Conway (1998), Islam and Thomas (1994), and Jones (1994).
91 Jones (1994).
92 See NRI (1999) for a detailed discussion of the options.

9 Consequences of poor food aid management

1 See the review in Barrett (2002a). Examples of more recent evidence on this point include Quisumbing (2003) and Yamano *et al.* (2003).
2 Schubert (1986), Clay and Stokke (1991), Clay (2000), and Yamano *et al.* (2003).
3 Yamano *et al.* (2003) is among the only studies of which we are aware that takes care to control for these effects. They find them to be substantial in their data from Ethiopia, tending to bias downwards the estimated effect of food ration receipts on child growth.
4 See WFP (2004a and 2004c).
5 See, for just one example, Médicins sans Frontières-Belgium (2001).
6 Coates *et al.* (2003), Maxwell (1999), Maxwell *et al.* (2003), and CARE/ERREC/WFP (2003).
7 Bonnard (1999) and Devereux (1998).
8 Barrett (2002a).
9 Clay *et al.* (1996), Barrett (2002a), and Marchione (2002).
10 Marchione (2000, 2002). This issue is now much higher on the WFP agenda (WFP, 2004c).
11 UNICEF (1990) and Strauss and Thomas (1998).
12 We thank Erin Lentz for undertaking a careful literature search on the topic of food aid dependency. The excellent annotated bibliography she generated on the subject (Lentz 2003) confirmed our prior impression that little solid empirical evidence has been published demonstrating "dependency" on food aid. People simply assume and assert dependency to exist, perhaps explain why it could occur in theory, or offer an anecdote or two rather than any systematic evidence. Most commonly, contemporary authors invoking the notion of dependency cite Isenman and Singer (1977), Lappé and Collins (1977), or Jackson and Eade (1982) but offer no evidence of their own.
13 We use the economic definition of "expenditure," i.e., including the value of all goods and services obtained through own production or transfers, not just purchases.
14 The empirical evidence in this paragraph comes from Lentz and Barrett (2004).
15 Little (2004).
16 Del Ninno *et al.* (2001).
17 Gainey (2000).
18 Kanbur *et al.* (1994), Barrett (2002a).
19 Jackson (1982) find significant labor market disincentives from food-for-work projects in various developing countries while Stevens (1979), Maxwell *et al.* (1994), von Braun *et al.* (1999), and Abdulai *et al.* (2001) find little or no evidence of labor market disincentive effects in various places in Sub-Saharan Africa.
20 There is a serious methodological problem as well in establishing the labor supply

effect of food aid receipt. Because food aid tends to respond positively to exogenous conditions – such as rainfall that affects the returns to labor on one's own fields, or employment options on the private labor markets – that likewise reduce labor demand, there will tend to be a spurious negative relationship between observed labor supply and food aid receipts in studies that fail to control adequately for the endogeneity of food aid receipts. Abdulai *et al.* (2004) is the only empirical study we know of that makes proper controls for this effect, which suggests that the limited empirical evidence available necessarily overstates the negative effects of food aid on recipients' labor supply.

21 Byerlee (1987).

22 McPeak (2002).

23 See McPeak (2003) on localized degradation and McPeak (2002) on food aid and fuelwood use.

24 Townsend (1994), Deaton (1997), and Lybbert *et al.* (2004).

25 See Albarran and Attanasio (2003), Cox and Jimenez (1995), Dercon and Krishnan (2003), Devereux (2002a), Jensen (1999), and Lentz and Barrett (2004).

26 Devereux (2002a).

27 Huysentruyt *et al.* (2002).

28 CARE (2003) personal communication to authors.

29 The key original papers are Schultz (1960) and Fisher (1963). Maxwell and Singer (1979) summarize this debate nicely.

30 See *The Economist*, "Food for Russia," November, 12, 1998, on Russia and Tschirley *et al.* (1996) and Donovan *et al.* (1999) on Mozambique.

31 Mohapatra *et al.* (1999).

32 Holden *et al.* (forthcoming) describe an analogous situation, where food for work schemes in the hilly Tigray region of northern Ethiopia that pay participants to construct soil and water conservation structures on private farmland appear to induce increased complementary private investment in soil conservation, leading to reduced erosion rates and sustainable increases in farm productivity and household incomes.

33 Large volumes of food aid can even affect the real exchange rate, making imported inputs and food cheaper and nontradable foods more expensive. Younger (1992) explains the phenomenon of aid-induced changes in real exchange rates and its effects on recipient economies. Mohapatra *et al.* (1999) provide a brief theoretical treatment of the issue as it relates to food aid in particular. See Gabre-Madhin *et al.* (2002) for a detailed discussion of food aid, technological change, and market price effects in the context of Asia and Sub-Saharan Africa.

34 Maxwell and Singer (1979), Nathan Associates (1990), Clay and Stokke (1991), and Shaw and Clay (1993) each review a range of prior studies on the impact of food aid on farmers' incentives and production levels in recipient countries. Interested readers are directed to those sources for detailed discussion of past empirical results and the methodological challenges surrounding trying to identify precisely the effect of food aid deliveries on recipient country producer incentives and agricultural output. Hall (1980) and Bezuneh *et al.* (2003) provide somewhat more recent and sophisticated empirical studies of this issue in Brazil and Tunisia, respectively, while Barrett *et al.* (1999) provide econometric evidence, based on national-level panel data (i.e., time series data on a cross-section of countries), that suggests a very modest, negative (and statistically insignificantly different from zero) effect of food aid on recipient country production in the year when food aid is received, with the effect vanishing within two years.

35 Abdulai *et al.* (2004).

36 Clay *et al.* (1996).

37 Recall that food aid monetization occurs almost exclusively with US food aid donations.

38 Rubey (1996).

39 Deaton and Laroque (1992, 1996).

40 Sen (1981a) and Ravallion (1987).
41 See Williams and Wright (1990) or Deaton and Laroque (1992, 1996) for a rigorous treatment of the dynamics of storable commodity prices.
42 Marchione (2002).

10 Recasting food aid's role: the general strategy

1 See Barrett and Carter (2002) and Barrett (2003) for more on this point.
2 For the more technically minded reader, the slightly more formal definition is that a poverty trap arises when there exist multiple stable dynamic equilibria in the relevant measure of welfare (e.g., income, expenditures, assets), at least one of which falls below the local poverty line. See Chapter 6 or Barrett (2003) for more detail.
3 These processes occur at all scales of analysis, from individual through multinational regions, giving rise to the concept of "fractal poverty traps" reflecting the similarity of the phenomenon of persistent poverty and bifurcated accumulation dynamics at all scales, from household to community to national levels (Easterly 2001; Barrett and Swallow 2003). Barrett and Swallow (2004) explain how the poverty traps approach usefully generalizes the sustainable livelihoods approach currently popular among many donors.
4 For example, asset-based approaches have been the subject of major recent conferences on poverty reduction in Canada (http://policyresearch.gc.ca/doclib/ Asset-Based_Approaches.pdf) and globally (http://www.tessproject.com/products/ seminarsandtraining/seminar%20series/Assets_Materials/Agenda.pdf) and are now are the centerpiece of the Ford Foundation's grantsmaking (http://www.fordfound. org/publications/recent_articles/docs/assets_bw.pdf).
5 See Dasgupta (1993, 1997), Loury (1981), and Strauss and Thomas (1998).
6 Recent programming, for example, the USAID Famine Prevention Framework for Ethiopia, appropriately place considerable emphasis on the concept of resilience (Marchione and Novick 2003).
7 Von Braun (1995), Ravallion (1999), Barrett *et al.* (2003), and Coady *et al.* (2003) discuss such schemes in detail.
8 Many of these points are summarized in the "Berlin Statement on Food Aid for Sustainable Food Security" (von Braun 2003).
9 See, for example, Duffield (2001), or Rieff (2002).
10 See Macrae and Leader (2000), but this has become an even larger concern given the extent to which food and other forms of humanitarian aid have been identified with belligerent parties in the Afghanistan and Iraq wars of 2001 and 2003.
11 "Monopsony" refers to the market power enjoyed by a single buyer, akin to the "monopoly" market power enjoyed by a single seller.
12 See the Sphere Guidelines (Sphere Project 2004) on assessment and delivery; Maxwell and Watkins (2003) on early warning, assessment, and monitoring/evaluation – as well as other components of humanitarian information systems; Sharp (2001), Jaspars and Shoham (1999), and Jaspars (2000) on targeting and alternative means of ensuring consumption by the most vulnerable; and Maxwell *et al.* (2003) or Seaman (2000) on measuring impact.
13 See Marchione (2002) or WFP (2004a, 2004b) on the nutritional content of US and WFP food aid, respectively, and the prioritization of nutritional quality among other policy objectives within a food aid program.
14 Surprising as it may seem to many industrial country readers, insufficient fat content in food aid rations is another nutritional concern. Cost and shelf life concerns typically limit the fat available in food aid although it is an essential macronutrient for human survival (WFP 2004a).
15 Collins (2001) and WFP (2004a, b). Many of these advances have been captured in UNHCR/UNICEF/WFP/WHO (2002) and Sphere Project (2004).

16 WFP (2003, p. 18).
17 See Barrett and McPeak (forthcoming) on the important distinction between "asset smoothing" and "consumption smoothing" and for evidence from northern Kenyan pastoralists that the poorest populations asset smooth – i.e., destabilize consumption in order to protect assets from following below critical thresholds – rather than consumption smooth – i.e., use assets as a buffer stock to reduce intertemporal variability in consumption. The same objectives of famine affected were noted in different language during the 1984–85 crisis in western Sudan (de Waal 1989).
18 Lybbert *et al.* (2004) present evidence that asset shocks among southern Ethiopian pastoralists are overwhelmingly idiosyncratic, meaning household-specific, although covariate risks due to rainfall also play an important role.
19 See World Bank (2002), WFP (2002), Devereux (2002b), Ravallion (2003), Raisin (2002), Barrett *et al.* (forthcoming), or Barrett and McPeak (forthcoming) for a more detailed discussion of safety nets.
20 Barrett and Clay (2003), Barrett *et al.* (forthcoming), or Holden *et al.* (forthcoming).
21 See McCaston (1999) and Barrett and Clay (2003) on the effects of self-targeting on labor deficit or malnourished households, and WFP (2002) on food for work activities among destitute households.
22 See Peppiat *et al.* (2001) on cash alternatives to food for work. See Ravallion (1991, 1999), Ravallion *et al.* (1993), von Braun (1995), and Coady *et al.* (2003) for evaluations of public works schemes based on cash versus food. See Barrett and Clay (2003) for evidence on prospective Ethiopian participants' differential valuation of cash versus in kind wage payments.
23 See Jalan and Ravallion (2000) for details on Trabajar.
24 The distinction and the nested relationship between humanitarian response and safety nets were captured in slightly different language by the debate in the mid-1990s over protecting lives or protecting livelihoods. See, for example, Davies (1996) or Lautze (1997).
25 See de Waal and Whiteside (2002), FANTA (2002a), or Kadiyala and Gillespie (2003).
26 See, for example, Haddad and Gillespie (2001), or FANTA (2002a).
27 See the Board on Natural Disasters (1999).
28 Unfortunately, this has been the general pattern in donor countries over the past 15–20 years, as short-sighted donor response has created a "relief trap" for donors intimately related to the "poverty trap" into which particular subpopulations are steadily falling (Barrett and Carter 2002).
29 See FEWSNET/CARE, December 2000.
30 World Bank (2002), Marchione and Novick (2003), and USAID (2004).
31 Strauss and Thomas (1998).
32 See, for example, Ahmed and Del Ninno (2001), and FANTA (2002b).
33 See WFP (2001c).
34 US GAO (2002) discusses some of these issues as well as operational challenges to the US Global Food for Education Initiative.
35 See Barrett and Heisey (2002), Jayne *et al.* (2002), and Lentz and Barrett (2004) for evidence on inertia in food aid distribution.
36 See ACDI-VOCA (2003), Africare (1996), or Savoie and Bamugye (2003) for examples of monetization as a tool for market development. However, while all of these address the "how-to" questions and note the positive impacts of monetization, none of them even mentions potential negative impacts.
37 See Tschirley and Howard (2003) and Abdulai *et al.* (2004) for more detail on food aid in support of market development, and Candler and Kumar (1998) on the Operation Flood experience.
38 The Bangladesh famine of 1974 arose under such circumstances. See Ravallion (1987) for a careful analysis of that event. Food aid monetization can be valuable in popping speculative price bubbles in such situations.

39 Barrett (1997).

40 We don't use the term "dump" lightly here, nor merely for dramatic effect. In international trade agreements, dumping refers to a situation of international price discrimination, where the price of a product sold in the importing country is less than the price of that product in the market of the exporting country. The 1967 Agreement on Anti-Dumping Practices, under the old Generalized Agreement on Tariffs and Trade (GATT), formally authorized measures to combat dumping. The 1994 GATT agreement that established the WTO elaborates on these in the Agreement on Implementation of Article VI, the Anti-Dumping Agreement. Monetization as currently practiced, frequently fits this definition.

41 One recent example was the development of new Title II Development Assistance Proposals (DAPs) by the Ethiopian Food Security Consortium in 2002, which successfully utilized food aid to leverage additional cash resources, reduced monetization, and increased the direct use of food in safety net activities. While monetization of Title II resources continues, it is at a lower level, and more appropriate cash resources were leveraged to meet cash program needs. Whether this change is sustainable or will be adopted elsewhere remains to be seen.

42 Weber *et al.* (1988), Maxwell *et al.* (2000), and Barrett (2002a).

43 Toward this end, there have been useful innovations in food security information systems to provide policymakers with the necessary information to permit this kind of analysis. For example, see the Regional Agricultural Trade Intelligence Network (RATIN), introduced by the FEWSNET project in East Africa, at: www.ratin.net.

44 USAID (2004).

45 Von Braun (2003).

46 See Barrett and Carter (2002) on poverty traps and relief traps.

47 For example, investigations by Malawi's National Audit Office and Anti-Corruption Bureau in mid-2002 concluded that the National Food Reserve Agency – which sold all 167,000 metric tons of maize it had held as national food reserves in the year to August 2001, mere months before the onset of a major food crisis – lost money in every area of maize handling, could not account for the proceeds of the maize sales, and ultimately cost the Malawian government about US$40 million due to mismanagement (US GAO 2003).

48 See, for example, Marchione and Sywulka (2004) for current USAID perspectives on the roles recipient communities might effectively play in food aid programming. Conning and Kevane (2001) offer a range of cautions about prospective pitfalls in community-based efforts.

49 See, for example, CARE (2003).

50 Clay (2003b).

51 Strategic Plan, 2004–2007 (WFP, 2003).

52 Harinaryan *et al.* (2000).

53 Von Braun (2003).

11 Recasting food aid's role: the particulars and the politics

1 As this book was being completed, the OECD/DAC launched a major international study of food aid tying, slated for release in autumn 2004.

2 See, for example, the September 2003 Berlin Statement (von Braun 2003).

3 This has not always been possible, as in the Democratic People's Republic of Korea, where independent monitoring has not been permitted by government, where access to some areas has been completely banned, and where interpreters have been assigned by the government.

4 Landlocked countries such as Burundi, Ethiopia, Malawi, Rwanda, and Zambia would be prime candidates.

5 Shaw (2001) and Clay (2003b) go into greater detail in criticizing "multi-bi" aid in

which bilateral donors tie their contributions to uses in particular emergencies (e.g., Afghanistan, Bosnia, or Iraq in recent years) rather than others regardless of the relative merits of using food aid across the different settings.

6 Equal value could be established based on moving average global market prices over the preceding three or four years.

7 The IMF's CFF provides loans to member country governments in response to exogenous commodity price shocks, whether for exports or cereals imports. CFF has proved difficult to use and administer (IMF 2004). The EAF provides emergency assistance to member states with urgent balance of payments financing needs in the wake of natural disasters or armed conflicts. Both EAF and CFF loans, however, carry interest and must be repaid in 3–5 years. In 2000 the IMF also eliminated its Buffer Stock Financing Facility, which used to help poor countries build up strategic reserves.

8 Orden (2004).

9 Von Braun (2003).

10 This paragraph and the next draw heavily on and update figures from Barrett and Carter (2002).

11 Twenty countries originally signed the Convention on the Organization for Economic Co-operation and Development on 14 December 1960: Austria, Belgium, Canada, Denmark, France, Germany, Greece, Iceland, Ireland, Italy, Luxembourg, Netherlands, Norway, Portugal, Spain, Sweden, Switzerland, Turkey, United Kingdom, and the United States. Australia, Finland, Japan, and New Zealand joined over the ensuing decade. Much more recently, the Czech Republic, Hungary, Korea, Mexico, Poland, and the Slovak Republic have all joined the OECD since 1993, bringing membership to 30 nations as of 2004.

12 US GAO (2003).

13 See Anderson (2004) for details on the studies that produce these estimates.

14 Van Beers and de Moor (2001).

15 *The Economist*, "Sour Subsidies," April 17, 2004, p. 11.

16 See World Bank (2003) for these estimates and Anderson (2004) for a broader summary of the cost and benefits of trade liberalization and the termination of agricultural subsidies.

17 See Anderson (2004) and Orden (2004) for reviews of a range of technical studies of the global costs of agricultural trade barriers and subsidy programs.

18 The Cairns Group, formed in 1986, represents agricultural exporting countries that support global liberalization of agricultural trade. The member states are Argentina, Australia, Bolivia, Brazil, Canada, Chile, Colombia, Costa Rica, Guatemala, Indonesia, Malaysia, New Zealand, Paraguay, Philippines, South Africa, Thailand, and Uruguay.

19 We do not propose set quantitative limits on monetization but rather agreed conditions under which monetization would be permitted: when (1) food availability through local markets is insufficient to provide for the population's minimum nutritional needs; (2) there is no prospective conflict of interest on the part of the recipient agency (as can exist with respect to the non-profit arms of for-profit agribusinesses), and the monetized food can be used effectively either (a) to limit or prevent a price spike that could harm poor consumers, or (b) develop local food processing, storage or marketing capacity that can be expected to increase employment and/or reduce marketing margins within a reasonable period of three to five years. These recommendations generally conform with those made by Tschirley and Howard (2003).

20 US GAO (1995a, 1995b).

21 The authorization for more flexible procurements in developing countries could readily prohibit procurements from other high- or middle-income exporting countries (e.g., Argentina, Australia, Brazil, Canada, France).

22 OMB (2001, p. 3).

23 Ibid., p. 65.

24 See Bonnard *et al.* (2002) for an evaluation of USAID's PL 480 Title II Development Food Aid Program.

25 See Sachs (2004) for a strong argument in favor of renewed professionalization of international development within the US government.

26 Shaw (2001) documents the WFP's experience with school feeding in detail.

27 Trueblood and Shapouri (2002) and Natsios (2003).

28 See Burnside and Dollar (2000) for empirical evidence on the aid-policy interaction effect.

29 For example, investigations by Malawi's National Audit Office and Anti-Corruption Bureau in mid-2002 concluded that the National Food Reserve Agency – which sold all 167,000 metric tons of maize it had held as national food reserves in the year to August 2001, mere months before the onset of a major food crisis – lost money in every area of maize handling, could not account for the proceeds of the maize sales, and ultimately cost the Malawian government about US$40 million due to mismanagement (US GAO 2003).

30 See Maxwell and Watkins (2003).

31 See Hoddinott and Kinsey (2001), Quisumbing (2003), and Yamano *et al.* (2003) for rigorous statistical evidence on the adverse effects of shocks on child growth performance and the palliative effects of food aid on child nutritional status and subsequent growth performance.

32 World Food Programme (2003, 2004a, 2004b).

33 As of early 2003, the membership of the Coalition for Food Aid consisted of Adventist Development and Relief Agency International, ACDI/VOCA, Africare, American Red Cross, CARE, Catholic Relief Services, Counterpart International, Food for the Hungry International, International Orthodox Christian Charities, International Relief and Development, Mercy Corps, OIC International, Save the Children, and World Vision.

34 NGOs also use other US food aid programs, but the overwhelming majority of NGO resources comes from Title II.

35 In summer 2004, OXFAM's official position stated that

> Although food aid has played and will continue to play a critical role in poverty reduction efforts, it has also been misused by some policymakers to pursue political and commercial purposes at the expense of publicly declared humanitarian objectives. Evidence shows that food aid has peaked in years when cereal prices were low and stocks particularly high. Food aid should be provided exclusively through untied financial grants, to be used for the purchase of food by the recipient country. Where it is provided in the form of stocks, this should be provided on grant terms within the framework of programs operated by specialized UN agencies, or non-governmental organizations. All ties between food aid and commercial aid programs should be broken, including a prohibition on the use of export credits and "blending" of food aid with commercial exports.

We thank Jennifer Brant of OXFAM America for providing the exact wording.

36 Sachs (2004).

37 US emergency food aid to Ethiopia is channeled through NGOs via a separate funding mechanism.

38 The discrepancy between the two methods arises due to the fact that shipments-level analyses focus on bulk commodities (e.g., corn, wheat) where prices for identical products can be matched in source and destination markets. This necessarily eliminates higher value-to-weight commodities (e.g., corn-soy or wheat-soy blend, nonfat dried milk powder) for which shipping is a lower share of total costs.

39 The maritime industry won a court suit arguing that cargo preference provisions applied to government-supported agricultural export programs. Subjecting such exports to the added costs associated with cargo preference threatened, however, to render

American agricultural exports under those programs uncompetitive internationally. Hence the 1985 Cargo Preference Compromise, which increased cargo preference's coverage to 75 percent of food aid shipments and added other costly restrictions, such as set-asides for Great Lakes ports. The Compromise was subsequently reaffirmed in the 1990, 1996 and 2002 Farm Bills.

40 As this book went to press, the US Government Accountability Office (the GAO's new name as of July 2004) was completing a study requested by the Senate on shipping lines' double dipping through MSP and cargo preference restrictions on food aid and other government-impelled international shipments.

41 The Maritime Security Act was signed into law by President Clinton in October 1996. The law authorized a ten-year Maritime Security Program for 47 vessels, funded through regular annual appropriations. MSP, which is run by the Department of Transportation's Maritime Administration, provides the Department of Defense with access to US-flag, US-citizen crewed ships, intermodal equipment, terminal facilities and management services during national emergencies in exchange for annual subsidies paid directly to shipping firms, currently $2.1 million per ship.

42 Blandford and Boisvert (2004).

43 Jim Cornelius, Canadian Foodgrains Bank, personal communication.

44 See, for example, Andrew Natsios' introduction to the USAID White Paper on US Foreign Aid (USAID 2004). It is important to note, however, as emergency and development assistance of all kinds are increasingly linked to security issues, that the operational independence and impartiality of humanitarian actors are increasingly threatened, so there are important trade-offs to consider in suggesting a stronger linkage. See, for example, Macrae and Leader (2000) or Rieff (2002).

45 Skees (2000) provides an excellent, accessible discussion of some of the potential roles for capital markets in addressing natural disasters.

46 More precisely, we estimate that eliminating Title I would yield budgetary savings of approximately $234 million annually, the average for the program over fiscal years 2000–3 – a significantly lower estimate than those made by GAO (1995a, 1995b). Reducing bureaucratic overlap between USDA and USAID would (conservatively) bring long-term gains of $6 million annually in administrative and personnel costs. Authorizing procurement of commodities overseas could reduce freight costs on approximately 30 percent of emergency shipments by 30 percent, yielding $19 million annually. Finally, a 10 percent reduction in non-emergency Title II food aid would save $43 million each year.

Bibliography

Aaltola, M. (1999) Emergency Food Aid as a Means of Political Persuasion in North Korea. *Third World Quarterly*, 20(2), 371–386.

Abbott, P.C. (1979) Modeling International Grain Trade with Government Controlled Markets. *American Journal of Agricultural Economics*, 61(1), 22–31.

Abbott, P.C. and McCarthy, F.D. (1982) The Welfare Costs of Tied Food Aid. *Journal of Development Economics*, 11(1), 63–79.

Abdulai, A., Barrett, C.B., and Hazell, P. (2004a) Food Aid for Market Development in Sub-Saharan Africa. Working Paper, International Food Policy Research Institute, Washington, DC.

Abdulai, A., Barrett. C.B. and Hoddinott, J. (2004). Does Food Aid *Really* Have Disincentive Effects? New Evidence from Sub-Saharan Africa. Working Paper, Cornell University, Ithaca, New York.

ACDI/VOCA (Agricultural Cooperative Development International and Volunteers in Overseas Cooperative Assistance) (2003) *Monetization: Best Practices Manual.* 1st edn. ACDI/VOCA. Mimeo. Washington, DC.

Adato, M. and Meinzen-Dick, R. (2002) *Assessing the Impact of Agricultural Research on Poverty Using the Sustainable Livelihoods Framework.* EPTD Discussion Paper No. 89/FCND Discussion Paper No. 128. Washington, DC: International Food Policy Research Institute.

Africare (1996) *Africare Food for Development Handbook.* Chapter V. Monetization. Washington, DC: Africare.

Ag Biotech Reporter (2002) The Politics of Hunger Overshadow Africa's Plight, 19(10), 1–3.

Agjournal (2001) Soy Growers Want to Help Needy Become Food Buyers. February 25. Available online at http://www.agjournal.com/story.cfm?story_id=1129.

Ahmed, A.U. and Arends-Kuenning, M. (2003) *Do Crowded Classrooms Crowd Out Learning? Evidence from the Food for Education Program in Bangladesh*, Food Consumption and Nutrition Division Discussion Paper No. 149. Washington, DC: International Food Policy Research Institute.

Ahmed, A.U. and del Ninno, C. (2001) *Food for Education Program in Bangladesh: An Evaluation of its Impact on Educational Attainment and Food Security.* Washington, DC: International Food Policy Research Institute.

Albarran, P. and Attanasio, O.P. (2003) Limited Commitment and Crowding Out of Private Transfers: Evidence from a Randomised Experiment. *Economic Journal*, 113(486), C77–C85.

Alderman, H. (2002) Do Local Officials Know Something We Don't? Decentralization of Targeted Transfers in Albania. *Journal of Public Economics*, 83(3), 375–404.

Alderman, H. and Paxson, C.H. (1992) Do the Poor Insure? A Synthesis of the Literature on Risk and Consumption in Developing Countries, World Bank Policy Research Working Paper WPS 1008. Washington, DC: World Bank.

Alexander, C. and Wyeth, J. (1994) Cointegration and Market Integration: An Application to the Indonesian Rice Market. *Journal of Development Studies*, 30(1): 303–328.

Allen, L. and Gillespie, S. (2001) *What Works? A Review of the Efficacy and Effectiveness of Nutrition Interventions*. United Nations Administrative Committee on Coordination Sub-Committee on Nutrition (ACC/SCN) Nutrition Policy Paper No. 19, in cooperation with the Asian Development Bank. Manila: Asian Development Bank.

Amha, W., Stepanek, J., Jayne, T.S. and Negassa, A. (1997) Meeting Food Aid and Price Stabilization Objectives Through Local Grain Purchase: A Review of the 1996 Experience, Working Paper No. 7, Ethiopia Ministry of Economic Development and Cooperation Grain Market Research Project, Addis Ababa.

Anderson, K. (2004) Subsidies and Trade Barriers. Copenhagen Consensus Challenge Paper working paper. Available online at http://www.copenhagenconsensus.com/Files/Filer/CC/Papers/Subsidies_and_Trade_Barriers_140504.pdf.

Anderson, M. (1996) *Do No Harm: Supporting Local Capacities for Peace through Aid*. Cambridge: Collaborative for Development Action, Local Capacities for Peace Project.

Ball, R. and Johnson, C. (1996) Political, Economic, and Humanitarian Motivations for PL 480 Food Aid: Evidence from Africa. *Economic Development and Cultural Change*, 44(3), 515–537.

Ballenger, N. and Mabbs-Zeno, C. (1992) Treating Food Security And Food Aid Issues at the GATT. *Food Policy*, 17(4), 264–276.

Barrett, C.B. (1995). Madagascar: An Empirical Test of the Market Relaxation–State Compression Hypothesis. *Development Policy Review*, 13(4), 391–406.

Barrett, C.B. (1996) Market Analysis Methods: Are Our Enriched Toolkits Well-Suited To Enlivened Markets? *American Journal of Agricultural Economics*, 78(3), 825–829.

Barrett, C.B. (1997) Liberalization and Food Price Distributions: ARCH-M Evidence from Madagascar. *Food Policy*, 22(2), 155–173.

Barrett, C.B. (1998) Food Aid: Is It Development Assistance, Trade Promotion, Both or Neither? *American Journal of Agricultural Economics*, 80(3), 566–571.

Barrett, C.B. (2001a) Does Food Aid Stabilize Food Availability? *Economic Development and Cultural Change*, 49(2), 335–349.

Barrett, C.B. (2001b) Measuring Integration and Efficiency in International Agricultural Markets. *Review of Agricultural Economics*, 23(1), 19–32.

Barrett, C.B. (2002a) Food Security and Food Assistance Programs. In B.L. Gardner and G. Rausser (eds), *Handbook of Agricultural Economics*, vol. 2B. Amsterdam: Elsevier.

Barrett, C.B. (2002b) Food Aid and Commercial International Food Trade. Background paper prepared for the Trade and Markets Division, Organization for Economic Co-operation and Development.

Barrett, C.B. (2002c) Food Aid Effectiveness: "It's The Targeting, Stupid!" Paper prepared for the Policy Service, Strategy and Policy Division, World Food Programme.

Barrett, C.B. (2003) Rural Poverty Dynamics: Development Policy Implications. Address to the 25th triennial meeting of the International Association of Agricultural Economists, Durban, South Africa.

Barrett, C.B., Bezuneh, M. and Aboud, A. (2001) Income Diversification, Poverty Traps and Policy Shocks in Côte d'Ivoire and Kenya. *Food Policy*, 26(4), 367–384.

Barrett, C.B. and Carter, M.R. (2002) Can't Get Ahead for Falling Behind: New Directions for Development Policy to Escape Poverty and Relief Traps. *Choices*, 16(4), 35–38.

Barrett, C.B., Chabari, F., Bailey, D., Little, P.D. and Coppock, D.L. (2003) Livestock Pricing in the Northern Kenyan Rangelands. *Journal of African Economies*, 12(2), 127–155.

Barrett, C.B. and Clay, D.C. (2003) Self-Targeting Accuracy in the Presence of Imperfect Factor Markets: Evidence from Food-for-Work in Ethiopia. *Journal of Development Studies*, 39(5), 152–180.

Barrett, C.B. and Heisey, K.C. (2002) How Effectively Does Multilateral Food Aid Respond To Fluctuating Needs? *Food Policy*, 27(5–6), 477–491.

Barrett, C.B., Holden, S. and Clay, D.C. (forthcoming) Can Food-For-Work Programs Reduce Vulnerability? In S. Dercon (ed.), *Insurance Against Poverty*. Oxford: Oxford University Press.

Barrett, C.B. and Li, J.R. (2002) Distinguishing Between Equilibrium and Integration in Spatial Price Analysis. *American Journal of Agricultural Economics*, 84(2), 292–307.

Barrett, C.B. and McPeak, J.G. (forthcoming) Poverty Traps and Safety Nets. In A. DeJanvry and R. Kanbur (eds), *Poverty, Inequality and Development: Essays in Honor of Erik Thorbecke*. Amsterdam: Kluwer.

Barrett, C.B., Mohapatra, S. and Snyder, D.L. (1999) The Dynamic Effects of U.S. Food Aid. *Economic Inquiry*, 37(4), 647–656.

Barrett, C.B. and Swallow, B.M. (2003) Fractal Poverty Traps. Working Paper, Cornell University, Ithaca, New York.

Barrett, C.B. and Swallow, B.M. (2004) Dynamic Poverty Traps and Rural Livelihoods. In F. Ellis and H.A. Freeman (eds), *Rural Livelihoods and Poverty Reduction Policies*. London: Routledge.

Basu, K. (1996) Relief Programs When It May be Better to Give Food Instead of Cash. *World Development*, 24(1), 91–96.

Baulch, B. (1997a) Testing for Food Market Integration Revisited. *Journal of Development Studies*, 33(1), 512–534.

Baulch, B. (1997b) Transfer Costs, Spatial Arbitrage, and Testing for Food Market Integration. *American Journal of Agricultural Economics*, 79(2), 477–487.

Baulch, B. and Hoddinott, J. (2000) *Economic Mobility and Poverty Dynamics in Developing Countries*. London: Frank Cass.

Beaton, G.H. and Ghassemi, H. (1982) Supplementary Feeding Programs for Young Children in Developing Countries. *American Journal of Clinical Nutrition*, 35, 864–916.

Becker, E. (2001) Level of Food Aid to Afghans Drops. *The New York Times*, November 30.

Behrman, J. and Deolalikar, A.B. (1989) Is Variety the Spice of Life? Implications for Calorie Intake. *Review of Economics and Statistics*, 71(3), 666–672.

Benson, C. (2000) The Food Aid Convention: An Effective Safety Net. In E. Clay and O. Stokke (eds), *Food Aid and Human Security*. London: Frank Cass.

Benson, C. and Clay, E.J. (1998) Additionality or Diversion? Food Aid to Eastern Europe and the Former Soviet Republics and the Implications for Developing Countries. *World Development*, 26(1), 31–44.

Besley, T. and Kanbur, R. (1990) The Principles of Targeting. Policy, Research and External Affairs Working Paper No. 385, World Bank, Washington, DC.

Bezuneh, M. and Deaton, B. (1997) Food Aid Impacts on Safety Nets: Theory and Evidence – A Conceptual Perspective on Safety Nets. *American Journal of Agricultural Economics*, 79, 672–677.

Bezuneh, M., Deaton, B.J. and Norton, G.W. (1988) Food Aid Impacts in Rural Kenya. *American Journal of Agricultural Economics*, 70(1), 181–191.

Bezuneh, M., Deaton, B. and Zuhair, S. (2003) Food Aid Disincentives: The Tunisian Experience. *Review of Development Economics*, 7(4), 609–621.

Binswanger, H. and Rosenzweig, M.R. (1993) Wealth, Weather Risk and the Composition and Profitability of Agricultural Investments, *Economic Journal*, 103, 56–78.

Blandford, D. and Boisvert, R.N. (2004) U.S. Policy for Agricultural Adjustment. Paper prepared for the International Agricultural Trade Research Consortium.

Board on Natural Disasters (1999) Mitigation Emerges as Major Strategy for Reducing Losses Caused by Natural Disasters. *Science*, 284, 1943–1947.

Bonnard, P. (1999) *Increasing the Nutritional Impacts of Agricultural Interventions*. Washington, DC: FANTA.

Bonnard, P. (2002) *HIV/AIDS Mitigation: Using What We Already Know*. Washington, DC: FANTA.

Bonnard, P., Haggerty, P., Swindale, A., Bergeron, G. and Dempsey, J. (2002) *Report of the Food Aid and Food Security Assessment: A Review of the Title II Development Food Aid Program*. A FANTA Project Report. Washington, DC: Academy for Educational Development.

Boudreau, T. (1998) *The Food Economy Approach: A Framework for Understanding Rural Livelihoods*, RRN Network Paper 26. London: Overseas Development Institute.

Bremer-Fox, J., Bailey, L., Lang, P. and Mervenne, M. (1990) *Experience with Auctions of Food Aid Commodities in Africa*, Volume I: *Summary of Field Experiences and Guidelines for Auction Design*. Final report by Nathan Associates to Africa Bureau, U.S. Agency for International Development, Washington, DC.

Brennan, D. (2003) Price Dynamics in the Bangladesh Rice Market: Implications for Public Intervention. *Agricultural Economics*, 29(1), 15–25.

Buchanan-Smith, M. and Davies, S. (1995) *Famine Early Warning and Response: The Missing Link*. London: IT Publications.

Burnside, C. and Dollar, D. (2000) Aid, Policies, and Growth. *American Economic Review* 90(4), 847–868.

But Will it Help? (1998) *The Economist*, 349(8094), 54.

Byerlee, D. (1987) The Political Economy of Third World Food Imports: The Case of Wheat. *Economic Development and Cultural Change*, 35(2), 307–328.

Campbell, W. and Harvey, P. (1998) *Food-Assisted Programming in the Greater Horn of Africa*. Atlanta: CARE.

Canadian International Development Agency (2003) *Food Aid Synthesis Report*. Ottawa: CIDA.

Candler, W. and Kumar, N. (1998) *India: The Dairy Revolution. The Impact of Dairy Development in India and the World Bank Contribution*. Washington, DC: The World Bank.

CARE (2001) *Benefits/Harms Analysis: A Practitioners Handbook*. Nairobi: CARE.

CARE (2003) *Managing Risk, Improving Livelihoods: Program Guidelines for Situations of Chronic Vulnerability*. Nairobi: CARE.

CARE/ERREC/WFP (2003) *Eritrea Rural Livelihood Security Assessment: Report of the Findings*. Asmara: CARE/ERREC/WFP.

Carney, D. (1998) *Sustainable Rural Livelihoods: What Contribution Can We Make?* London: Overseas Development Institute.

Cathie, J. (1982) *The Political Economy of Food Aid*. New York: St. Martin's Press.

Cathie, J. (1997) *European Food Aid Policy*. Brookfield, VT: Ashgate Publishing.

Cekan, J., MacNeil, A. and Loegering, S. (1996) *Monetisation: Linkages to Food Security?* Relief and Rehabilitation Network Paper 17. London: Overseas Development Institute.

Chambers, R. and Conway, G. (1992) *Sustainable Rural Livelihoods: Practical Concepts for the 21st Century*. IDS Discussion Paper 296. Brighton: Institute of Development Studies.

Charlton, M.W. (1992) *The Making of Canadian Food Aid Policy*. Montreal: McGill-Queens University Press.

Chite, R.M. (1999) *RS20269: Emergency Funding for Agriculture: A Brief History of Congressional Action, 1988–June 1999*. Congressional Research Service Report for Congress, Washington, DC.

Christensen, C. (2000) The New Policy Environment for Food Aid: The Challenge of Sub-Saharan Africa. *Food Policy*, 25(2), 255–268.

Clapp, J. (2004) The Political Economy of Food Aid in an Era of Agricultural Bio-technology. Working Paper, Trent University, Peterborough, ONT.

Claudon, M. and Gutner, T. (eds) (1992) *Putting Food on What Was the Soviet Table*. Albany, NY: New York University Press.

Clay, D.C., Molla, D. and Habtewold, D. (1999) Food Aid Targeting in Ethiopia: A Study of Who Needs It and Who Gets It. *Food Policy*, 24(3), 391–409.

Clay, E.J. (1986) Rural Public Works and Food-for-Work: A Survey. *World Development*, 14(10/11), 1237–1286.

Clay, E.J. (2000) *Reforming Food Aid: Time to Grasp the Nettle?* ODI Briefing Paper 1. London: Overseas Development Institute.

Clay, E.J. (2003a) *Commentary on the "Berlin Statement on Food Aid and Food Security."* London: Overseas Development Institute.

Clay, E.J. (2003b) Responding to Change: WFP and the Global Food Aid System. *Development Policy Review*, 21(5–6), 697–709.

Clay, E.J. and Benson, C. (1990) Acquisition of Commodities in Developing Countries for Food Aid in the 1980s. *Food Policy*, 15(1), 27–43.

Clay, E.J., Dhiri, S. and Benson, C. (1996) *Joint Evaluation of European Union Programme Food Aid – Synthesis Report*. London: Overseas Development Institute.

Clay, E.J. and Stokke, O. (eds) (1991) *Food Aid Reconsidered: Assessing the Impact on Third World Countries*. London: Frank Cass.

Clay, E.J. and Stokke, O. (eds) (2000) *Food Aid and Human Security*. London: Frank Cass.

Coady, D., Grosh, M. and Hoddinott, J. (2003) Targeting Outcomes Redux. Working Paper, International Food Policy Research Institute, Washington, DC.

Coates J., Webb, P. and Houser, R. (2003) *Measuring Food Insecurity: Going Beyond Indicators of Income and Anthropometry*. Food and Nutrition Technical Assistance Paper. Washington, DC: Academy for Educational Development.

Cohen, R. (2001) The Hungry Country. *New York Times*, December 9.

Cohen, R. (2002) Aid Meant for the Hungry. *New York Times*, May 16.

Colding, B. and Pinstrup-Andersen, P. (1999) Denmark's Contribution to the World Food Programme: A Success Story. *Food Policy*, 24(1), 93–108.

Collins, S. (2001) Changing the Way We Address Severe Malnutrition during Famine. *The Lancet*, 358, 498–501.

Committee on Commodity Problems, Consultative Sub-Committee on Surplus Disposal (2003) *Thirty-Ninth Report to the CCP*, Sixty-second Session (Rome). Available online at http://www.fao.org/DOCREP/MEETING/005/Y8286e.htm

Conning, J. and Kevane, M. (2001) *Community Based Targeting Mechanisms for Social Safety Nets*, World Bank Social Protection Paper no. 102. Washington, DC: World Bank.

Conway, J. (1998) *National Food Security Reserves: A Comparative Assessment with Specific Reference to Ethiopia*. Norwich: Natural Resources Institute.

Corbett, J. (1988) Famine and Household Coping Strategies. *World Development*, 16(12), 1099–1112.

Council on Foreign Relations (2003) *Fact Sheet on Foreign Aid*. Washington, DC.

Cox, D. and Jimenez, E. (1992) Social Security and Private Transfers in Developing Countries: The Case of Peru. *World Bank Economic Review*, 6(1), 155–169.

Cox, D. and Jimenez, E. (1995) Private Transfers and the Effectiveness of Public Income Redistribution in the Philippines. In D. van de Walle and K. Nead (eds), *Public Spending and the Poor: Theory and Evidence*. Baltimore, MD: Johns Hopkins University Press.

Darcy, J. and Hoffmann, C. (2003) *According to Need? Needs Assessment and Decision Making in the Humanitarian Sector*. Humanitarian Policy Group Report 15. London: Overseas Development Institute.

Dasgupta, P. (1993) *An Inquiry into Well-Being and Destitution*. Oxford: Oxford University Press.

Dasgupta, P. (1997) Nutritional Status, the Capacity for Work, and Poverty Traps. *Journal of Econometrics*, 77(1), 5–37.

Davies, S. (1996) *Adaptable Livelihoods: Coping with Food Insecurity in the Malian Sahel*. London: Macmillan Press.

Dearden, P.J. and Ackroyd, P.J. (1989) Reassessing the Role of Food Aid. *Food Policy*, 14(3), 218–231.

Deaton, A. (1997) *The Analysis of Household Surveys*. Baltimore, MD: Johns Hopkins University Press.

Deaton, A. and Laroque, G. (1992) On the Behavior of Commodity Prices. *Review of Economic Studies*, 59, 1–23.

Deaton, A. and Laroque, G. (1996) Competitive Storage and Commodity Price Dynamics. *Journal of Political Economy*, 104, 896–923.

Delgado, C.L. and Miller, C.P.J. (1985) Changing Food Patterns in West Africa. *Food Policy*, 10, 55–61.

Del Ninno, C., Dorosh, P.A., Smith, L.C. and Roy, D.K. (2001) *The 1998 Floods in Bangladesh: Disaster Impacts, Household Coping Strategies, and Response*. Washington, DC: International Food Policy Research Institute.

Del Rosso, J.M. and Marek, T. (1996) *Class Action: Improving School Performance in the Developing World Through Better Health and Nutrition*. Washington, DC: World Bank.

Dercon, S. (1995) On Market Integration and Liberalisation: Method and Application to Ethiopia. *Journal of Development Studies*, 32 (4), 112–143.

Dercon, S. and Krishnan, P. (2003) Does Food Aid Reduce Vulnerability? Working Paper, University of Oxford.

Devaney, B., Bilheimer, L. and Schore, J. (1990) *The Savings in Medicare Costs for Newborns and Their Mothers from Prenatal Participation in the WIC Program*. Washington, DC: Mathematica Policy Research.

Devereux, S. (1993) *Theories of Famine*. London: Harvester Wheatsheaf.

Devereux, S. (1998) *The Impact of WFP Development Assistance: Effective Approaches for Food Aid Interventions*. Brighton: Institute for Development Studies.

Devereux, S. (1999) Targeting Transfers: Innovative Solutions to Familiar Problems. *IDS Bulletin*, 30(2), 61–74.

Devereux, S. (2002a) *The Malawi Famine of 2002: Causes, Consequences and Policy Lessons*. Brighton: Institute for Development Studies.

Devereux, S. (2002b) *Social Protection for the Poor: Lessons from Recent International Experience*. Brighton: Institute for Development Studies.

Devereux, S. and Hoddinott, J. (1999) Improving Food Needs Assessment Methodologies, Working Paper, International Food Policy Research Institute, Washington, DC.

Devereux, S. and Maxwell, S. (eds) (2001) *Food Security in Sub-Saharan Africa*. London: ITDG Publishing.

de Waal, A. (1989) *Famine that Kills: Darfur, Sudan, 1984–85*. Oxford: Clarendon Press.

de Waal, A. (1997) *Famine Crimes: Politics and the Disaster Relief Industry in Africa.* Bloomington, IN: Indiana University Press.

de Waal, A. and Whiteside, A. (2002) New Variant Famine: AIDS and Food Crisis in southern Africa. *Lancet*, 362, 1234–1237.

Diven, P.J. (2001) The Domestic Determinants of US Food Aid Policy. *Food Policy*, 26(3), 455–474.

Donovan, C., Myers, R., Tschirley, D. and Weber, M. (1999) The Effects of Food Aid on Maize Prices in Mozambique. In G.H. Peters and J. von Braun (eds), *Food Security, Diversification and Resource Management: Refocusing the Role of Agriculture?* Proceedings of the Twenty-Third International Conference of Agricultural Economists. Brookfield, VT: Ashgate.

Doornbos, M., van Dorsten, F., Mitra, M. and Terhal, P. (1990) *Dairy Aid and Development: India's Operation Flood.* Indo-Dutch Studies on Development Alternatives 3. London: Sage Publications.

Dorosh, P.A., Ninno, C. and Sahn, D.E. (1995) Poverty Alleviation in Mozambique: A Multi-market Analysis of the Role of Food Aid. *Agricultural Economics*, 13(1), 89–99.

Drèze, J. and Sen, A. (1989). *Hunger and Public Action.* Oxford: Clarendon Press.

Duffield, M. (2001) *Global Governance and the New Wars.* London: Zed Books.

Dugger, C. (2004) To Help Poor be Pupils, Not Wage Earners, Brazil Pays Parents. *New York Times*, January 3.

Easterly, W.R. (2001) *The Elusive Quest for Growth: Economists' Adventures and Misadventures in the Tropics.* Cambridge, MA: MIT Press.

Eide, A. (1999) Human Rights Requirements to Social and Economic Development: The Case of the Right to Food and Nutrition Rights. Chapter 16 in U. Kracht and M. Schulz (eds), *Food Security and Nutrition: The Global Challenge.* New York: St. Martin's Press.

Ellis, F. (1998) Household Strategies and Rural Livelihood Diversification. *Journal of Development Studies*, 35(1), 1–38.

Enders, W. (1995) *Applied Econometric Time Series.* New York: John Wiley and Sons.

EuronAid (1995) *NGO Code of Conduct on Food Aid and Food Security.* Brussels: EuronAid.

Fackler, P.L. and Goodwin, B.K. (2002) Spatial Price Analysis. In B.L. Gardner and G.C. Rausser (eds), *Handbook of Agricultural Economics.* Amsterdam: Elsevier Science.

Fafchamps, M. and Gavian, S. (1996) The spatial integration of livestock markets in Niger. *Journal of African Economies*, 5(3), 366–405.

FANTA (2002a) *Potential Uses of Food Aid to Support HIV/AIDS Mitigation Activities in Sub-Saharan Africa*, Food and Nutrition Technical Assistance. Washington, DC: FANTA.

FANTA (2002b) *Report of the Food Aid and Food Security Assessment: A Review of Title II Development Food Aid Programs.* Washington, DC: AED.

FAO (2002) Global Information and Early Warning System, *Special Report: FAO/WFP Crop and Food Supply Assessment Mission to the Democratic People's Republic of Korea.* July 29, p. 4. Rome: FAO.

Farzin, Y.H. (1991) Food Aid: Positive or Negative Economic Effects in Somalia? *Journal of Developing Areas*, 25(2), 261–282.

Ferdous, H. (2001) The Children of Shamshatoo. Available online at http://www.un.org/news/hd/latest/afghan/shamshatoo.html

FEWSNET/CARE (2000) The Year in Review; Lessons for the Future. *Greater Horn of Africa Food Security Update*, 3, December. Nairobi: FEWSNET and CARE.

Figa-Talamanca, I. (1985) *Nutritional Implications of Food Aid: An Annotated Bibliography.* FAO Food and Nutrition Paper No. 33. Rome: FAO.

Fisher, F.M. (1963) A Theoretical Analysis of the Impact of Food Surplus Disposal on

Agricultural Production in Recipient Countries. *Journal of Farm Economics*, 45(4), 863–875.

Fitzpatrick, J. and Storey, A. (1989) Food Aid and Agricultural Disincentives. *Food Policy*, 14(3), 241–247.

FIVIMS (2002) *Measurement and Assessment of Food Deprivation and Undernutrition*. Report of Scientific Symposium. Rome: FAO/FIVIMS

Food and Agriculture Organization of the United Nations (1995) *Impact of the Uruguay Round on Agriculture*. Rome: FAO.

Food and Agriculture Organization of the United Nations (2002) *State of Food Insecurity 2002*. Rome: FAO.

Food and Agriculture Organization of the United Nations (2004) *State of Food Insecurity 2004*. Rome: FAO.

Food and Nutrition Technical Assistance (FANTA) Project (2002) *A Review of the Title II Development Food Aid Program*. Washington, DC: Academy for Educational Development.

Food for Peace (2003) *Concept Paper for Strategic Plan, 2004–2008*. Washington, DC: USAID/ Office of Food for Peace.

Frumkin, P. and Kim, M.T. (2001) Strategic Positioning and the Financing of Nonprofit Organizations: Is Efficiency Rewarded in the Contributions Marketplace? *Public Administration Review*, 61(3), 266–275.

Gabbert, S. and Weikard, H.-P. (2000) The Poor Performance of the Rich – Bilateral Versus Multilateral Food Aid Allocation. *Quarterly Journal of International Agriculture*, 39(2), 199–218.

Gabre-Madhin, E., Barrett, C.B. and Dorosh, P. (2002) Technological Change and Price Effects in Agriculture: Conceptual and Comparative Perspectives. In T. Bonger, E. Gabre-Madhin and S. Babu (eds), *Agriculture Technology Diffusion and Price Policy*. Washington, DC: Ethiopian Development Research Institute and the International Food Policy Research Institute.

Gainey, V. (2000) The Impact of Food Aid on Agriculture and Poverty Alleviation in Africa: An Assessment. Paper from panel discussion at the Africa Centre, London. Available at http://www.africacentre.org.uk/foodaid.htm

Gardner, B.L. (2002) *American Agriculture in the Twentieth Century: How It Flourished and What It Cost*. Cambridge, MA: Harvard University Press.

Gebremedhin, B. and Swinton, S.M. (2000) Reconciling Food-for-Work Project Feasibility with Food Aid Targeting in Tigray, Ethiopia. *Food Policy*, 26(1), 85–95.

Gilbert, C.L. (1993) Domestic Price Stabilization Schemes for Developing Countries. In S. Claessens and R. Duncan (eds), *Managing Commodity Price Risk in Developing Countries*. Baltimore, MD: Johns Hopkins University Press.

Gilbert, C.L. (1996) A Model of US Cereals Food Aid Flows with an Application to Trade Liberalisation. *Journal of Agricultural Economics*, 47(2), 143–157.

Grigsby, S.E. and Dixit, H.-P. (1986) *Alternative Export Strategies and U.S. Agricultural Policies for Grains and Oilseeds, 1950–83*. Washington, DC: USDA Economic Research Service Staff Report AGES 860616.

Guardian, (2001) Afghanistan on Edge of Humanitarian Catastrophe *Guardian*, October 21. Available online at http://www.Guardian.co.uk

Gupta, S., Clements, B. and Tiongson, E.R. (2002) Foreign Aid and Consumption Smoothing: Evidence from Global Food Aid, Working Paper, International Monetary Fund Fiscal Affairs Department, Washington, DC.

Haddad, L. and Frankenberger, T. (2003) *Integrating Relief and Development to Accelerate Reductions in Food Insecurity in Shock-Prone Areas*, FFP Occasional Paper 2. Washington, DC: USAID Office of Food for Peace.

Haddad, L. and Gillespie, S. (2001) *Effective Food and Nutrition Policy Responses to HIV/AIDS: What We Know and What We Need to Know.* Food consumption and nutrition division. Washington, DC: International Food Policy Research Institute.

Hall, L.L. (1980) Evaluating the Effects of P.L. 480 Wheat Imports on Brazil's Grain Sector. *American Journal of Agricultural Economics*, 62(1), 19–28.

Hamilton, J.S. (1994) *Time Series Analysis.* Princeton, NJ: Princeton University Press.

Hammond, L. and Maxwell, D. (2002). The Ethiopian Crisis of 1999–2000: Lessons Learned, Questions Unanswered. *Disasters*, 26(3), 262–279.

Hanrahan, C.E. (2002) *Agricultural Export and Food Aid Programs.* Issue Brief for Congress IB98006. Washington, DC: Congressional Research Service.

Harinaryan, A., Solberg, H. and Hubbel, C. (2000) Best Practices: Review of NGOs in the Use of Food Resources. Paper prepared for CARE Food Aid Policy Review. Somerville, MA: Feinstein International Famine Centre, Tufts University.

Harvey, P. (2003) *HIV/AIDS: What are the Implications for Humanitarian Action? A Literature Review.* London: Overseas Development Institute.

Herrmann, R., Prinz, C. and Schenck, P. (1992) The Relationship between Food Aid and Food Trade: Theoretical Analysis and Quantitative Results. In M. Bellamy and B. Greenshields (eds), *Issues in Agricultural Development: Sustainability and Cooperation*, International Association of Agricultural Economists Occasional Paper No. 6, Aldershot.

Hertel, T.W. (ed.) (1997) *Global Trade Analysis: Modeling and Applications.* Cambridge: Cambridge University Press.

Hoddinott, J. (1999) *Targeting: Principles and Practice*, Technical Guide no. 9. Washington, DC: IFPRI.

Hoddinott, J., Cohen, M.J. and Bos, M.S. (2004) Re-defining the role of food aid. Mimeo. Washington, DC: IFPRI.

Hoddinott, J. and Kinsey, B.H. (2001) Child Growth in the Time of Drought. *Oxford Bulletin of Economics and Statistics*, 63(4), 409–436.

Hoffman, W.L., Gardner, B.L., Just, R.E. and Hueth, B.M. (1994) The Impact of Food Aid on Food Subsidies in Recipient Countries. *American Journal of Agricultural Economics*, 76(3), 733–743.

Holden, S.T., Barrett, C.B. and Hagos, F. (forthcoming) Food for Work for Poverty Reduction and the Promotion of Sustainable Land Use: Can It Work? *Environment and Development Economics.*

Hopkins, R.F. (1984) The Evolution of Food Aid: Towards a Development First Regime. *Food Policy*, 9(4), 345–362.

Hyde, H. International Relations Committee Hearing. *Congressional Record* ONLINE 1 November 2001. Available online at http://www.house.gov/international_relations, viewed September 23, 2002.

Hyden, G. and Reutlinger, S. (1992) Foreign Aid in a Period of Democratization: The Case of Politically Autonomous Food Funds. *World Development* 20(9), 1253–1260.

Huysentruyt, M., Barrett, C.B. and McPeak, J.G. (2002) Social Identity and Manipulative Interhousehold Transfers among East African Pastoralists, Working Paper, Cornell University, Ithaca, New York.

International Federation of the Red Cross (1995) *Red Cross/NGO Code of Conduct.* Geneva: IFRC.

International Federation of Red Cross and Red Crescent Societies (2003) *World Disaster Report 2003.* Geneva: IFRCRCS.

International Grains Council (1999) *Food Aid Convention 1999.* London: International Grains Council.

International Monetary Fund (2004) *Review of the Compensatory Financing Facility*. Report prepared by the Policy Development and Review Department. Washington, DC: IMF.

IRIN (2003) Ethopia: Interview with Prof Jeffrey Sachs, UN special adviser on Millennium Goals, Addis Ababa, 28 July.

Isenman, P.J. and Singer, H.W. (1977) Food Aid: Disincentive Effects and their Policy Implications, *Economic Development and Cultural Change*, 25, 205–237.

Islam, N. and Thomas, S. (1994) *Foodgrain Price Stabilisation in Developing Countries: Issues and Experiences in Asia*. Washington, DC: International Food Policy Research Institute.

Jackson, T. and Eade, D. (1982) *Against the Grain: The Dilemma of Project Food Aid*. Oxford: Oxfam.

Jalan, J. and Ravallion, M. (2000) Income Gains to the Poor from Workfare: Estimates for Argentina's Trabajar Program. Unpublished World Bank manuscript.

Jaspars, S. (2000) *Solidarity or Soup Kitchens? A Review of Principles and Practice for Food Distribution in Conflict*. London: Overseas Development Institute/NutritionWorks.

Jaspars, S. and Shoham, J. (1999) Targeting the Vulnerable: A Review of the Necessity and Feasibility of Targeting Vulnerable Households. *Disasters*, 23(4), 359–372.

Jayne, T.S., Strauss, J., Yamano, T. and Molla, D. (2001) Giving to the Poor? Targeting of Food Aid in Rural Ethiopia. *World Development*, 29(5), 887–910.

Jayne, T.S., Strauss, J., Yamano, T. and Molla, D. (2002) Targeting of Food Aid in Rural Ethiopia: Chronic Needs or Inertia? *Journal of Development Economics*, 68(2), 247–288.

Jensen, R. (1999) Public Transfers, Private Transfers, and the "Crowding Out" Hypothesis: Evidence from South Africa. Mimeo. John F. Kennedy School of Government, Cambridge, MA.

Jepma, C.J. (1991) *The Tying of Aid*. Paris: Development Centre of the Organization for Economic Co-operation and Development.

Jones, S. (1994) Food Security Reserve Policy in Ethiopia: A Case Study of Experience and Implications. *Disasters*, 18(2), 140–151.

Kadiyala, S. and Gillespie, S. (2003) *Rethinking Food Aid to Fight HIV/AIDS*. Food Consumption and Nutrition Division Discussion Paper 159. Washington, DC: International Food Policy Research Institute.

Kanbur, R., Keen, M. and Tuomala, M. (1994) Labor Supply and Targeting in Poverty Alleviation Programs. *World Bank Economic Review*, 8(2), 191–211.

Kerven, C. (1992) *Customary Commerce: A Historical Reassessment of Pastoral Livestock Marketing in Africa*. London: Overseas Development Institute.

Khan, A.Z.M.O. (1999) Tigers and Butterflies: The 1998 Bangladesh Floods and Food Security. Working Paper, Harvard University Asia Center, Cambridge, MA.

Kielman, A., Ajello, C. and Kielman, N. (1982) Nutrition Intervention: An Evaluation of Six Studies. *Studies in Family Planning*, 13(8/9), 246–257.

Konandreas, P., Sharma, R. and Greenfield, J. (2000) The Uruguay Round, the Marrakesh Decision and the Role of Food Aid. In E. Clay and O. Stokke (eds), *Food Aid and Human Security*. London: Frank Cass.

Kracht, U. (1999) Hunger, Malnutrition and Poverty: Trends and Prospects Towards the 21st Century. Chapter 2 in U. Kracht and M. Schulz (eds), *Food Security and Nutrition: The Global Challenge*. New York: St. Martin's Press.

Krishna, A., Kristjanson, P., Radeny, M. and Nindo, W. (2003) Comparing Pathways out of Poverty in Kenya and India. Working Paper, International Livestock Research Institute, Nairobi.

LaFranchi, H. (2001) Massive Food Aid as a Tool of Diplomacy. *Christian Science*

Monitor, 21 November. Available online at http://www.csmonitor.com/2001/1123/p1s1-usgn.html

Lantos, C.A. International Relations Committee Hearing. *Congressional Record* ONLINE 1 November 2001. Available online at http://www.house.gov/international_relations

Lappé, F.M. and Collins, J. (1977) *Food First: Beyond the Myth of Scarcity*. Boston, MA: Houghton-Mifflin.

Lautze, S. (1997) *Saving Lives and Livelihoods: The Fundamentals of a Livelihood Strategy*. Addis Ababa: Feinstein International Famine Center, Tufts University.

Lautze, S., Aklilu, Y., Raven-Roberts, A., Young, H., Kebede, G. and Leaning, J. (2003) *Risk and Vulnerability in Ethiopia. Report for USAID*. Addis Ababa: Feinstein International Famine Center, Tufts University.

Lavy, V. (1990) Does Food Aid Depress Food Production? The Disincentive Dilemma in the African Context, Working Paper, World Bank, Washington, DC.

Lentz, E. (2003) Annotated Bibliography of Food Aid Disincentive Effects. Mimeo. Cornell University.

Lentz, E. and Barrett, C.B. (2004) Food Aid Targeting, Shocks and Private Transfers among East African Pastoralists. Working Paper, Cornell University, Ithaca, New York.

Leon, J. and Soto, R. (1995) Structural Breaks and Long Run Trends in Commodity Prices. World Bank Policy Research Working Paper No. 1406, Washington, DC.

Light, P.S. (2000) *Making Nonprofits Work: A Report on the Tides of Nonprofit Management Reform*. Washington, DC: Brookings Institution.

Little, P.D. (2004) Food Aid Dependency in Rural Ethiopia: Myth or Reality? Working Paper, University of Kentucky, Lexington, KY.

Longen, K.A. (1983) The Effect of Federal Purchases of Surplus Commodities on Prices of Selected Commodities. MS Thesis, Department of Agricultural Economics, University of Maryland.

Loury, G.C. (1981) Intergenerational Transfers and the Distribution of Earnings. *Econometrica*, 49(4), 843–867.

Lybbert, T.J., Barrett, C.B., Desta, S. and Coppock, D.L. (2004) Stochastic Wealth Dynamics and Risk Management among a Poor Population. *Economic Journal*, 114(498), 750–777.

Mabaya, E. (2003) Smallholder Agricultural Markets in Zimbabwe: Organization, Spatial Integration and Equilibrium. PhD dissertation, Cornell University.

McCaston, M.K. (1999) The Shortcomings of Food Aid Targeting: Food-for-Work Programs and Human Energy Expenditure. Paper presented to the Society for Applied Anthropology, Tucson, Arizona, April.

MacDonald, J.M., Handy, C.R. and Plato, G.E. (1998) *Food Procurement by USDA's Farm Service Agency*. Washington, DC: US Department of Agriculture Economic Research Service.

MacDonald, J.M., Handy, C.R. and Plato, G.E. (2002) Competition and Prices in USDA Commodity Procurement. *Southern Economic Journal*, 69(1), 128–143.

McPeak, J.G. (2002) Fuelwood Gathering and Use in Northern Kenya. Mimeo. Department of Public Administration, Syracuse University, New York.

McPeak, J.G. (2003) Analyzing and Addressing Localized Degradation in the Commons. *Land Economics* 79(4), 515–536.

McPeak, J.G. (2004a) Risk Sharing and Asset Transfers: The Role of Livestock Transfers in Northern Kenya. Mimeo. Department of Public Administration, Syracuse University, New York.

McPeak, J.G. (2004b) Contrasting Income Shocks with Asset Shocks: Livestock Sales in Northern Kenya. *Oxford Economic Papers*, 56, 263–284.

McPeak, J.G. and Barrett, C.B. (2001) Differential Risk Exposure and Stochastic Poverty Traps among East African Pastoralists. *American Journal of Agricultural Economics*, 83(3), 674–679.

Macrae, J. (2002) *International Humanitarian Action: A Review of Policy Trends*. London: Overseas Development Institute.

Macrae, J., Bradbury, M., Jaspars, S., Johnson, D. and Duffield, M. (1997) Conflict, the Continuum, and Chronic Emergencies: A Critical Analysis of the Scope for Linking Relief, Rehabilitation and Development Planning in Sudan. *Disasters*, 21(3), 223–243.

Macrae, J. and Leader, N. (2000) *Shifting Sands: The Search for Coherence Between Political and Humanitarian Responses to Complex Political Emergencies*. HPG Report 8. London: ODI.

Maizels, A. and Nissanke, M. (1984) Motivations for Aid to Developing Countries. *World Development*, 12(6), 879–900.

Marchione, T.J. (1996) The Right to Food in the Post-Cold War Era. *Food Policy*, 21(1), 83–102.

Marchione, T.J. (2000) Title II food aid and the nutrition of children in Latin America and the Caribbean. *Food and Nutrition Bulletin*, 21(1), 65–72.

Marchione, T.J. (2002) Foods Provided through U.S. Government Emergency Food Aid Programs: Policies and Customs Governing Their Formulation, Selection and Distribution. *Journal of Nutrition*, 132, 2104S–2111S.

Marchione, T.J. and Novick, P. (2003) *Decreasing Vulnerability: Building a Resilience Safety Net*. Report prepared for Office of Food and Humanitarian Assistance. Washington, DC: USAID/Ethiopia.

Marchione, T.J. and Sywulka, S. (2004) Interactions with the Recipient Community in Targeted Food and Nutrition Programs. Unpublished manuscript.

Martens, B. (1990) The Economics of Triangular Food Aid Transactions. *Food Policy*, 15(1), 13–26.

Martinez, S.W. and Dixit, P.M. (1992) *Domestic Food Assistance Programs: Measuring the Benefits to Producers*. Washington, DC: USDA Economic Research Service.

Martorell, R. (1993) Enhancing Human Potential in Guatemalan Adults through Improved Nutrition in Early Childhood. *Nutrition Today*, 27, 6–13.

Mathys, E. and Kebede, E. (2000) Monitoring the Impact of Food Aid: The SC(UK) Programme in North and South Wollo Ethiopia in 2000. Addis Ababa: Save the Children (UK).

Maxwell, D. (1999) Programs in Chronically Vulnerable Areas: Challenges and Lessons Learned. *Disasters*, 23(4), 373–384.

Maxwell, D. (2001) *An NGO Perspective on the Right to Food: Experiences of CARE International in Chronically Vulnerable Areas*. Nairobi: CARE.

Maxwell, D. (2002) Why Do Famines Persist? A Brief Review of Ethiopia 1999–2000. *IDS Bulletin*, 33(4), 48–54.

Maxwell, D., Levin, C., Armar-Klemesu, M., Ruel, M., Morris, S. and Ahiadeke C. (2000). *Urban Livelihoods, Food and Nutrition Security in Greater Accra*. IFPRI Research Report 112. Washington, DC: International Food Policy Research Institute.

Maxwell, D. and Maunder, N. (2003) Genetically Modified Crops and Food Security: Outlines of the Debate. *Greater Horn of Africa Food Security Policy Review*, 23. Nairobi: CARE.

Maxwell D. and Watkins, B. (2003) Humanitarian Information Systems and Emergencies in the Greater Horn of Africa: Logical Components and Logical Linkages. *Disasters*, 27(2), 72–90.

Maxwell, D., Watkins, B., Wheeler, R. and Collins, G. (2003) *The Coping Strategies Index:*

A Tool for Rapidly Monitoring Food Security in Emergencies. Field Methods Manual. Nairobi: CARE and WFP

Maxwell, S. and Frankenberger, T. (1992) *Household Food Security: Concepts, Indicators and Measurements: A Technical Review.* New York and Rome: UNICEF and IFAD.

Maxwell, S., Belshaw, D. and Lirenso, A. (1994) The Disincentive Effect of Food-for-Work on Labour Supply and Agricultural Intensification in Ethiopia. *Journal of Agricultural Economics,* 45, 351–359.

Maxwell, S. and Singer, H.W. (1979) Food Aid to Developing Countries: A Survey. *World Development,* 7(3), 225–47.

Médicins sans Frontières-Belgium (2001) *Nutritional Survey, Denan, Ogaden, Ethiopia September 7–10, 2001.* Addis Ababa: MSF-Belgium.

Mendez-England and Associates (1996) *Final Report: Shaping the Future of Monetization – An Evaluation of the PL 480 Title Monetization Program.* Report for the USAID Office of Food for Peace. Washington, DC: USAID.

Merbis, M. and Nubé, M. (2001). Food Aid: Selected Problems of Implementation and International Coordination. Centre for World Food Studies, Vrije Universiteit Amsterdam, unpublished report to the Netherlands Ministry of Foreign Affairs.

Miljkovic, D. (1999) The Law of One Price in International Trade: A Critical Review. *Review of Agricultural Economics,* 21(1), 126–139.

Mohapatra, S., Barrett, C.B., Snyder, D.L. and Biswas, B. (1999) Does Food Aid Really Discourage Food Production? *Indian Journal of Agricultural Economics,* 54(2), 212–219.

Morduch, J. (1995) Income Smoothing and Consumption Smoothing. *Journal of Economic Perspectives,* 9, 103–114.

Mustard, A. (2003) An Unauthorized History of FAS. *Foreign Service Journal,* 80(5), 36–43.

Mutume, G. (2003) Africa Struggles for Global Attention. *Africa Recovery,* 17(2), 10–11.

Nathan Associates, Inc. (1990) *Food Aid Impacts on Commercial trade: A Review of the Quantitative Evidence.* Consulting report to Bureau for Food for Peace, United States Agency for International Development, Washington, DC.

National Research Council, Board on Agriculture (1989) *Investing in Research: A Proposal to Strengthen the Agricultural, Food, and Environmental System.* Washington, DC: National Academy Press.

Natsios, A.S. (2003) Testimony Before the United States Senate Committee on Foreign Relations. February 25.

Natural Resources Institute (1999) *Review of Role, Size and Structure of the Ethiopia Food Security Reserve: Final Report.* Norwich: Natural Resources Institute.

Neun, J. (2000) *Missed Opportunities or Latent Potential for Poverty Reduction and Alleviation in Ethiopia.* Addis Ababa: EU Local Food Security Unit.

Newbery, D. (1989) The Theory of Food Price Stabilization. *Economic Journal,* 99(4), 1065–1082.

Newbery, D.M.G. and Stiglitz, J.E. (1981) *The Theory of Commodity Price Stabilization.* Oxford: Clarendon Press.

New York Times (2002) The Hypocrisy of Farm Subsidies. Editorial, December 1.

Noland, M. (2000) *Avoiding the Apocalypse: The Future of the Two Koreas.* Washington, DC: Institute for International Economics.

Nord, M., Kabbani, N., Tiehen, L., Andrews, M., Bickel, G. and Carlson, S. (2002) *Household Food Security in the United States 2001.* Food Assistance and Nutrition Research Report 29. Washington, DC: United States Department of Agriculture Economic Research Service.

Office of Management and Budget, Executive Office of the President (2001) *The President's Management Agenda*. Washington, DC: OMB.

Olson, M. (1965) *The Logic of Collective Action: Public Goods and the Theory of Groups*. Cambridge, MA: Harvard University Press.

Orden, D. (2004) *Review of U.S. Farm Policies: International Context, Effects on Developing Countries, and Food Aid in this Policy Nexus*. International Food Policy Research Institute report to CARE USA, Washington, DC.

Organization for Economic Co-operation and Development (2003) Export Competition Issues Related to Food Aid. Mimeo.

Oshaug A. and Barthe-Eide, W. (1997) The World Food Summit: A Milestone in Developing a Human Rights Approach to Food and Nutrition. *World Hunger Notes: The World Food Summit*. Washington, DC: Available online at http://www.worldhunger.org

Osmani, S.R. and Chowdhury, O.H. (1983) Short Run Impacts of Food for Work Programme in Bangladesh. *Bangladesh Development Studies*, 11(1/2), 135–190.

Paarlberg, R. (1985) *Food Trade and Foreign Policy*. Ithaca, NY: Cornell University Press.

Palasakas, T.B. and Harriss-White, B. (1993) Testing Market Integration: New Approaches with Case Material from the West Bengal Food Economy. *Journal of Development Studies*, 30(3), 1–57.

Payne, P. and Lipton, M. (1994) *How Third World Rural Households Adapt to Dietary Energy Stress* Washington, DC: International Food Policy Research Institute.

Peppiatt, D., Mitchell, J. and Holzman, P. (2001) *Cash Transfers and Emergencies: Evaluating Benefits and Assessing Risks*. Humanitarian Practice Network Paper 35. London: Overseas Development Institute.

Pinstrup-Andersen, P. (ed.) (1988) *Food Subsidies in Developing Countries*. Baltimore, MD: Johns Hopkins University Press.

Pinstrup-Andersen, P., Pandya-Lorch, R. and Rosegrant, M. (1997) *The World Food Situation: Recent Development, Emerging Issues and Long-Term Prospects*. 2020 Vision Food Policy Report. Washington, DC: International Food Policy Research Institute.

Piot, P., Pinstrup Andersen, P., Gillespie, S., and Haddad, L. (2002) *AIDS and Food Security*. Rome: IFPRI.

Piwoz, E. (2004) *Nutrition and HIV/AIDS: Evidence, Gaps and Priority Actions*. SARA Project (Support for Analysis and Research in Africa). Washington, DC: USAID.

Quisumbing, A. (2003) Food Aid and Child Nutrition in Rural Ethiopia. *World Development*, 31(7), 1309–1324.

Raisin, J. (2001) *Beyond the Merry-Go-Round to the Relief-Development Continuum*. Addis Ababa: USAID Mission to Ethiopia.

Raisin, J. (2002) *Development with the Poor. The Transitional Asset Protection System: A Middle Road to Social Protection*. Addis Ababa: USAID Mission to Ethiopia.

Rami, H. (2002) *Food Aid is not Development*. Addis Ababa: UN Emergencies Unit for Ethiopia.

Ravallion, M. (1986) Testing Market Integration. *American Journal of Agricultural Economics*, 68(1), 102–109.

Ravallion, M. (1987) *Markets and Famines*. Oxford: Oxford University Press.

Ravallion, M. (1991) Reaching the Rural Poor through Public Employment: Arguments, Lessons, and Evidence from South Asia. *World Bank Research Observer* 6(1), 153–176.

Ravallion, M. (1997) Famines and Economics. *Journal of Economic Literature*, 35(3), 1205–1242.

Ravallion, M. (1999) Appraising Workfare. *World Bank Research Observer*, 14(1), 31–48.

Ravallion, M. (2003) Targeted Transfers in Poor Countries: Revisiting the Trade-Offs and Policy Options. Working Paper, World Bank, Washington, DC.

Ravallion, M., Datt, G. and Chaudhuri, S. (1993) Does Maharashtra's Employment Guarantee Scheme Guarantee Employment? Effects of the 1988 Wage Increase. *Economic Development and Cultural Change*, 41(2), 251–275.

Reed, B.A. and Habicht, J.-P. (1998) Sales of Food Aid as a Sign of Distress, not Excess. *The Lancet*, 351, 128–130.

Relief Development Institute (1987) *A Study of Triangular Transactions and Local Purchases in Food Aid*, Occasional Paper No. 11. Rome: WFP.

Reutlinger, S. (1999) From "Food Aid" to "Aid for Food": Into the 21st Century. *Food Policy*, 24(1), 7–15.

Reutlinger, S. and Bigman, D. (1981) Feasibility, Effectiveness, and Costs of Food Security Alternatives in Developing Countries. In A. Valdes (ed.), *Food Security for Developing Countries*. Boulder, CO: Westview Press.

Reutlinger, S. and Katona-Apte, J. (1984) The Nutritional Impact of Food Aid: Criteria for the Selection of Cost-Effective Foods. *Food and Nutrition Bulletin*, 6(4), 1–10.

Ridenour, A. (2003) Feed the World: Bush Challenges European Ban on Genetically-Modified Foods, National Center for Public Policy Research. Available online at http://www. nationalcenter.org/TSR6203.html.

Rideout, M. (1999) Community Managed Targeting of Emergency Food Aid: Does it Ever Work? *Field Exchange*, 7(July 1999), 18–20.

Rieff, D. (2002) *A Bed for the Night: Humanitarianism in Crisis*. New York: Simon and Schuster.

Rogers, B.L. (2002) *Proposed Exit Strategy for Title II Food Security Programs in Honduras*. Somerville, MA: School of Nutrition, Tufts University.

Rose-Ackerman, S. (1982) Charitable Giving and "Excessive" Fundraising. *Quarterly Journal of Economics*, 97(2), 193–212.

Rosegrant, M.W., Paisner, M.S., Meijer, S. and Witcover, J. (2001) *Global Food Projections to 2020: Emerging Trends and Alternative Futures*. Washington, DC: International Food Policy Research Institute.

Rosset, P. (2002) U.S. Opposes Right to Food at World Summit. *World Editorial and International Law*, June 30.

Rubey, L. (1996) *Draft USAID Principles for Title II Food Aid Monetization*. Washington, DC: USAID.

Rush, D. (1987) *The National WIC Evaluation: An Evaluation of the Special Supplemental Food Program for Women, Infants, and Children (WIC)*, 3 vols. Washington, DC: Research Triangle Institute.

Ruttan, V.W. (ed.) (1993) *Why Food Aid?* Baltimore, MD: Johns Hopkins University Press.

Ruttan, V.W. (1995) *United States Development Assistance Policy: The Domestic Politics of Foreign Economic Assistance*. Baltimore, MD: Johns Hopkins University Press.

Ruttan, V.W. (1996) Does Aid Have a Future? *Choices* (first quarter 1995), reprinted as pp. 122–126 in H.W. Ayer (ed.), *The Best of Choices*. Ames, IA: American Agricultural Economics Association.

Sachs, J.D. (2004) Don't Know, Should Care. *New York Times*, June 5.

Salama, P., Assefa, F., Talley, L., Spiegel, P., van der Veen, A. and Gotway, C. (2001) Malnutrition, Measles, Mortality and the Humanitarian Response During a Famine in Ethiopia. *Journal of the American Medical Association*, 286(5), 563–571.

Sanford, S. and Habtu, Y. (2002) *Emergency Response Interventions in Pastoral Areas of Ethiopia*. Addis Ababa: DFID.

Saran, R. and Konandreas, P. (1991) An Additional Resource? A Global Perspective on Food Aid Flows in Relation to Development Assistance. In E.J. Clay and O. Stokke (eds), *Food Aid Reconsidered: Assessing the Impact on Third World Countries*. London: Frank Cass.

Savoie, R. and Bamugye, G. (2003) Capacity Building in the Private Sector: Secondary Impacts of Small-Lot Sealed Bid Tenders. *Food Forum*, 64(1). Available online at http://www.foodaid.org/pdf/docs/foodforum/2003Q2/ACDIVOCA.pdf

Schubert, J.N. (1986) The Social, Developmental and Political Impacts of Food Aid. In W.P. Browne and D.F. Hadwiger (eds), *World Food Policies: Toward Agricultural Interdependence*. Boulder, CO: Lynne Rienner.

Schultz, T.W. (1960) Value of U.S. Farm Surpluses to Underdeveloped Countries. *Journal of Farm Economics*, 42(5), 1019–1030.

Seaman, J. (ed.) (2000) *The Food Economy Approach*. London: Save the Children - UK.

Sen, A. (1981a) *Poverty and Famines: An Essay on Entitlement and Deprivation*. Oxford: Clarendon Press.

Sen, A. (1981b) Ingredients of Famine Analysis: Availability and Entitlements, *Quarterly Journal of Economics*, 96(3), 433–464.

Seoul reviews rice deal with North. (2002) BBC News, July 3.

Shapouri, S. and Missiaen, M. (1990) *Food Aid: Motivation and Allocation Criteria*. Economic Research Service Foreign Agricultural Economic Report 240. Washington, DC: USDA.

Shapouri, S. and Rosen, S. (1987). *Effect of Fiscal Austerity on African Food Imports*. Economic Research Service Foreign Agricultural Economic Report 230. Washington, DC: USDA.

Shapouri, S. and Rosen, S. (2003) *Food Security Assessment*. United States Department of Agriculture Economic Research Service Report GFA-14. Washington, DC: USDA.

Sharp, K. (1998) *Between Relief and Development: Targeting Food Aid for Disaster Prevention in Ethiopia*, RRN Network Paper 27. London: Overseas Development Institute.

Sharp, K. (2001) *An Overview of Targeting Approaches for Food Assisted Programming*. Atlanta: CARE.

Shaw, D.J. (2001) *The UN World Food Programme and the Development of Food Aid*. New York: Palgrave.

Shaw, D.J. and Clay, E. (eds) (1993) *World Food Aid: Experiences of Recipients and Donors*. Portsmouth, NH: Heinemann.

Shaw, D.J. and Singer, H.W. (1996) A Future Food Aid Regime: Implications of the Final Act of the Uruguay Round. *World Development*, 21(4/5), 447–460.

Shoham, J. (1999a) Community Managed Targeting – Tanzania (Post-script). *Field Exchange*, 7(July), 20.

Shoham, J. (1999b) Special Focus on Targeting. *Field Exchange*, 8(November), 4.

Singer, H.W. (1989) The African Food Crisis and the Role of Food Aid. *Food Policy*, 14, 196–220.

Singer, H.W., Wood, J. and Jennings, T. (1987) *Food Aid: The Challenge and the Opportunity*. Oxford: Oxford University Press.

Skees, J.R. (2000) A Role for Capital Markets in Natural Disasters: A Piece of the Food Security Puzzle. *Food Policy*, 25(3), 365–378.

Smith, L.C. (1998) Can FAO's Measure of Chronic Undernourishment Be Strengthened? *Food Policy*, 23(5), 425–445.

Smith, L.C. and Aduayom, D. (2004) Measuring Food Insecurity Using Household Expenditures Surveys: New Estimates from Sub-Saharan Africa. Mimeo. International Food Policy Research Institute.

Smith, M.E. and Lee, D.R. (1994) Overseas Food Aid Programs. In M.C. Hallberg, R.G.F. Spitze, and D.E. Ray (eds), *Food, Agriculture, and Rural Policy into the Twenty-First Century: Issues and Trade-Offs*. Boulder, CO: Westview Press.

Speaker Hastert (2003) American Agriculture Can Help Solve World Hunger, Tells House Science Committee, Europeans Exacerbating Food Problems in Africa. Available online at http://speaker. house.gov/library/intrelations/030612ag.shtml

Sphere Project (2000) *Humanitarian Charter and Minimum Standards in Disaster Response.* Oxfam Publishing/Sphere Project.

Sphere Project (2004) *Humanitarian Charter and Minimum Standards in Disaster Response,* rev. edn. Oxfam Publishing/Sphere Project.

Srinivasan, T.N. (1989) Food Aid: A Cause of Development Failure or an Instrument for Success? *World Bank Economic Review,* 3(1), 39–65.

Stevens, C. (1979) *Food Aid and the Developing World: Four African Case Studies.* London: Croom Helm.

Strauss, J. and Thomas, D. (1995) Human Resources: Empirical Modeling of Household and Family Decisions. In J. Behrman and T.N. Srinivasan (eds), *Handbook of Development Economics,* Vol. 3A. Amsterdam: Elsevier Press.

Strauss, J. and Thomas, D. (1998) Health, Nutrition, and Economic Development, *Journal of Economic Literature,* 36, 766–817.

Suarez, N.R. (1994) *U.S. Agricultural Exports Under Public Law 480.* United States Department of Agriculture Economic Research Service Statistical Bulletin No. 876. Washington, DC: USDA.

Swindale, A., Deitchler, M., Cogill, B. and Marchione, T. (2004) *The Impact of Title II Maternal and Child Health and Nutrition Programs on the Nutritional Status of Children.* Occasional Paper No. 4. Washington, DC: USAID/Office of Food for Peace.

Taylor, D. and Byerlee, D. (1991) Food Aid and Food Security: A Cautionary Note. *Canadian Journal of Agricultural Economics,* 39(1), 163–175.

Teka, T., Alemayehu and Gebremariam, A. (1999) *Cross-Border Livestock Trade and Food Security in the Southern and Southeastern Ethiopia Borderlands,* OSSREA Development Research Report Series No. 1. Addis Ababa: OSSREA.

Teklu, T. and Asefa, S. (1999) Who Participates in Labor-Intensive Public Works in Sub-Saharan Africa? Evidence from Rural Botswana and Kenya. *World Development,* 27(2), 431–438.

Thurow, R. and Kilman, S. (2003) As U.S. Food Aid Policy Enriches Farmers, Poor Nations Cry Foul, Sending Crops, Not Cash, Eases American Gluts, Ignores Local Surpluses. *Wall Street Journal,* September 11.

Timmer, C.P. (1989) Food Price Policy: The Rationale for Government Intervention. *Food Policy,* 14(1), 17–27.

Timmer, C.P. (1996) Does Bulog Stabilize Rice Prices in Indonesia? Should It Try? *Bulletin of Indonesian Studies,* 32(1), 46–74.

Tinbergen, J. (1956) *Economic Policy: Principles and Design.* Amsterdam: North Holland.

Townsend, R. (1994) Risk and Insurance in Village India. *Econometrica,* 62(2), 539–592.

Trueblood, M.A. and Shapouri, S. (2002) Food Insecurity in the Least Developed Countries and the International Response. Working Paper, United States Department of Agriculture Economic Research Service, Washington, DC.

Trueblood, M.A., Shapouri, S. and Henneberry, S. (2001) *Policy Options to Stabilize Food Supplies: A Case Study of Southern Africa.* United States Department of Agriculture Economic Research Service Agriculture Information Bulletin No. 764. Washington, DC: USDA.

Tschirley, D., Donovan, C. and Weber, M.T. (1996) Food Aid and Food Markets: Lessons from Mozambique. *Food Policy,* 21(1), 189–209.

Tschirley, D and Howard, J. (2003) Title II Food Aid and Agricultural Development in Sub-Saharan Africa: Towards a Principled Argument for When and When Not to Monetize. MSU International Development Working Paper No. 81, Department of Agricultural Economics, Michigan State University, East Lansing, MI.

Tyers, R. and Anderson, K. (1992) *Disarray in World Food Markets: A Quantitative Assessment.* Cambridge: Cambridge University Press.

UNAIDS Barnett, T. and Whiteside, W. (2000) *Guidelines for Studies of the Social and Economic Impact of HIV/AIDS.* Geneva: UNAIDS Best Practice Collection.

UNAIDS and WHO (2002) *AIDS Epidemic Update.* Geneva: UNAIDS and WHO.

UNICEF (1990) *Strategy for Improved Nutrition of Children and Women in Developing Countries.* New York: UNICEF Policy Review Paper.

United Nations Conference on Trade and Development (2003) *Review of Maritime Transport 2003.* Geneva: UNCTAD.

United Nations Economic and Social Council (1999) *The Right to Adequate Food (Art. 11).* E/C.12/1999/5, General Comment Number 12. New York: UN.

United Nations High Commissioner for Refugees, United Nations Children's Fund, World Food Programme and World Health Organization (2002) *Food and Nutrition Needs in Emergencies.* Rome: WFP.

United States Agency for International Development (various years) *U.S. International Food Assistance Report.* Washington, DC: USDA.

United States Agency for International Development, Office of Inspector General (2001) *Audit of USAID's Cargo Preference Reimbursements Under Section 901d of the Merchant Marine Act of 1936.* Audit Report No. 9-000-01-003-P (March 30, 2001). Washington, DC: USDA.

United States Agency for International Development, Office of Food for Peace (2004) *Strategic Plan for 2004–2008*, Second Draft. Washington, DC: USDA.

United States Agency for International Development (2004) *US Foreign Aid: Meeting the Challenges of the 21st Century.* Bureau for Policy and Program Coordination. Washington, DC: USDA.

United States Department of Agriculture Foreign Agricultural Service (2001) *Report to Congress on Food Aid Monetization.* Washington, DC: USDA.

United States Department of Agriculture, National Agricultural Statistics Service (2002) *Crop Production–Acreage–supplement (PCP-BB).* June 28, 2002. Available online at http://usda.mannlib.cornell.edu/reports/nassr/field/pcp-bba/.

United States General Accounting Office (1984). *Opportunities for Greater Cost Effectiveness In Public Law 480, Title I Food Purchases.* Report GAO/NSIAD-84–69. Washington, DC: GAO.

United States General Accounting Office (1990) *Cargo Preference Requirements: Their Impact on U.S. Food Aid Programs and the U.S. Merchant Marine.* Report to the Chairman, Committee on Agriculture, House of Representatives. Washington, DC: GAO.

United States General Accounting Office (1994a) *Inadequate Accountability for U.S. Donations to the World Food Program.* Report GAO/NSIAD-94–29. Washington, DC: GAO.

United States General Accounting Office (1994b) *Cargo Preference Requirements: Objectives Not Significantly Advanced When Used in U.S. Food Aid Programs.* Report GAO/GGD-94–215. Washington, DC: GAO.

United States General Accounting Office (1994c) *Maritime Industry: Cargo Preference Laws – Estimated Costs and Effects.* Report GAO/RCED-95–34. Washington, DC: GAO.

United States General Accounting Office (1994d) *Private Voluntary Organizations' Role In Distributing Food Aid.* Report GAO/NSIAD-95–35. Washington, DC: GAO.

United States General Accounting Office (1995) *Food Aid: Competing Goals and Requirements Hinder Title I Program Results*, GAO/GGD-95-68. Washington, DC: GAO.

United States General Accounting Office (1999) *North Korea Restricts Food Aid Monitoring*. Report GAO/NSIAD-00-35. Washington, DC: GAO.

United States General Accounting Office (2000) *U.S. Food Aid Program to Russia Had Weak Internal Controls*. Report GAO/NSIAD/AIMD-00-329. Washington, DC: GAO.

United States General Accounting Office (2002) *Global Food for Education Initiative Faces Challenges for Successful Implementation*. Report GAO-020328. Washington, DC: GAO.

United States General Accounting Office (2003a) *Sustained Efforts Needed to Help Southern Africa Recover from Food Crisis*. Report GAO-03-644. Washington, DC: GAO.

United States General Accounting Office (2003b) *Lack of Strategic Focus and Obstacles to Agricultural Recovery Threaten Afghanistan's Stability*. Report GAO-03-607. Washington, DC: GAO.

USAID (1995) *Food Aid and Food Security Policy*. Washington, DC: USAID.

USDA Economic Research Service Analysis of Provisions of the Farm Bill. Available online at http://www.ers.usda.gov/Features/FarmBill/Analysis

USDA's Russian Food Aid Program: Hearing before the Committee on Agriculture. 106th Cong., 1st Session (1994). Available online at http://commdocs.house.gov/committees/ag/hag 10636.000/hag10636_0f.htm.

US Grains Council *Global Update* (2003), January 31. Available online at http://www. ncga.com/public_policy/PDF/Letter_EU_Moratorium.pdf.

van Beers, C. and de Moor, A. (2001) *Public Subsidies and Policy Failures: How Subsidies Distort the Natural Environment, Equity and Trade and How to Reform Them*. Cheltenham: Edward Elgar.

von Braun, J. (ed.) (1995) *Employment for Poverty Reduction and Food Security*. Washington, DC: International Food Policy Research Institute.

von Braun, J. (2003) *Berlin Statement on Food Aid for Sustainable Food Security*. International Workshop on Food Aid – Contributions and Risks to Sustainable Food Security. September 2–4, Berlin, Germany.

von Braun, J. and Huddleston, B. (1988) *Implications of Food Aid for Price Policy in Recipient Countries*. In J.W. Mellor and R. Ahmed (eds), *Agricultural Price Policy for Developing Countries*. Baltimore, MD: Johns Hopkins University Press.

von Braun, J., Teklu, T. and Webb, P. (1999) *Famine in Africa: Causes, Responses, and Prevention*. Baltimore, MD: Johns Hopkins University Press.

Washington Post (1992) Aid for Russian Democracy. April 2.

Webb, P. and Reardon, T. (1992). Drought Impact and Household Response in East and West Africa. *Quarterly Journal of International Agriculture*, 3(2), 230–246.

Webb, P. and Rogers, B. (2003) *Addressing the "In" in Food Insecurity*. FFP Occasional Paper no. 1. Washington, DC: USAID Office of Food for Peace.

Weber, M.T., Staatz, J.M., Holtzman, J.S., Crawford, E.W. and Bernsten, R.H. (1988) Informing Food Security Decisions in Africa: Empirical Analysis and Policy Dialogue. *American Journal of Agricultural Economics*, 70(5), 1044–1052.

Whitehouse, M. (1999) Many Ask Whom US Food Aid in Russia is Helping. *New York Times*, March 16.

Wijga, A. (1983) *The Nutritional Impact of Food-For-Work Programmes*. Wageningen University report presented to the 10th session of the ACC/SCN.

Williams, J.C. and Wright, B.D. (1990) *Storage and Commodity Markets*. New York: Cambridge University Press.

Windfuhr, M. (n.d.) *Food is a Human Right*. Heidelberg: Food First Information and Action Network (FIAN).

World Bank (1986) *Poverty and Hunger: Issues and Options for Food Security in Developing Countries*. Washington, DC: World Bank.

World Bank (2002). *Social Protection Sector Strategy: From Safety Net to Springboard*. Social Protection Division. Washington, DC: World Bank.

World Bank (2003) *Global Economic Prospects 2004: Realizing the Development Promise of the Doha Agenda*. Washington, DC: World Bank.

World Food Programme (1999) *Emergency Needs Assessment: Guidelines*. Rome: WFP Technical Support Service (ODT).

World Food Programme (2000) *Food and Nutrition Handbook*. Rome: WFP Nutrition Unit.

World Food Programme (2001a) *2000 Food Aid Flows*. Rome: WFP.

World Food Programme (2001b) *Enabling Development: Food Assistance in South Asia*. New Delhi: Oxford University Press.

World Food Programme (2001c) *School Feeding Works for Girls' Education*. Rome: WFP.

World Food Programme (2001d) *WFP, Food Security and HIV/AIDS*. Rome: WFP.

World Food Programme (2002) *Directions for Planning and Implementation of Effective Employment Generation Schemes*. Addis Ababa: WFP.

World Food Programme (2003) *Strategic Plan (2004–2007)*. Rome: WFP.

World Food Programme (2004a) *Nutrition in Emergencies: WFP Experiences and Challenges*. Rome: WFP.

World Food Programme (2004b) *Food for Nutrition: Mainstreaming Nutrition in WFP*. Rome: WFP.

World Food Programme (2004c) *Micronutrient Fortification: WFP's Experience and Ways Forward*. Rome: WFP.

Yager, L. (2002) Food Aid: Experience of U.S. Programs Suggests Opportunities for Improvement. Testimony before the Subcommittee on Oversight of Government Management, Restructuring and the District of Columbia, Committee on Governmental Affairs, US Senate, June 4, 2002. Report GAO-02-801T.

Yamano, T., Alderman, H. and Christiaensen, L. (2003) Child Growth, Shocks, and Food Aid in Rural Ethiopia, Working Paper, World Bank, Washington, DC.

Young, C.E. and Wescott, P.C. (1996) *The 1996 US Farm Act Increases Market Orientation*. Washington, DC: USDA Economic Research Service.

Young, H., Jaspars, S., Brown, R., Frize, J., and Khogali, H. (2001) *Food-Security Assessments in Emergencies: A Livelihoods Approach*, Humanitarian Practice Network (HPN) Network Paper 36. London: Overseas Development Institute.

Younger, S. (1992) Aid and the Dutch Disease: Macroeconomic Development When Everybody Loves You. *World Development*, 20(11), 1587–1597.

Zeigler, M.M. (2003) Political Food Fight in Southern Africa. *The Brandywine Review of Faith and International Affairs*, 1(1), 3–10.

Index

United States Agency for International Development (USAID) 20, 26, 38, 235; Bellmon Analyses 190–1; development food aid 235; Famine Early Warning System Network 157; Gramm-Rudman-Hollings Act 43; local purchases 234; NGOs 63; raisins 34; safety nets 209; Title II 21, 23, 130, 212, 238; Title III 21; *see also* Food for Peace; General Accounting Office

United States Department of Agriculture (USDA) 21, 26, *84*, 238; annual food security assessments 153; corn shipments 166; domestic food procurement 235; Economic Research Service 267n4; FAPC 20; humanitarian aid 26–7; nonfat dry milk 34; program food aid 214; school feeding program 90; Total Quality Systems Audit 178; wheat shipments 166; *see also* Commodity Credit Corporation; Food for Progress; Foreign Agricultural Service

United States Department of Defense 93

United States Department of Transportation 20

United States food aid 4, 5, 20–6, 216; Doha 73; Ethiopia 48, 218; monetization 135–6, 224; OMB 26, 235; poverty reduction 245; Public Law 480 231–2; regulations 217–18; Russia 28–31; WTO 21, 72

United States Maritime Administration 20

United States National Research Council 152–3

Universal Declaration of Human Rights 4, 57, 111, 112–13

Uruguay Round Agreement on Agriculture (URAA) 70, 72–3, 80–1, 232, 233

USAID: *see* **United States Agency for International Development**

USDA: *see* **United States Department of Agriculture**

usual marketing requirements (UMR) 69–70, 71, 73, 80

Uzbekistan 47

vegetable oil 90, 149

Vietnam 10–11, 39

Vietnam War 48

vulnerability 124–5, 127, 196, 207, 211

Vulnerability Assessment and Mapping, WFP 157

wages 144–5, 206, 212

war: food aid 45–8, 105, 221; humanitarian access 112; hunger 8

water supplies 177

WFP: *see* **World Food Programme**

wheat: international market 52; prices 32, 52; shipments 91, 160, 182; US 29, 33, 37

wheat flour 90

women: household heads 125, 145; livelihood security 125; malnutrition 118, 129–30, 220; mortality rates 129; rights 113

Women, Infants and Children Special Supplemental Program 132

World Bank 108, 167, 209, 232

World Disaster Report 44

World Food Conference 61, 114

World Food Crisis (1973–1974) 108; Africa 39; causes 27; changes 107; early warning system 153; multilateralism 61; WFP 219–20

World Food Programme (WFP) 13, 15, 61; Afghanistan 47, 64–5; bilateral aid 60–1; Canada 53–4; child nutrition 41–2n6; delivery 219–20; depoliticizing food aid 62–3; distribution 14, 263n41; emergency food aid 62, 64–5, 124; EU 56; food security 107; fortified foods 148–9; freight forwarders 94; Global Food Aid Compact 229; Maize Train operation 159; Millennium Development Goals 129, 271n17; monetization ceased 135; NGOs 63; nutrition 130, 204; recipient-oriented system 51; rights-based approach 111–12; shipments 273n6; soy products 33–4; strategic plans 204, 220; Vulnerability Assessment and Mapping 157; Vulnerable Group Development 272n30; world food crisis 219–20

World Food Summit 61, 111, 114

World Health Organization 45, 83

World Initiative for Soy in Human Health 33–4

World Trade Organization (WTO): donor countries 73; genetically modified foods 34, 86; Global Food Aid Compact 229; liberalization of trade 80–1; Public Law 480 242; URAA 70;